Dawn of the Arcana

13

Story & Art by
Rei Toma

characters

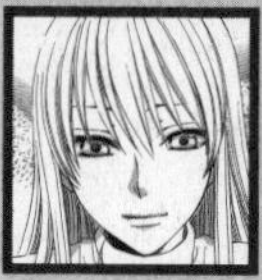

Sara
King Guran's concubine. Deceased.

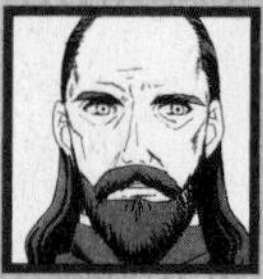

Guran
King of Belquat.

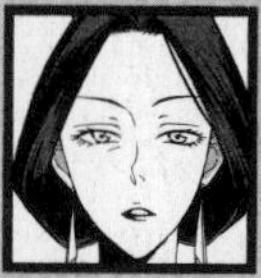

Rosenta
Queen of Belquat.

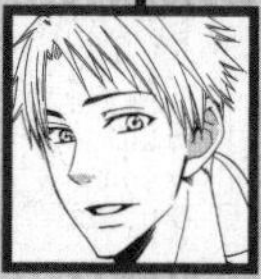

Cain
First-born prince of Belquat. Caesar's brother. He was killed by Loki.

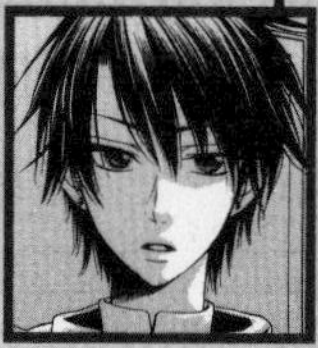

Caesar
The second-born prince of Belquat. He breaks up with Nakaba and marries Louise.

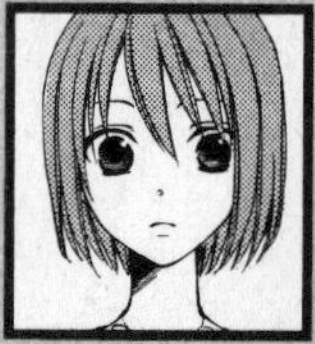

Nakaba
The princess royal of Senan. Strong of will and noble of spirit, she possesses a strange power.

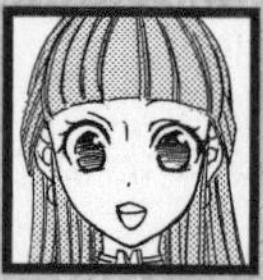

Lemiria
Bellinus's younger sister. Fond of her big brother.

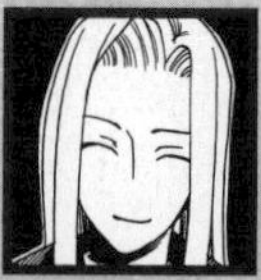

Bellinus
Caesar's attendant. Always cool and collected.

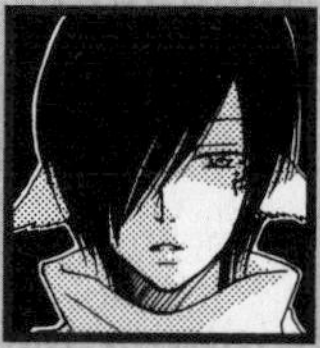

Loki
Nakaba's attendant. His senses of perception are unmatched.

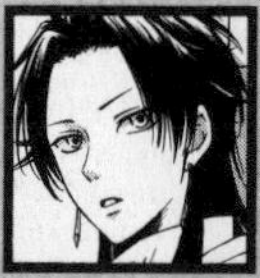

Adel
Successor to the throne of Senan. Married to Nakaba.

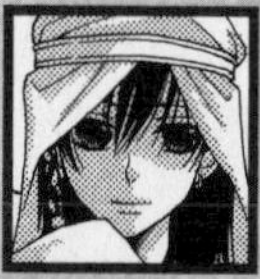

Akhil
Fifth-born prince of Lithuanel.

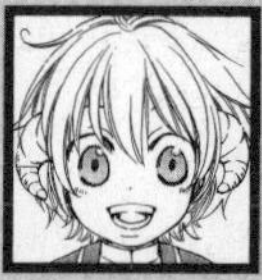

Rito
Nakaba's attendant.

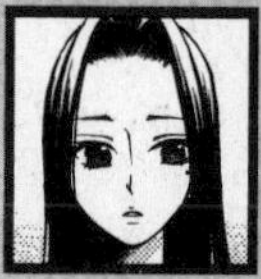

Louise
The daughter of a Belquat general.

story

Neighboring Kingdoms

Senan
A poor kingdom in the cold north of the island. Militarily weak.

Belquat
A powerful country that thrives thanks to its temperate climate.

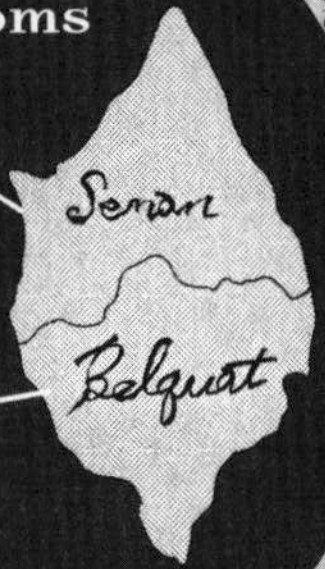
Senan
Belquat

• Wed to Prince Caesar as a symbol of the peace between their two countries, Nakaba is actually little more than a hostage. Unbeknownst to King Guran, she is a survivor of the race he tried to destroy for fear of their power. Nakaba herself possesses the Arcana of Time, so she can see the past and the future. The political marriage between Nakaba and Caesar gets off to a rocky start, but as they grow to know each other, they fall in love.

• In order to change a world full of absurd wars and battles for the throne, Caesar returns to Belquat while Nakaba is in Senan. They intend to become rulers of their respective countries and unite the two one day. They still think of each other often.

• When Caesar returns to Belquat, he does as his mother bids and marries Louise, who was formerly engaged to his late brother, Cain. Meanwhile, Nakaba returns to Senan and uses her Arcana power as a bargaining tool to marry Adel, who is next in line for the Senan throne.

• When the king of Senan falls ill and collapses, Nakaba forces him to draw up a will naming her as his heir, and she eventually becomes Senan's new ruler. When King Guran learns of her ascension, he decides to invade and claim Senan. Caesar is sent to the front lines.

• Through her Arcana of Time power, Nakaba knows that Caesar plans to rebel against Belquat. She meets with him and says she'll support his revolution provided that there will be real peace between their countries. They go to Belquat, but King Guran refuses to make peace. Caesar fights and kills him, after which Loki asks Nakaba to hand control of Senan over to him...!

Dawn of the Arcana

Volume 13

XII

XI

X

CONTENTS

· · · · · · · · · · · · · ·

IX

VIII

VII   VI

· ·

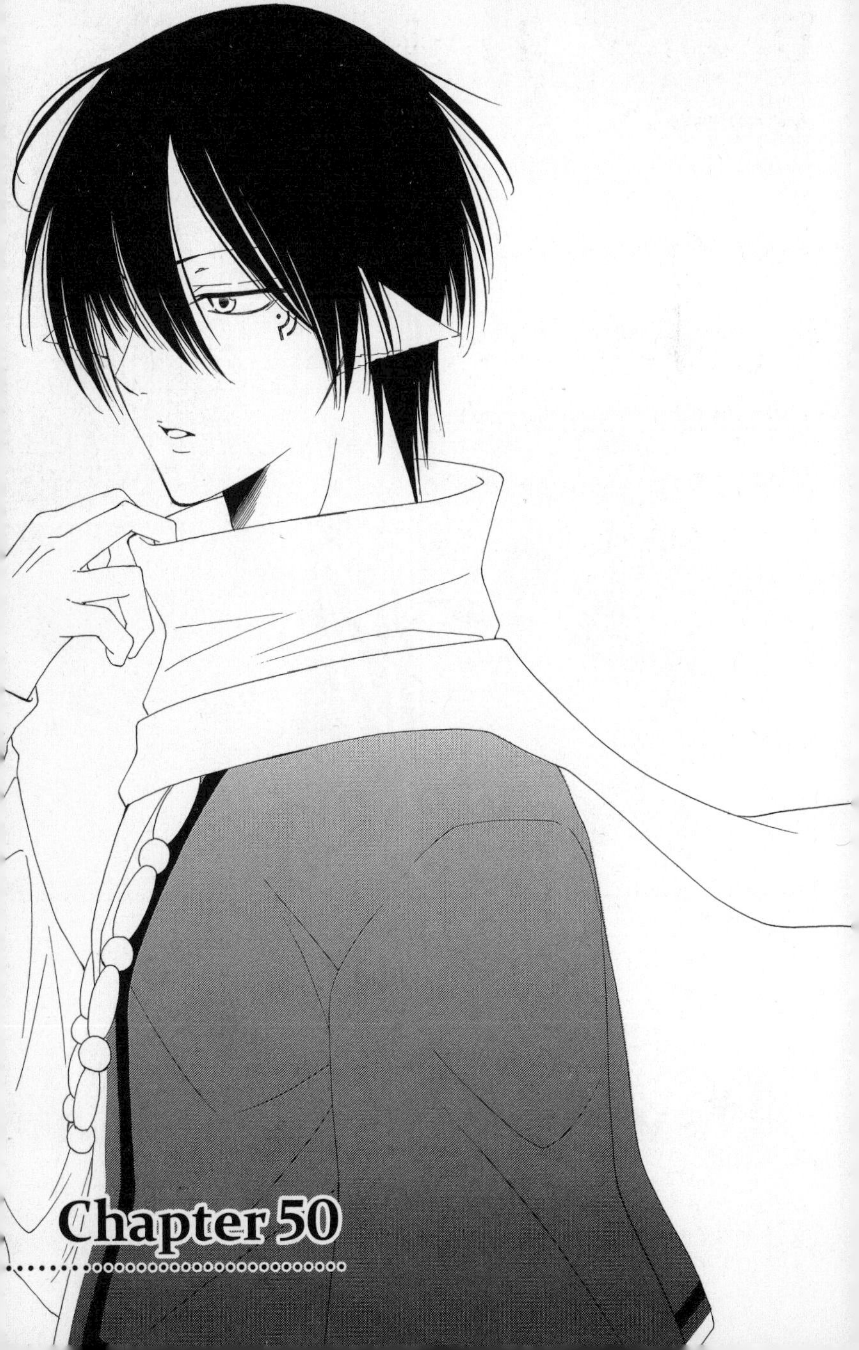
Chapter 50

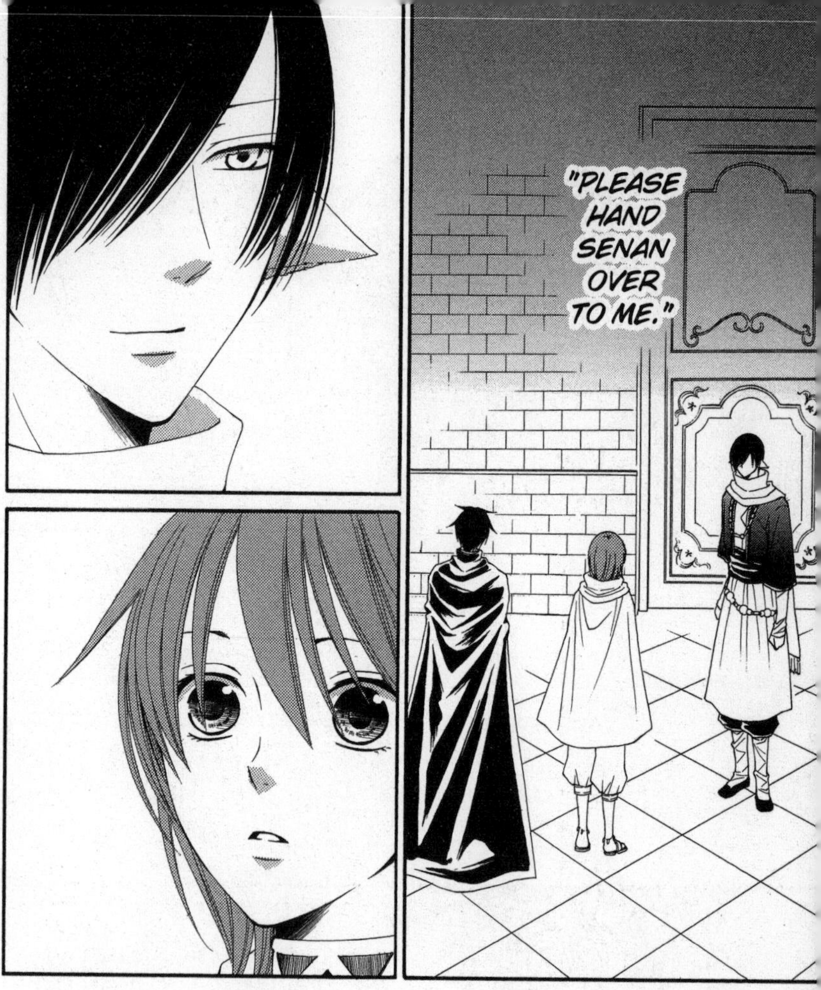
"PLEASE HAND SENAN OVER TO ME."

Dawn of the Arcana

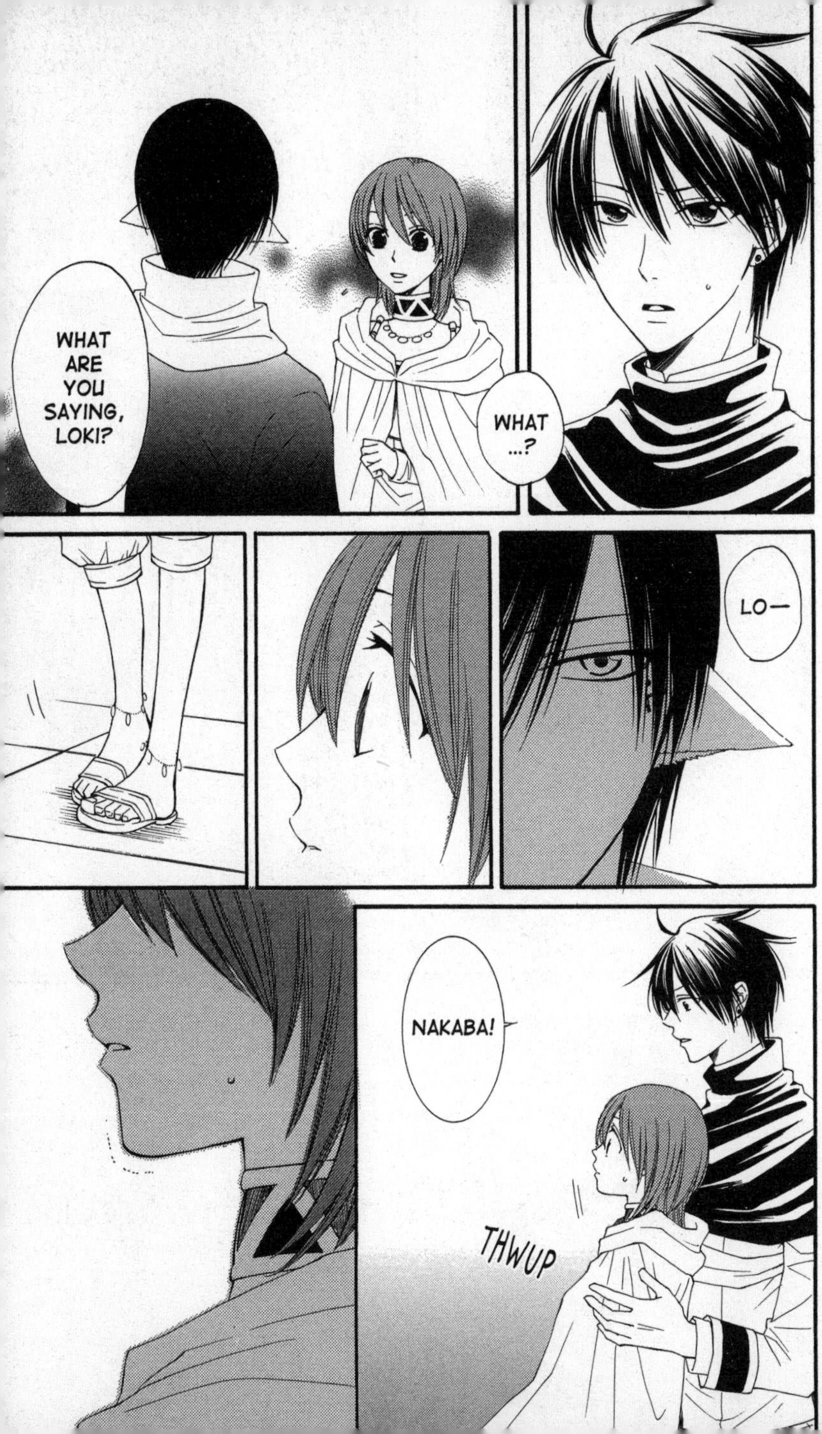
WHAT ...?
WHAT ARE YOU SAYING, LOKI?
LO—
NAKABA!
THWUP

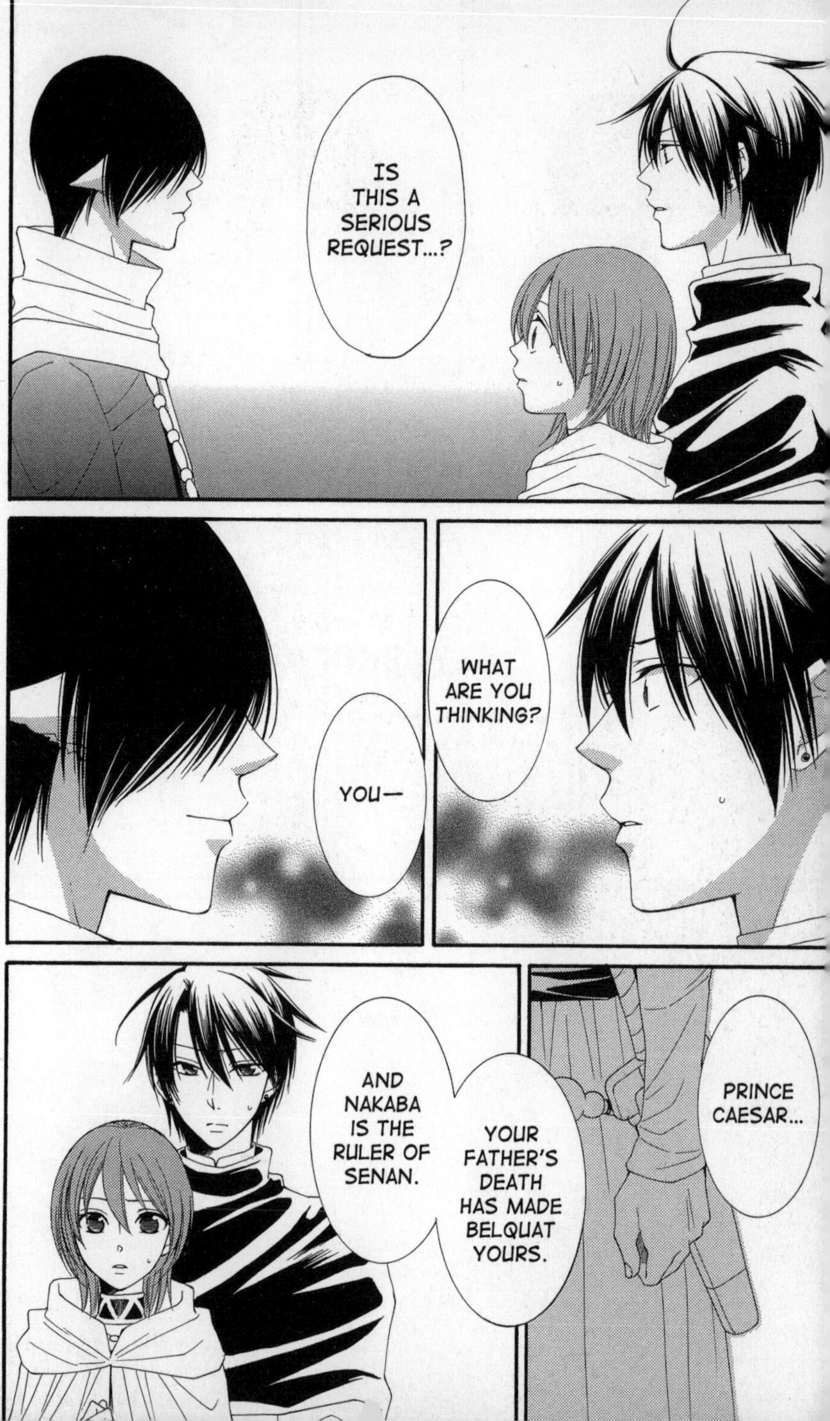
IS THIS A SERIOUS REQUEST...?
WHAT ARE YOU THINKING?
YOU—
PRINCE CAESAR...
YOUR FATHER'S DEATH HAS MADE BELQUAT YOURS.
AND NAKABA IS THE RULER OF SENAN.

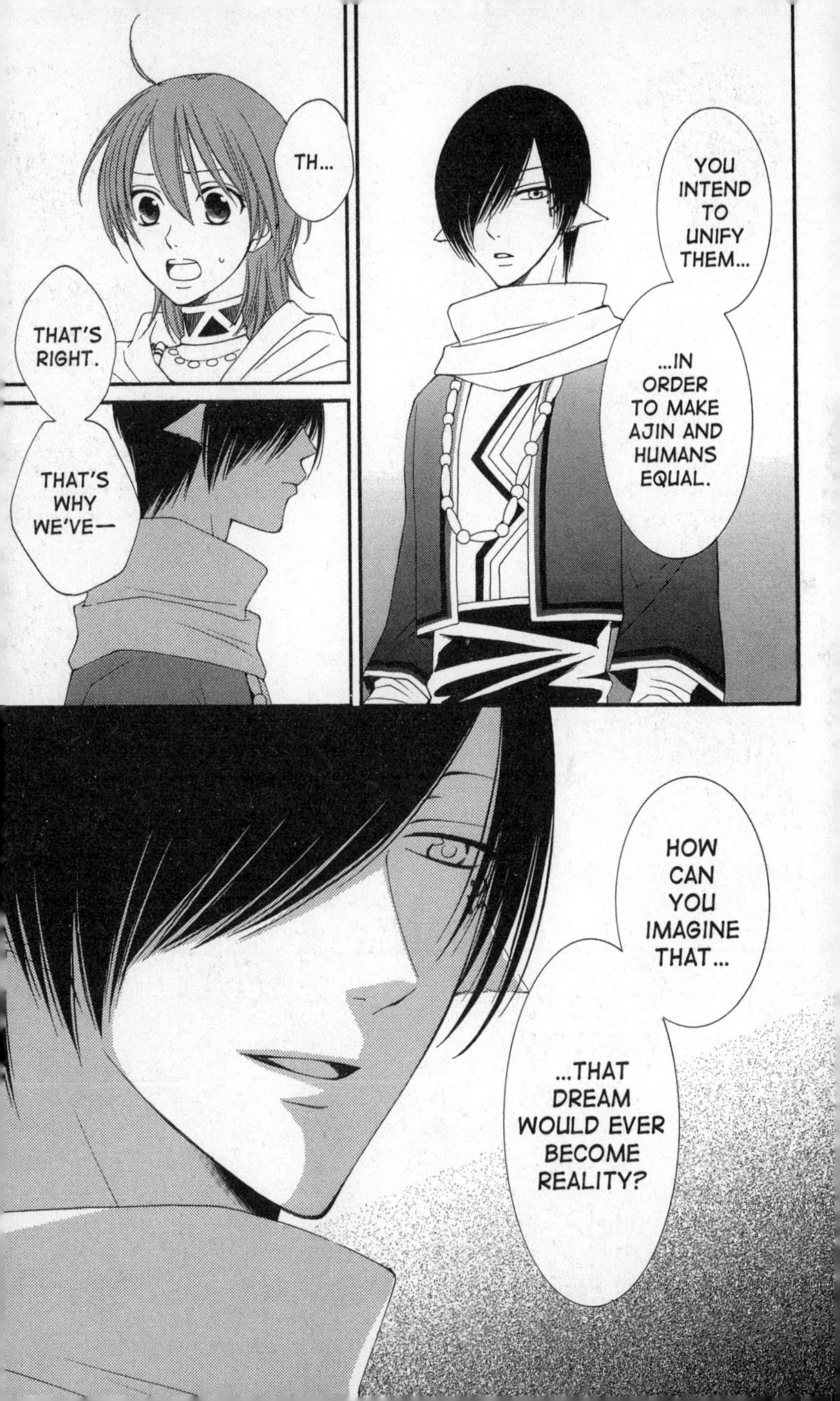
YOU INTEND TO UNIFY THEM...
...IN ORDER TO MAKE AJIN AND HUMANS EQUAL.
TH...
THAT'S RIGHT.
THAT'S WHY WE'VE—
HOW CAN YOU IMAGINE THAT...
...THAT DREAM WOULD EVER BECOME REALITY?

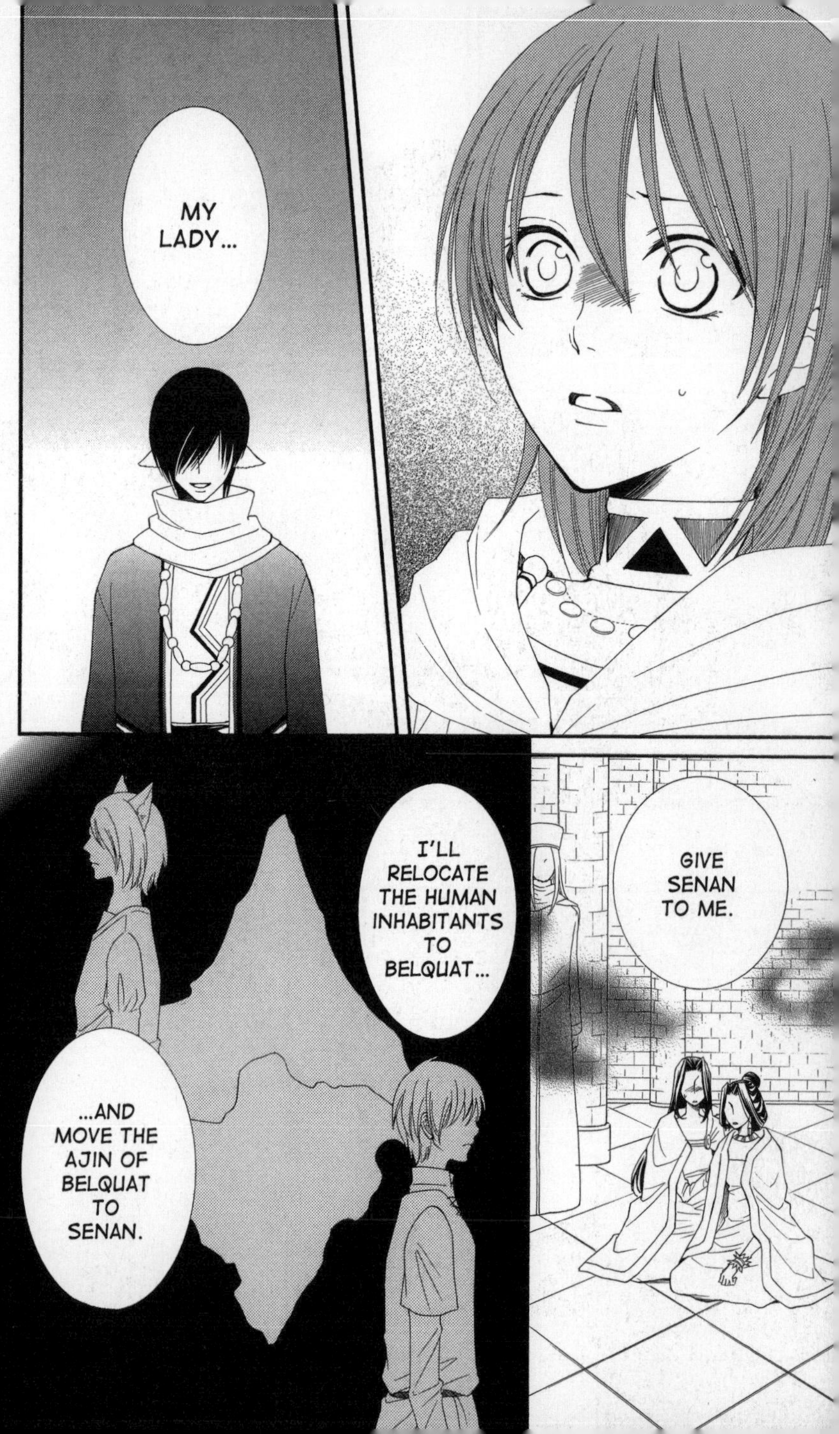
MY LADY...
GIVE SENAN TO ME.
I'LL RELOCATE THE HUMAN INHABITANTS TO BELQUAT...
...AND MOVE THE AJIN OF BELQUAT TO SENAN.

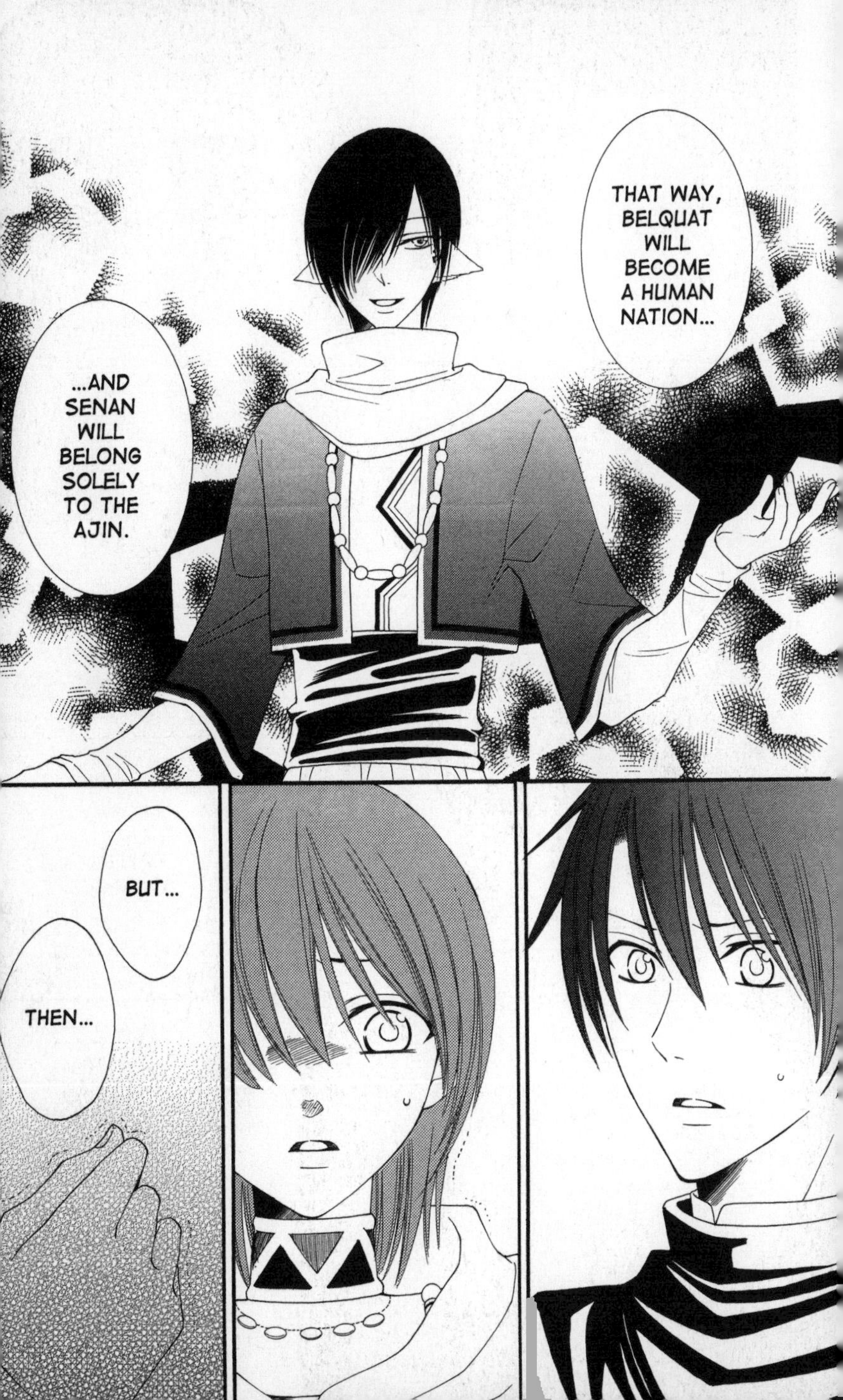
THAT WAY, BELQUAT WILL BECOME A HUMAN NATION...
...AND SENAN WILL BELONG SOLELY TO THE AJIN.
BUT...
THEN...

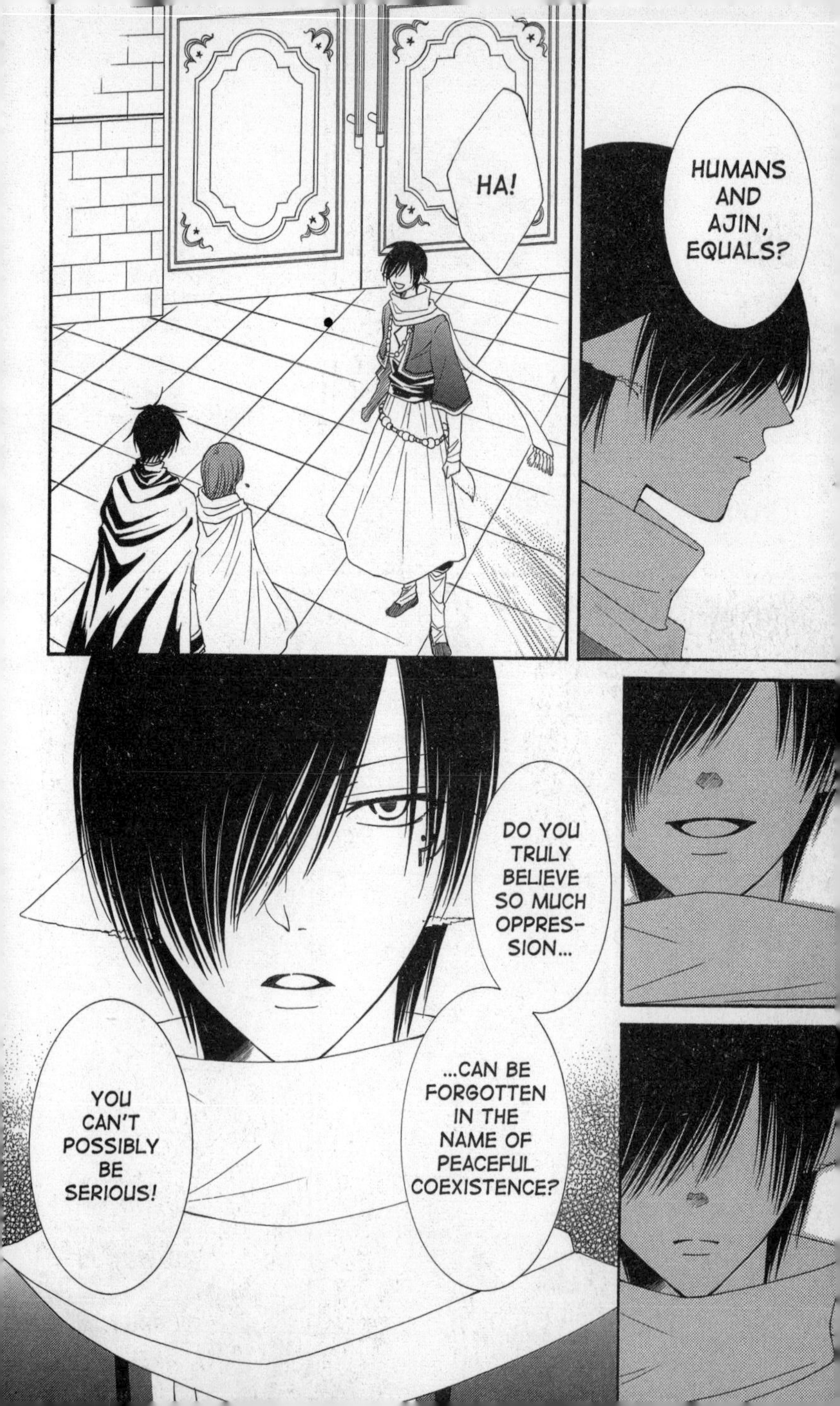
HUMANS AND AJIN, EQUALS?
HA!
DO YOU TRULY BELIEVE SO MUCH OPPRES-SION...
...CAN BE FORGOTTEN IN THE NAME OF PEACEFUL COEXISTENCE?
YOU CAN'T POSSIBLY BE SERIOUS!

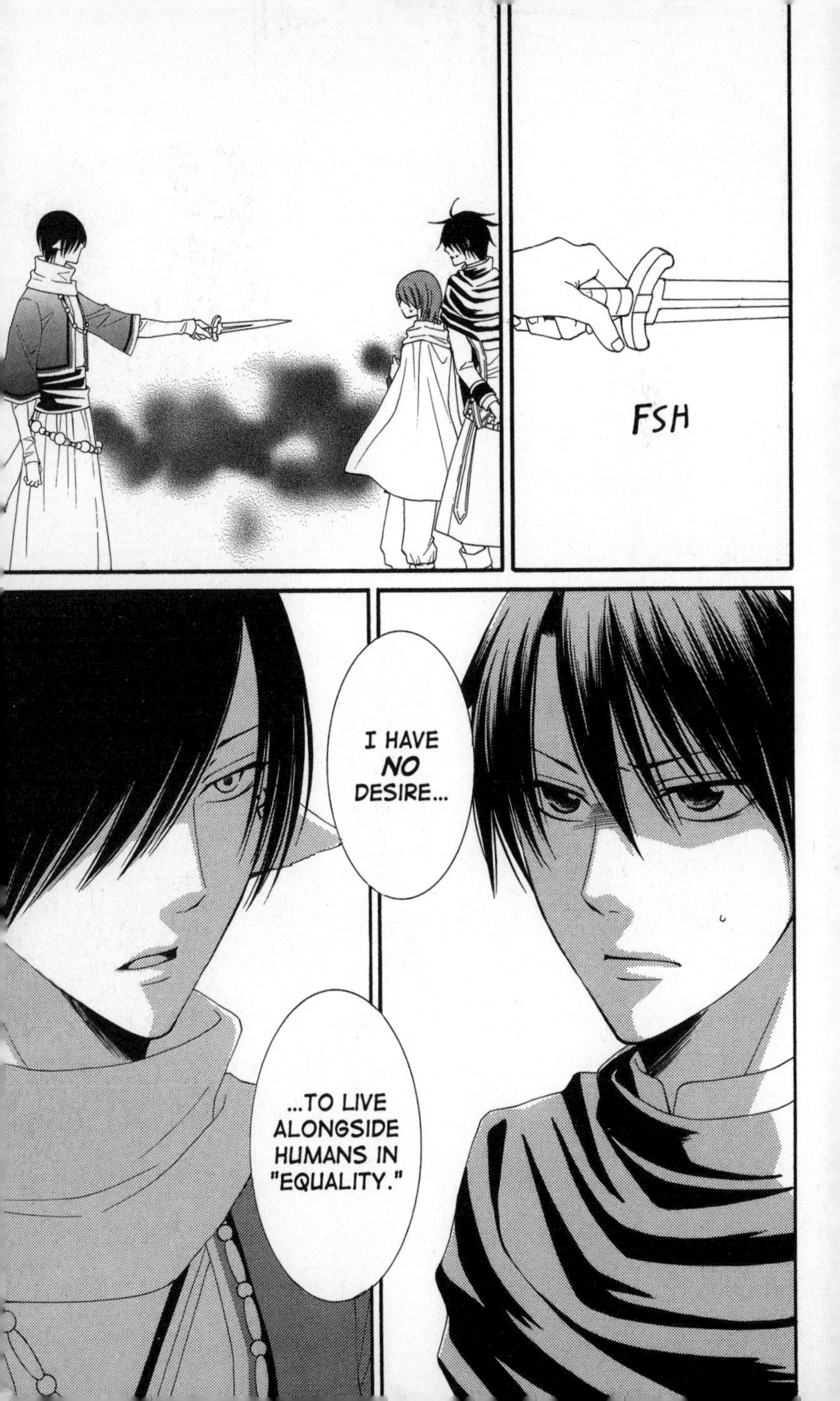
FSH
I HAVE NO DESIRE...
...TO LIVE ALONGSIDE HUMANS IN "EQUALITY."

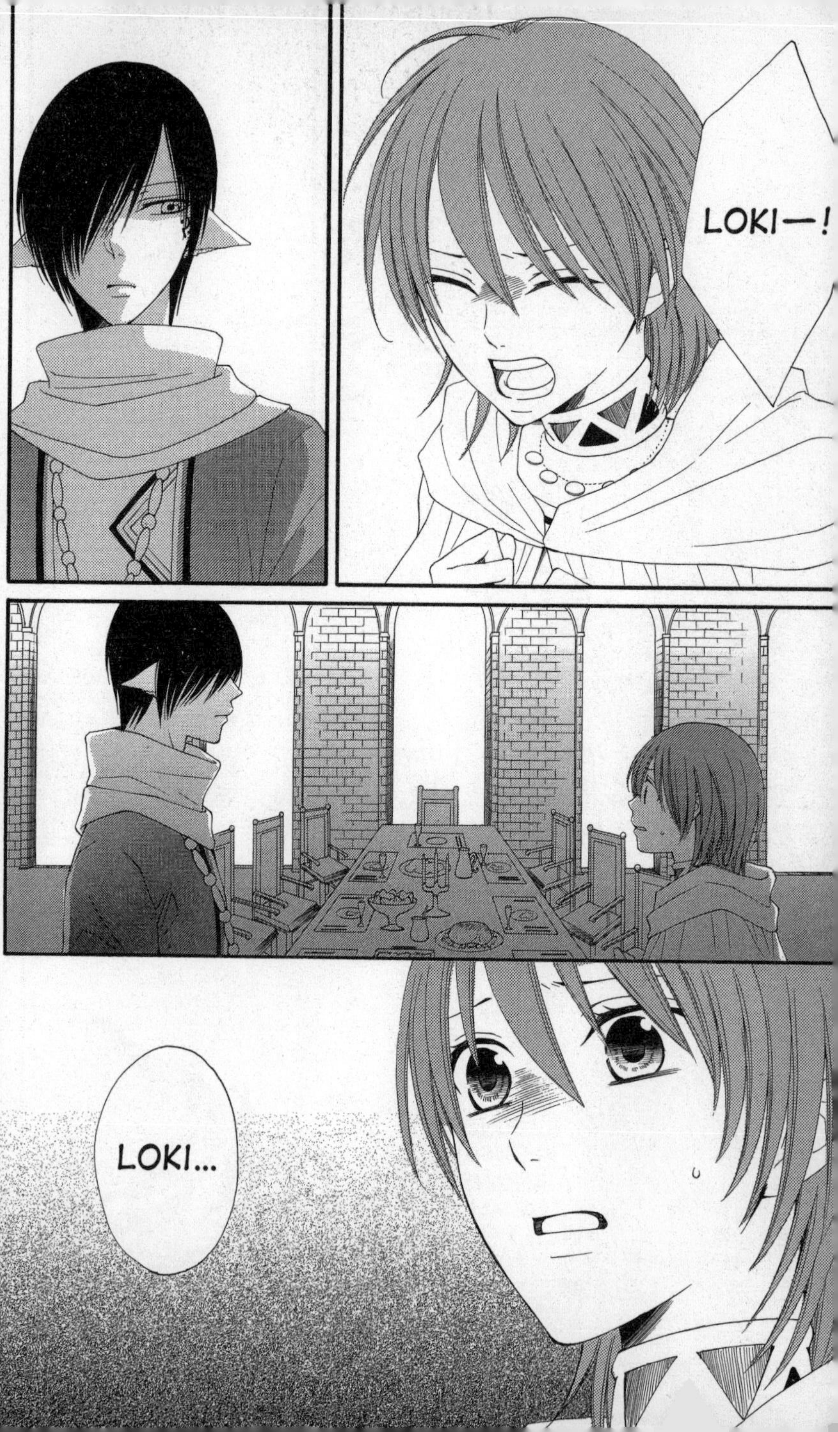
LOKI—!
LOKI...

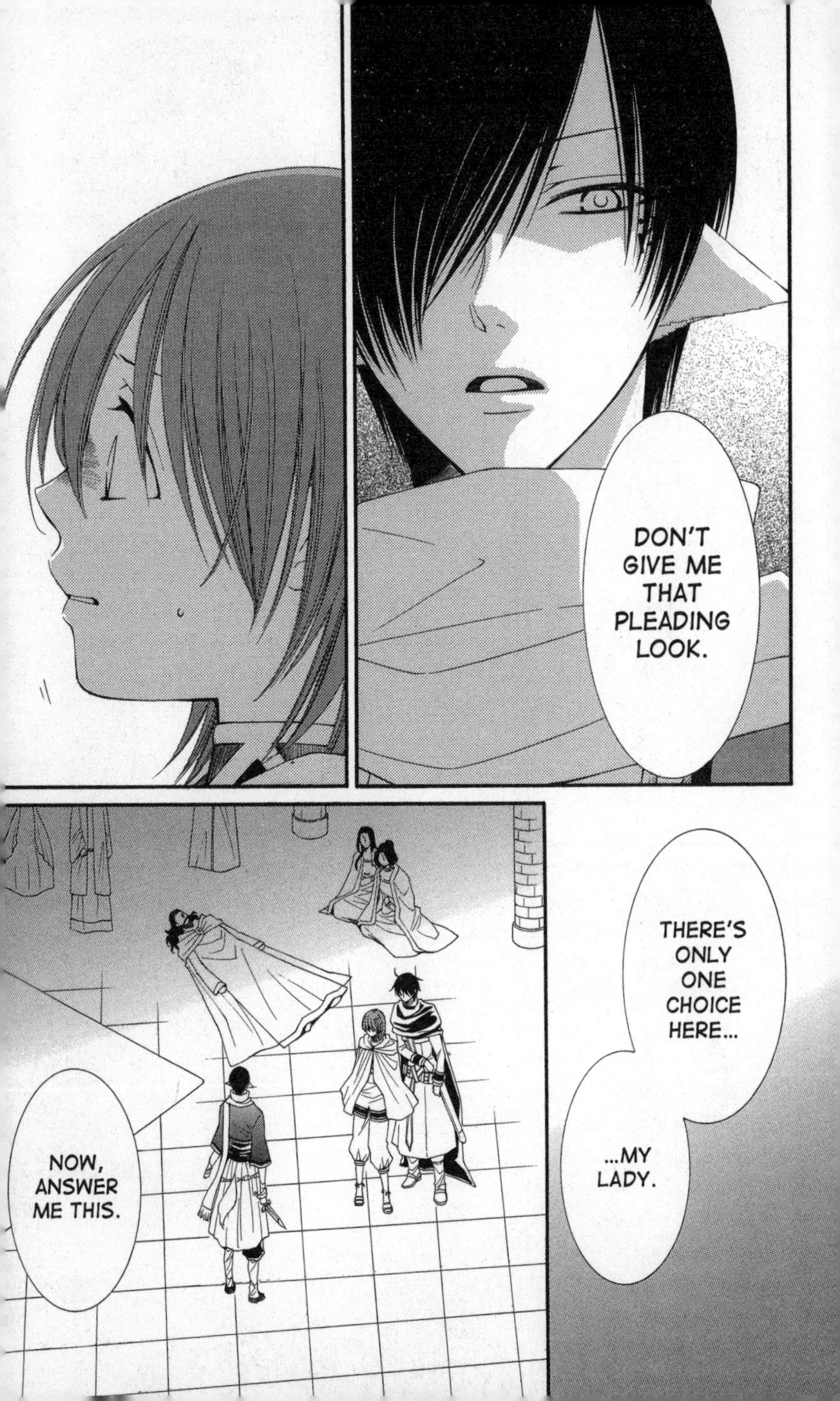
DON'T GIVE ME THAT PLEADING LOOK.
THERE'S ONLY ONE CHOICE HERE...
...MY LADY.
NOW, ANSWER ME THIS.

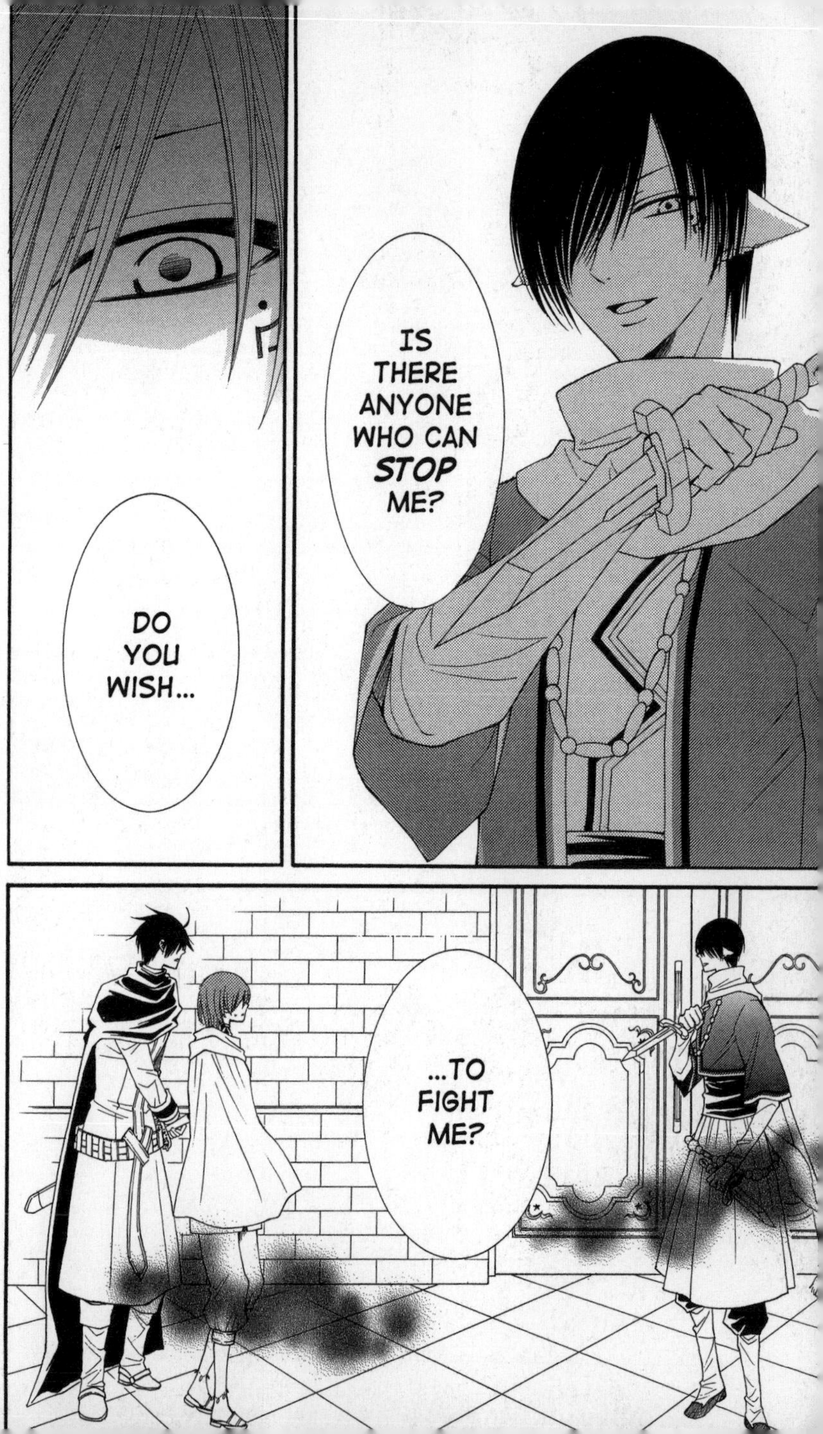
IS THERE ANYONE WHO CAN STOP ME?
DO YOU WISH...
...TO FIGHT ME?

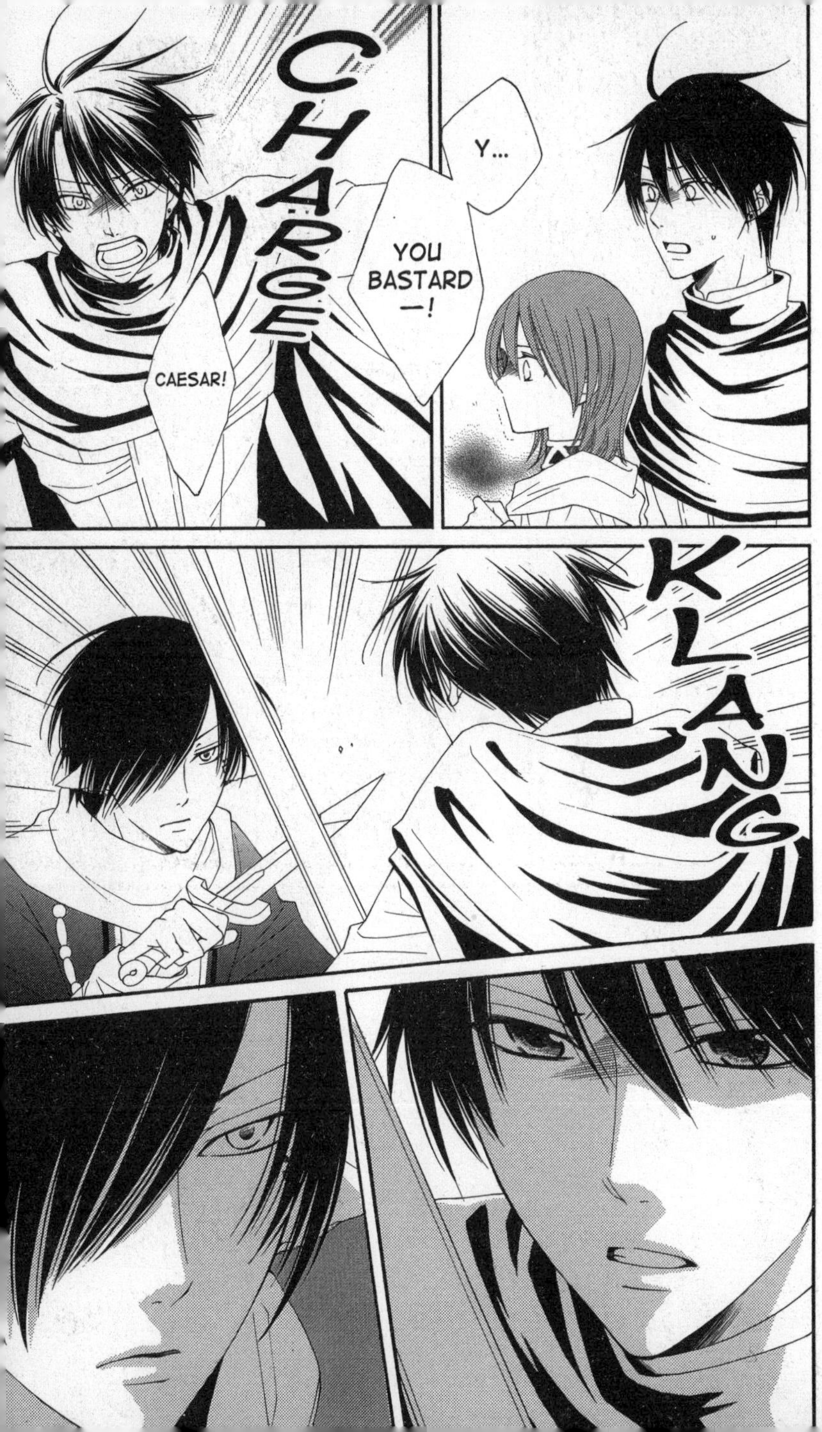
Y...
YOU BASTARD—!
CHARGE
CAESAR!
KLANG

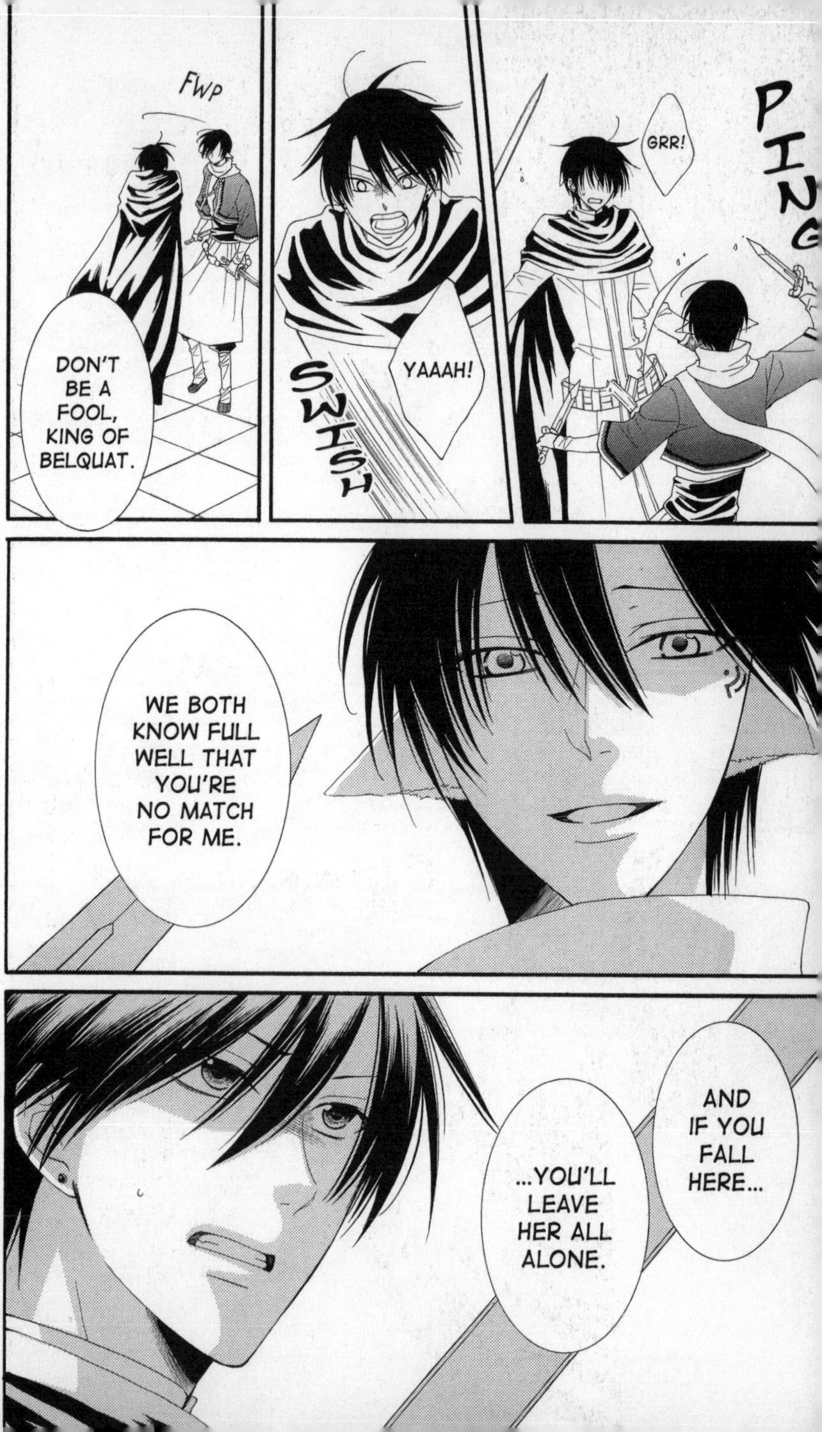
PING
GRR!
YAAAH!
SWISH
FWP
DON'T BE A FOOL, KING OF BELQUAT.
WE BOTH KNOW FULL WELL THAT YOU'RE NO MATCH FOR ME.
AND IF YOU FALL HERE...
...YOU'LL LEAVE HER ALL ALONE.

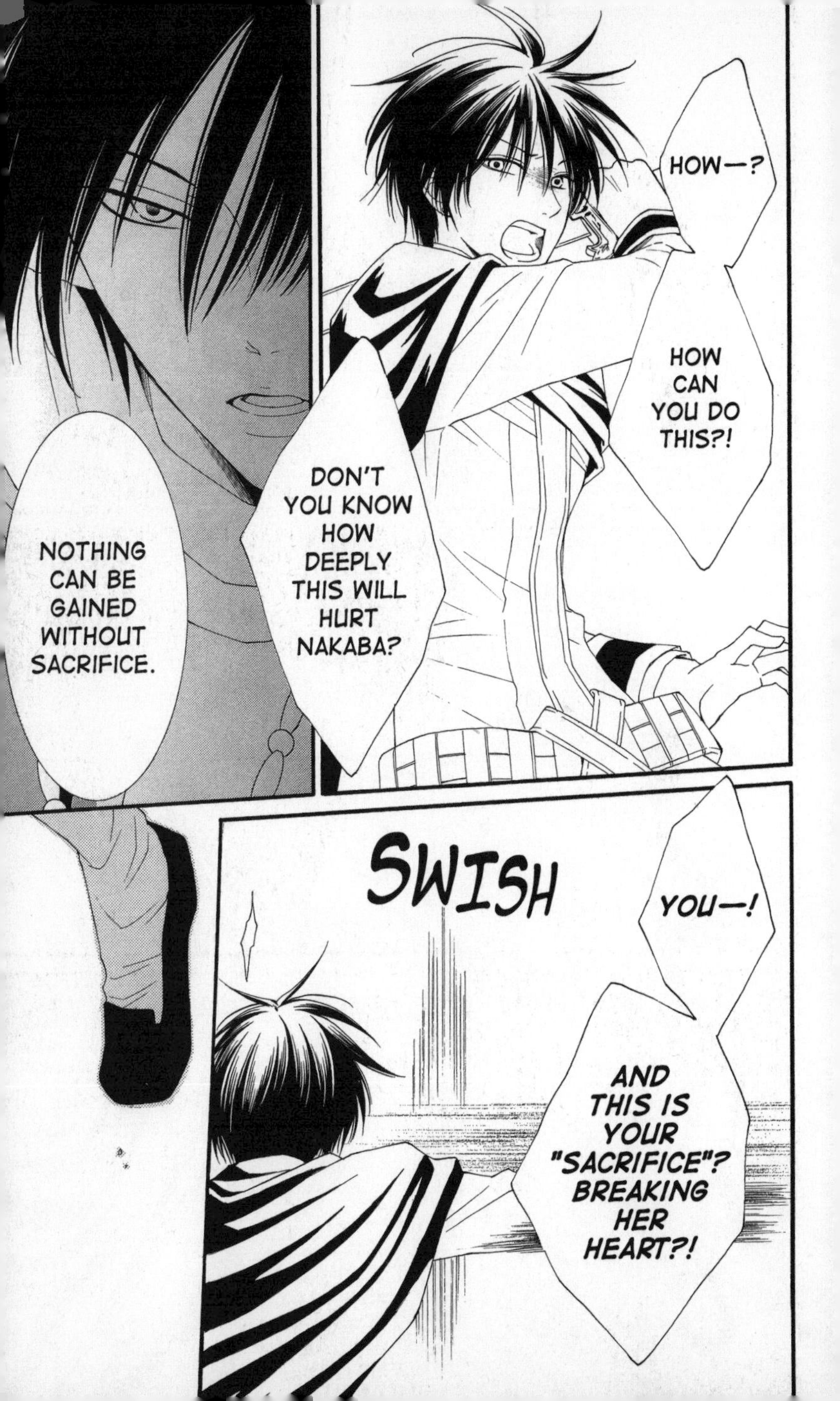
HOW—?
HOW CAN YOU DO THIS?!
DON'T YOU KNOW HOW DEEPLY THIS WILL HURT NAKABA?
NOTHING CAN BE GAINED WITHOUT SACRIFICE.
YOU—!
SWISH
AND THIS IS YOUR "SACRIFICE"? BREAKING HER HEART?!

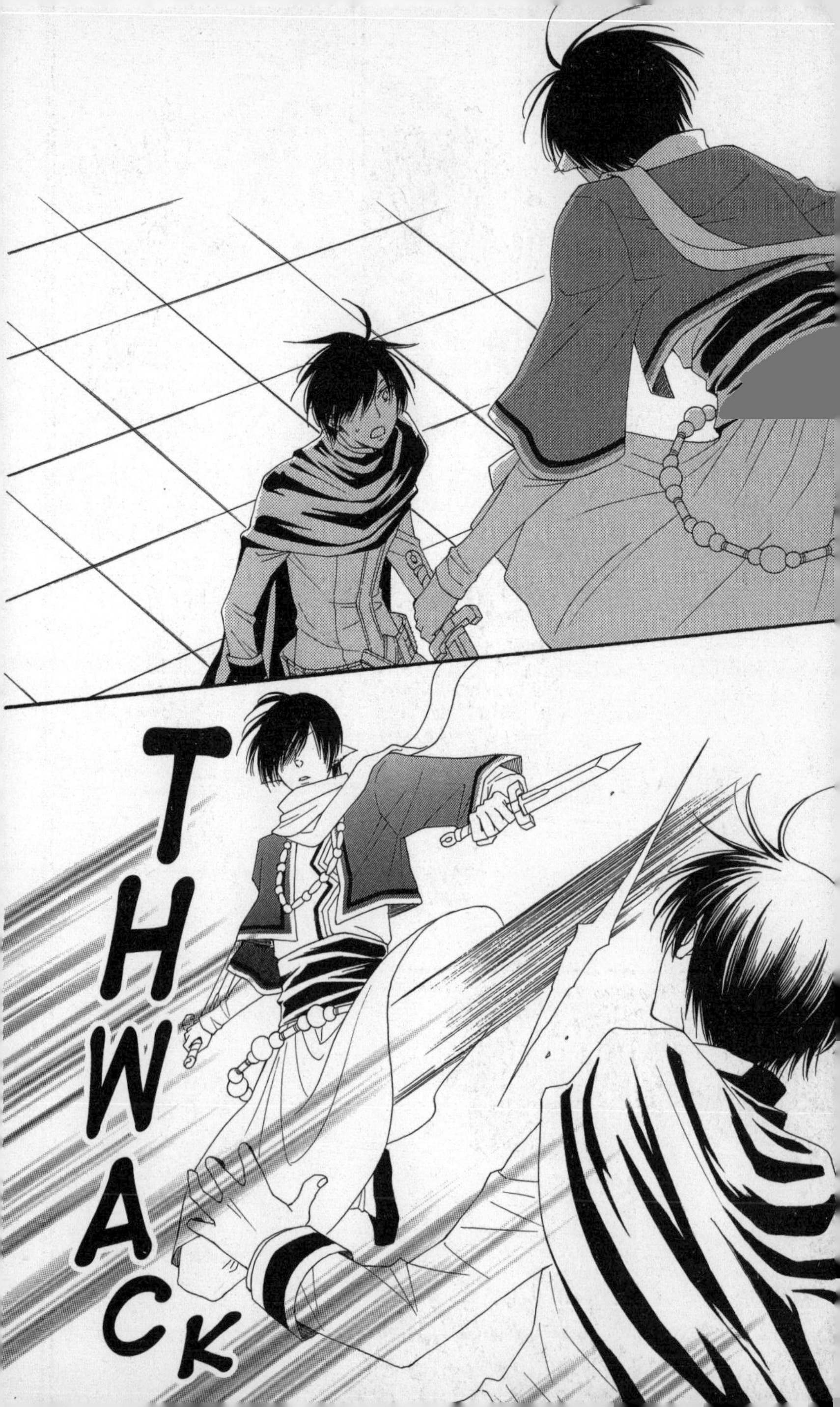
THWACK

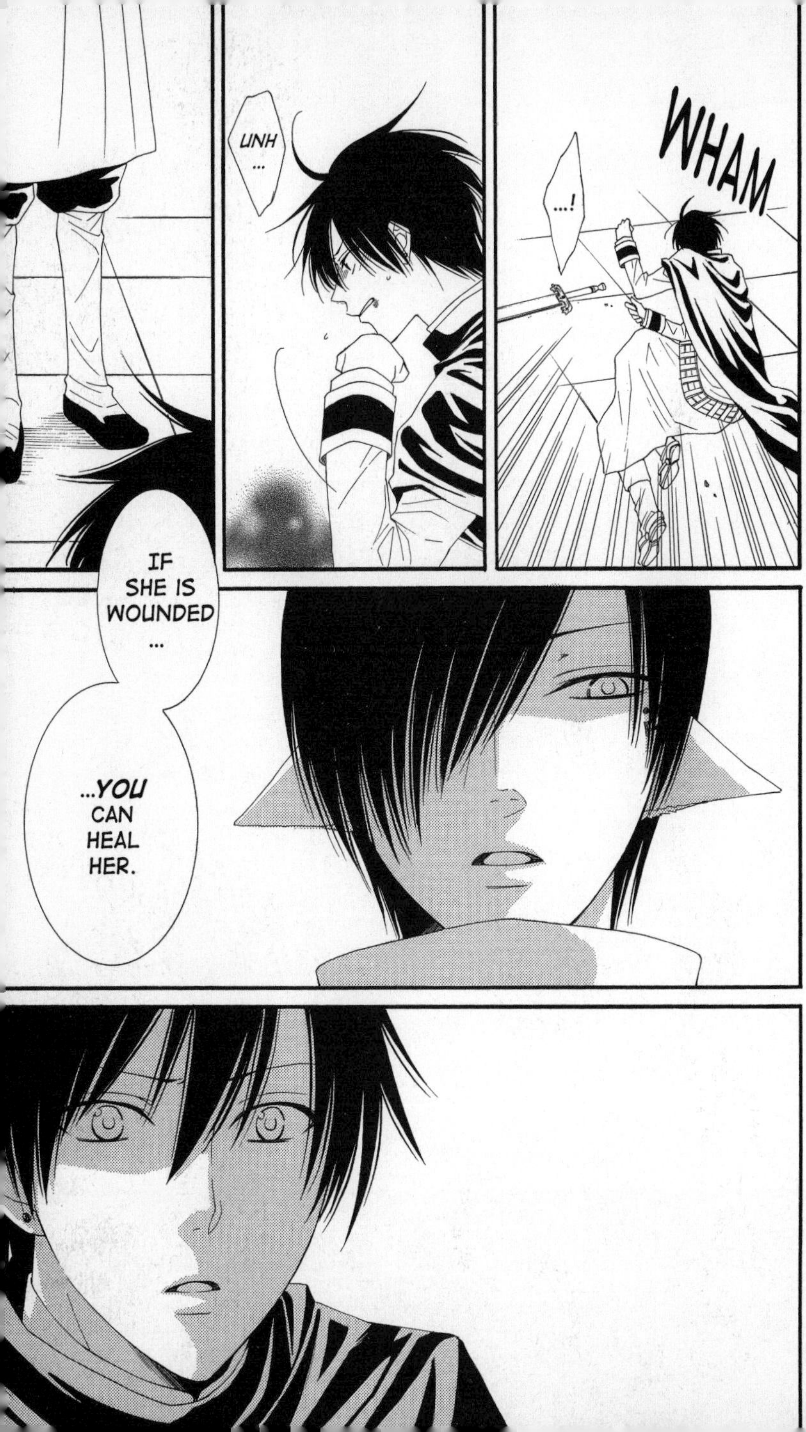
WHAM
...!
UNH ...
IF SHE IS WOUNDED ...
...YOU CAN HEAL HER.

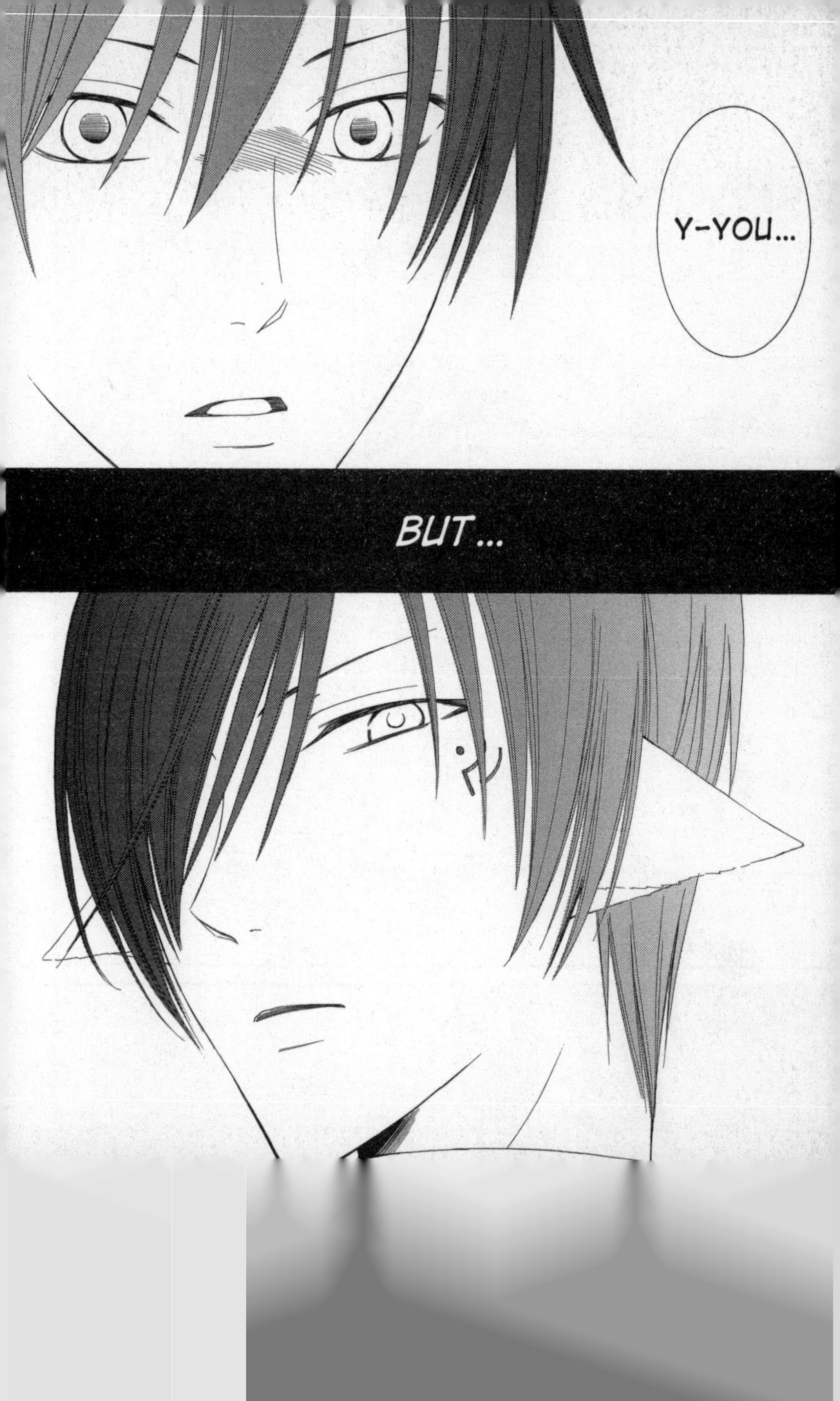
Y-YOU...
BUT...

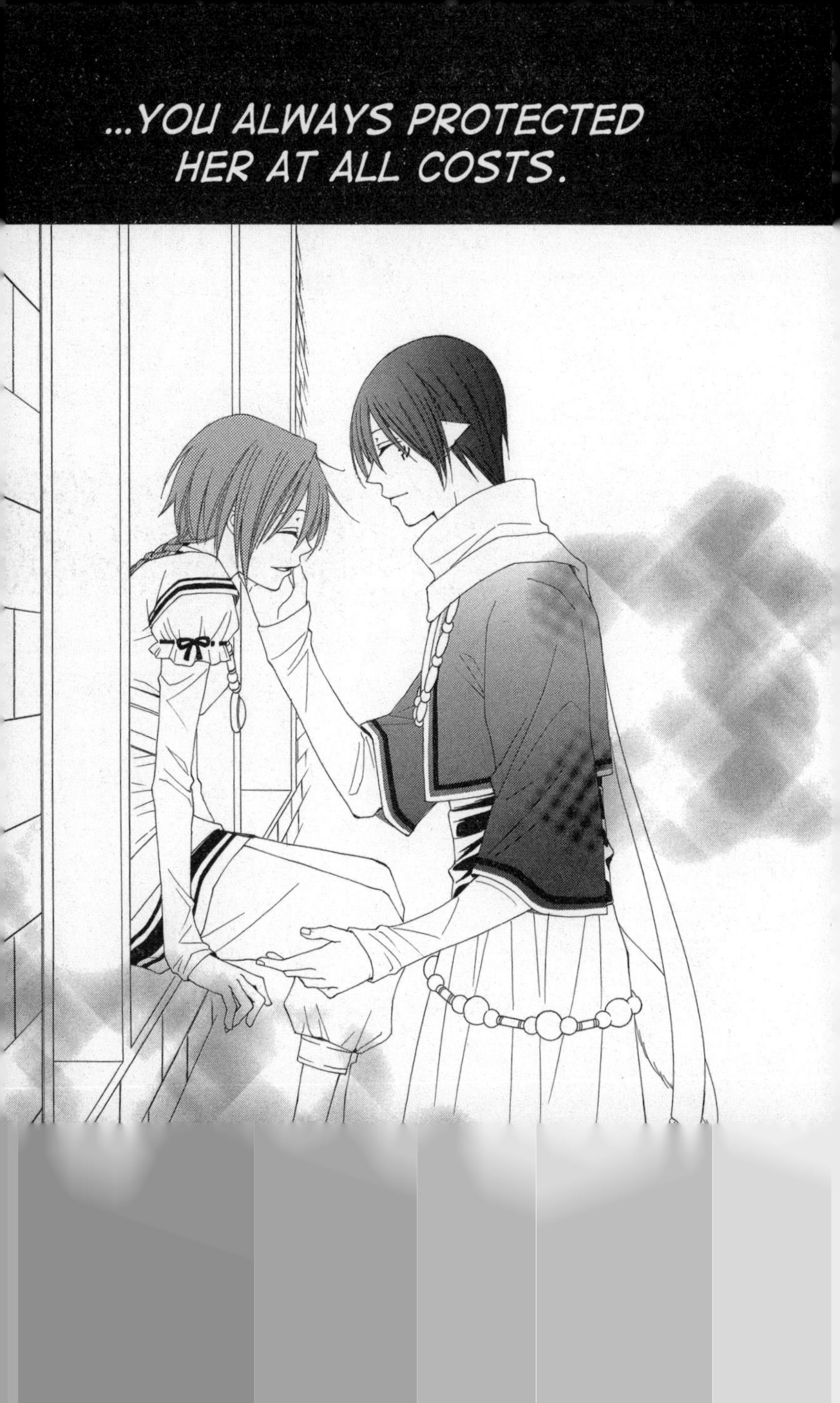
...YOU ALWAYS PROTECTED HER AT ALL COSTS.

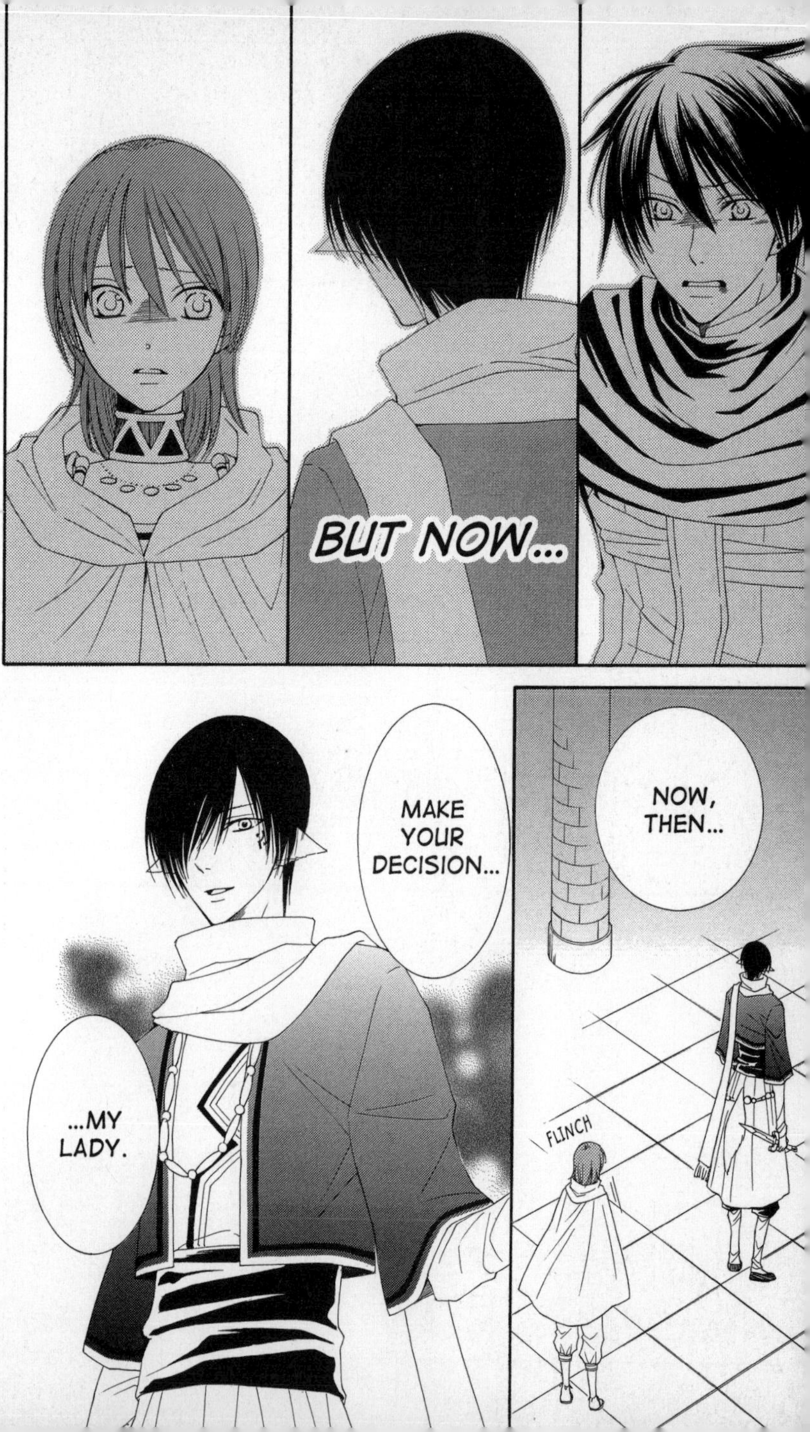
BUT NOW...
NOW, THEN...
FLINCH
MAKE YOUR DECISION...
...MY LADY.

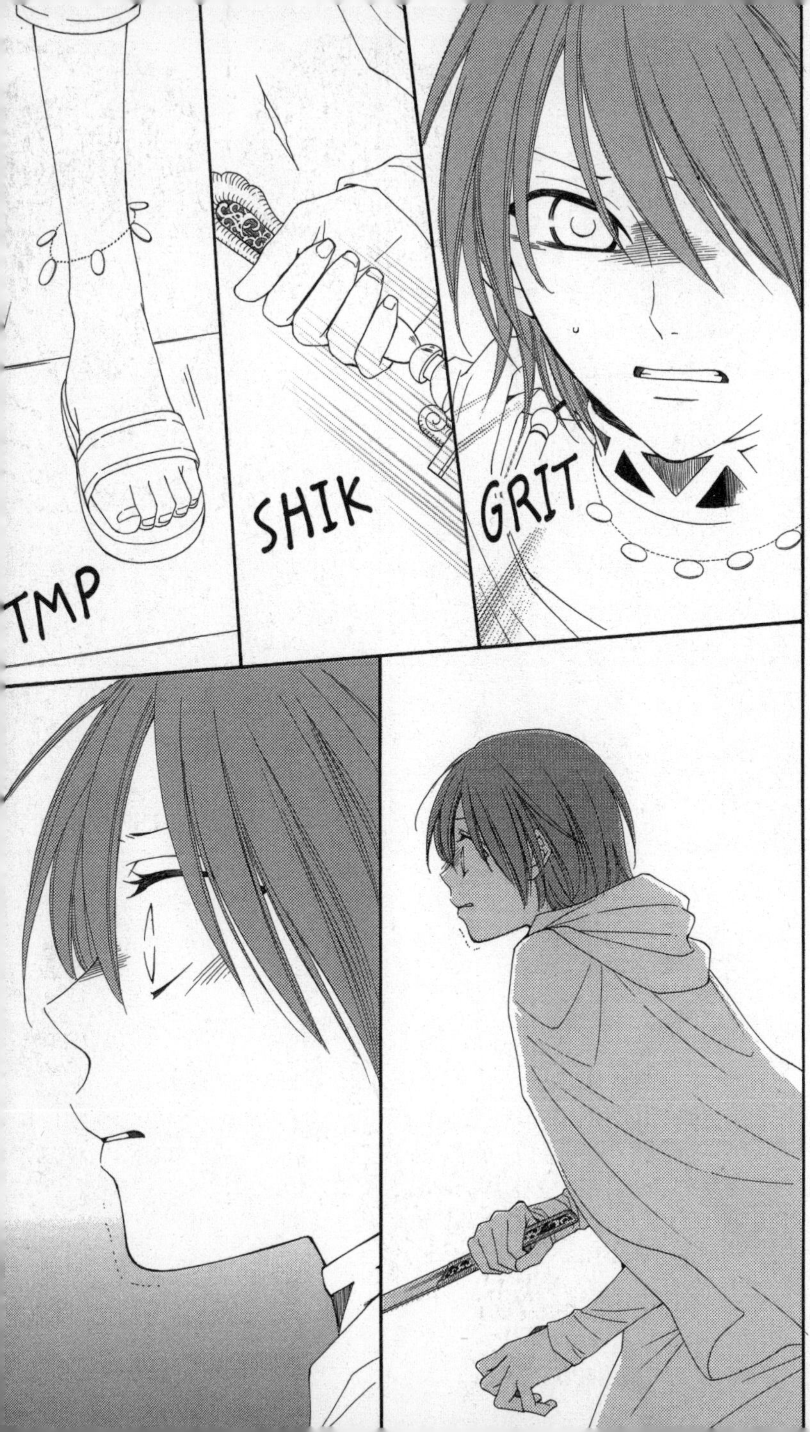
GRIT
SHIK
TMP

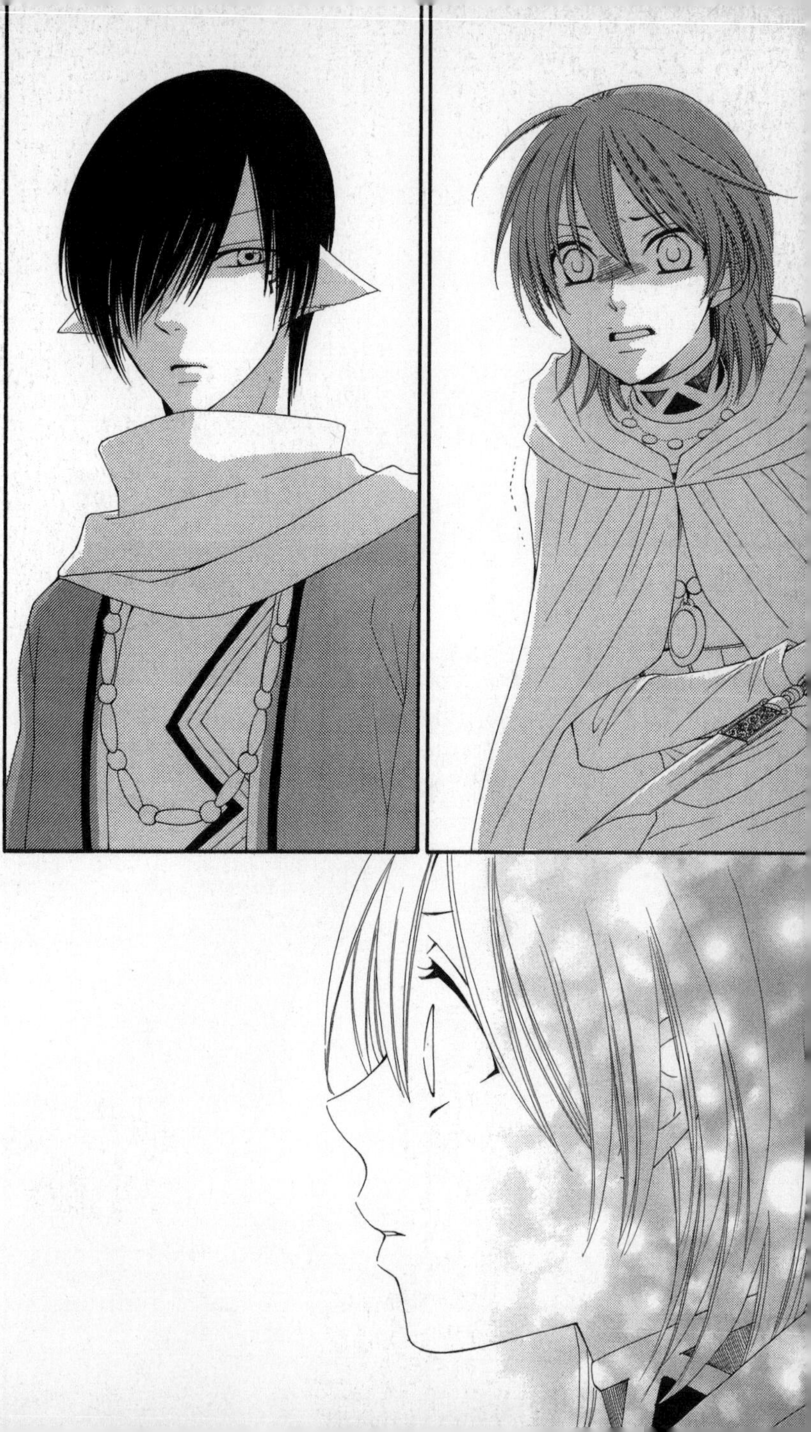

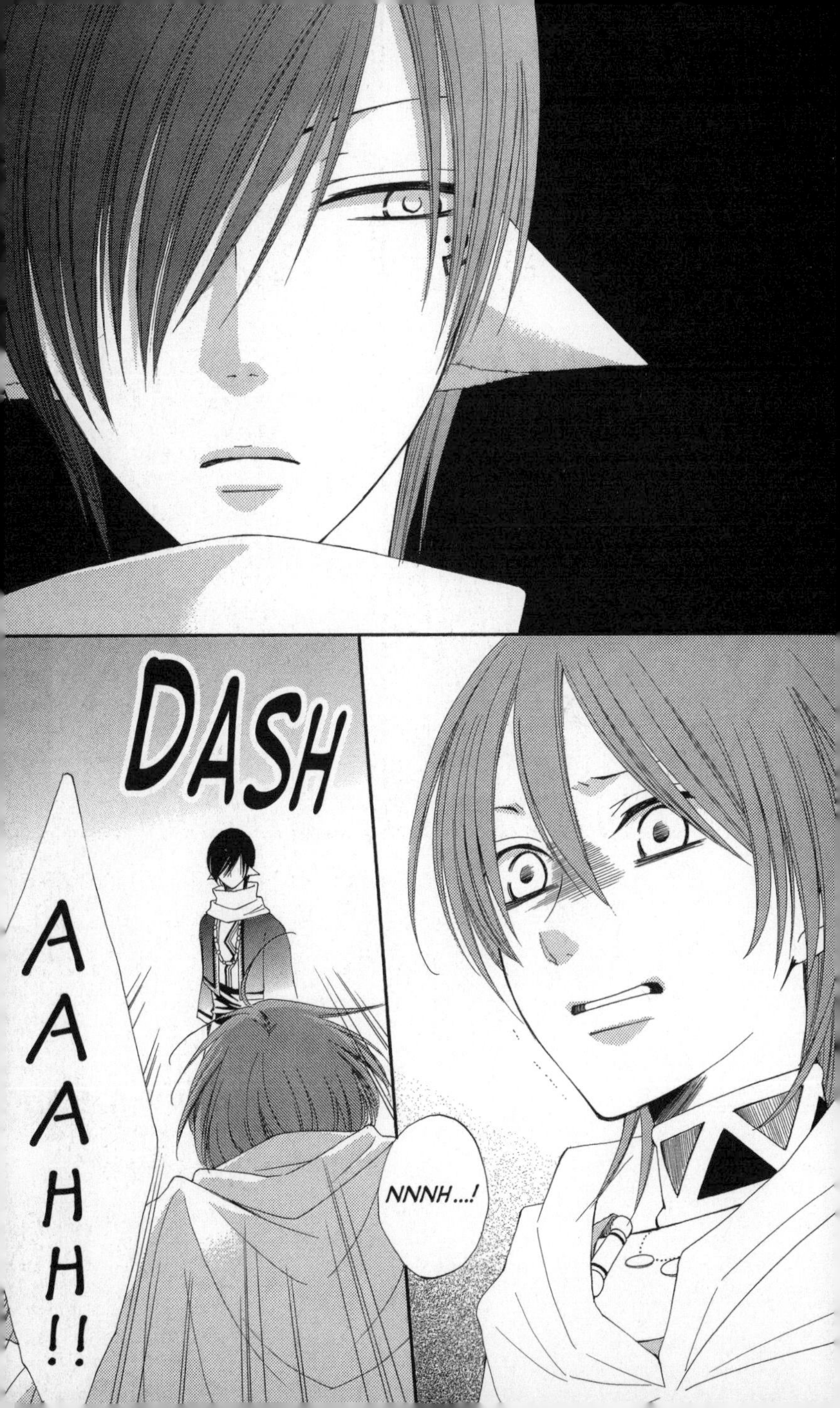
NNNH...!
DASH
AAAAHH!!

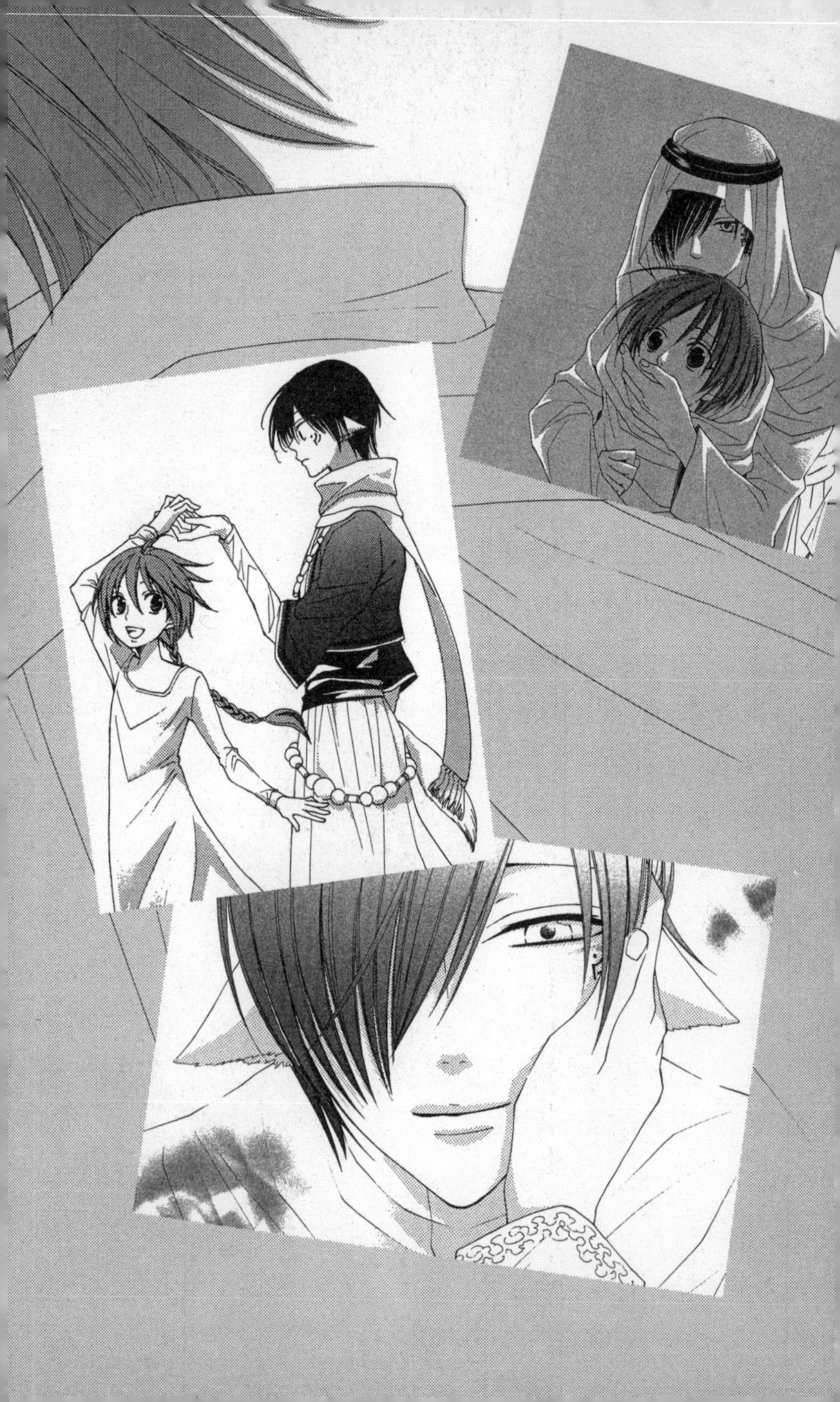

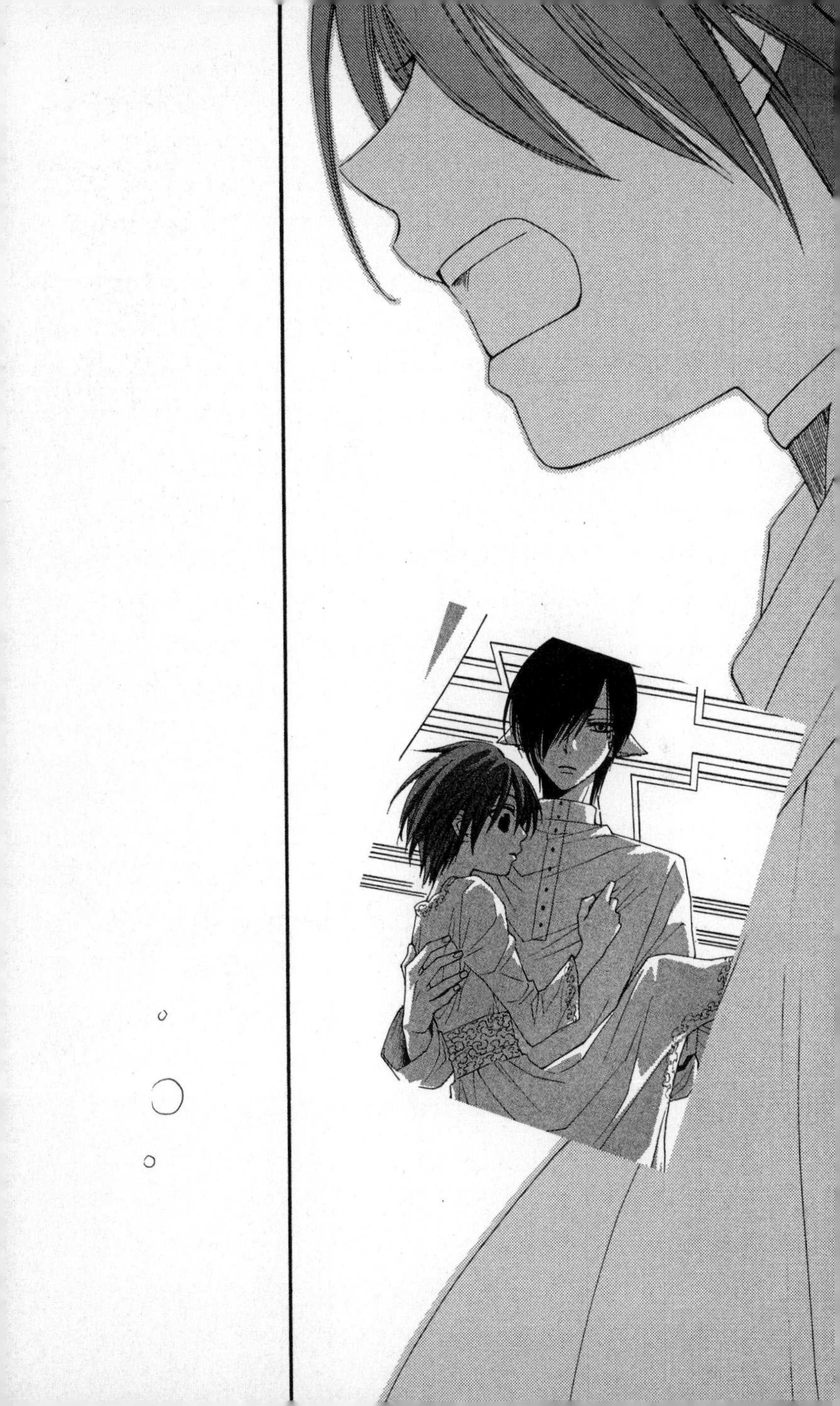

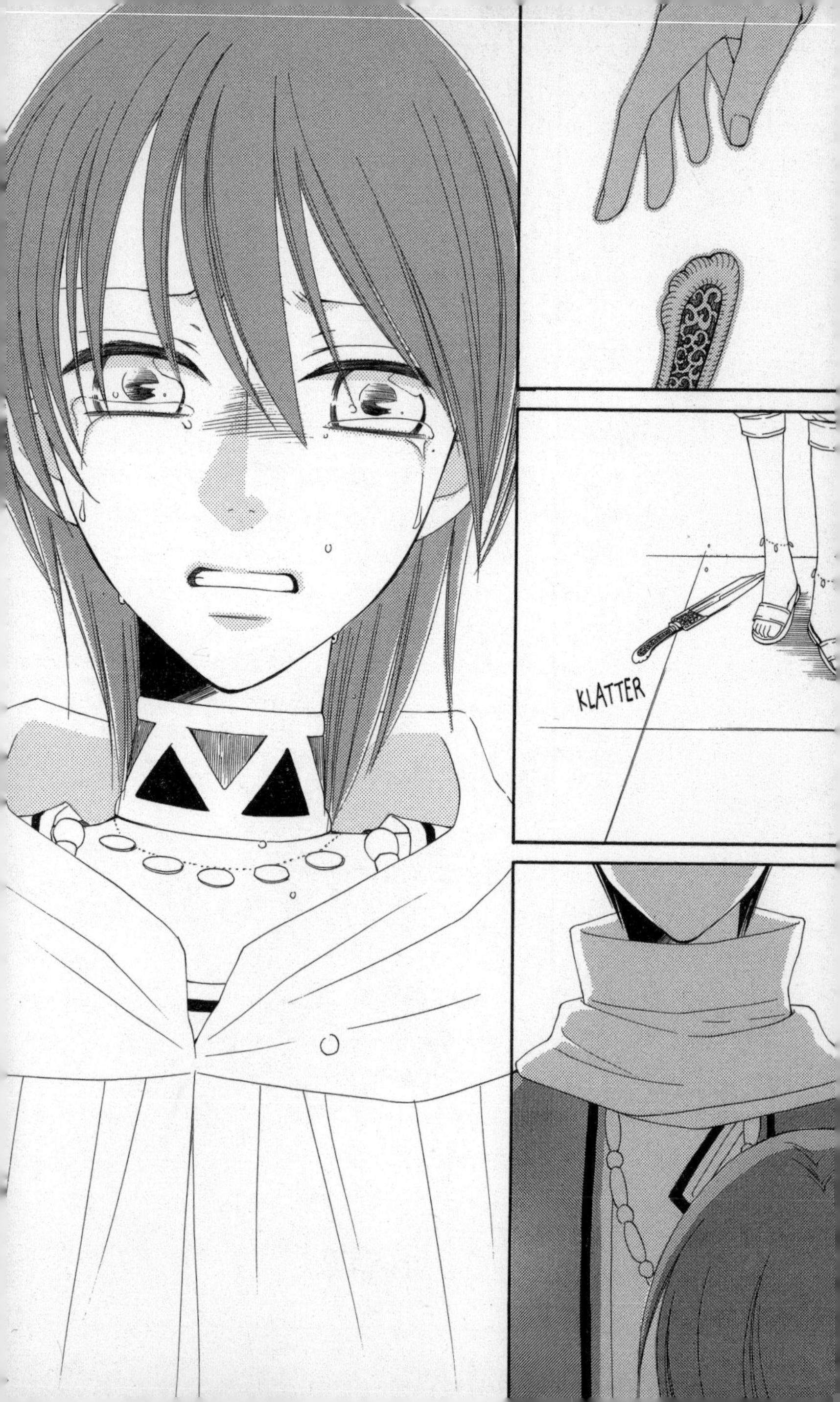
KLATTER

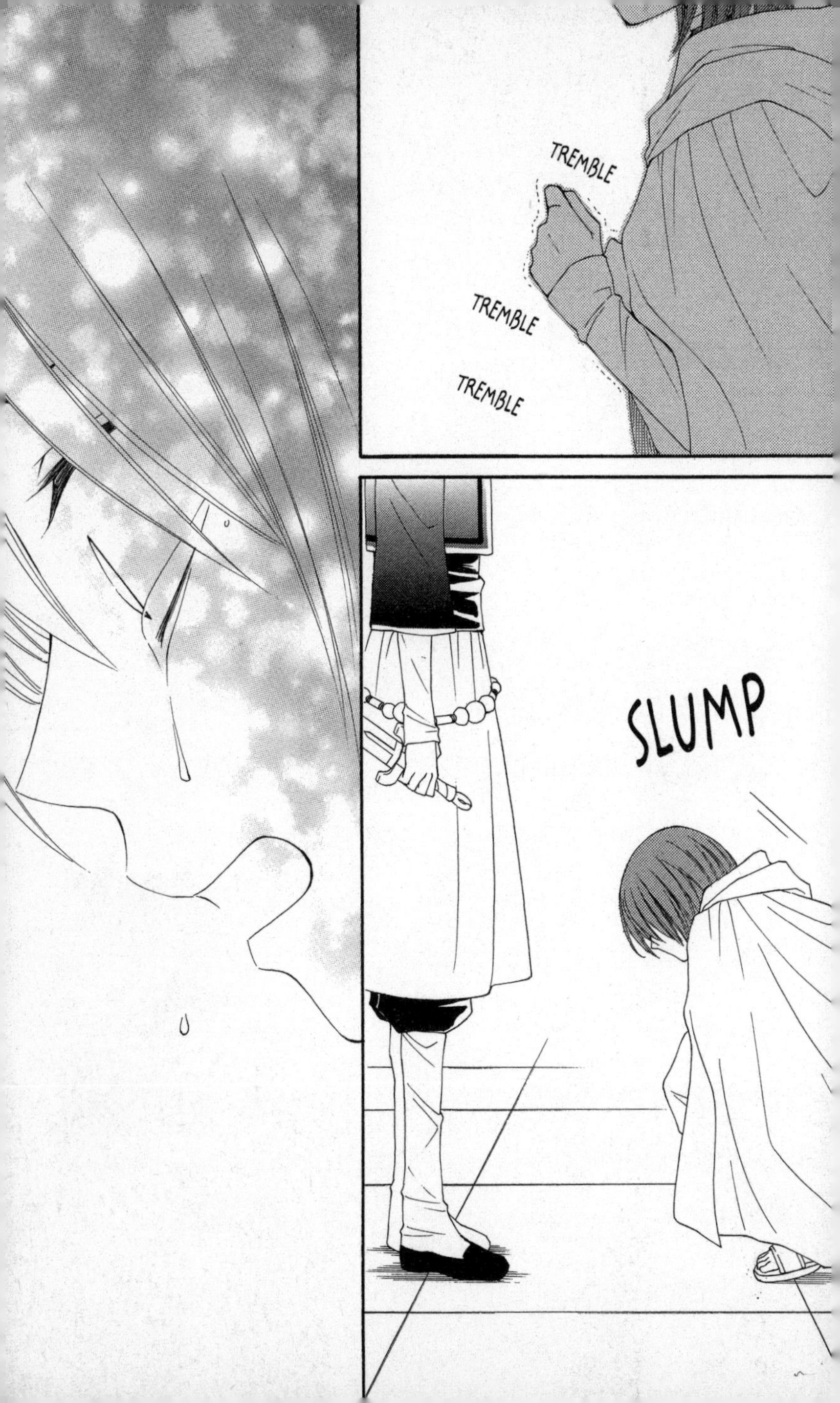
TREMBLE
TREMBLE
TREMBLE
SLUMP

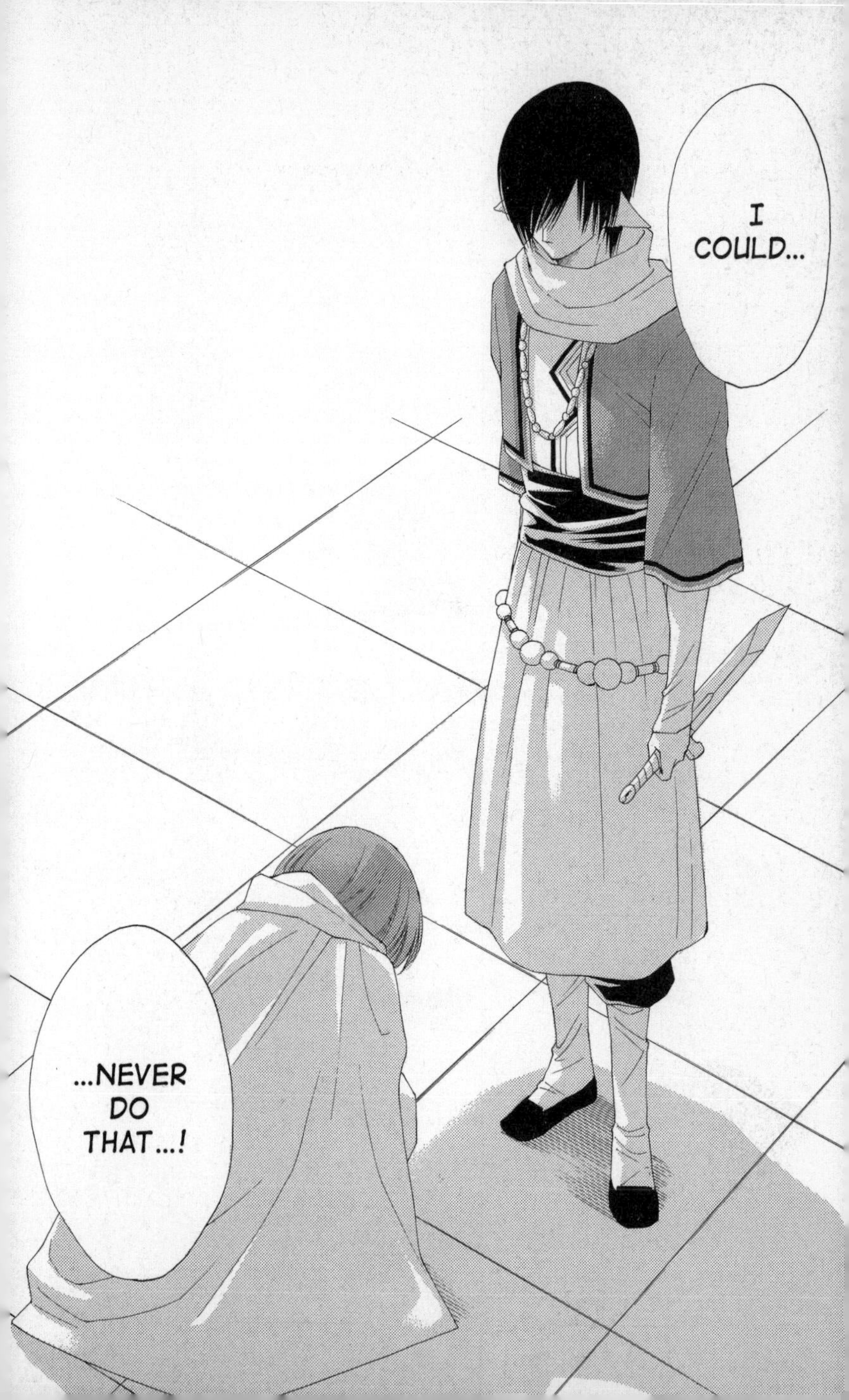
I COULD...
...NEVER DO THAT...!

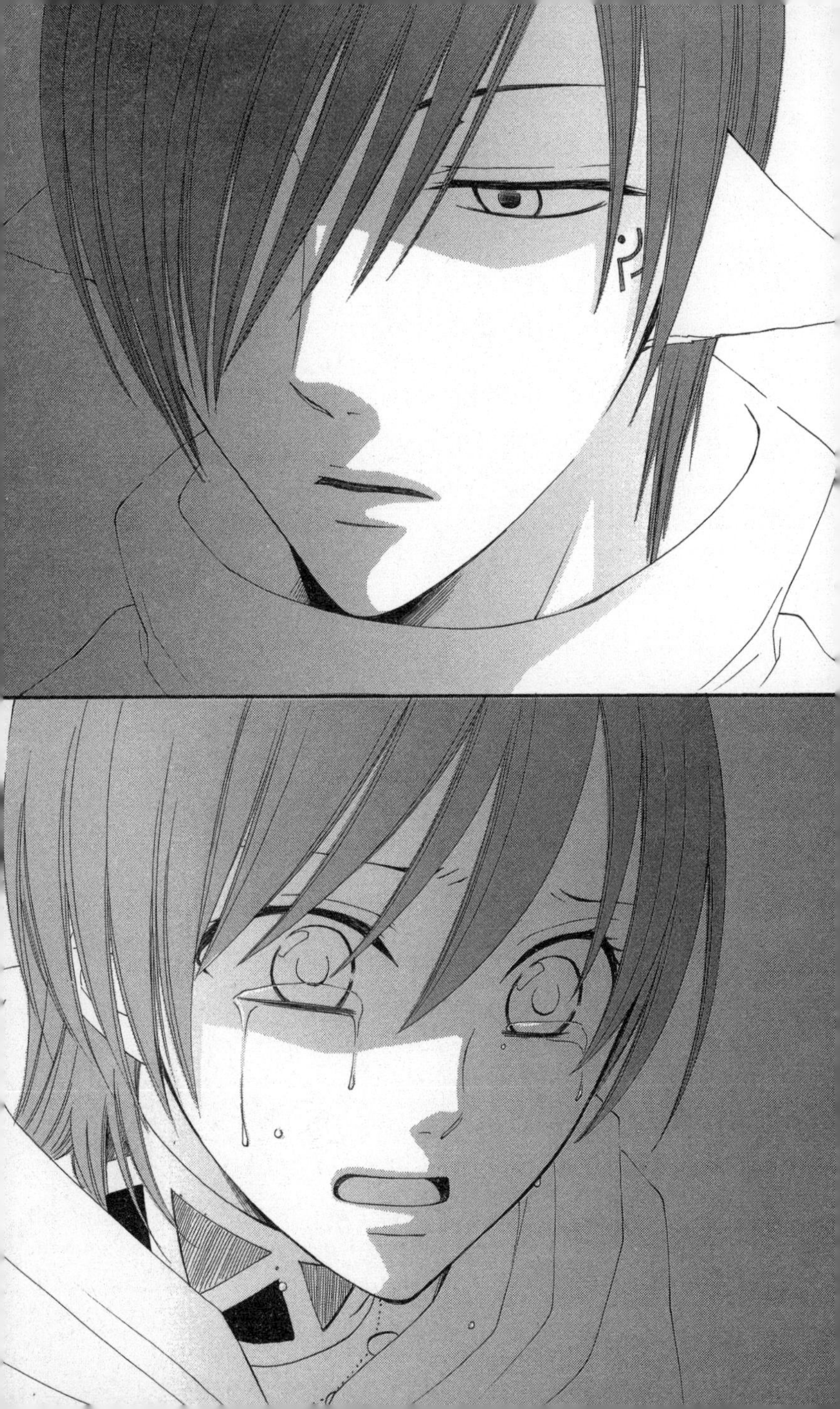

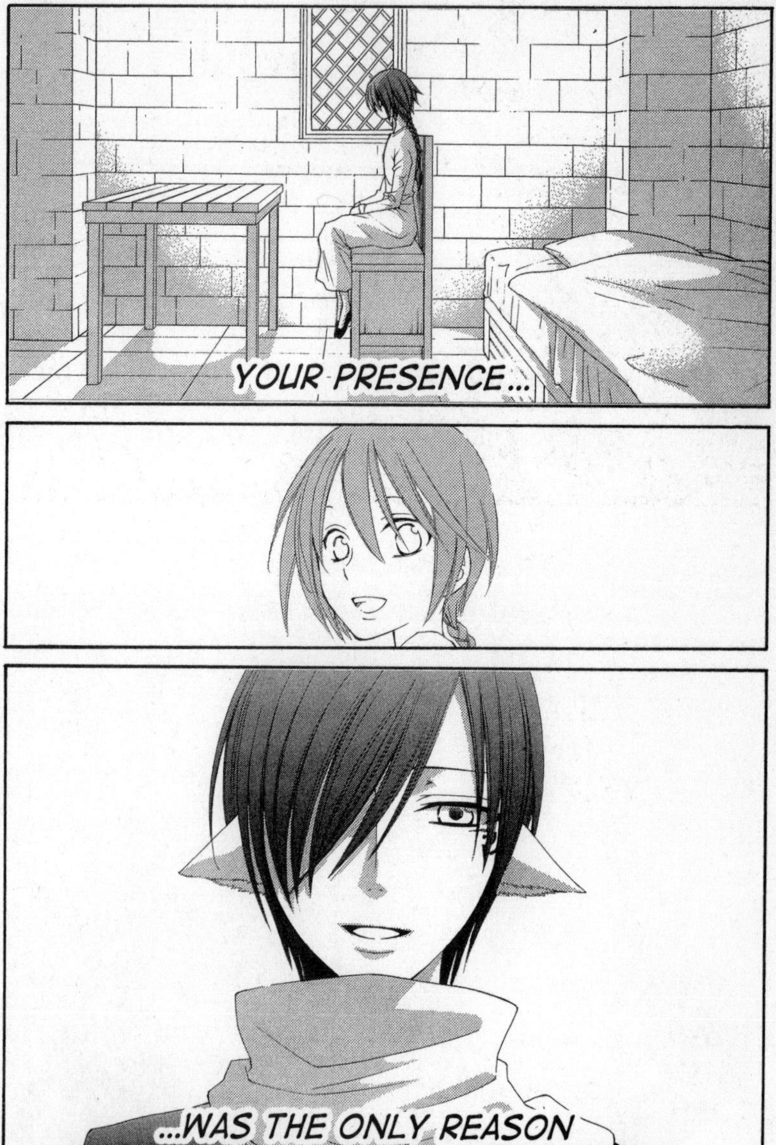
YOUR PRESENCE...
...WAS THE ONLY REASON I COULD ENDURE LIVING.

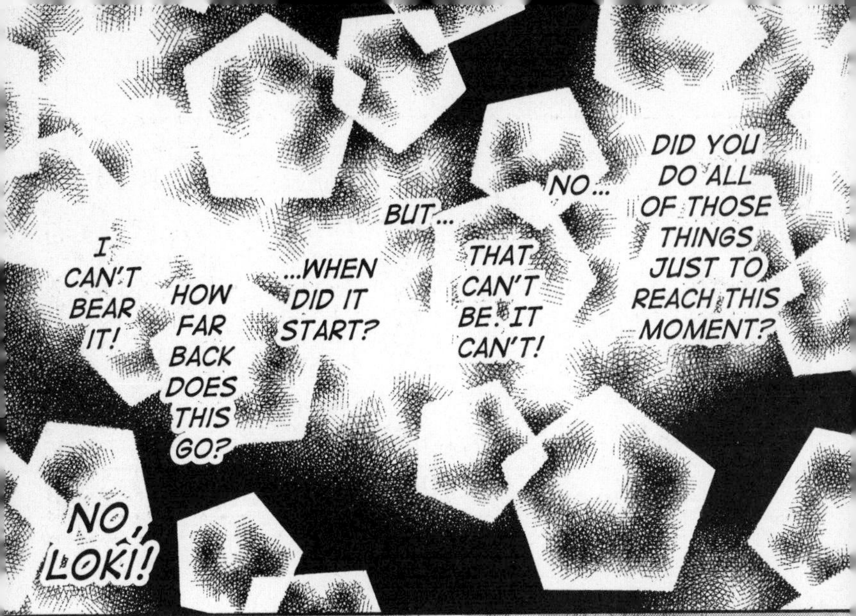
DID YOU DO ALL OF THOSE THINGS JUST TO REACH THIS MOMENT?
NO...
THAT CAN'T BE. IT CAN'T!
BUT...
...WHEN DID IT START?
HOW FAR BACK DOES THIS GO?
I CAN'T BEAR IT!
NO, LOKI!
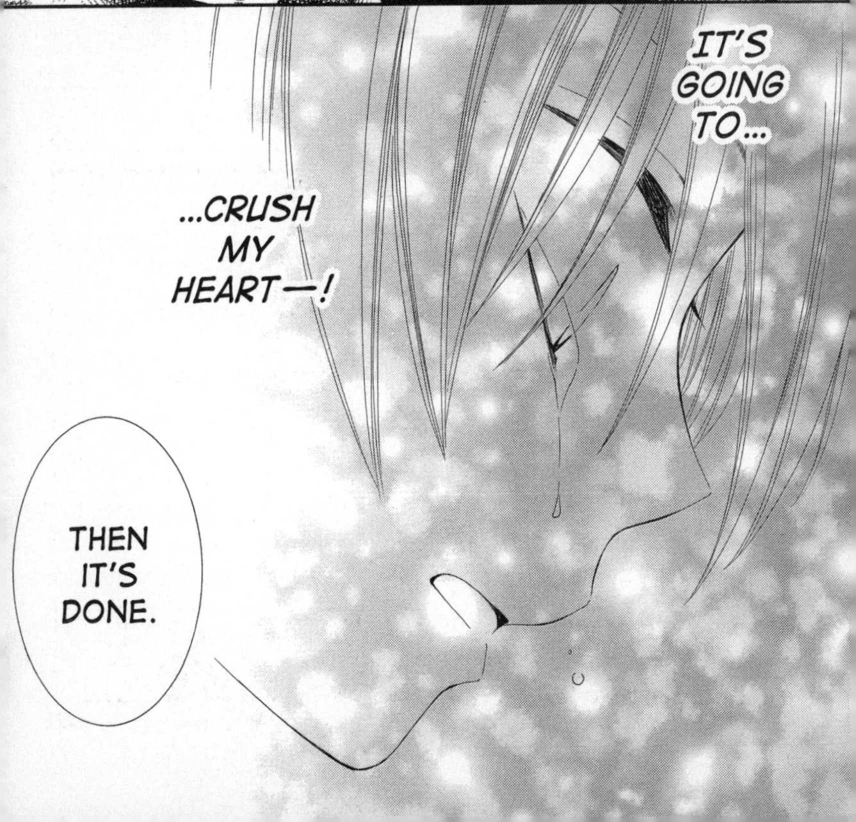
IT'S GOING TO...
...CRUSH MY HEART—!
THEN IT'S DONE.

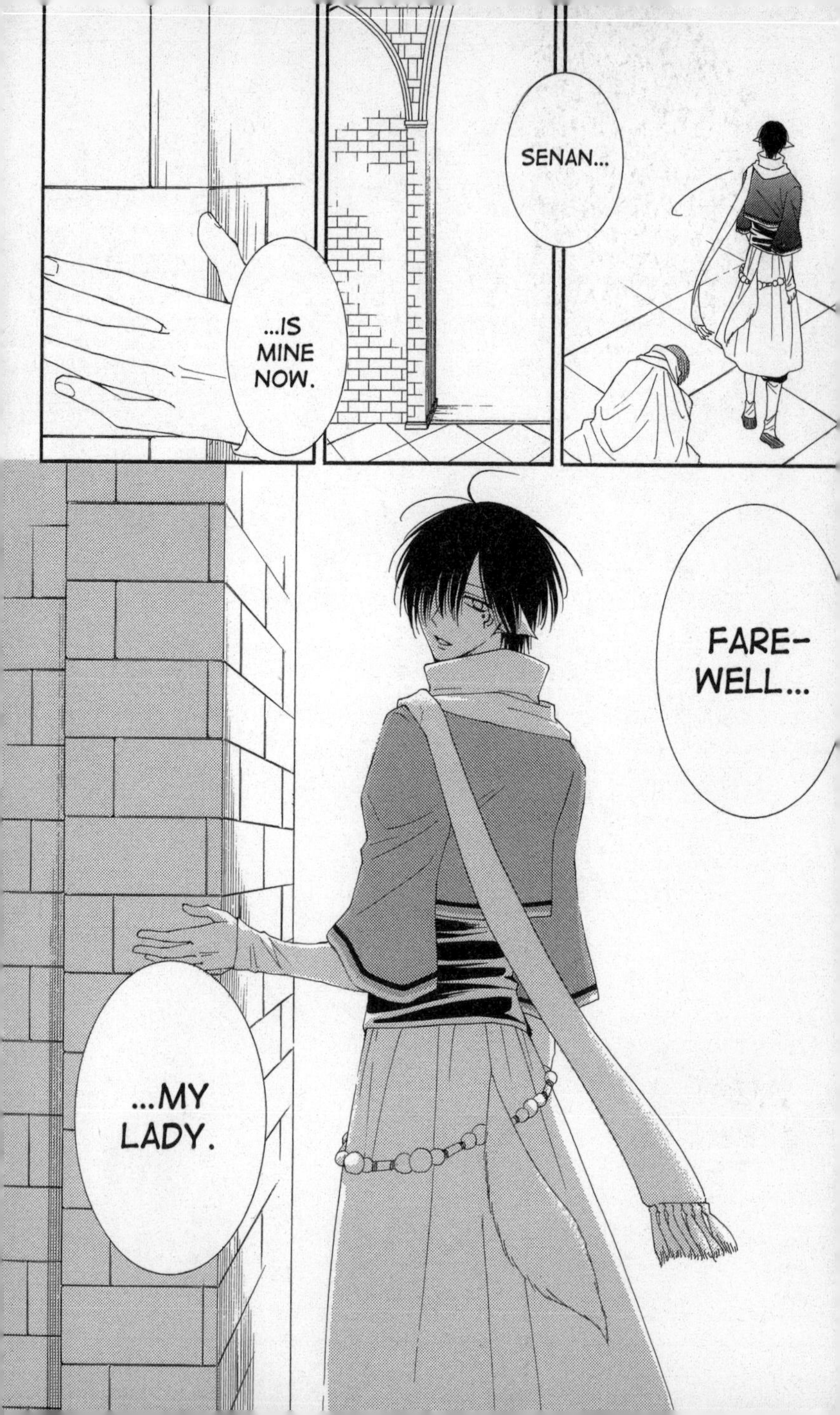
SENAN...
...IS MINE NOW.
FARE-WELL...
...MY LADY.

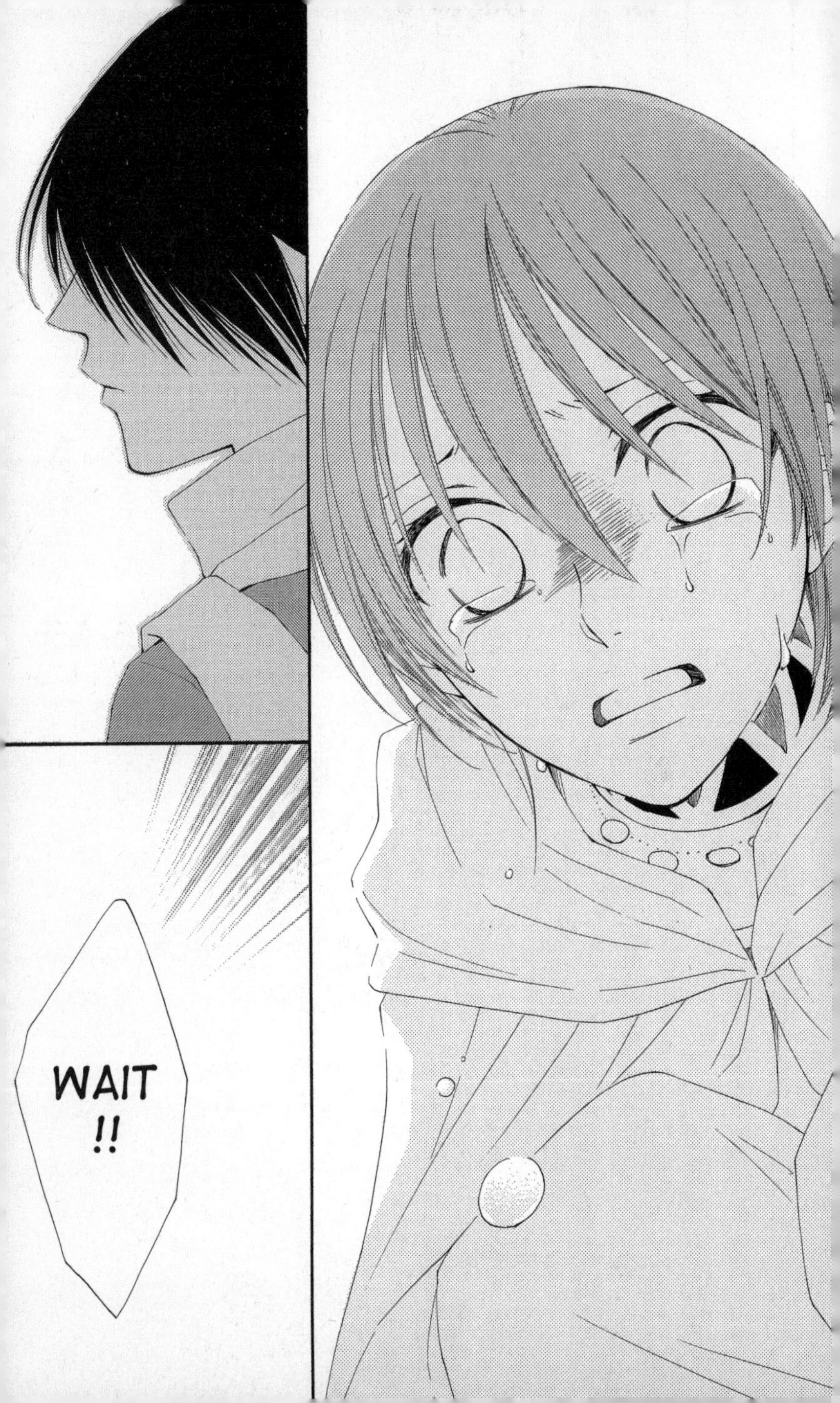
WAIT !!

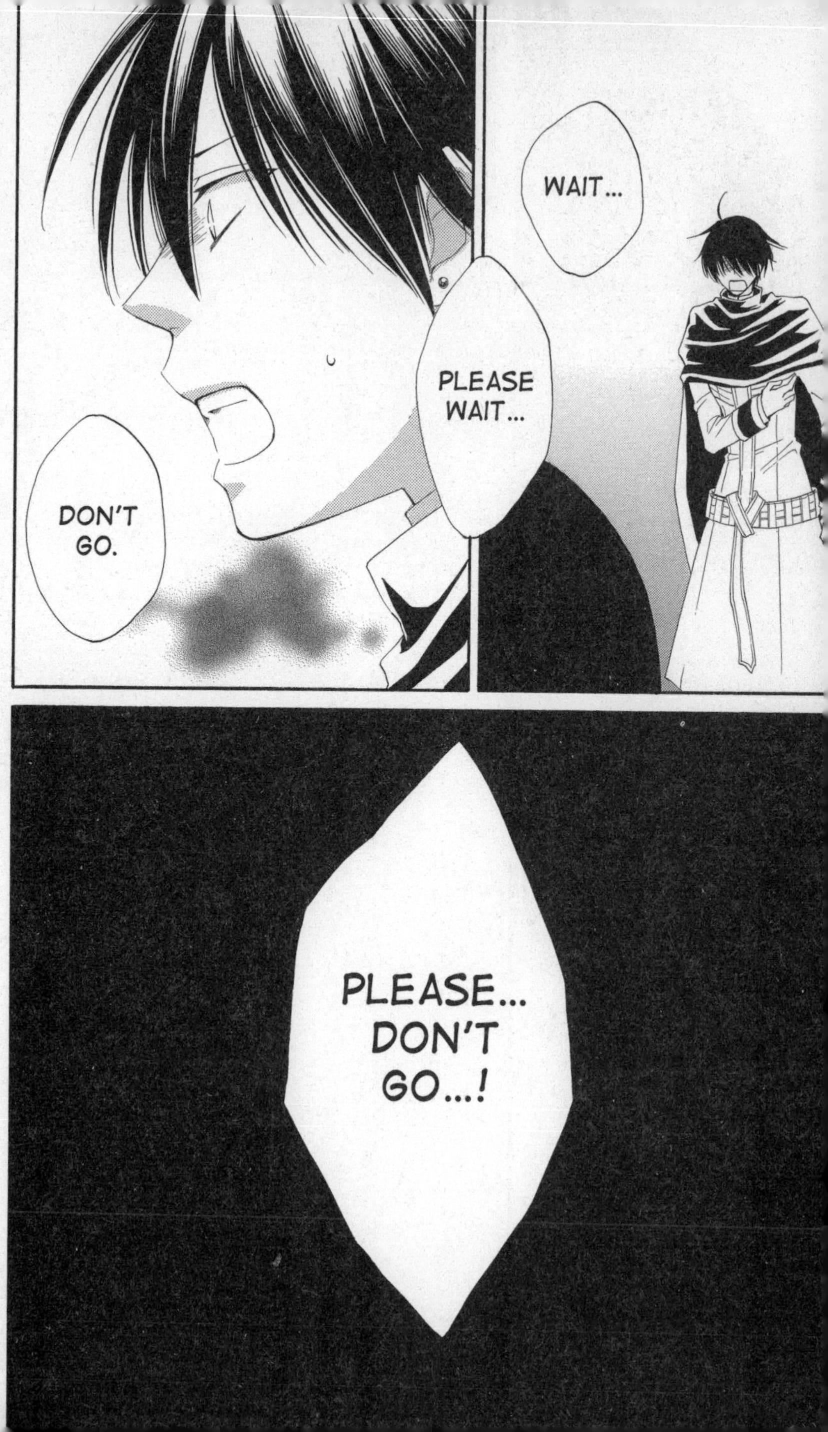
WAIT...
PLEASE WAIT...
DON'T GO.
PLEASE... DON'T GO...!

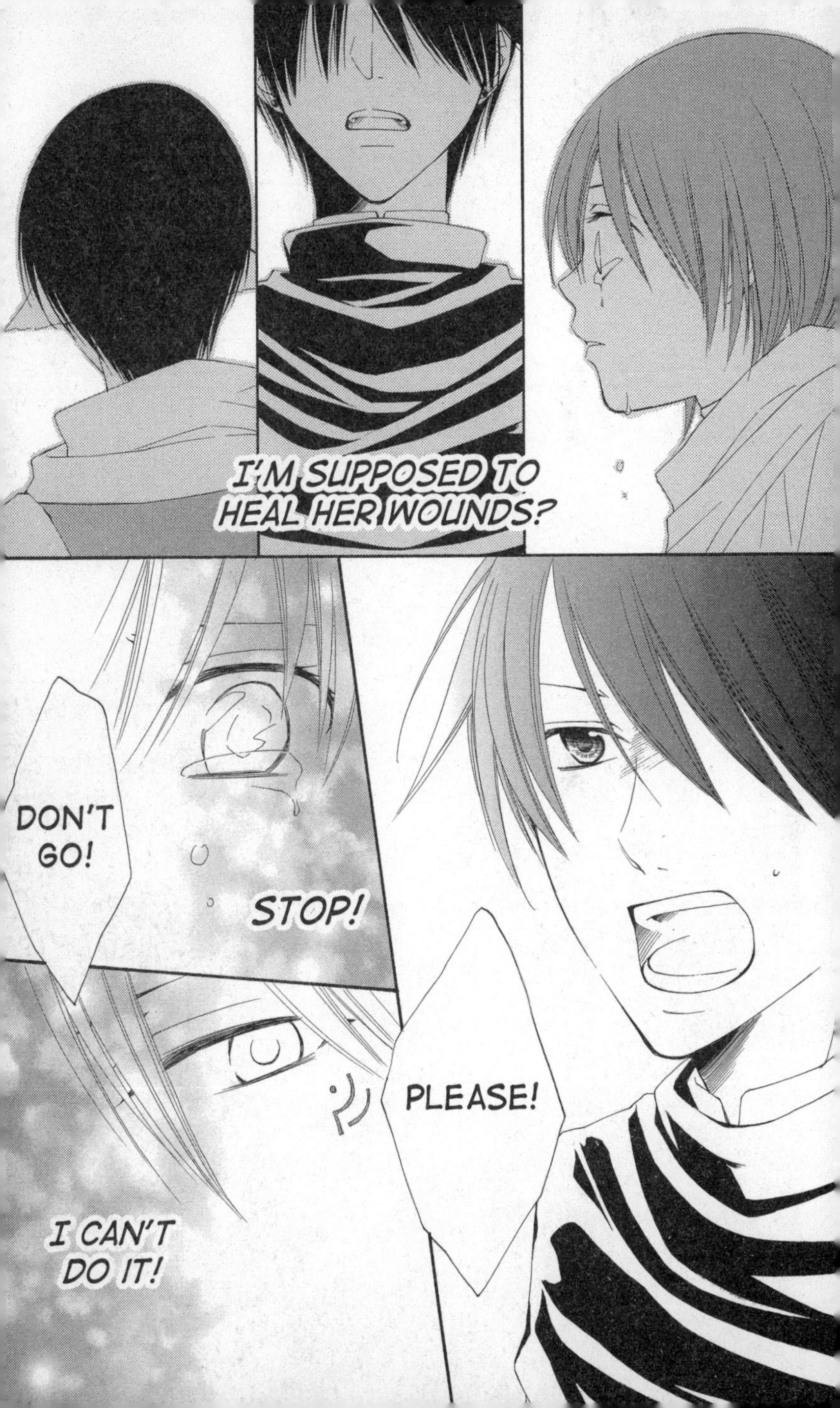
I'M SUPPOSED TO HEAL HER WOUNDS?
PLEASE!
DON'T GO!
STOP!
I CAN'T DO IT!

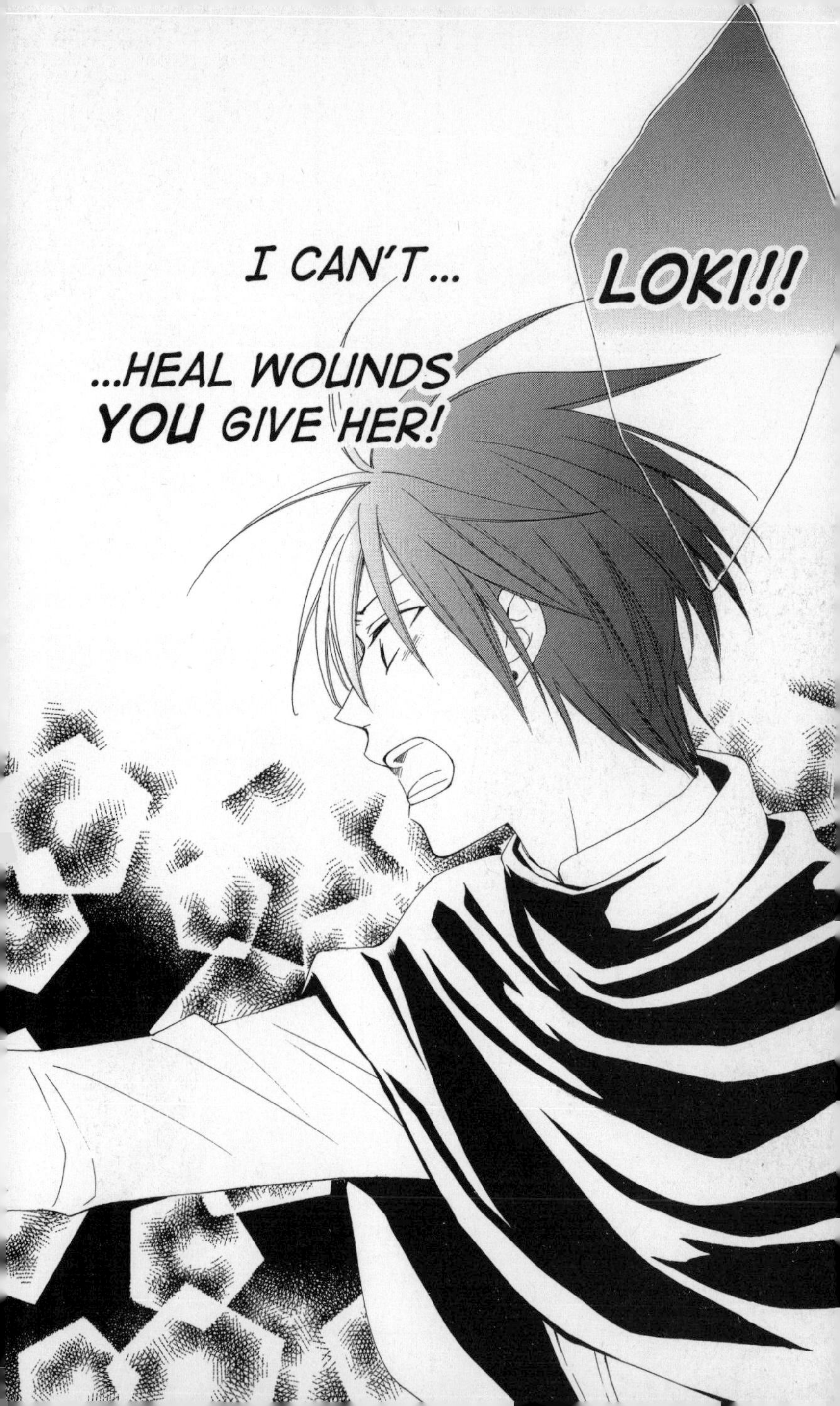
LOKI!!
I CAN'T...
...HEAL WOUNDS YOU GIVE HER!

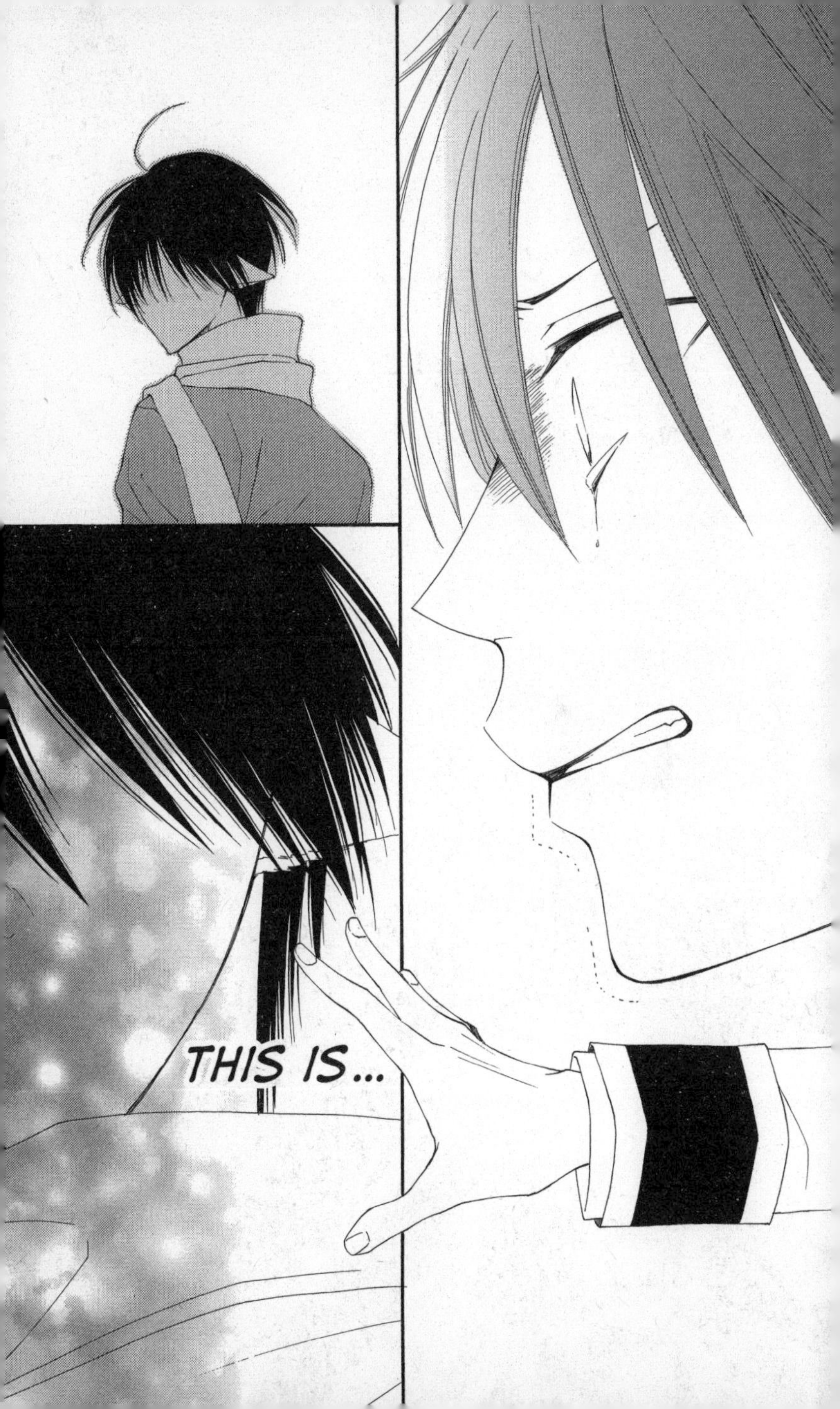
THIS IS...

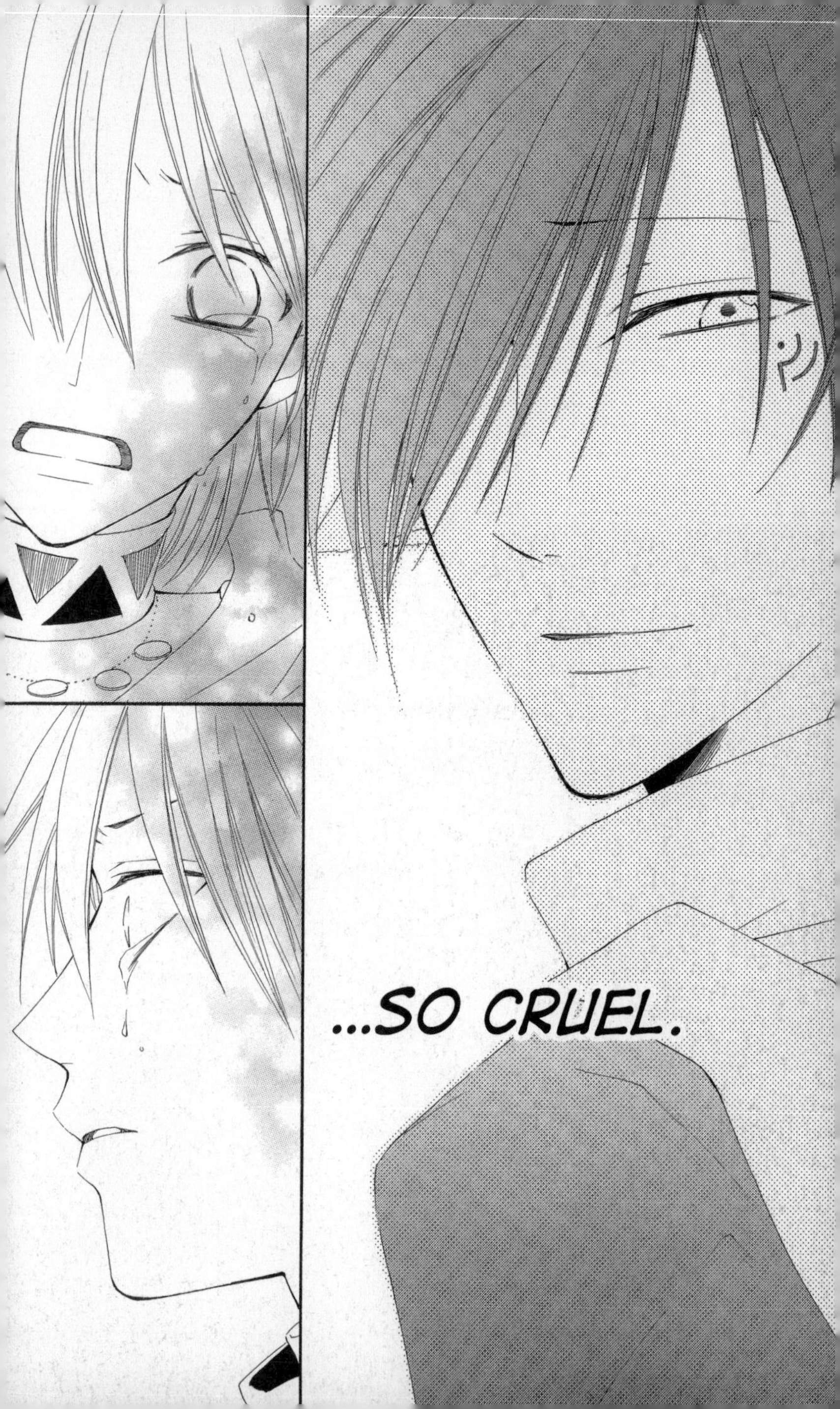
...SO CRUEL.

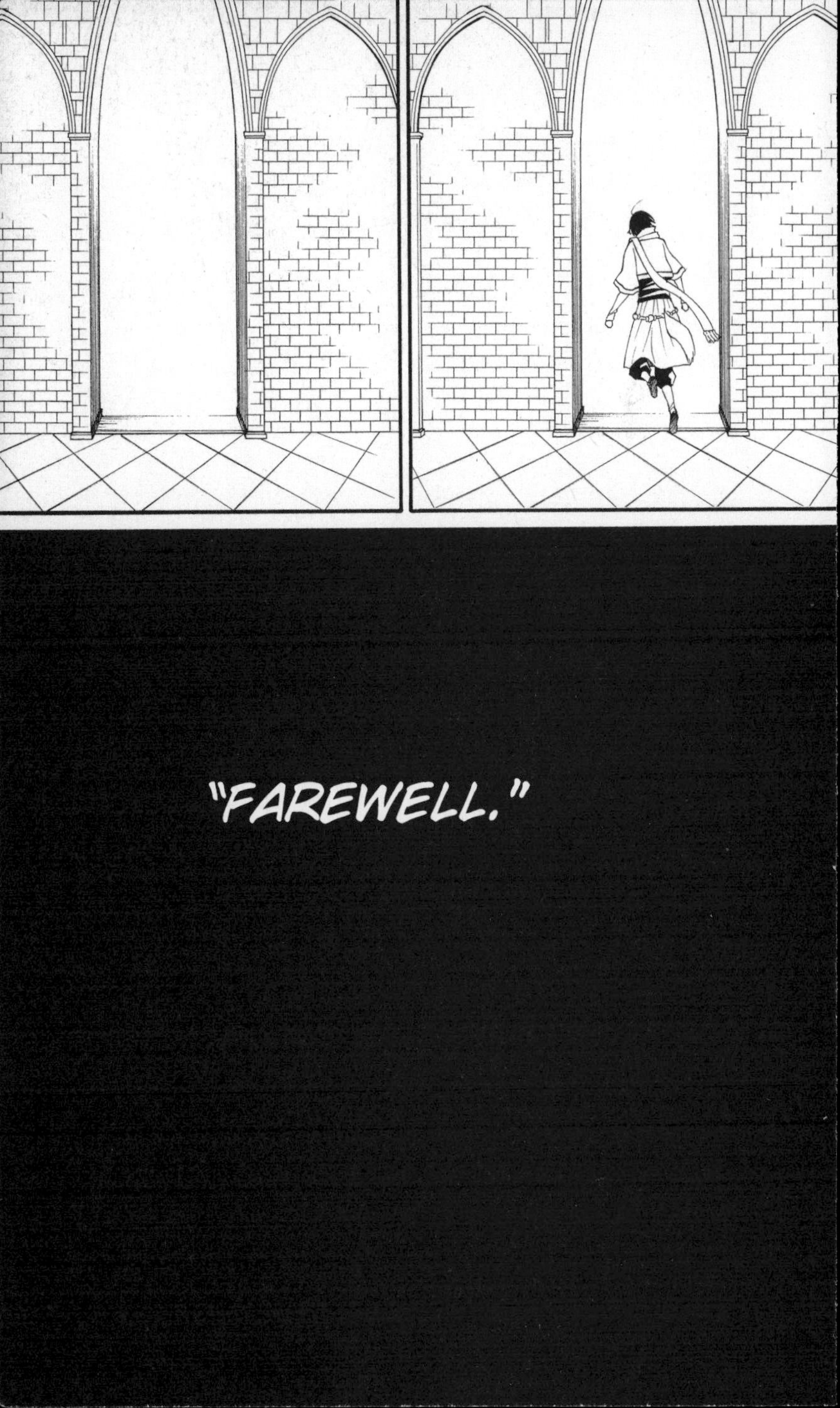
"FAREWELL."

Chapter 51

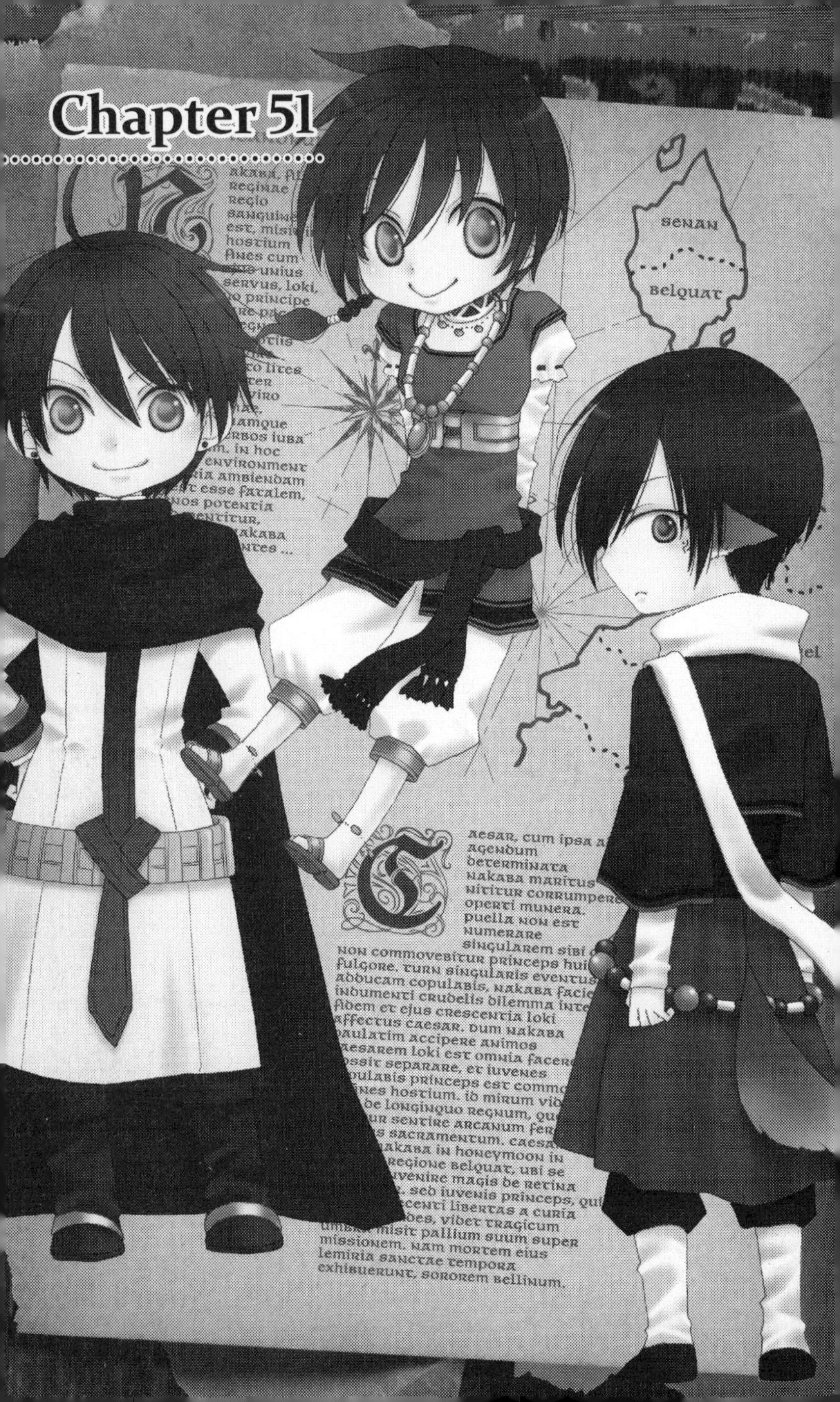

SENAN
BELQUAT
aesar, cum ipsa a
agendum
determinata
nakaba maritus
puella non est
numerare
singularem sibi
missionem. nam mortem eius
lemiria sanctae tempora
exhibuerunt, sororem bellinum.

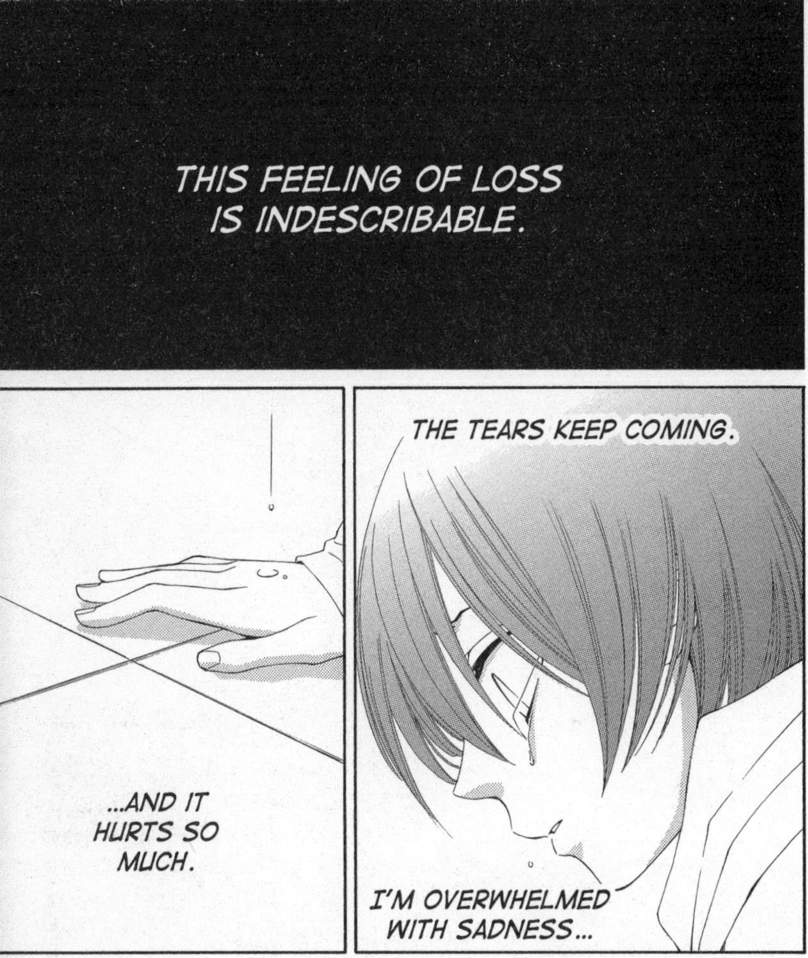
THIS FEELING OF LOSS IS INDESCRIBABLE.
THE TEARS KEEP COMING.
I'M OVERWHELMED WITH SADNESS...
...AND IT HURTS SO MUCH.

Dawn of the Arcana

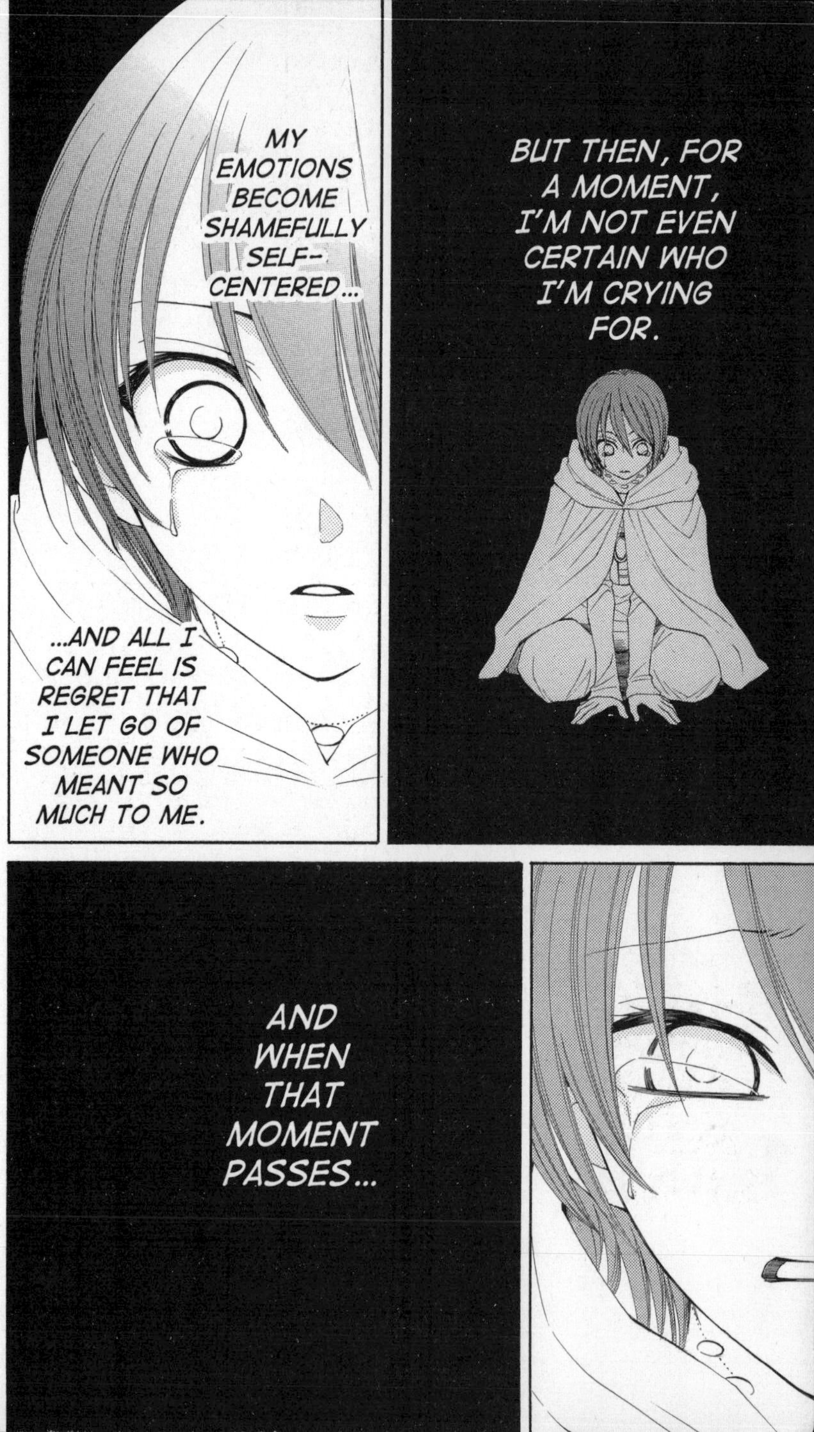
BUT THEN, FOR A MOMENT, I'M NOT EVEN CERTAIN WHO I'M CRYING FOR.
MY EMOTIONS BECOME SHAMEFULLY SELF-CENTERED...
...AND ALL I CAN FEEL IS REGRET THAT I LET GO OF SOMEONE WHO MEANT SO MUCH TO ME.
AND WHEN THAT MOMENT PASSES...

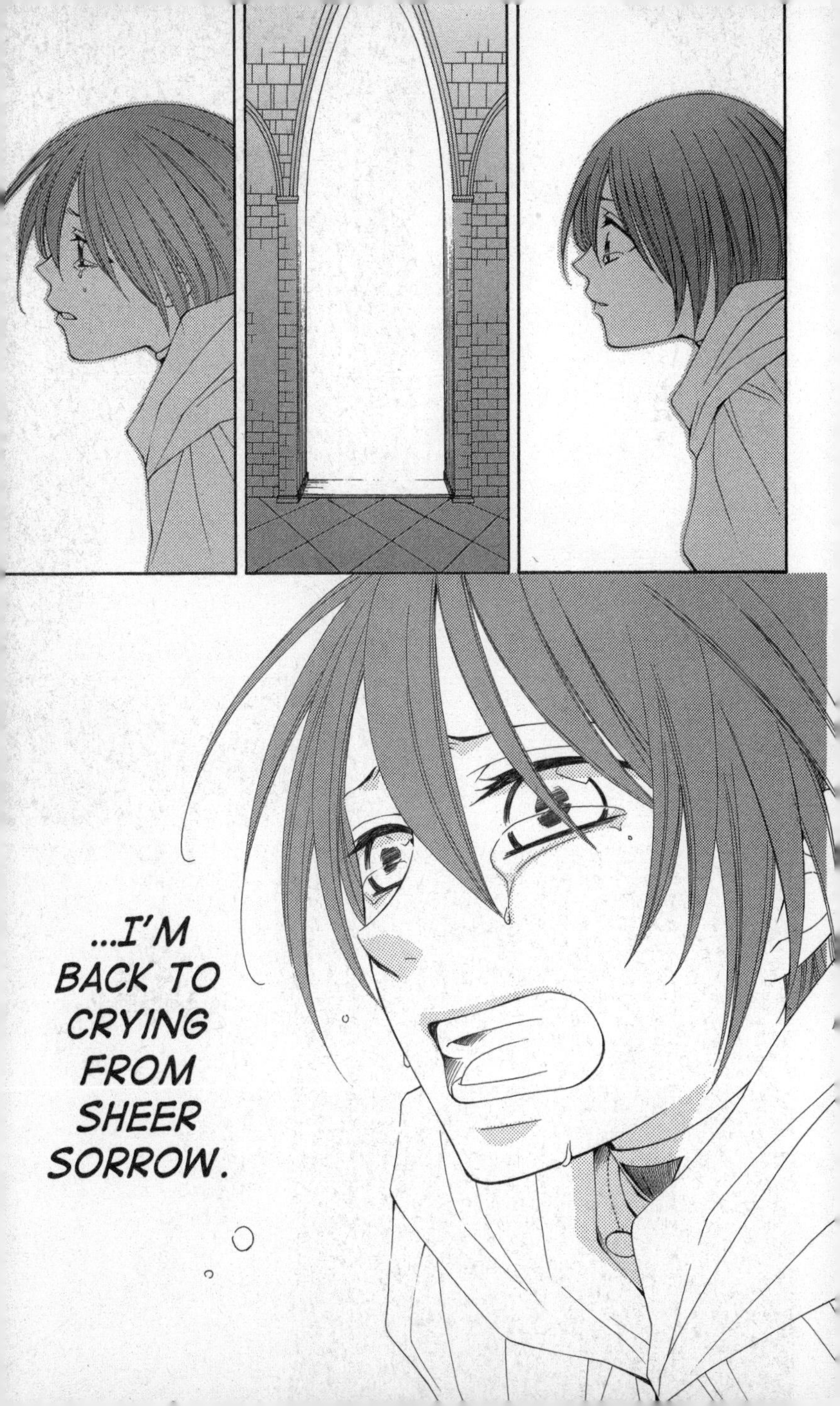
...I'M BACK TO CRYING FROM SHEER SORROW.

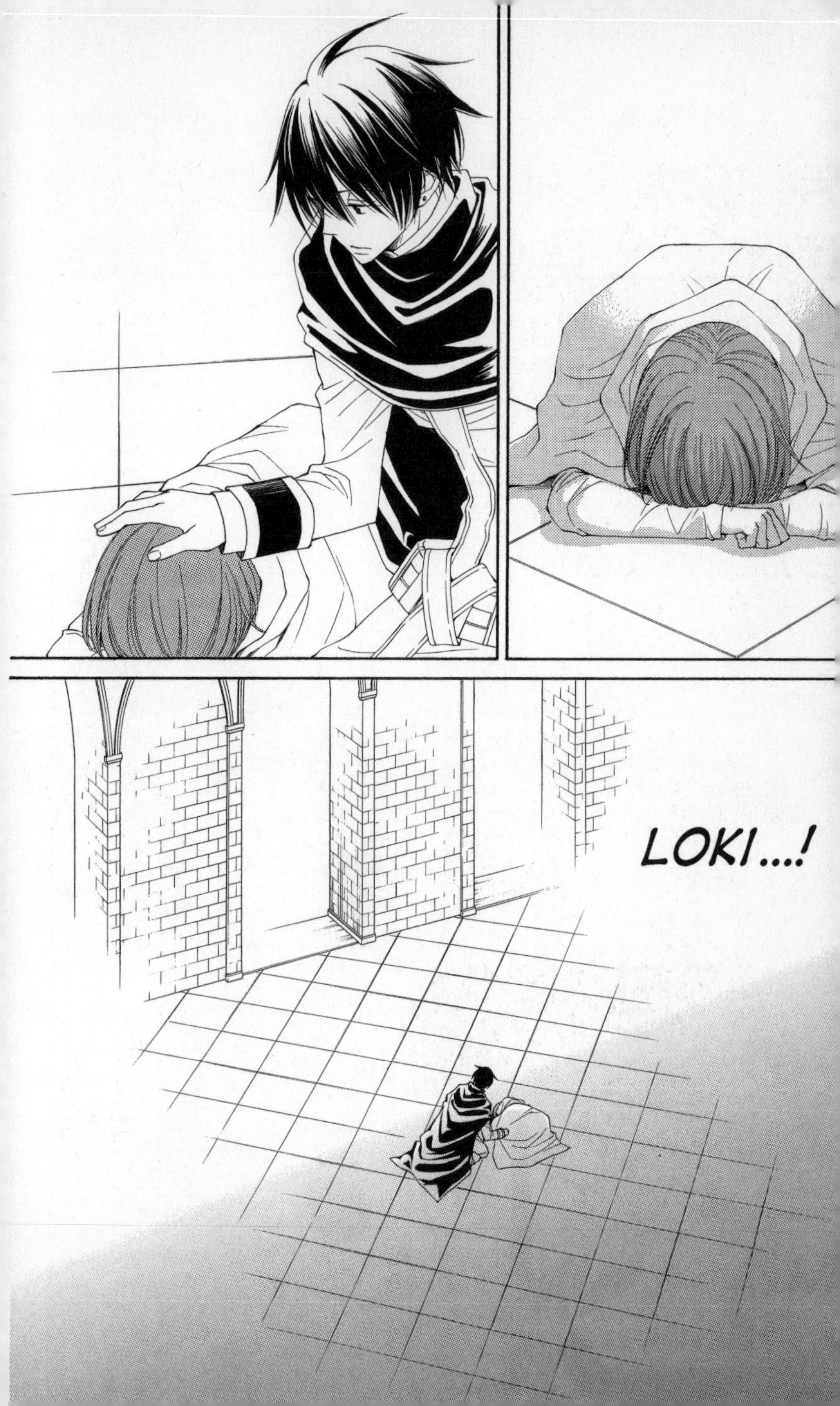
LOKI...!

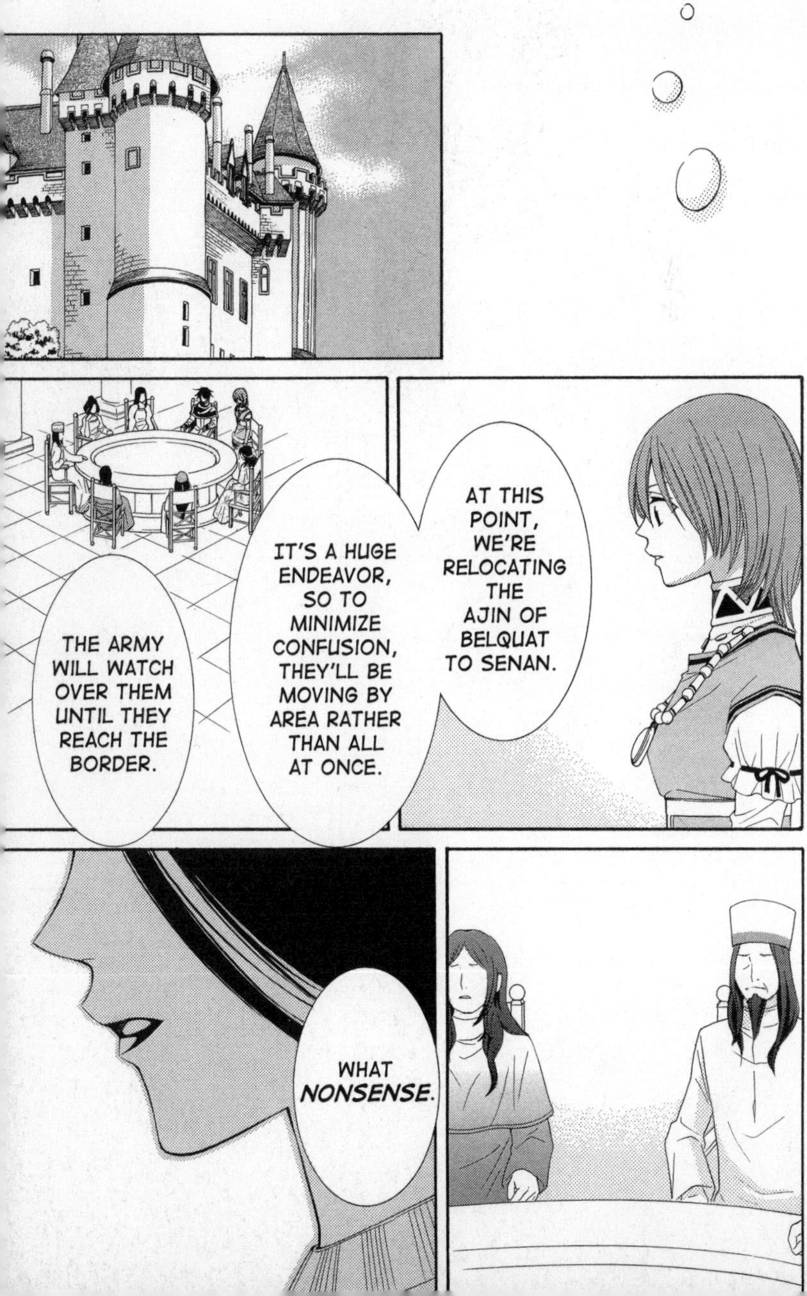
AT THIS POINT, WE'RE RELOCATING THE AJIN OF BELQUAT TO SENAN.
IT'S A HUGE ENDEAVOR, SO TO MINIMIZE CONFUSION, THEY'LL BE MOVING BY AREA RATHER THAN ALL AT ONCE.
THE ARMY WILL WATCH OVER THEM UNTIL THEY REACH THE BORDER.
WHAT *NONSENSE*.

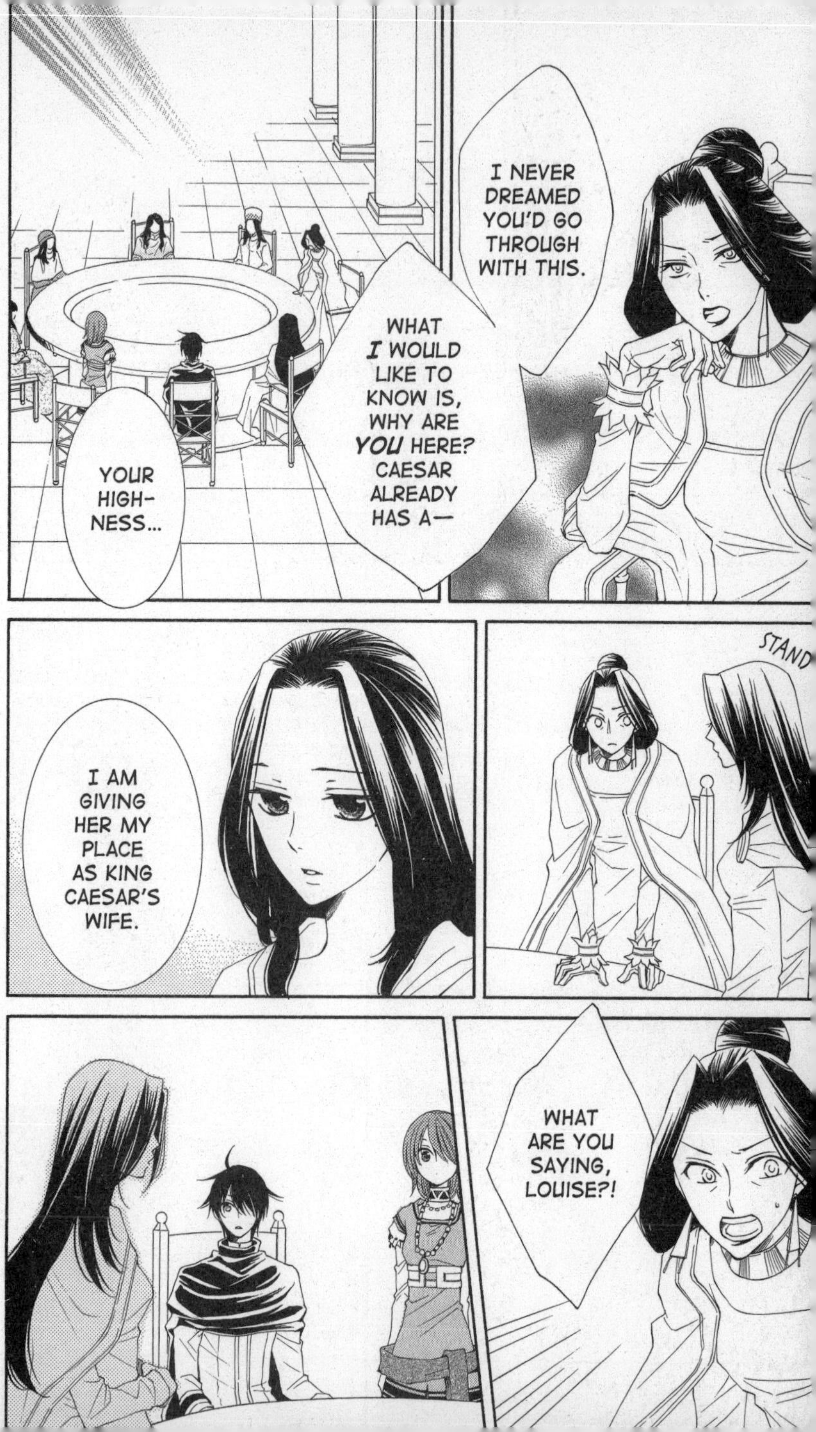
I NEVER DREAMED YOU'D GO THROUGH WITH THIS.
WHAT *I* WOULD LIKE TO KNOW IS, WHY ARE *YOU* HERE? CAESAR ALREADY HAS A—
YOUR HIGHNESS...
STAND
I AM GIVING HER MY PLACE AS KING CAESAR'S WIFE.
WHAT ARE YOU SAYING, LOUISE?!

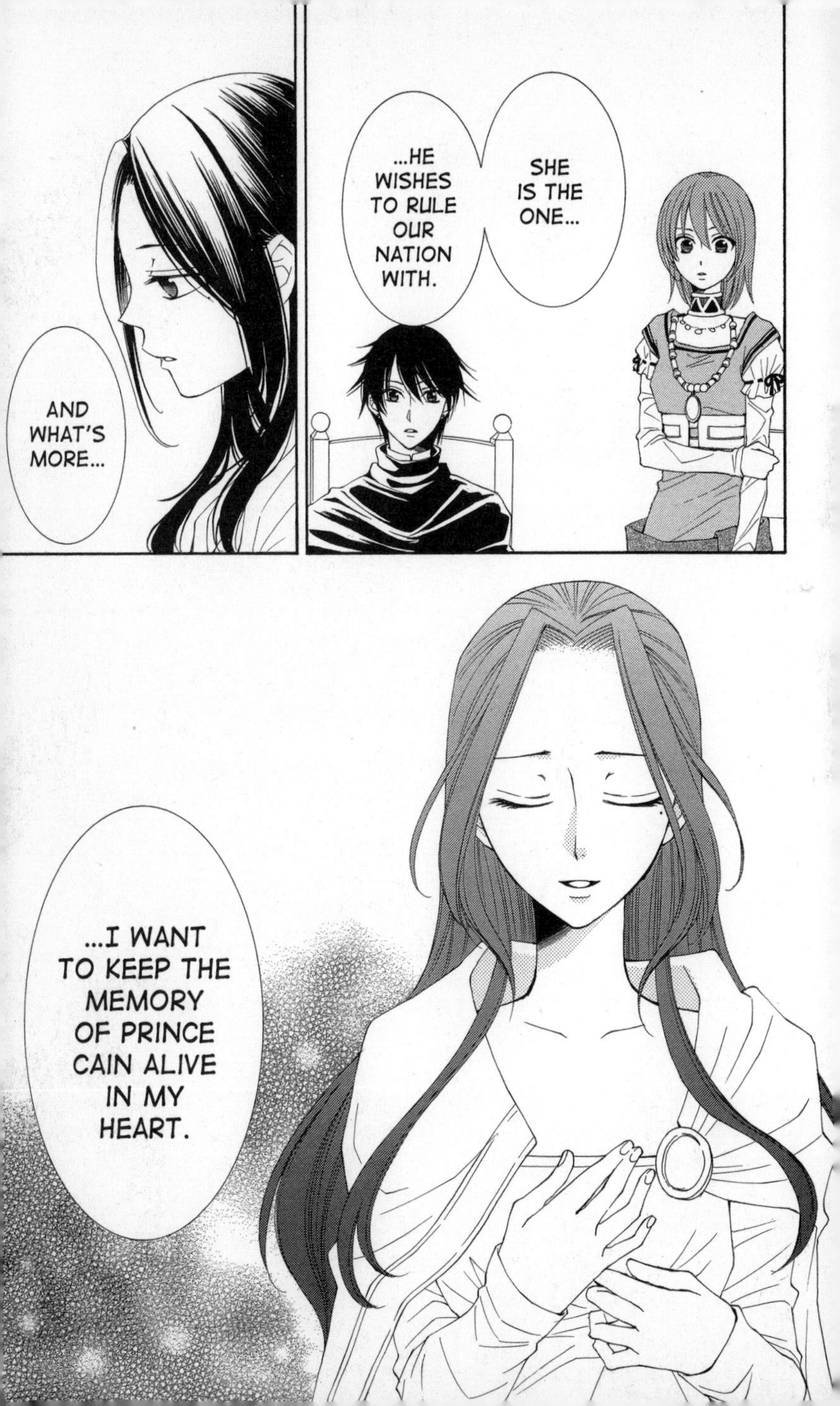
SHE IS THE ONE...
...HE WISHES TO RULE OUR NATION WITH.
AND WHAT'S MORE...
...I WANT TO KEEP THE MEMORY OF PRINCE CAIN ALIVE IN MY HEART.

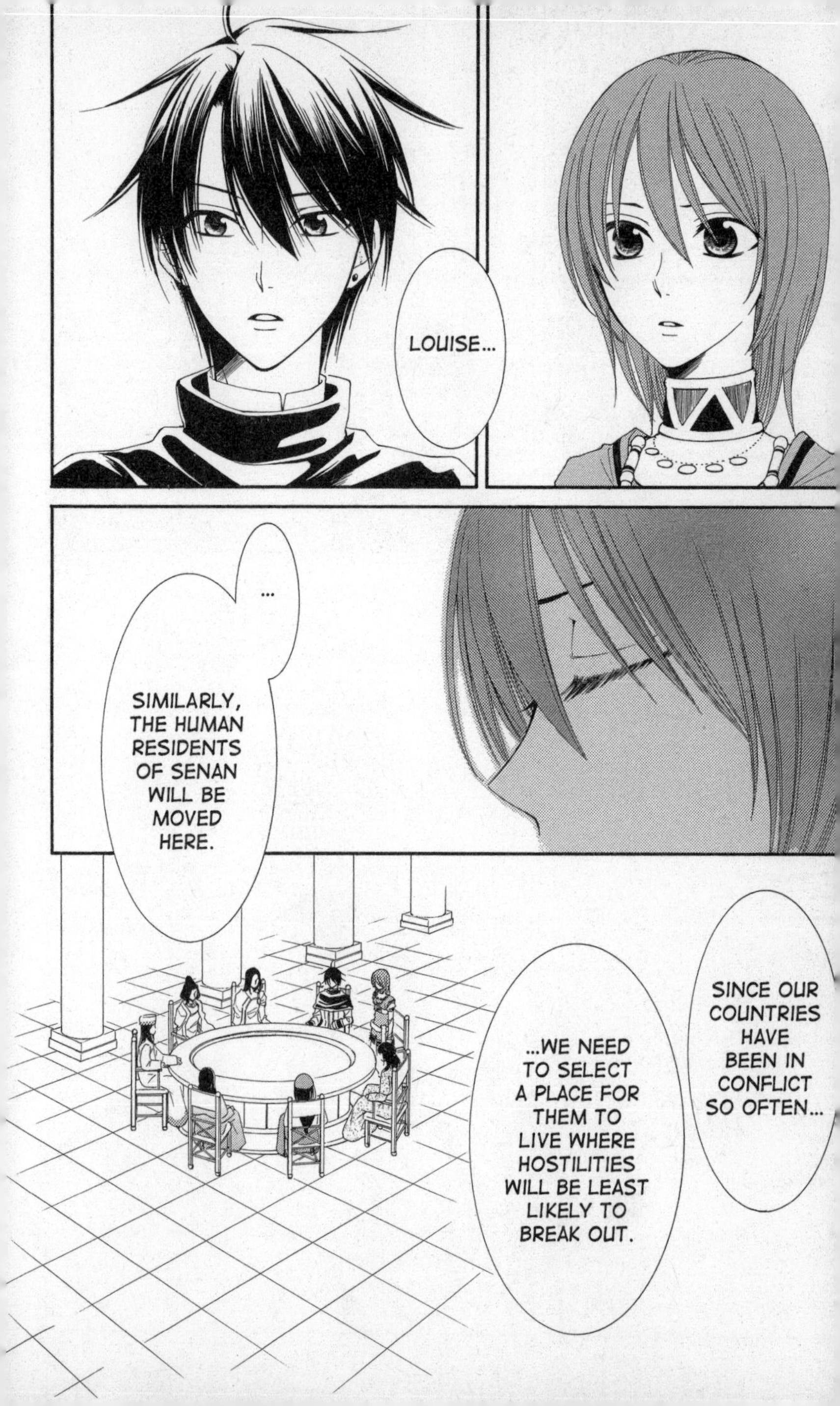
LOUISE...
...
SIMILARLY, THE HUMAN RESIDENTS OF SENAN WILL BE MOVED HERE.
SINCE OUR COUNTRIES HAVE BEEN IN CONFLICT SO OFTEN...
...WE NEED TO SELECT A PLACE FOR THEM TO LIVE WHERE HOSTILITIES WILL BE LEAST LIKELY TO BREAK OUT.

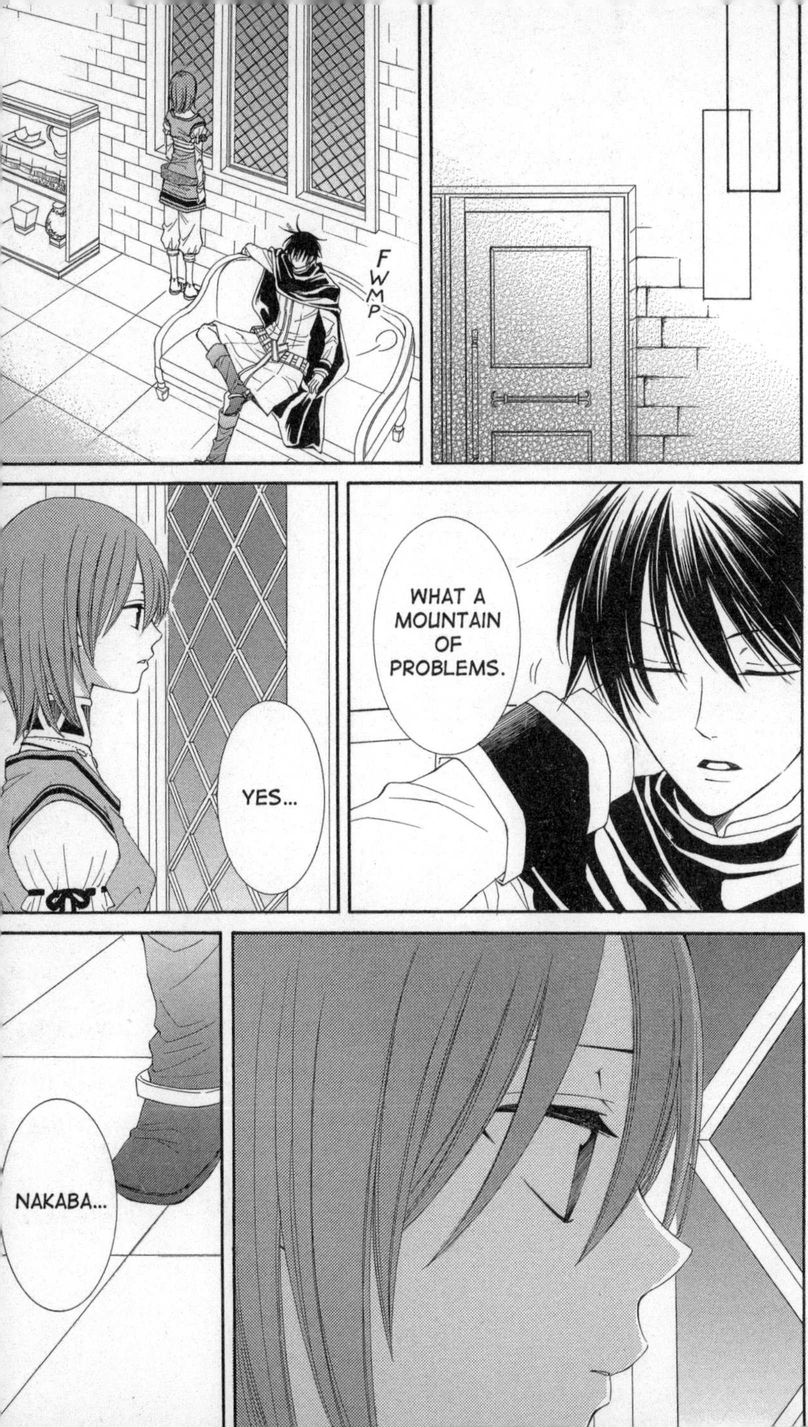
FWMP
WHAT A MOUNTAIN OF PROBLEMS.
YES...
NAKABA...

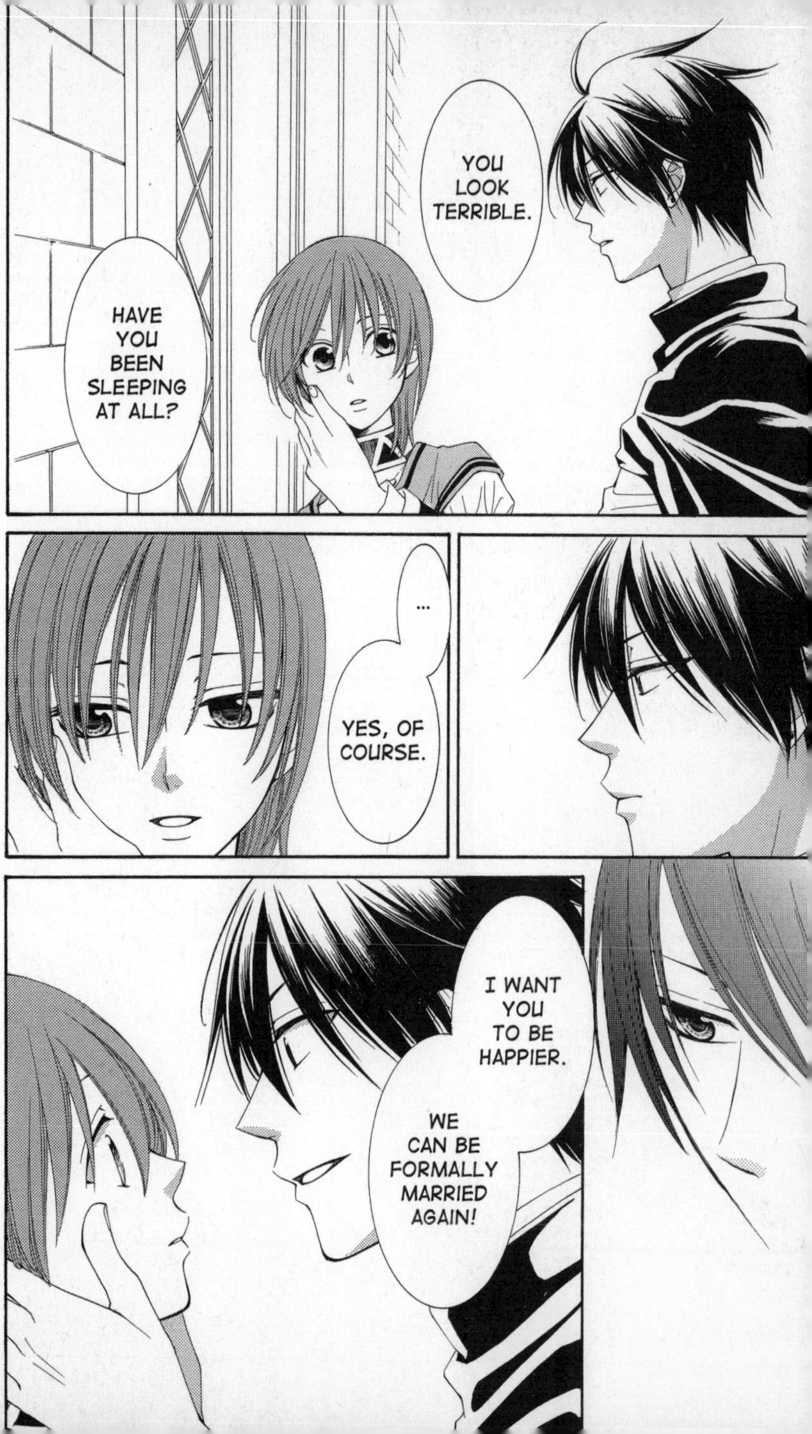
YOU LOOK TERRIBLE.
HAVE YOU BEEN SLEEPING AT ALL?
...
YES, OF COURSE.
I WANT YOU TO BE HAPPIER.
WE CAN BE FORMALLY MARRIED AGAIN!

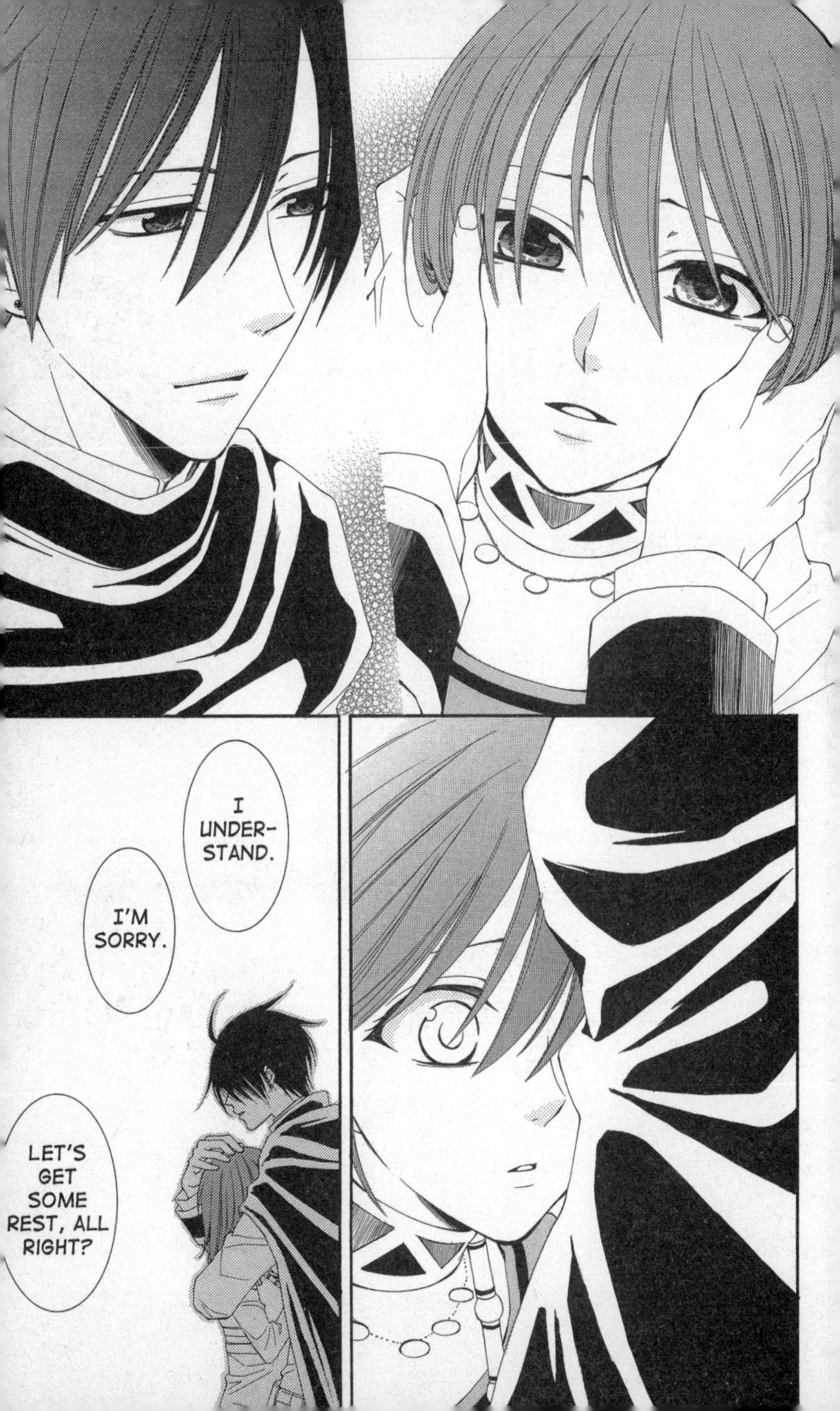
I UNDER-STAND.
I'M SORRY.
LET'S GET SOME REST, ALL RIGHT?

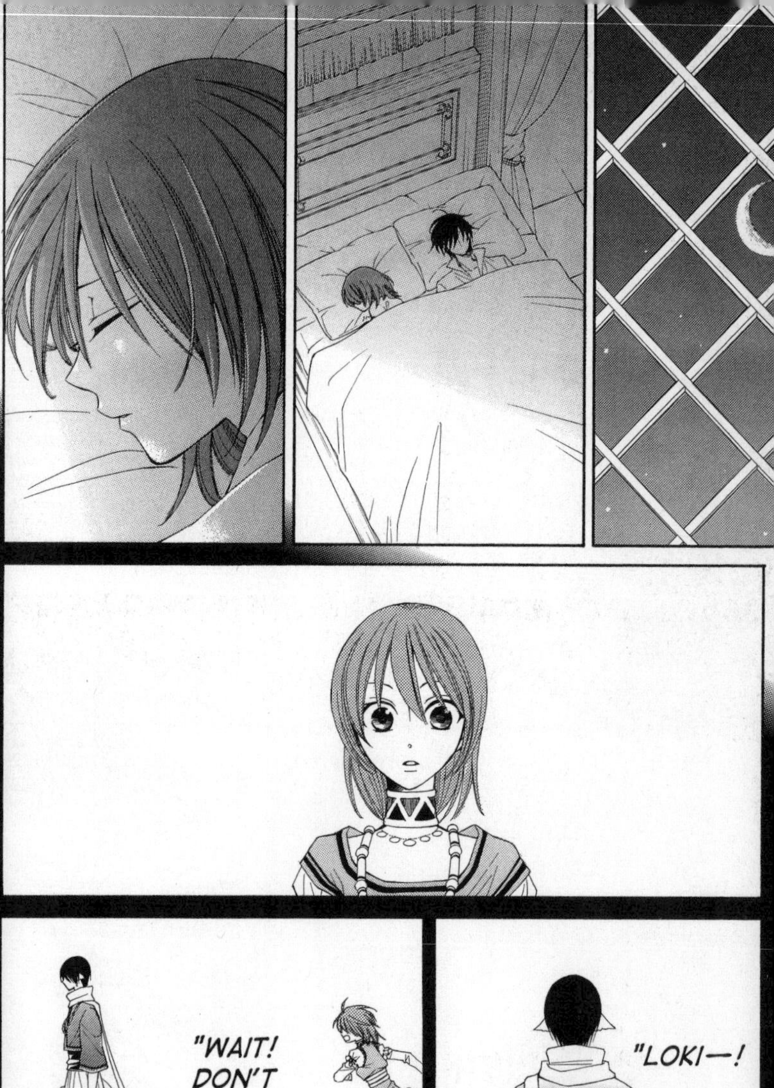
"LOKI—!
"WAIT! DON'T LEAVE ME!"

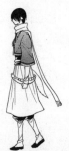

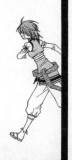

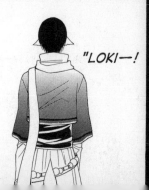

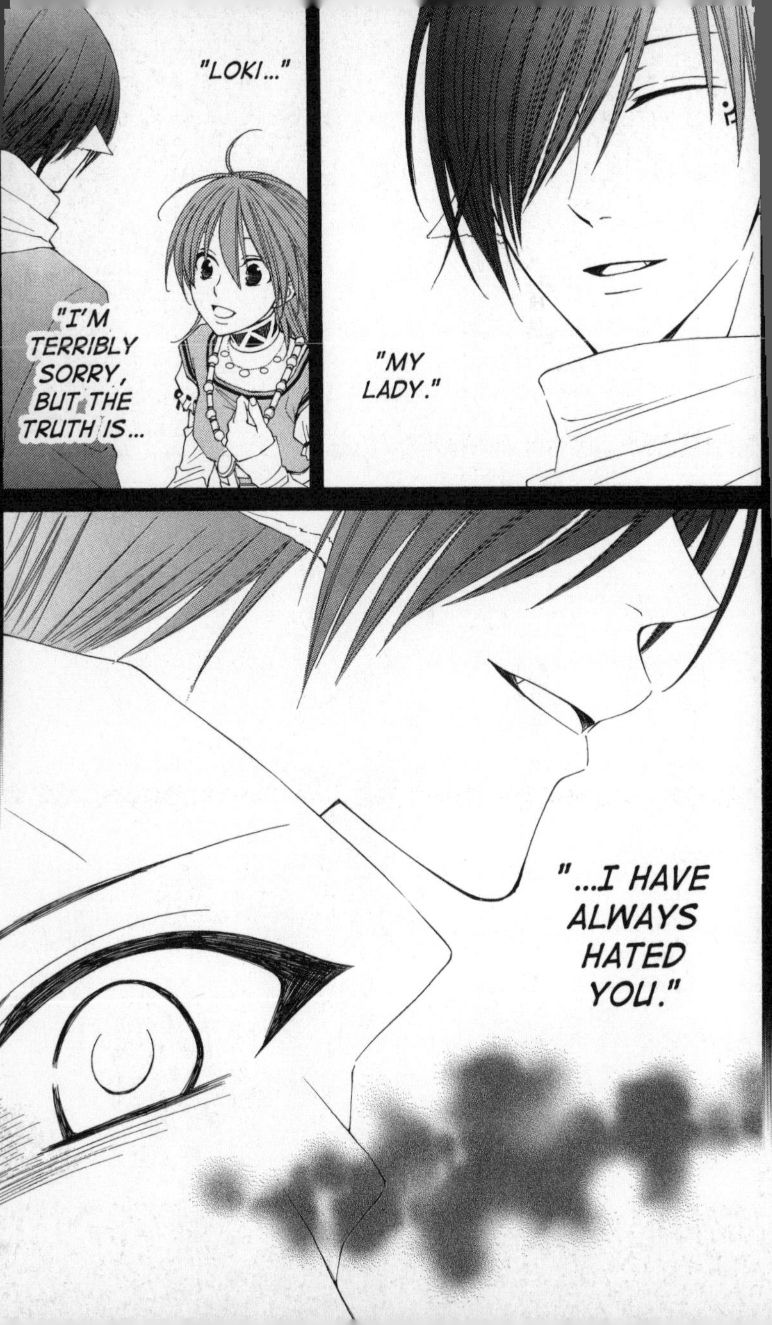
"MY LADY."
"LOKI..."
"I'M TERRIBLY SORRY, BUT THE TRUTH IS...
"...I HAVE ALWAYS HATED YOU."

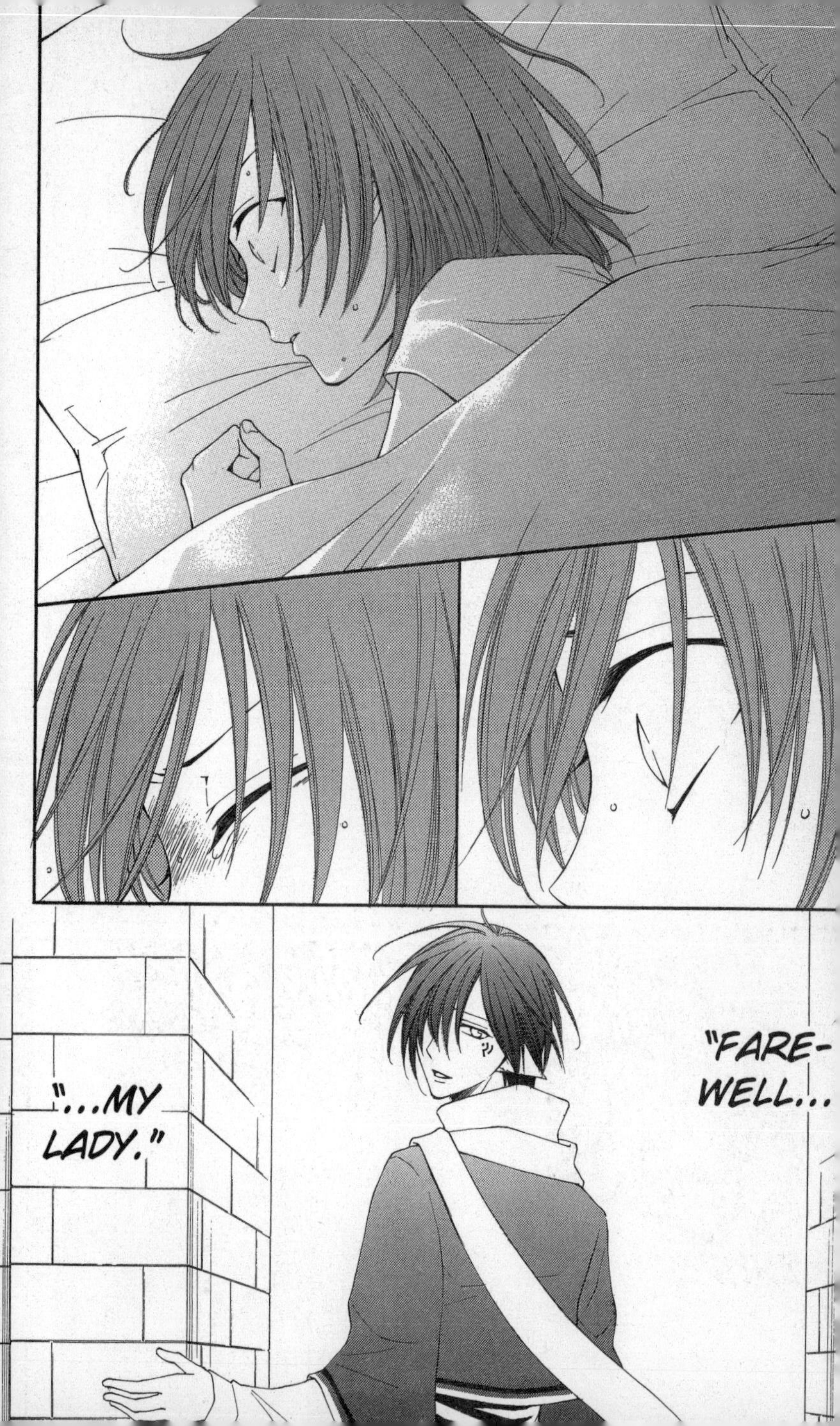
"FARE-WELL...
"...MY LADY."

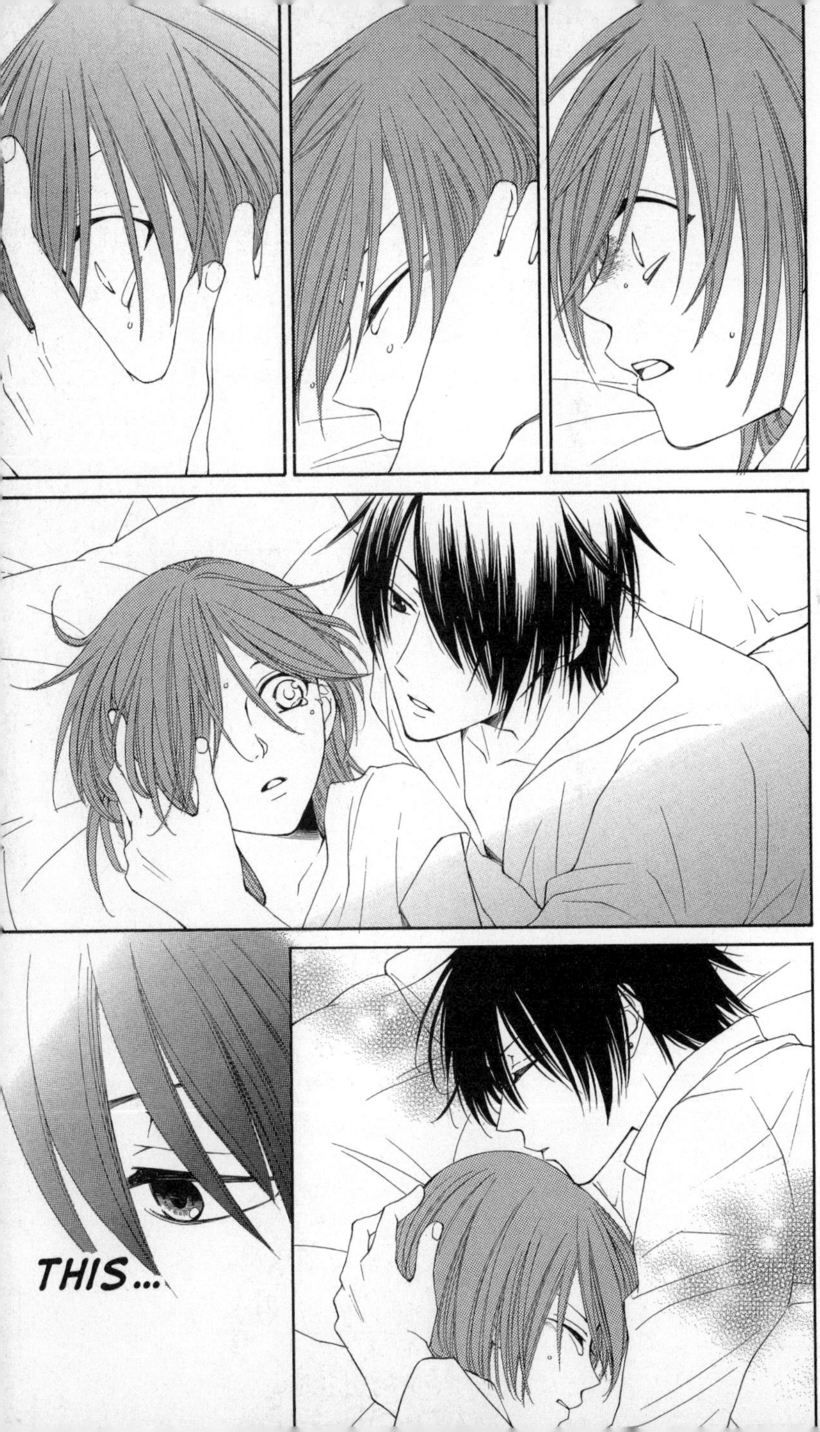
THIS...

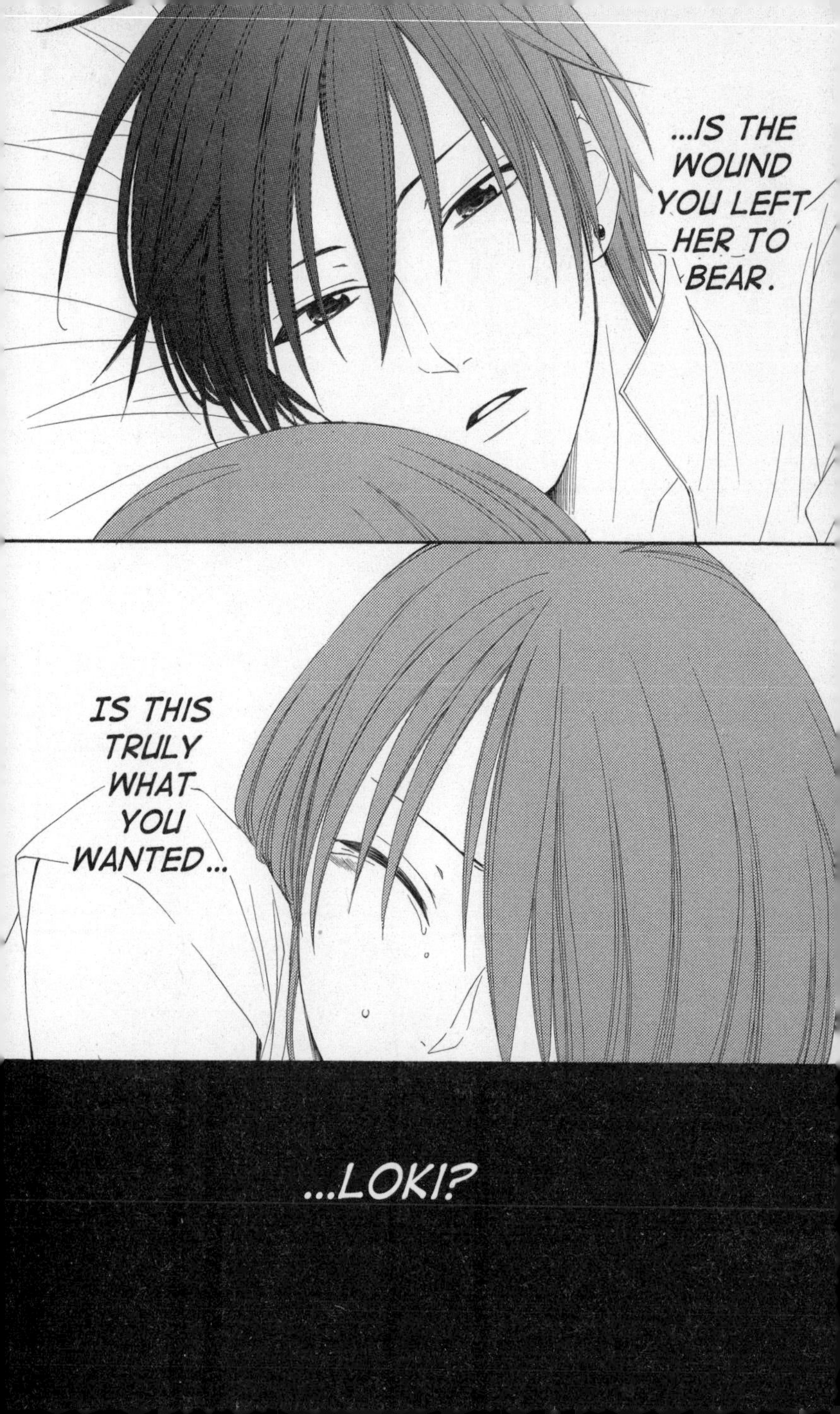
...IS THE WOUND YOU LEFT HER TO BEAR.
IS THIS TRULY WHAT YOU WANTED...
...LOKI?

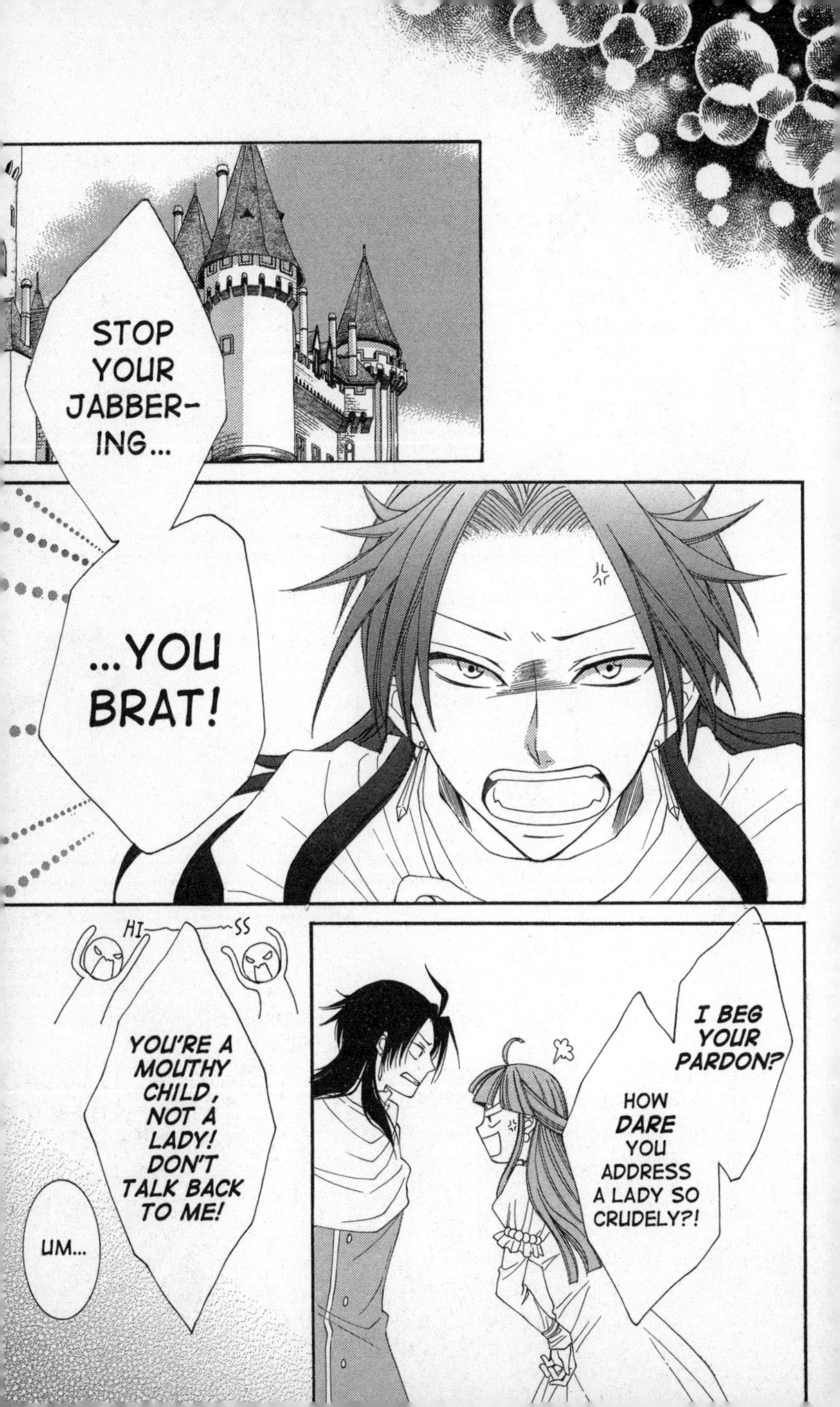
STOP YOUR JABBER-ING...
...YOU BRAT!
I BEG YOUR PARDON?
HOW DARE YOU ADDRESS A LADY SO CRUDELY?!
HI—SS
YOU'RE A MOUTHY CHILD, NOT A LADY! DON'T TALK BACK TO ME!
UM...

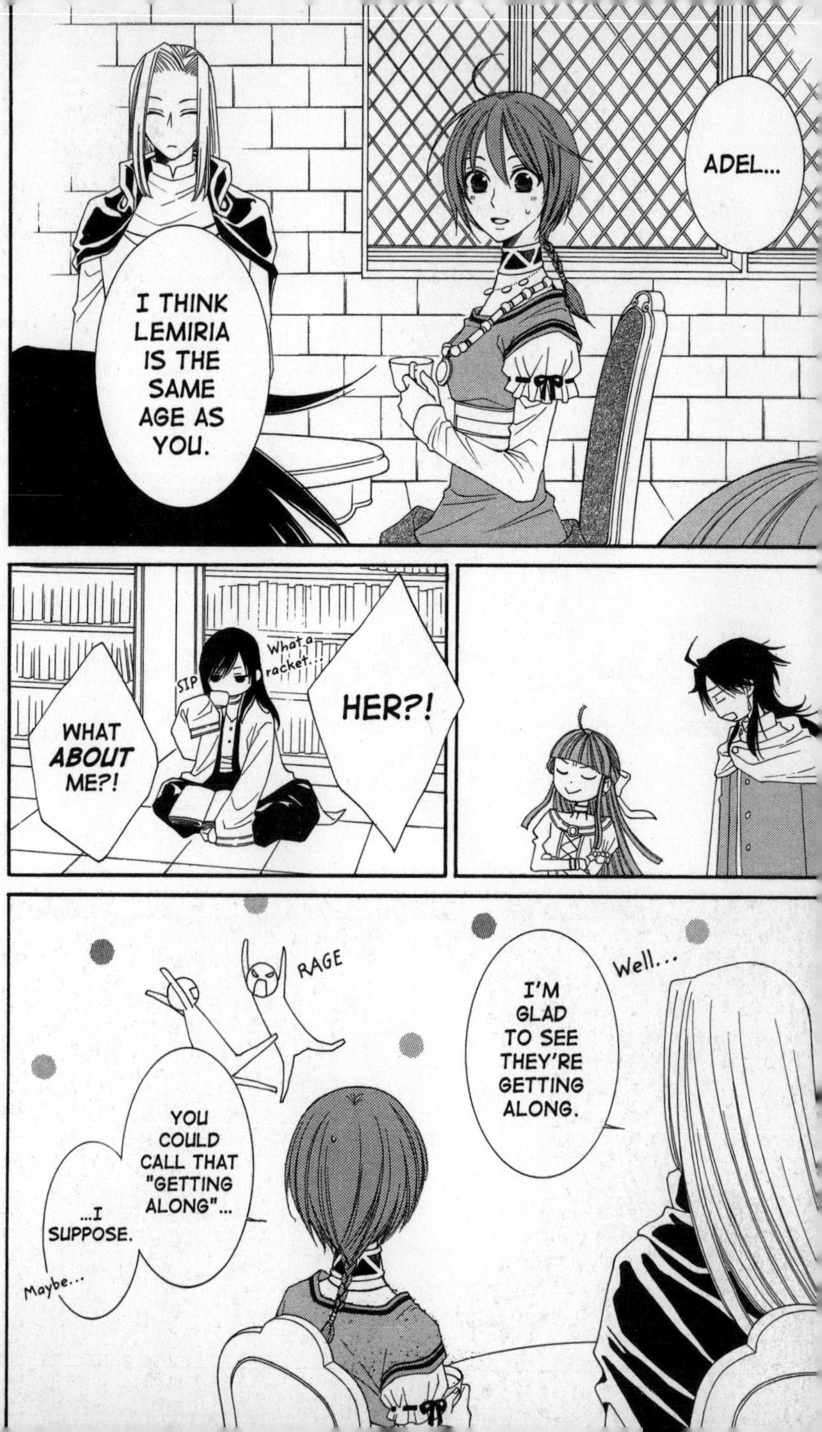
ADEL...
I THINK LEMIRIA IS THE SAME AGE AS YOU.
HER?!
What a racket...
SIP
WHAT ABOUT ME?!
Well...
I'M GLAD TO SEE THEY'RE GETTING ALONG.
RAGE
YOU COULD CALL THAT "GETTING ALONG"...
...I SUPPOSE.
Maybe...

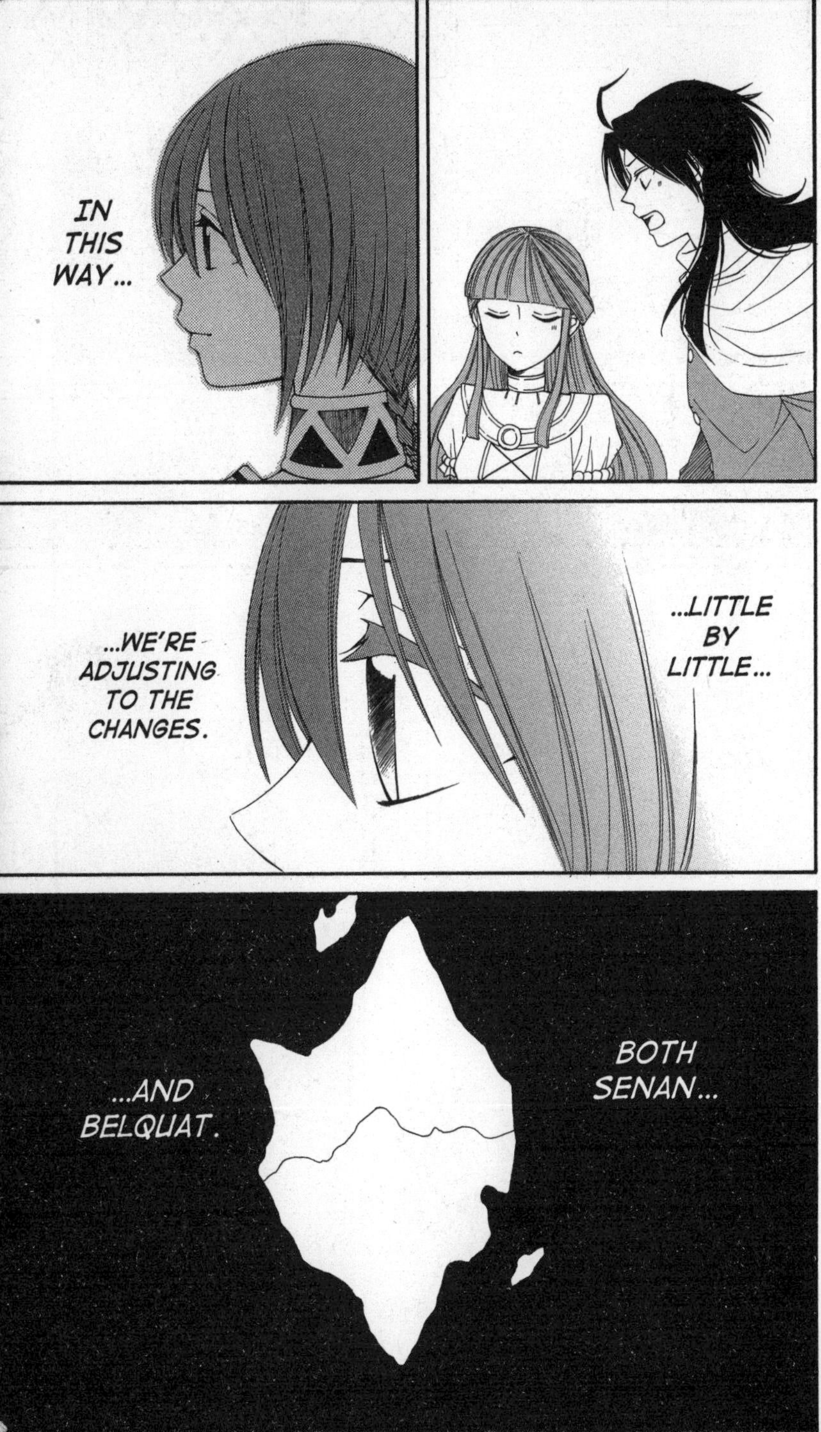
IN THIS WAY...
...LITTLE BY LITTLE...
...WE'RE ADJUSTING TO THE CHANGES.
BOTH SENAN...
...AND BELQUAT.

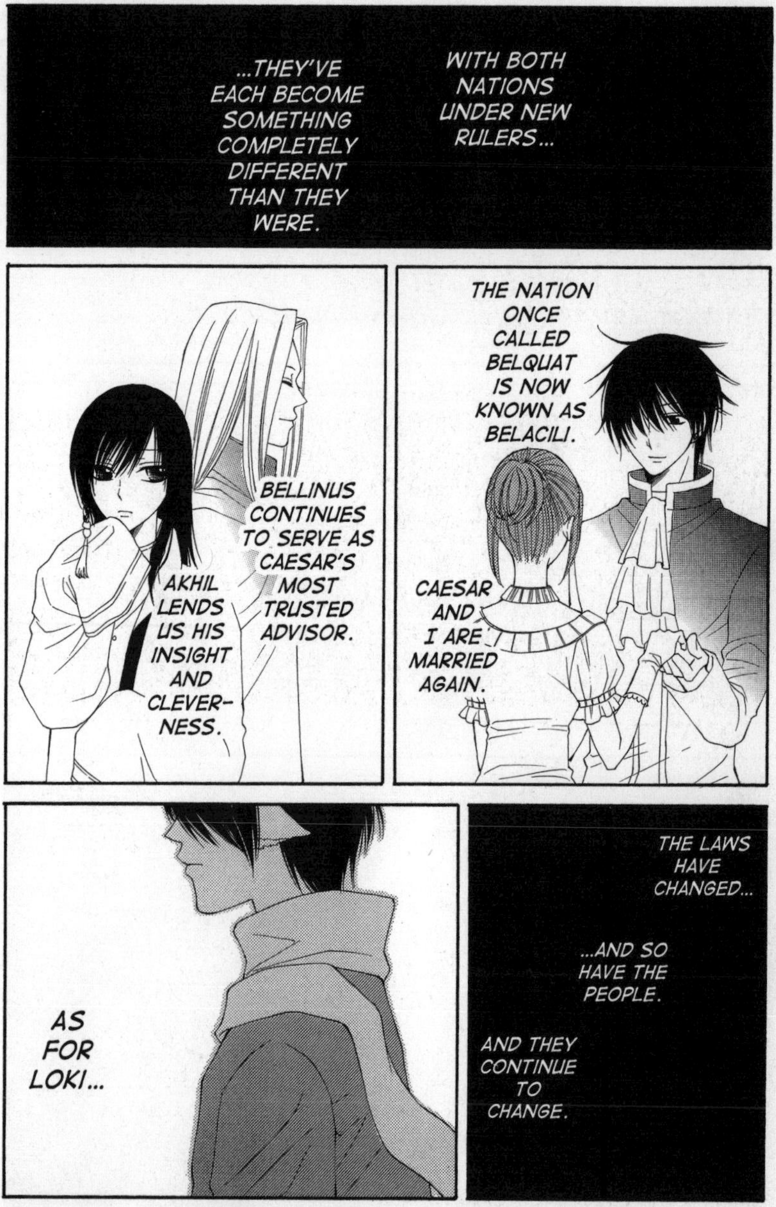
WITH BOTH NATIONS UNDER NEW RULERS...
...THEY'VE EACH BECOME SOMETHING COMPLETELY DIFFERENT THAN THEY WERE.
THE NATION ONCE CALLED BELQUAT IS NOW KNOWN AS BELACILI.
CAESAR AND I ARE MARRIED AGAIN.
BELLINUS CONTINUES TO SERVE AS CAESAR'S MOST TRUSTED ADVISOR.
AKHIL LENDS US HIS INSIGHT AND CLEVER-NESS.
THE LAWS HAVE CHANGED...
...AND SO HAVE THE PEOPLE.
AND THEY CONTINUE TO CHANGE.
AS FOR LOKI...

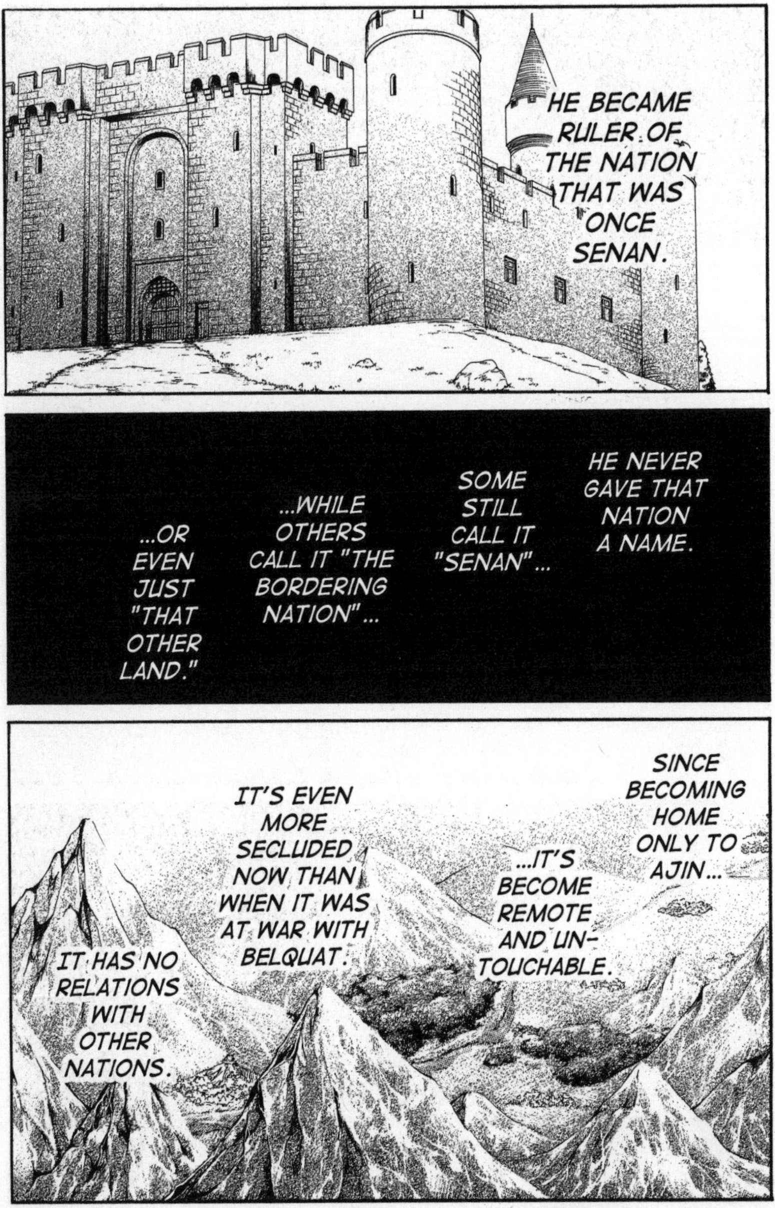
HE BECAME RULER OF THE NATION THAT WAS ONCE SENAN.
HE NEVER GAVE THAT NATION A NAME.
SOME STILL CALL IT "SENAN"...
...WHILE OTHERS CALL IT "THE BORDERING NATION"...
...OR EVEN JUST "THAT OTHER LAND."
SINCE BECOMING HOME ONLY TO AJIN...
...IT'S BECOME REMOTE AND UN-TOUCHABLE.
IT'S EVEN MORE SECLUDED NOW THAN WHEN IT WAS AT WAR WITH BELQUAT.
IT HAS NO RELATIONS WITH OTHER NATIONS.

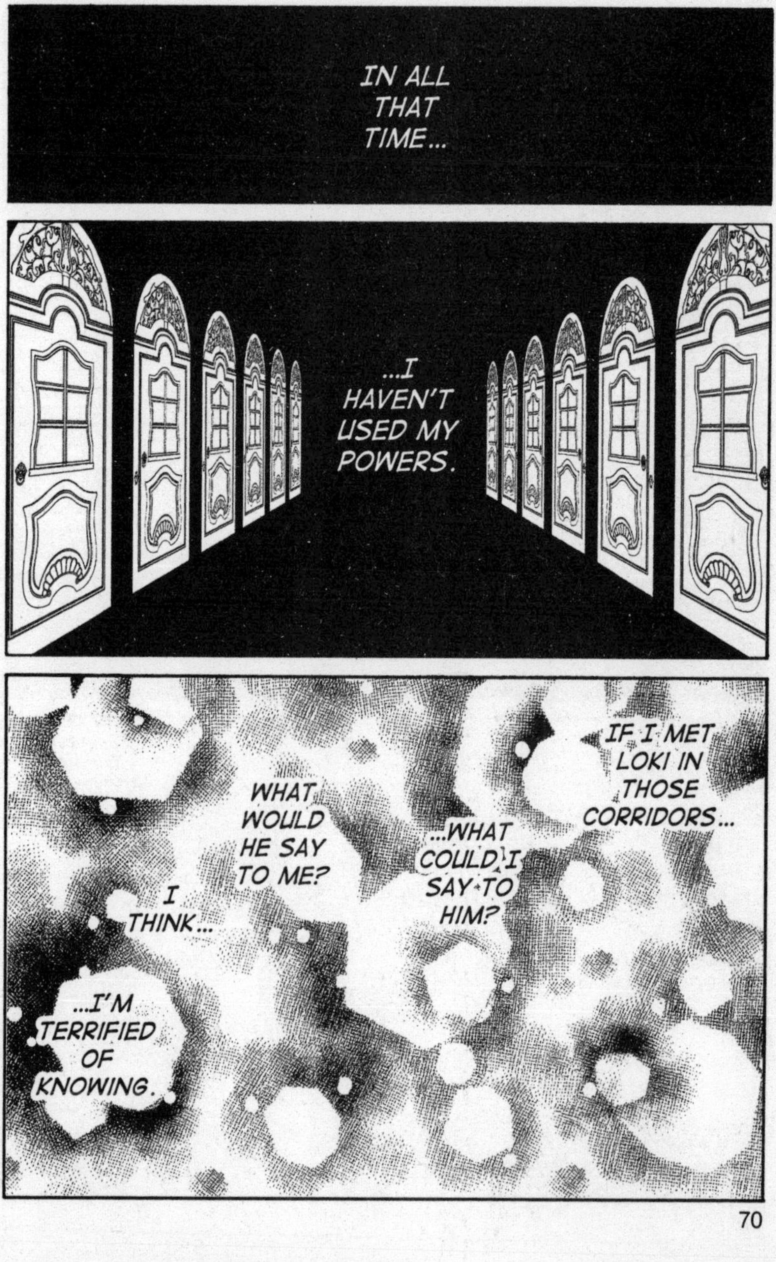
IN ALL THAT TIME...
...I HAVEN'T USED MY POWERS.
IF I MET LOKI IN THOSE CORRIDORS...
...WHAT COULD I SAY TO HIM?
WHAT WOULD HE SAY TO ME?
I THINK...
...I'M TERRIFIED OF KNOWING.

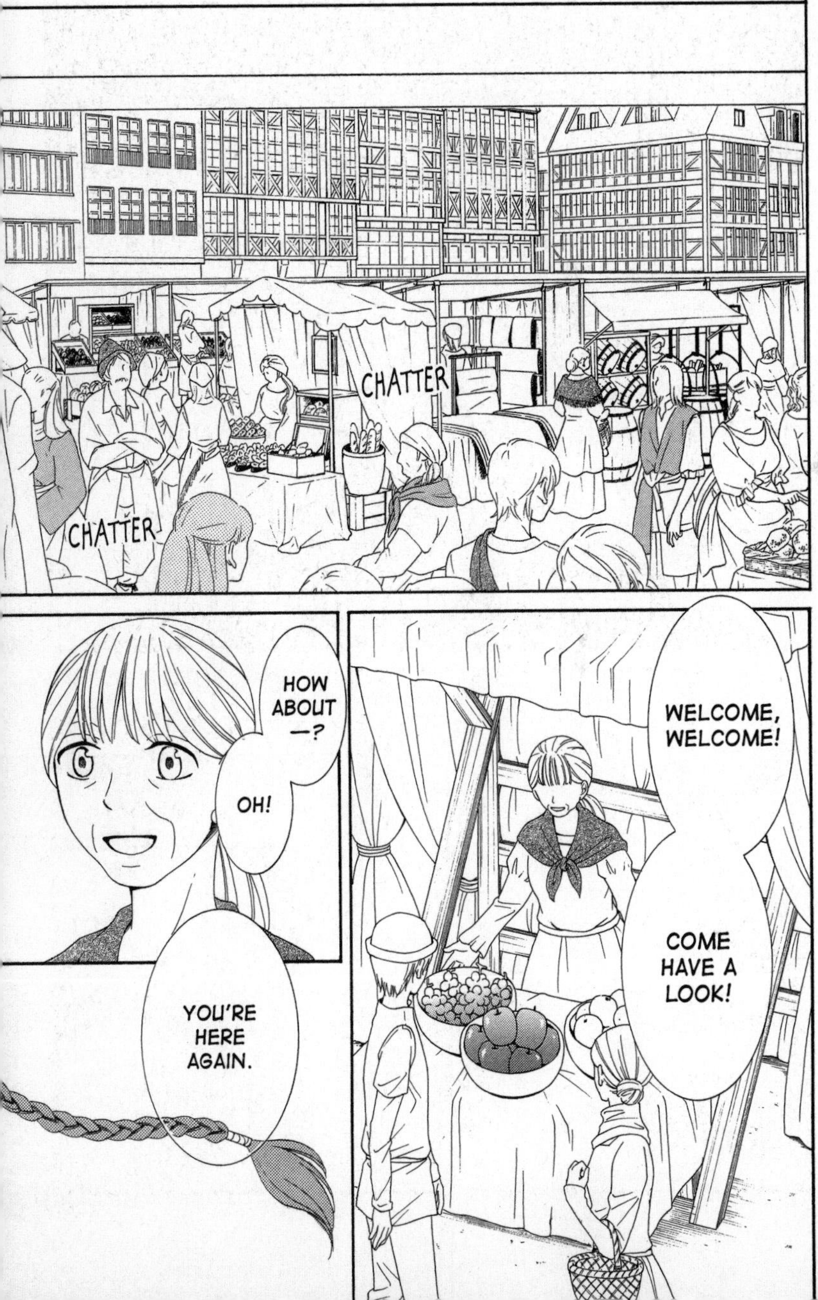
CHATTER
CHATTER
WELCOME, WELCOME!
COME HAVE A LOOK!
HOW ABOUT —?
OH!
YOU'RE HERE AGAIN.

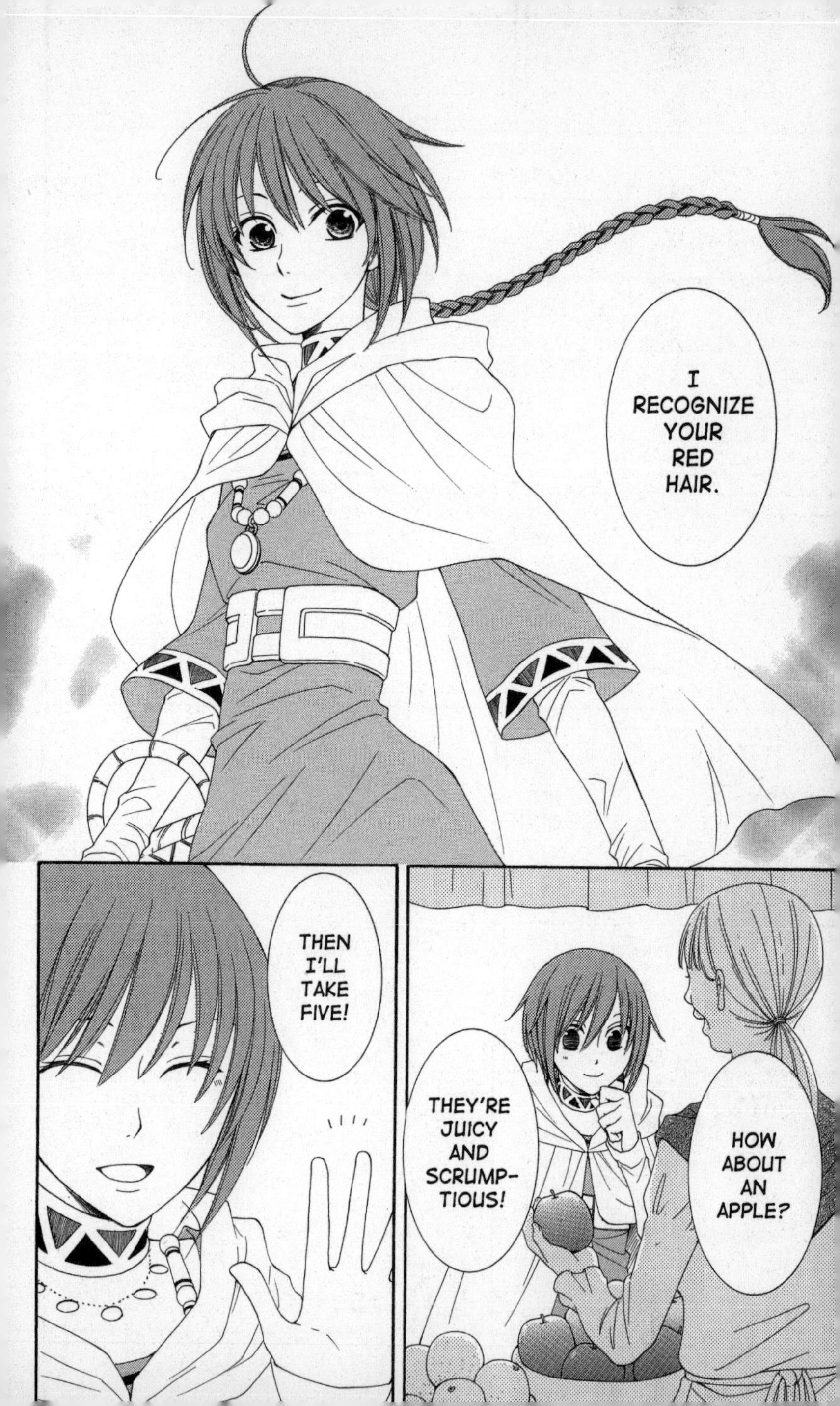
I RECOGNIZE YOUR RED HAIR.
HOW ABOUT AN APPLE?
THEY'RE JUICY AND SCRUMP-TIOUS!
THEN I'LL TAKE FIVE!

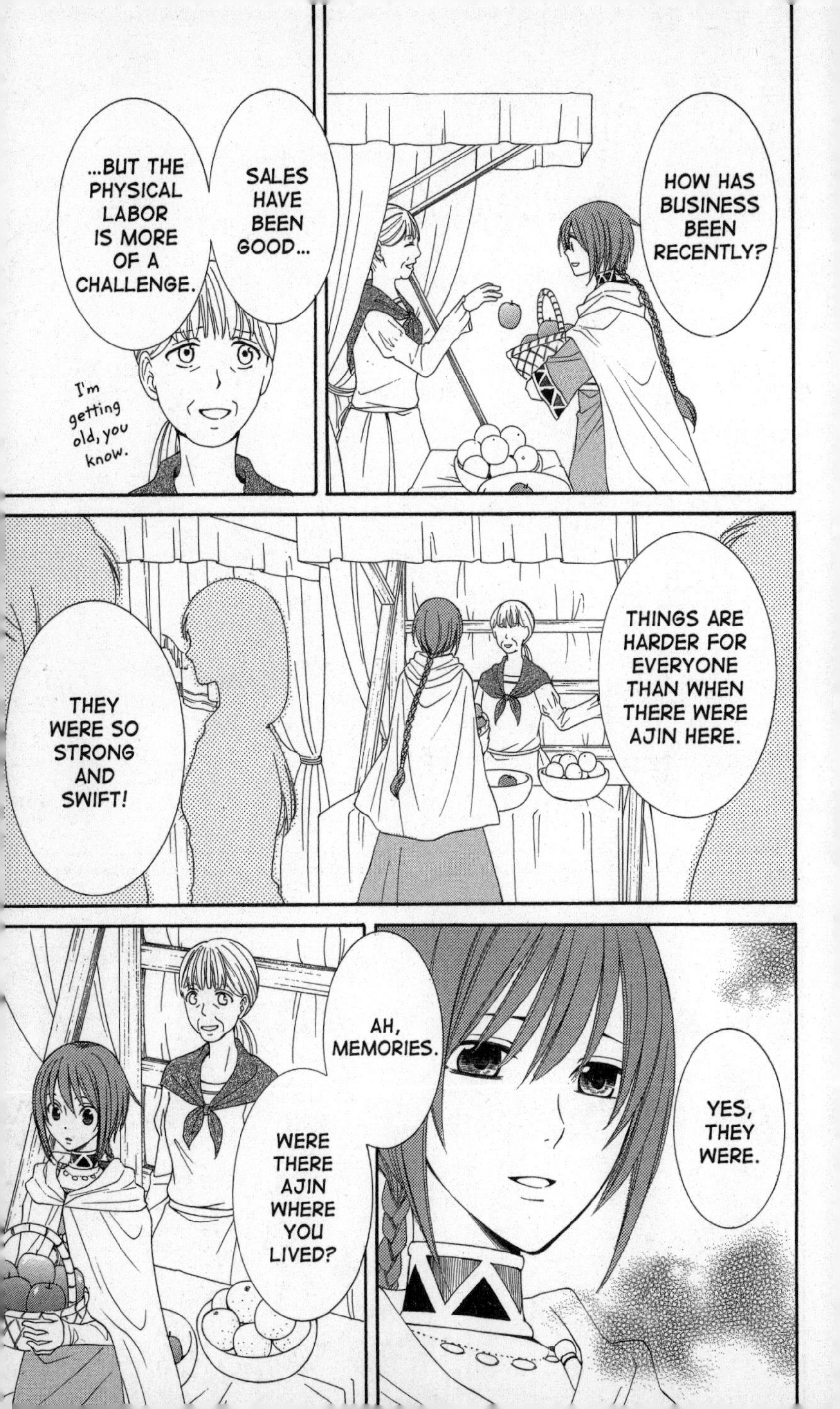
HOW HAS BUSINESS BEEN RECENTLY?
SALES HAVE BEEN GOOD...
...BUT THE PHYSICAL LABOR IS MORE OF A CHALLENGE.
I'm getting old, you know.
THINGS ARE HARDER FOR EVERYONE THAN WHEN THERE WERE AJIN HERE.
THEY WERE SO STRONG AND SWIFT!
YES, THEY WERE.
AH, MEMORIES.
WERE THERE AJIN WHERE YOU LIVED?

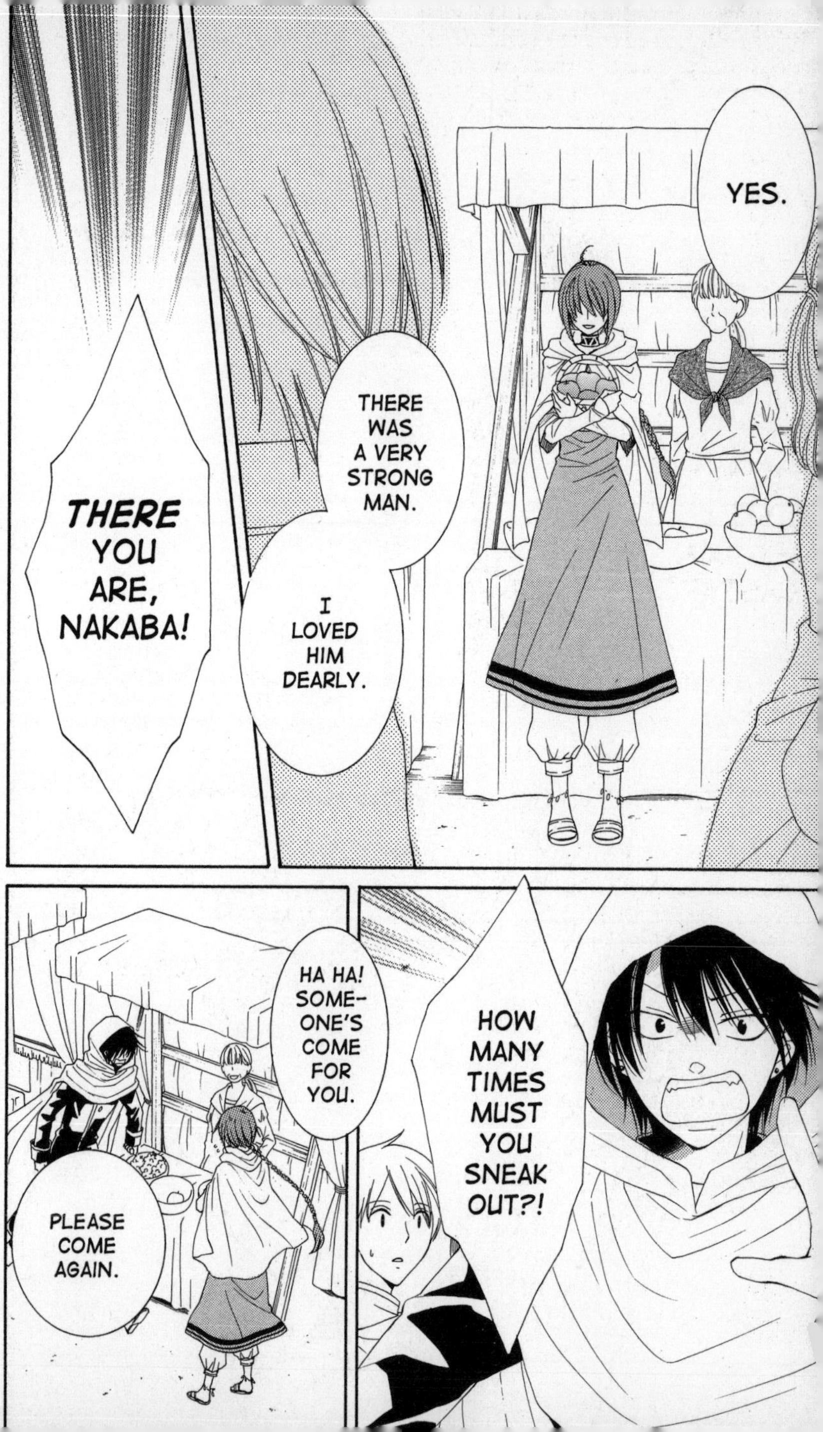
YES.
THERE WAS A VERY STRONG MAN.
I LOVED HIM DEARLY.
THERE YOU ARE, NAKABA!
HOW MANY TIMES MUST YOU SNEAK OUT?!
HA HA! SOME-ONE'S COME FOR YOU.
PLEASE COME AGAIN.

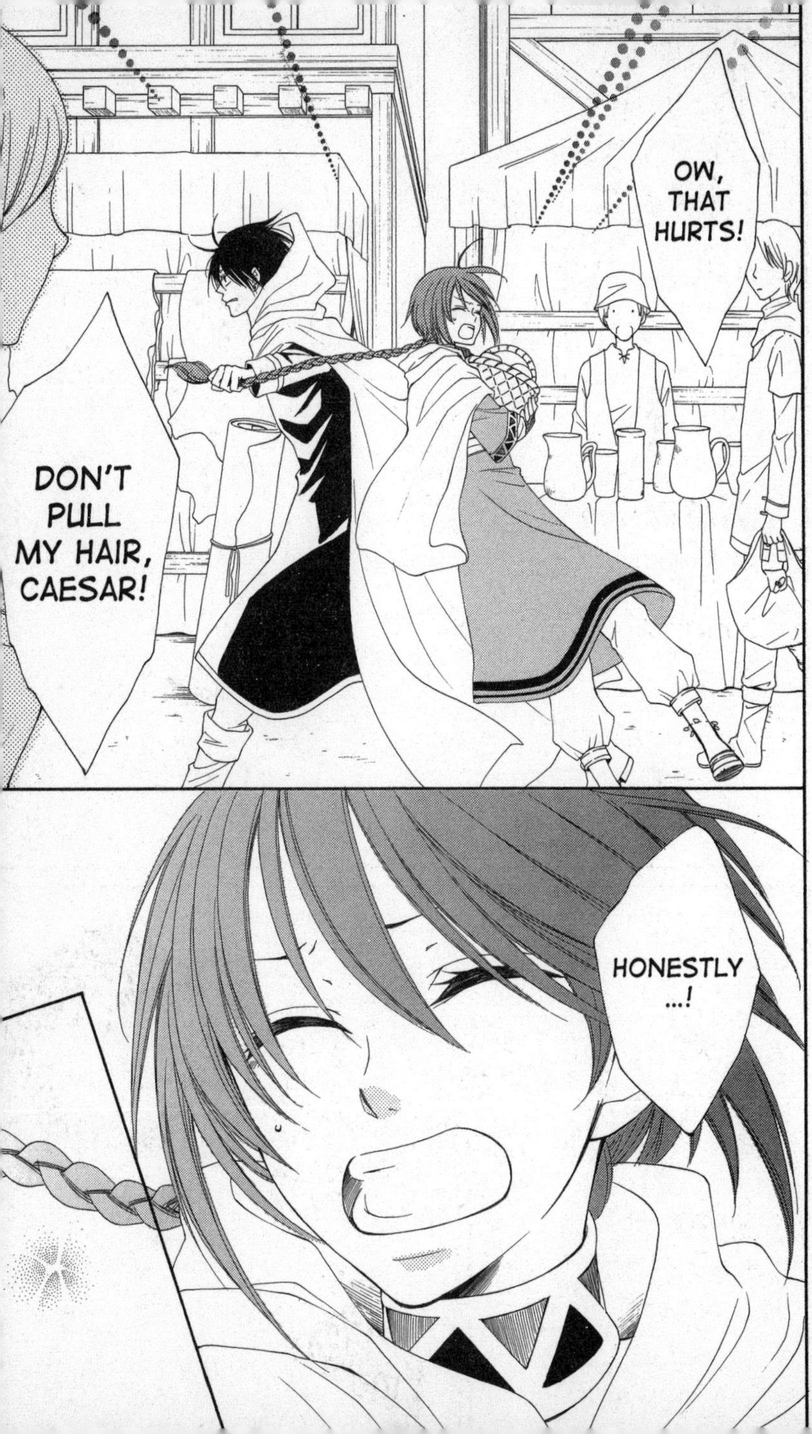
OW, THAT HURTS!
DON'T PULL MY HAIR, CAESAR!
HONESTLY ...!

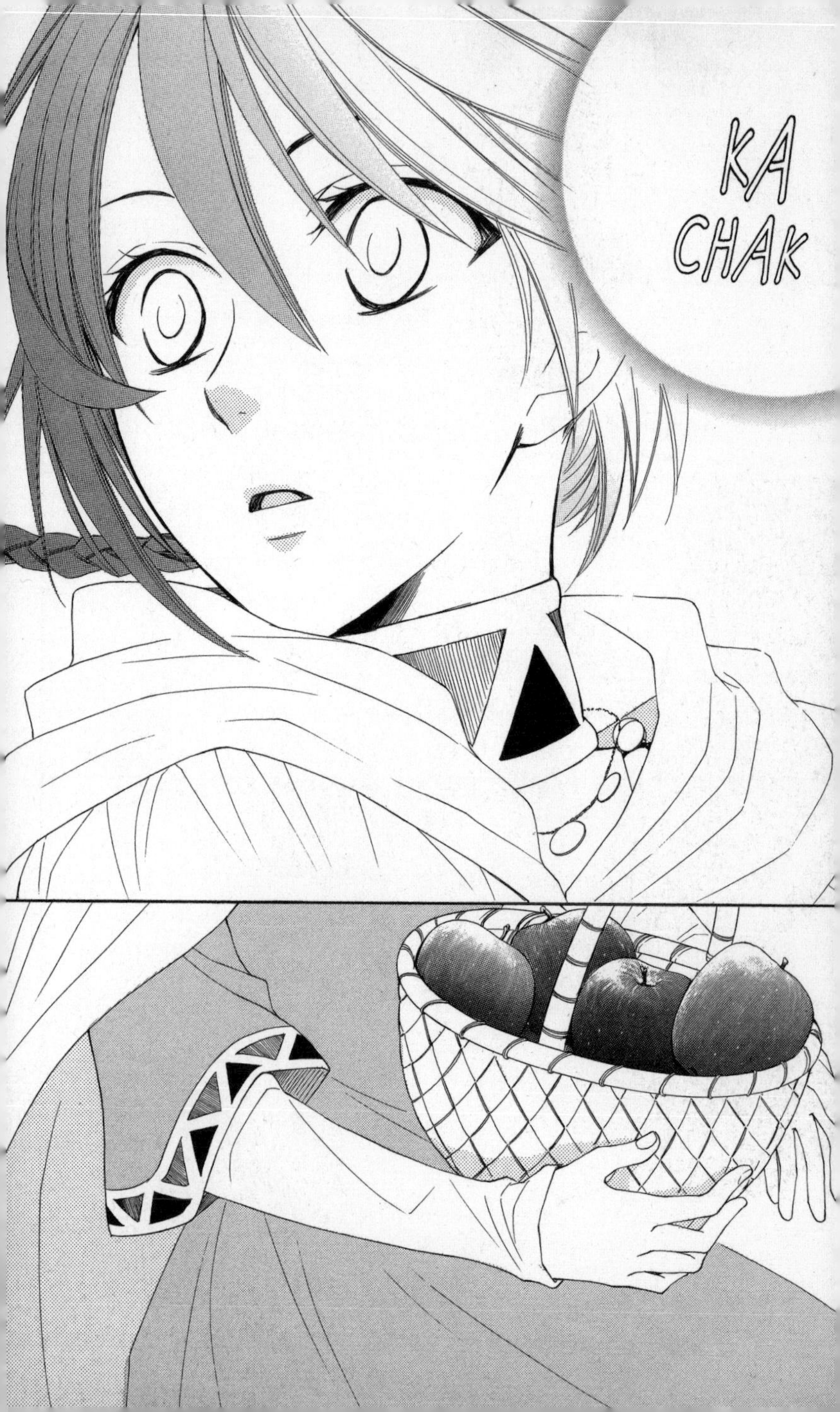
KA CHAK

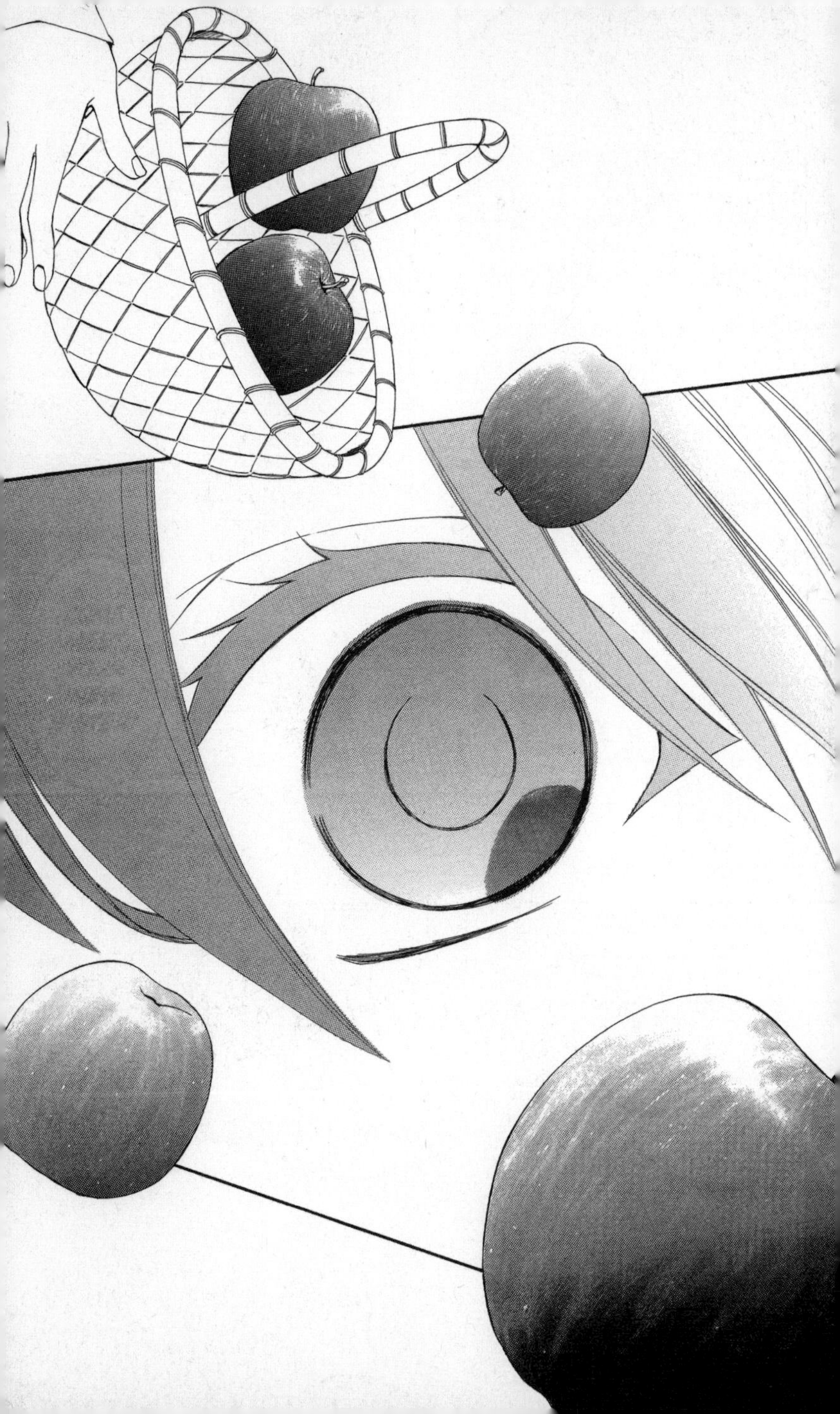

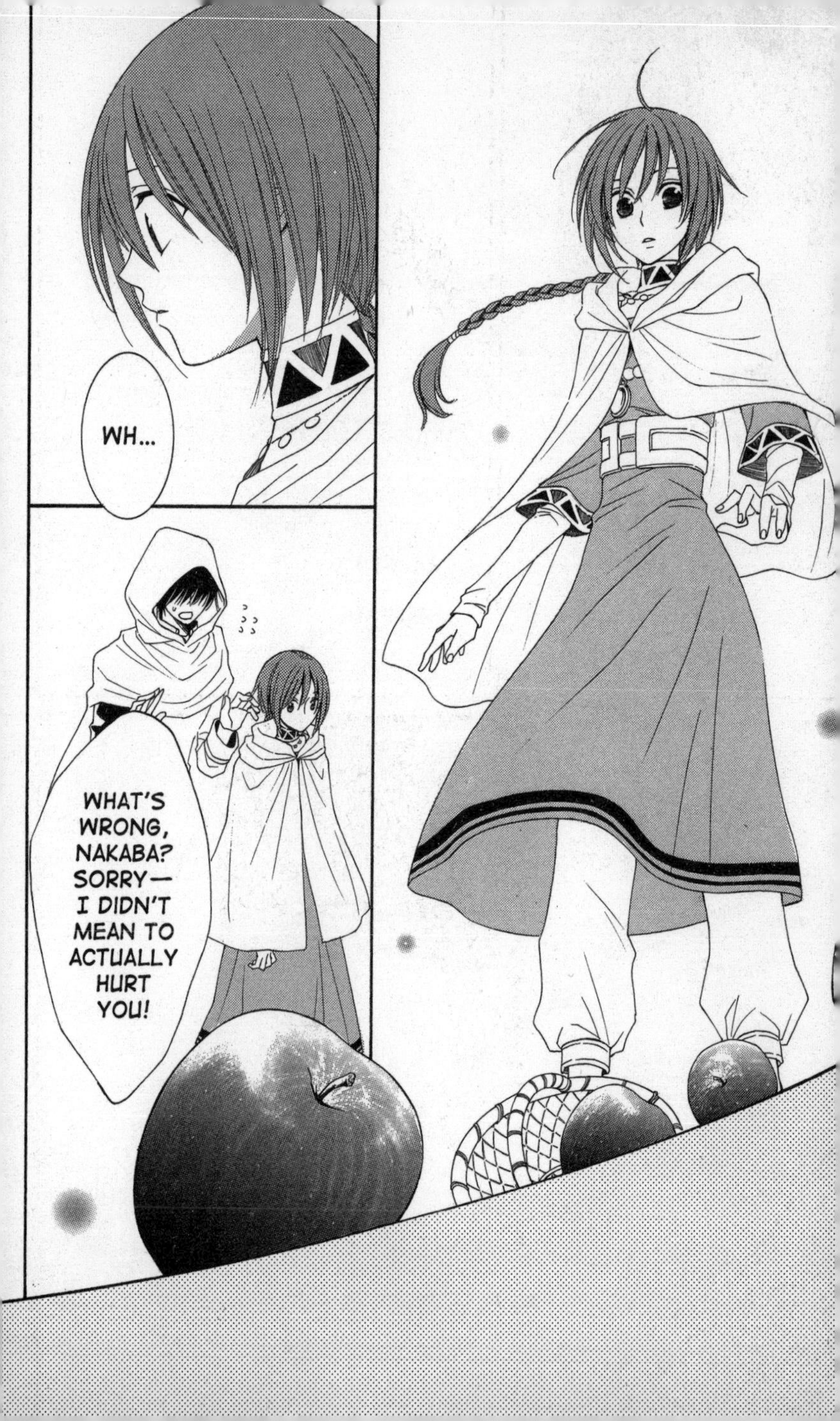
WH...
WHAT'S WRONG, NAKABA? SORRY— I DIDN'T MEAN TO ACTUALLY HURT YOU!

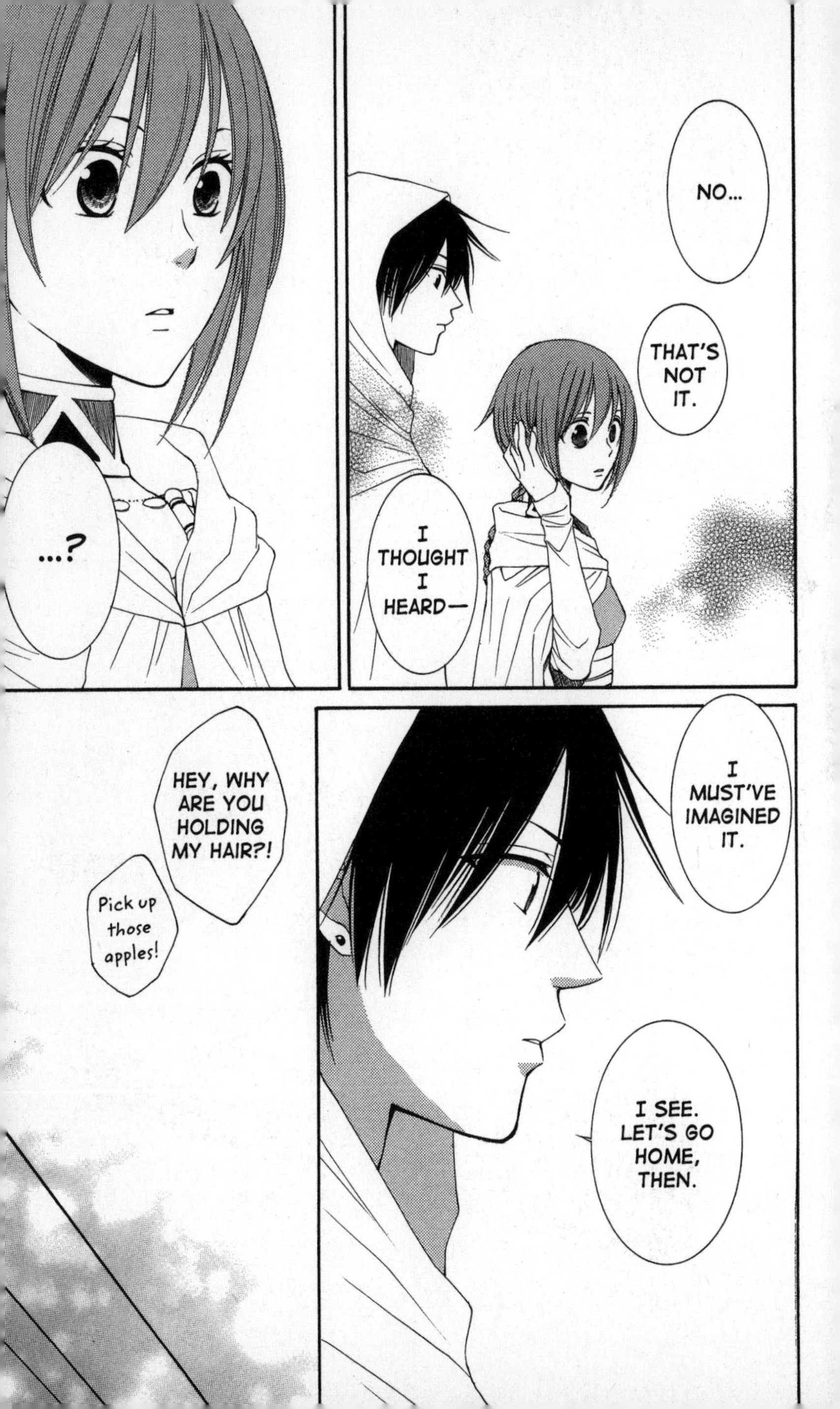
NO...
THAT'S NOT IT.
I THOUGHT I HEARD—
...?
I MUST'VE IMAGINED IT.
I SEE. LET'S GO HOME, THEN.
HEY, WHY ARE YOU HOLDING MY HAIR?!
Pick up those apples!

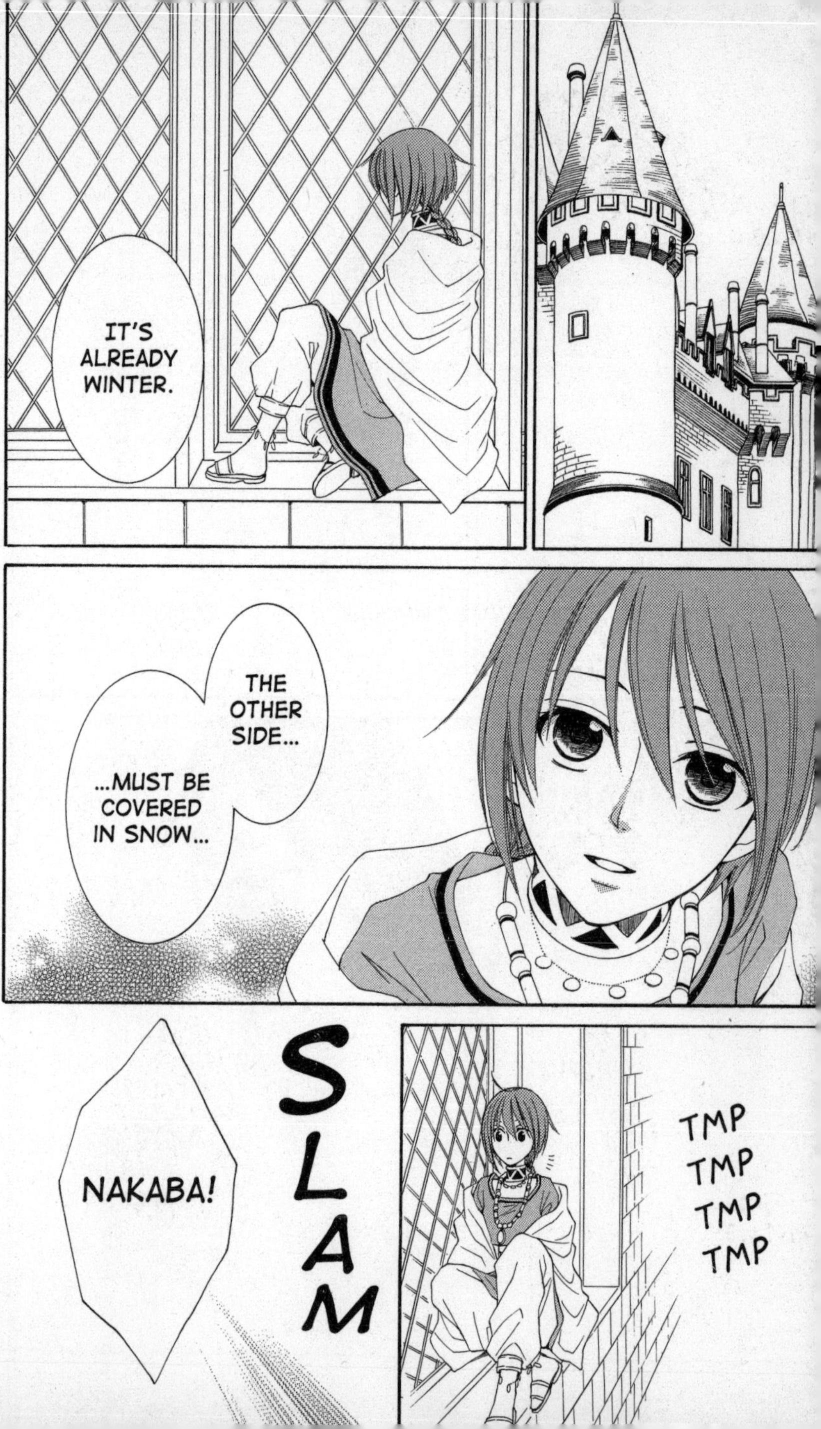
IT'S ALREADY WINTER.
THE OTHER SIDE...
...MUST BE COVERED IN SNOW...
TMP TMP TMP TMP
SLAM
NAKABA!

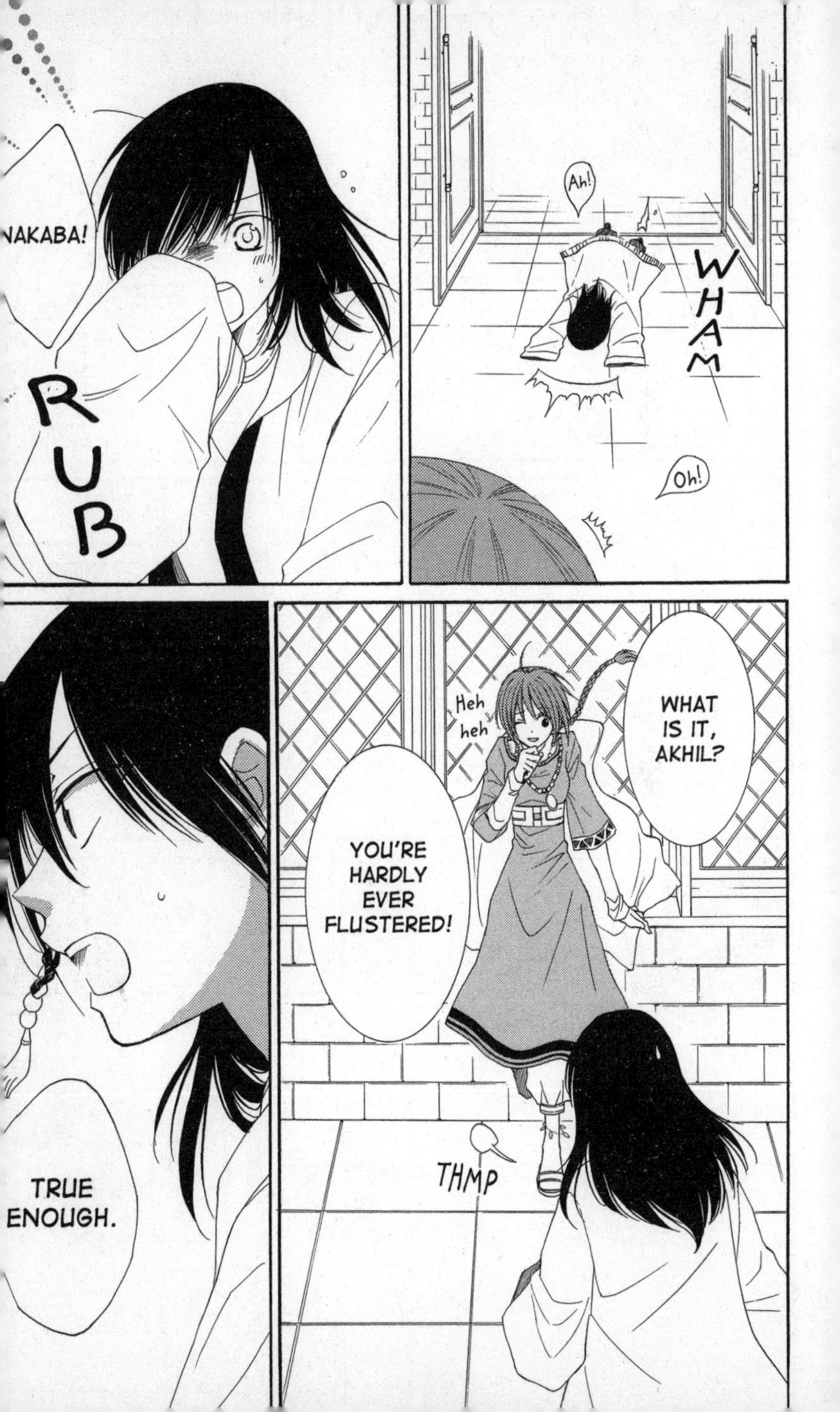
Ah!
WHAM
Oh!
NAKABA!
RUB
WHAT IS IT, AKHIL?
Heh heh
YOU'RE HARDLY EVER FLUSTERED!
THMP
TRUE ENOUGH.

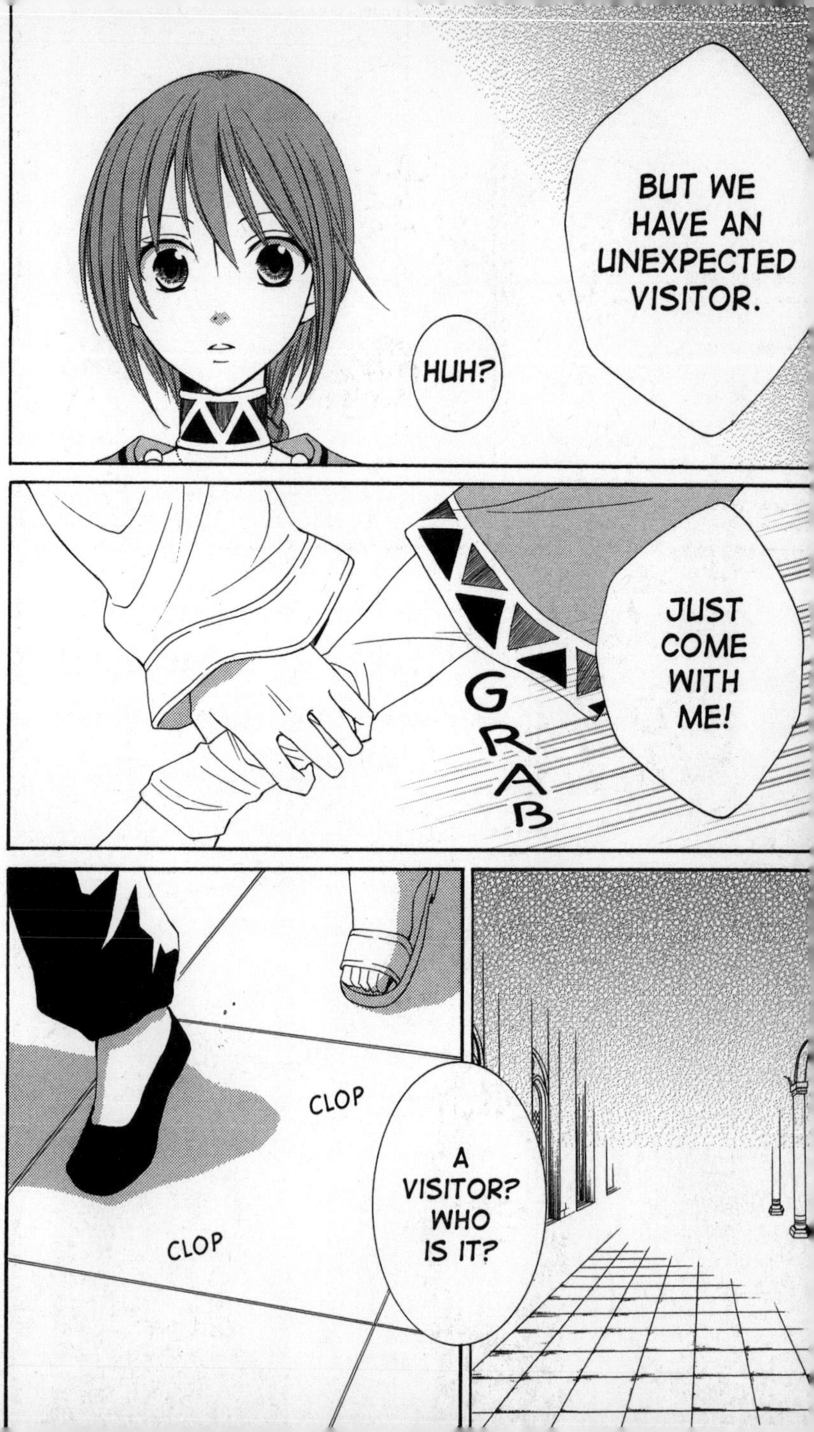
BUT WE HAVE AN UNEXPECTED VISITOR.
HUH?
JUST COME WITH ME!
GRAB
A VISITOR? WHO IS IT?
CLOP
CLOP

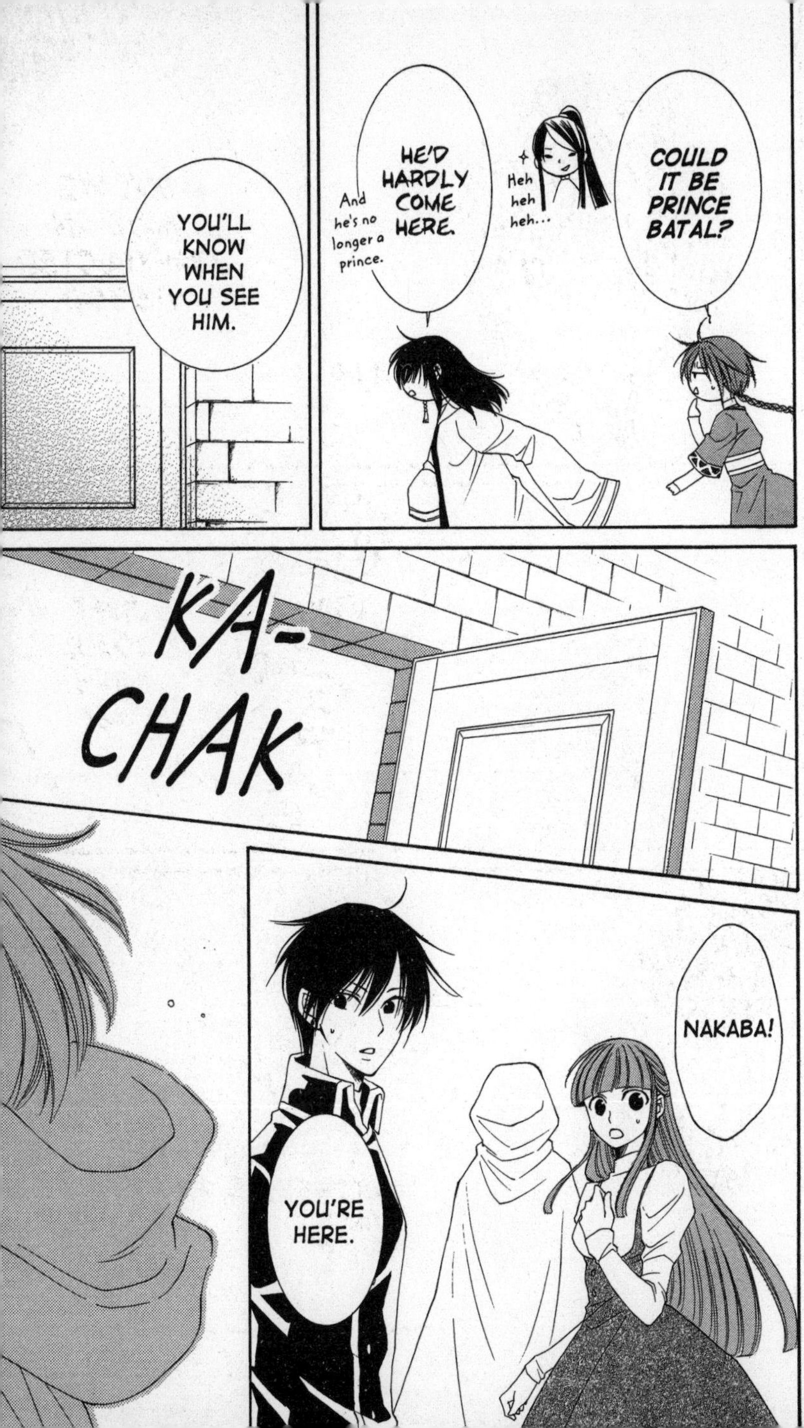
COULD IT BE PRINCE BATAL?
Heh heh heh...
HE'D HARDLY COME HERE.
And he's no longer a prince.
YOU'LL KNOW WHEN YOU SEE HIM.
KA-CHAK
NAKABA!
YOU'RE HERE.

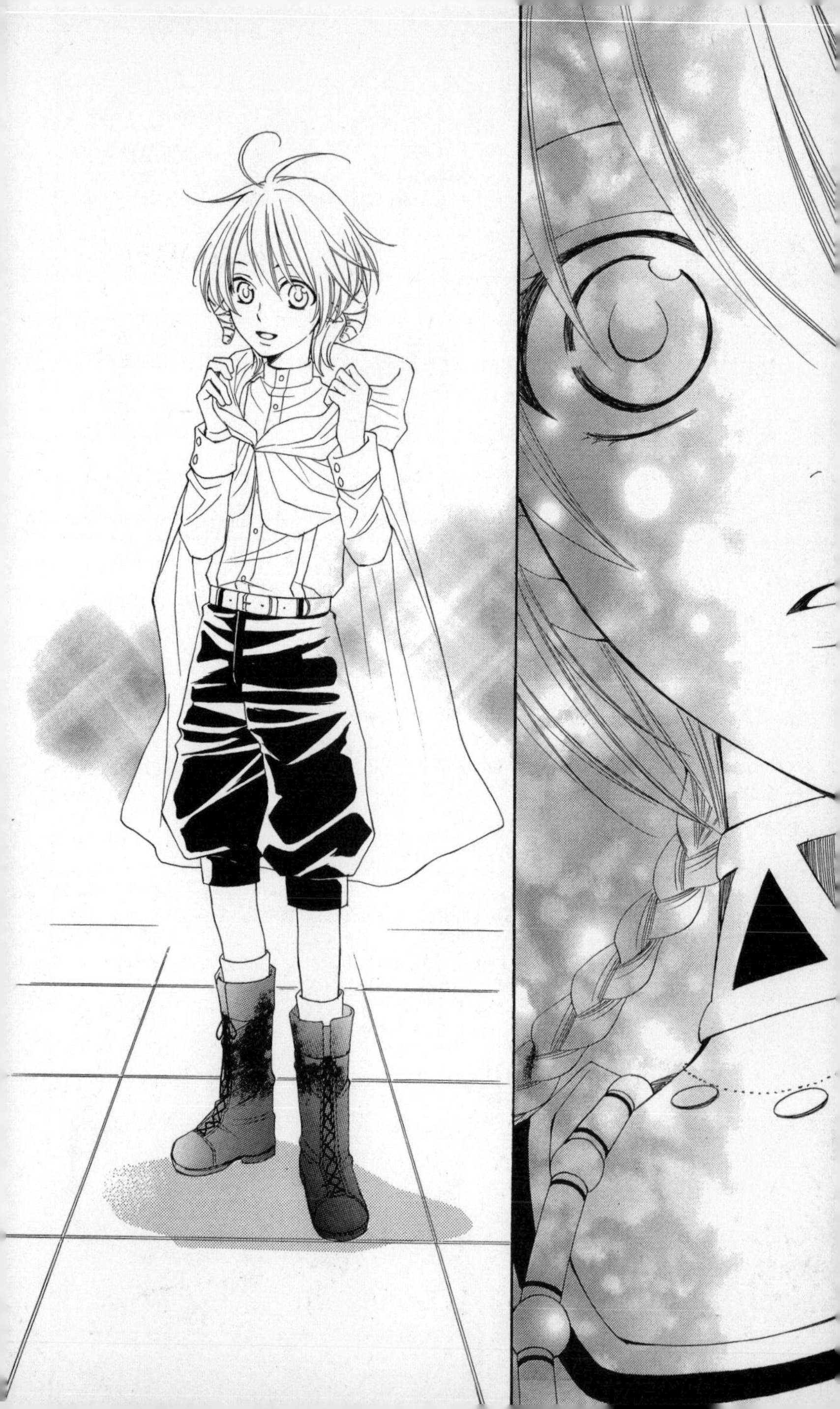

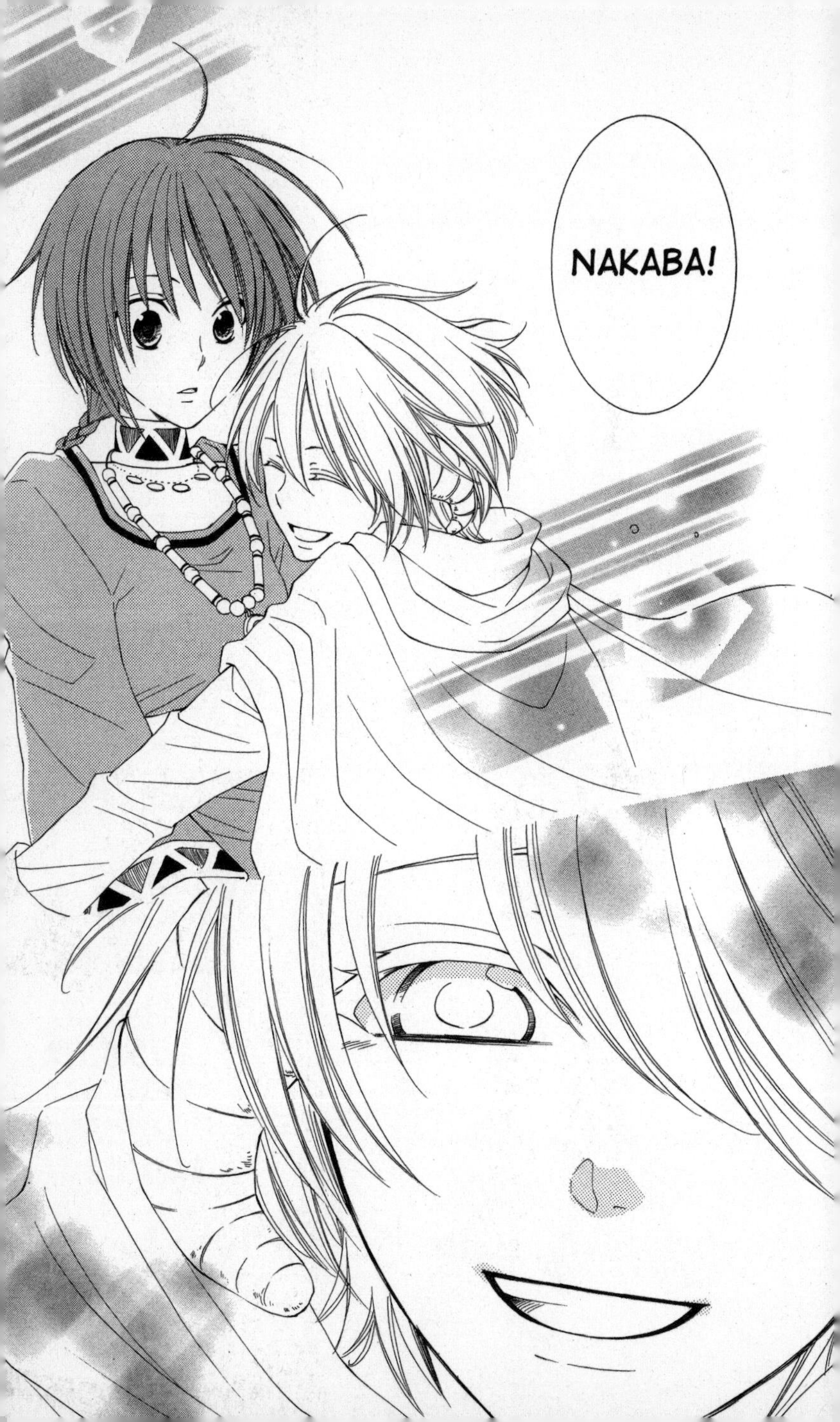
NAKABA!

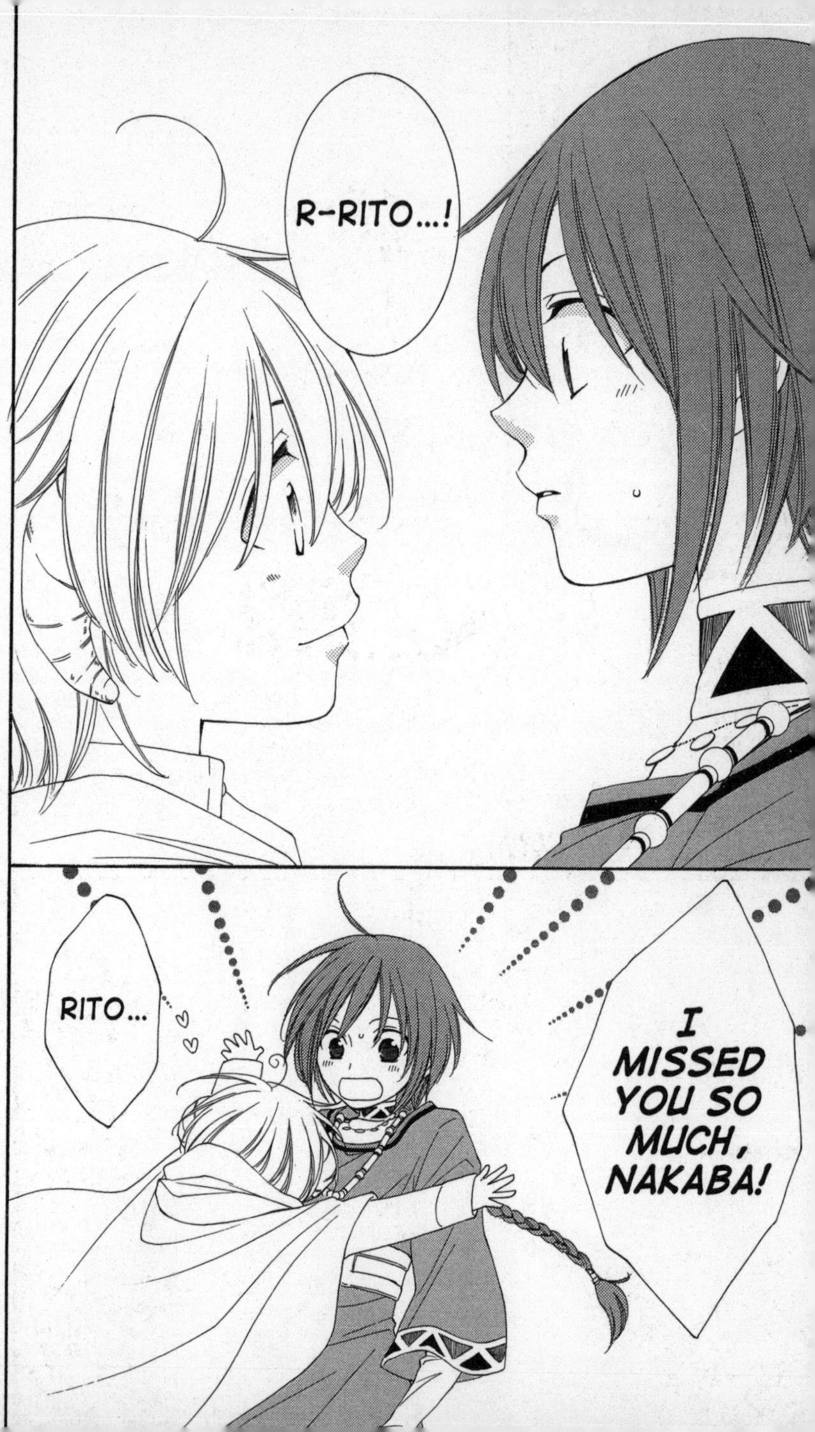
R-RITO...!
I MISSED YOU SO MUCH, NAKABA!
RITO...

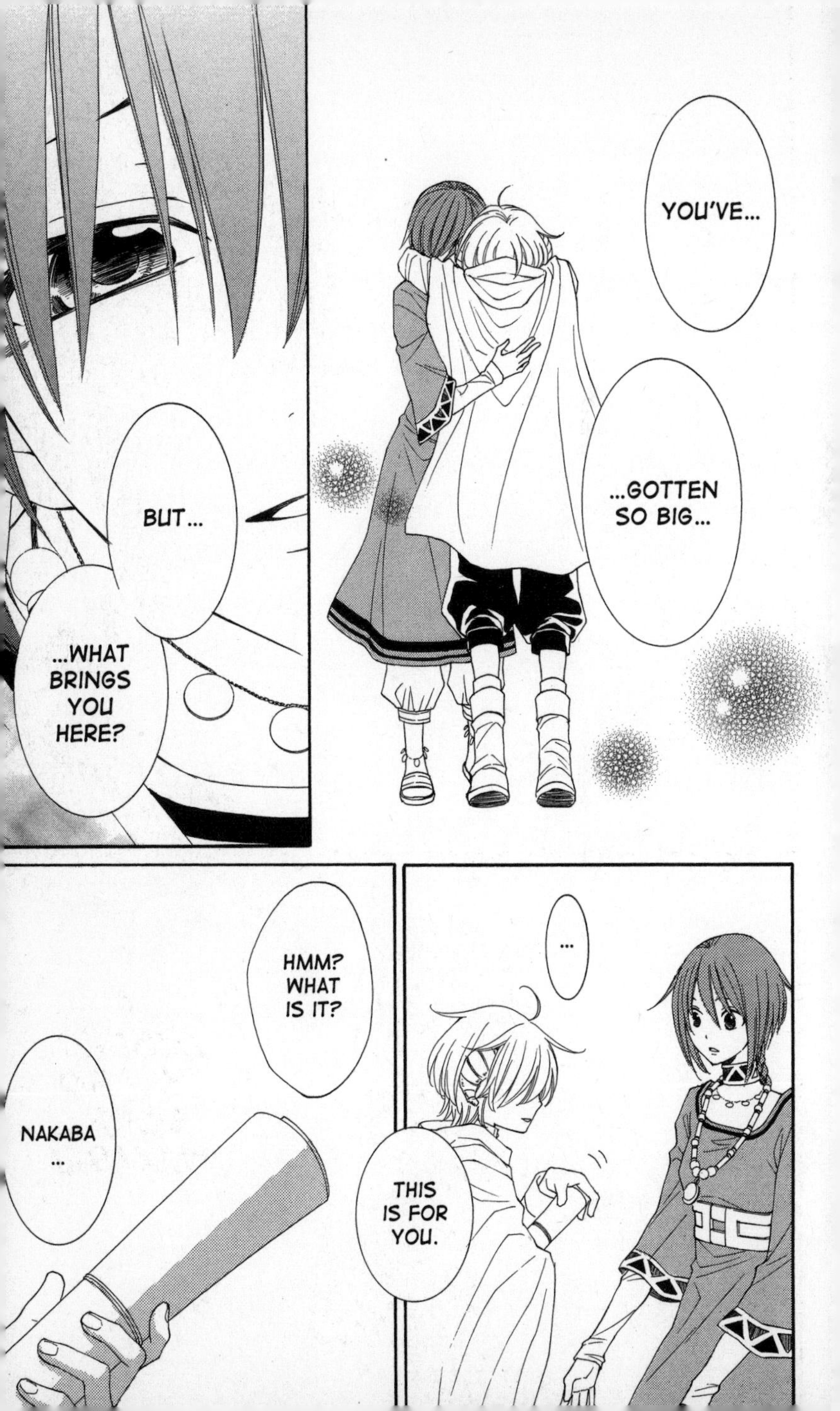
YOU'VE...
...GOTTEN SO BIG...
BUT...
...WHAT BRINGS YOU HERE?
...
THIS IS FOR YOU.
HMM? WHAT IS IT?
NAKABA ...

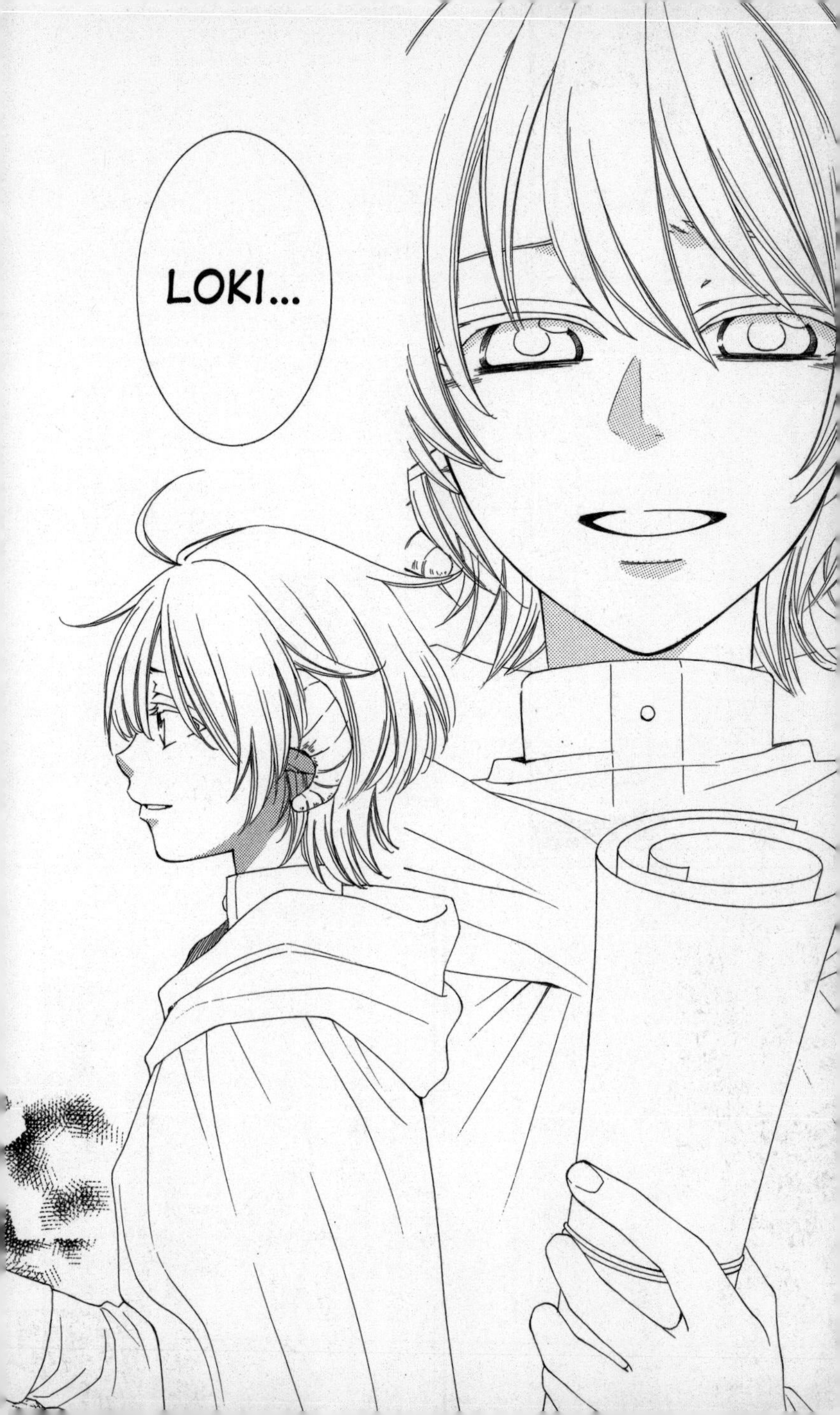
LOKI...

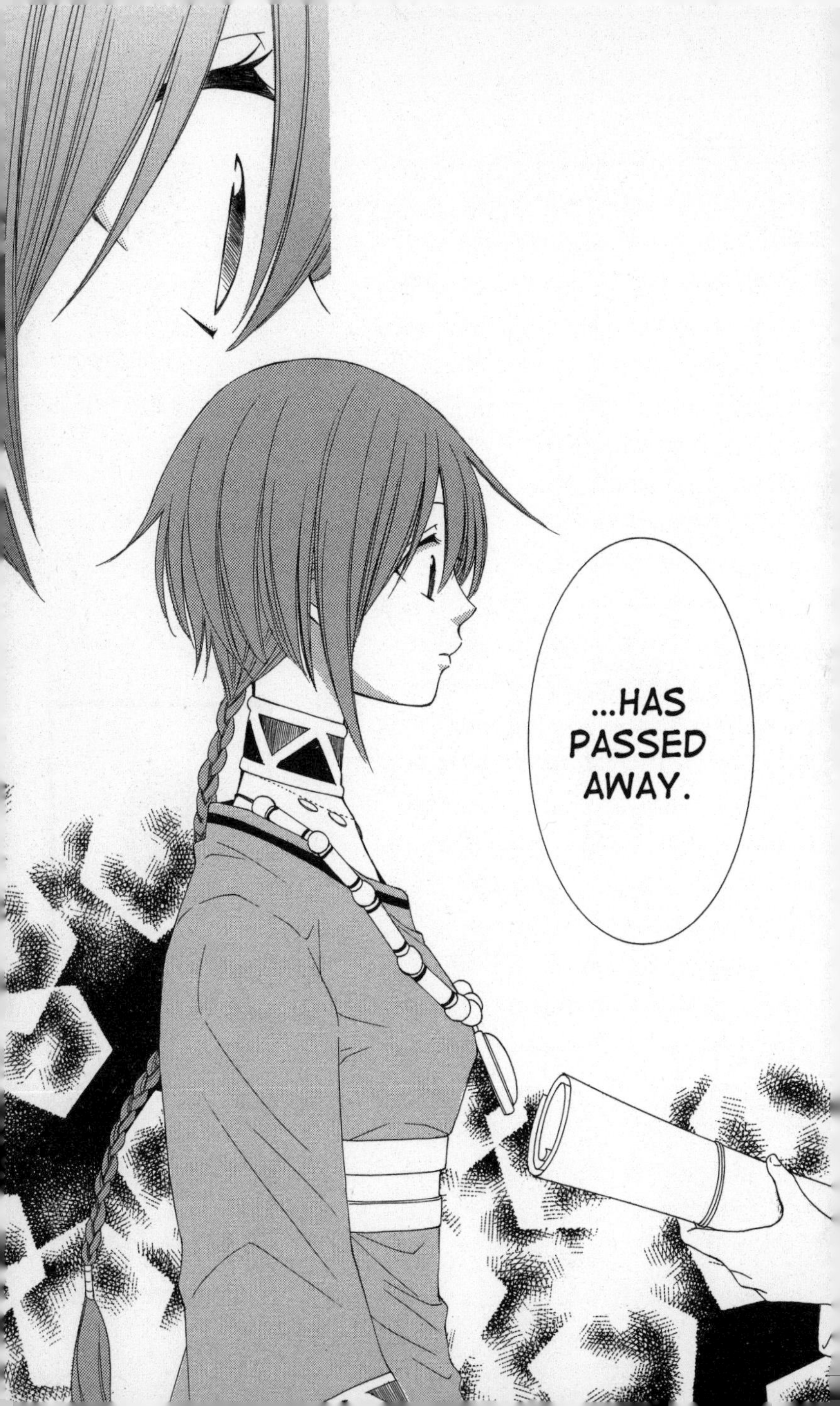
...HAS PASSED AWAY.

Chapter 52

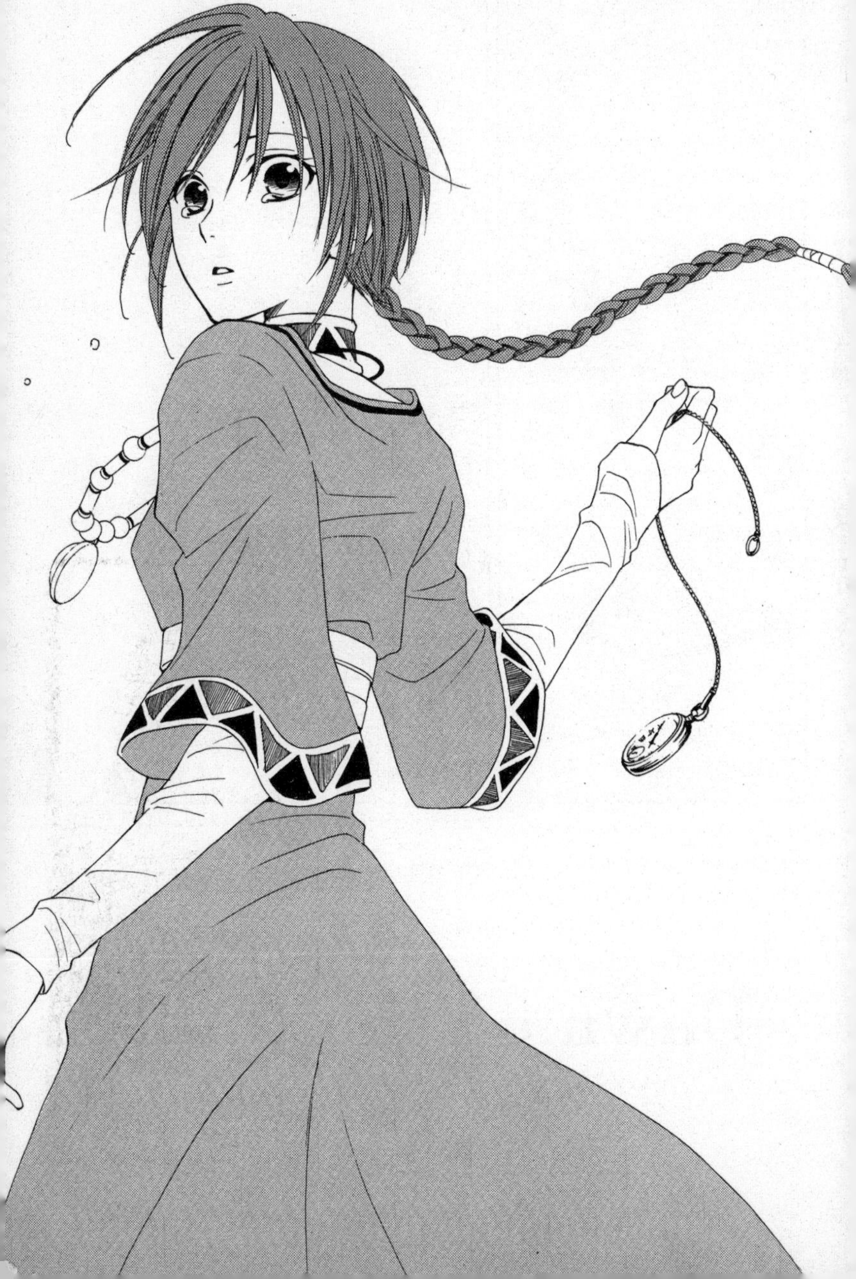

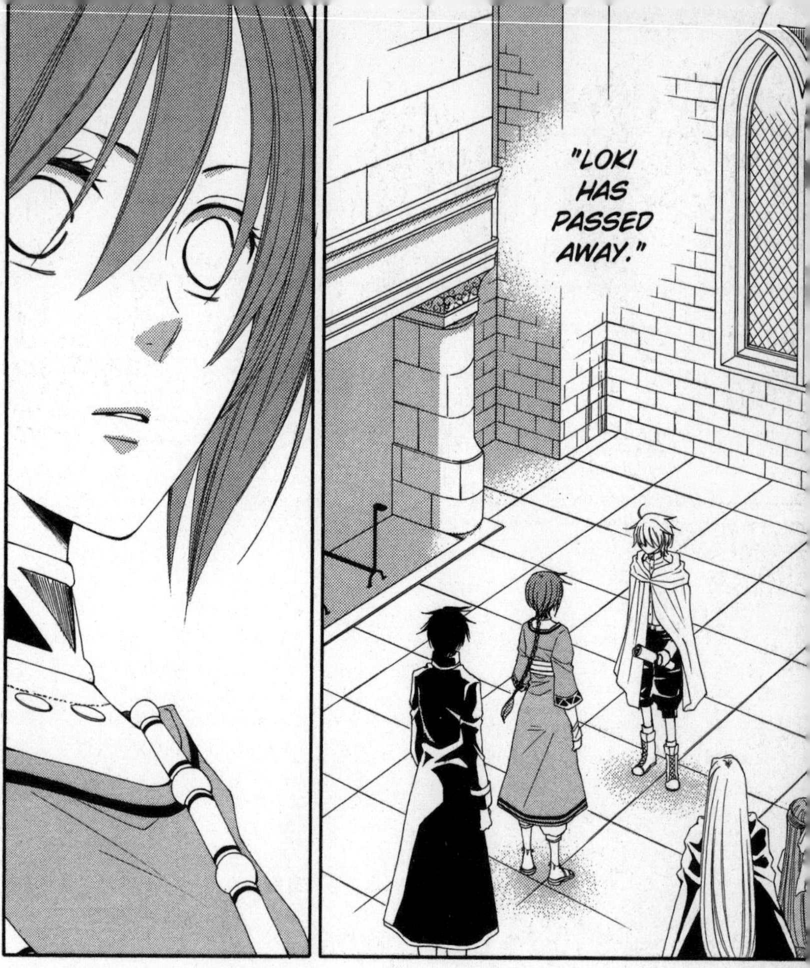
"LOKI HAS PASSED AWAY."

Dawn of the Arcana

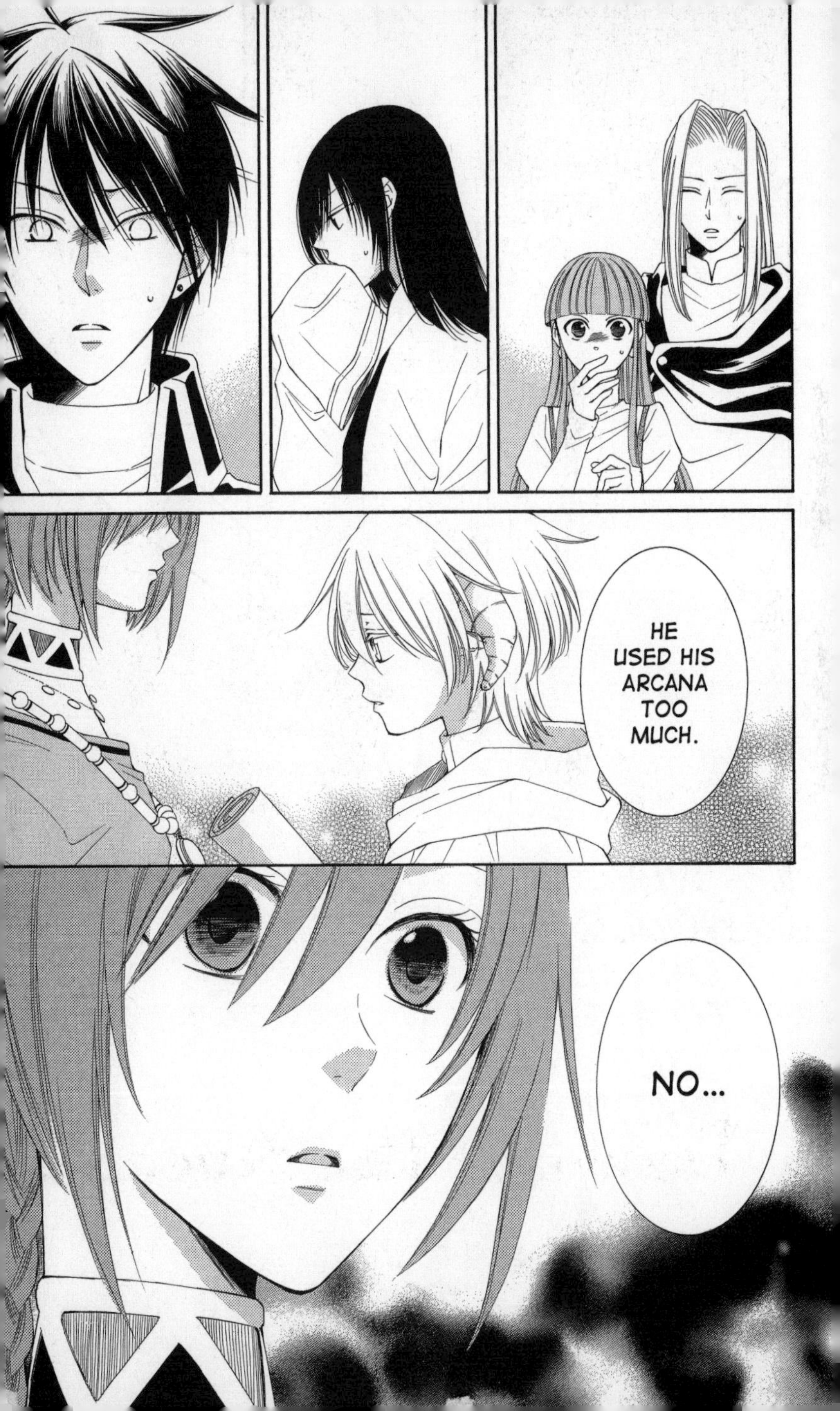
HE USED HIS ARCANA TOO MUCH.
NO...

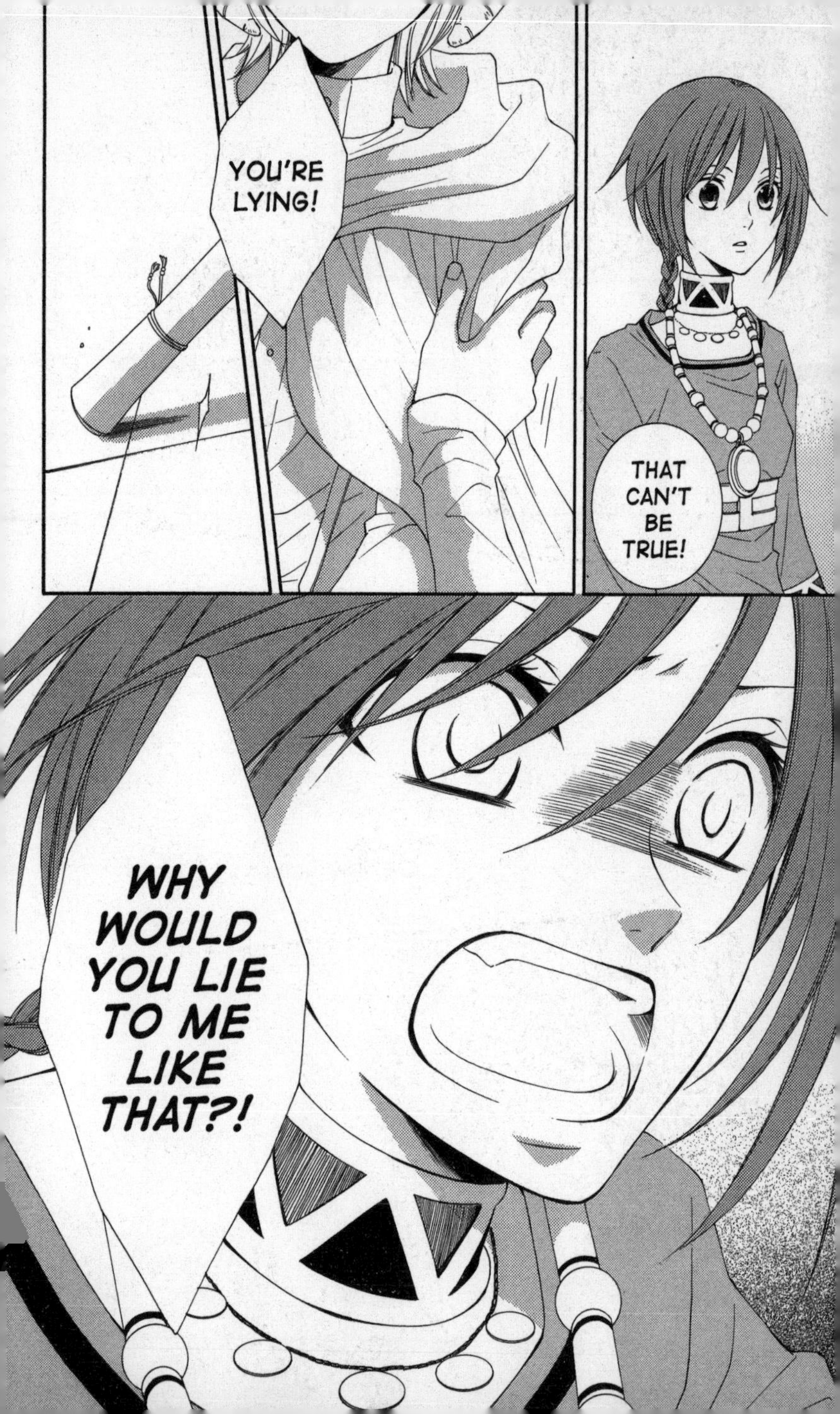
THAT CAN'T BE TRUE!
YOU'RE LYING!
WHY WOULD YOU LIE TO ME LIKE THAT?!

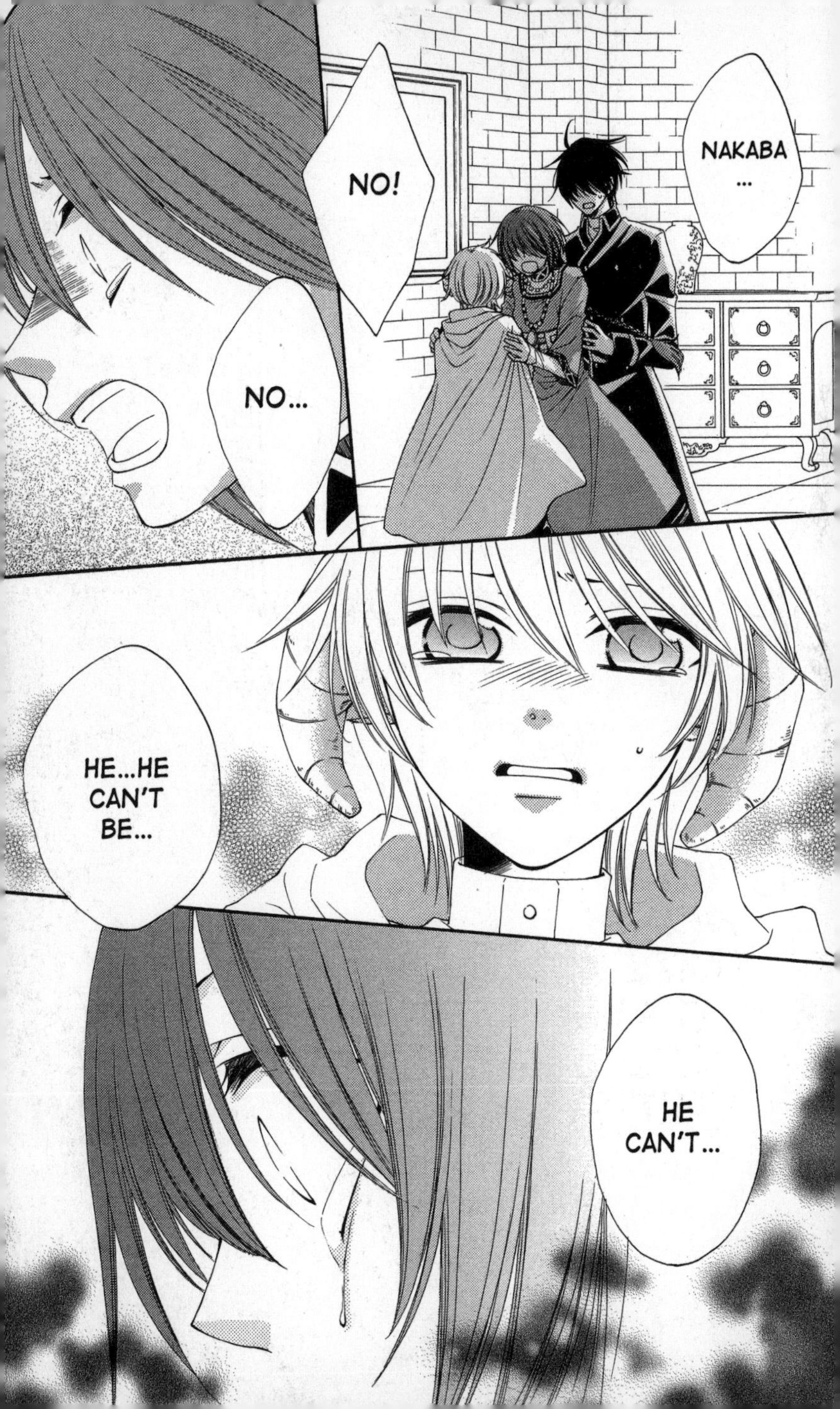
NAKABA ...
NO!
NO...
HE...HE CAN'T BE...
HE CAN'T...

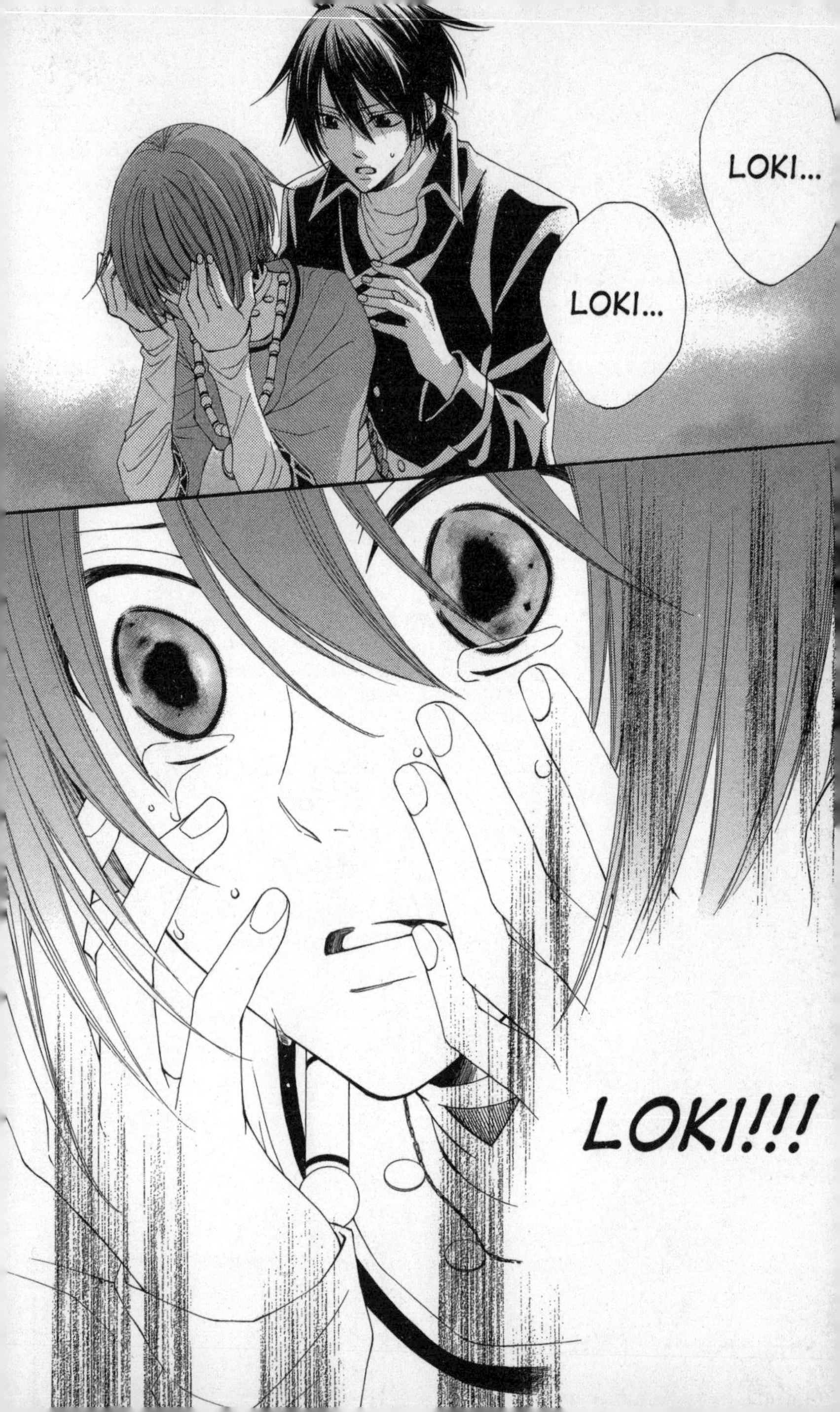
LOKI...
LOKI...
LOKI!!!

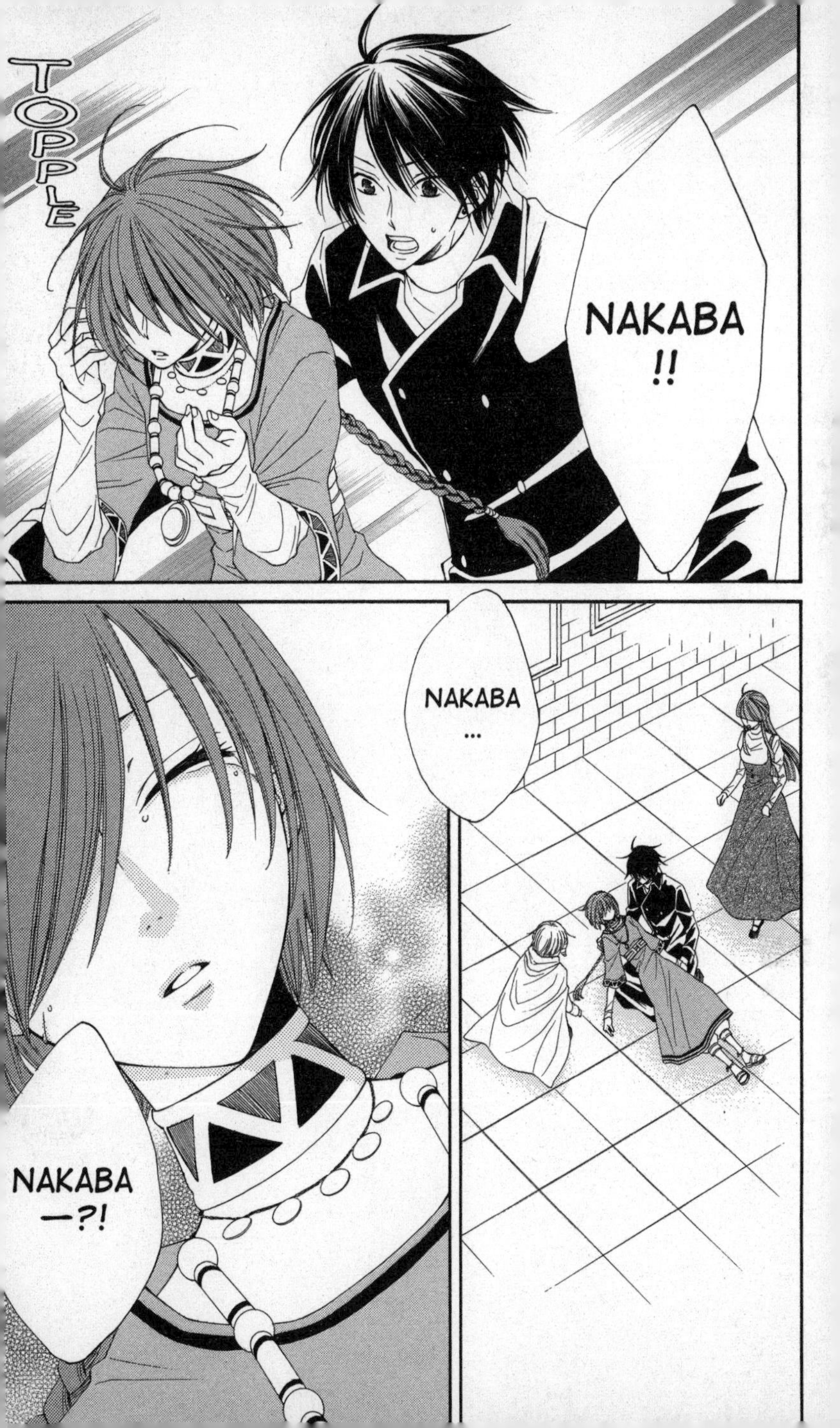
NAKABA!!
TOPPLE
NAKABA...
NAKABA—?!

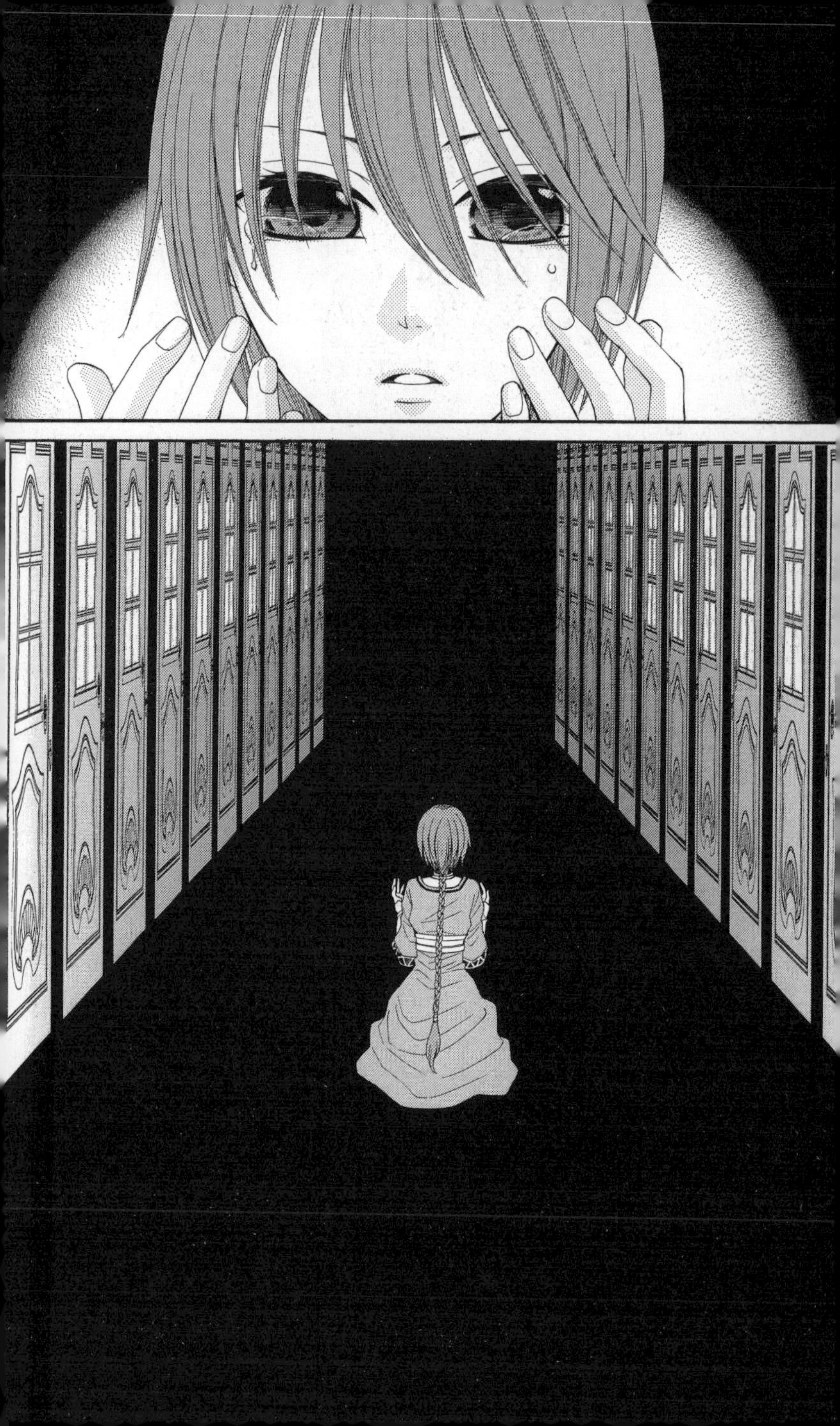

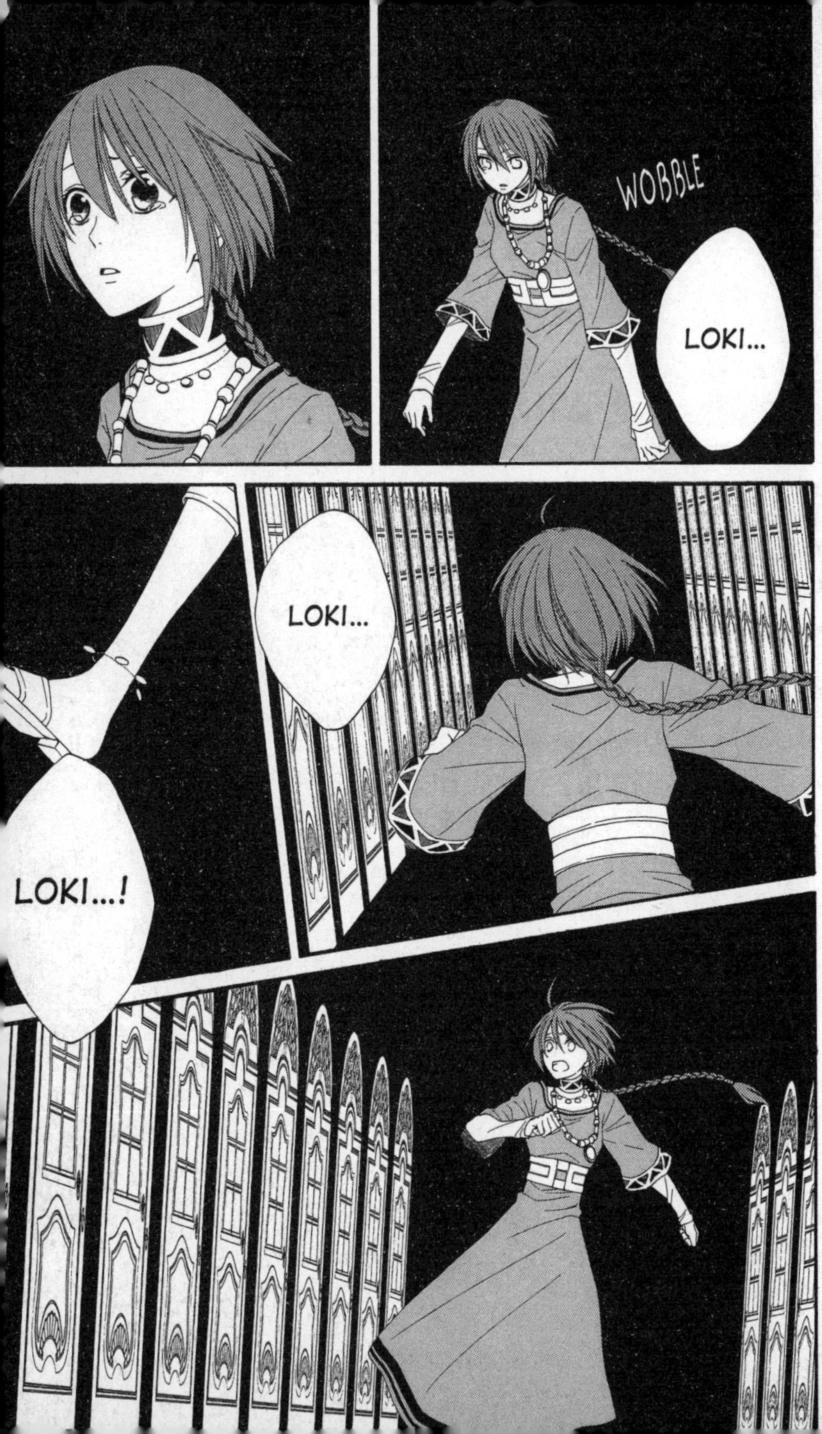
WOBBLE
LOKI...
LOKI...
LOKI...!

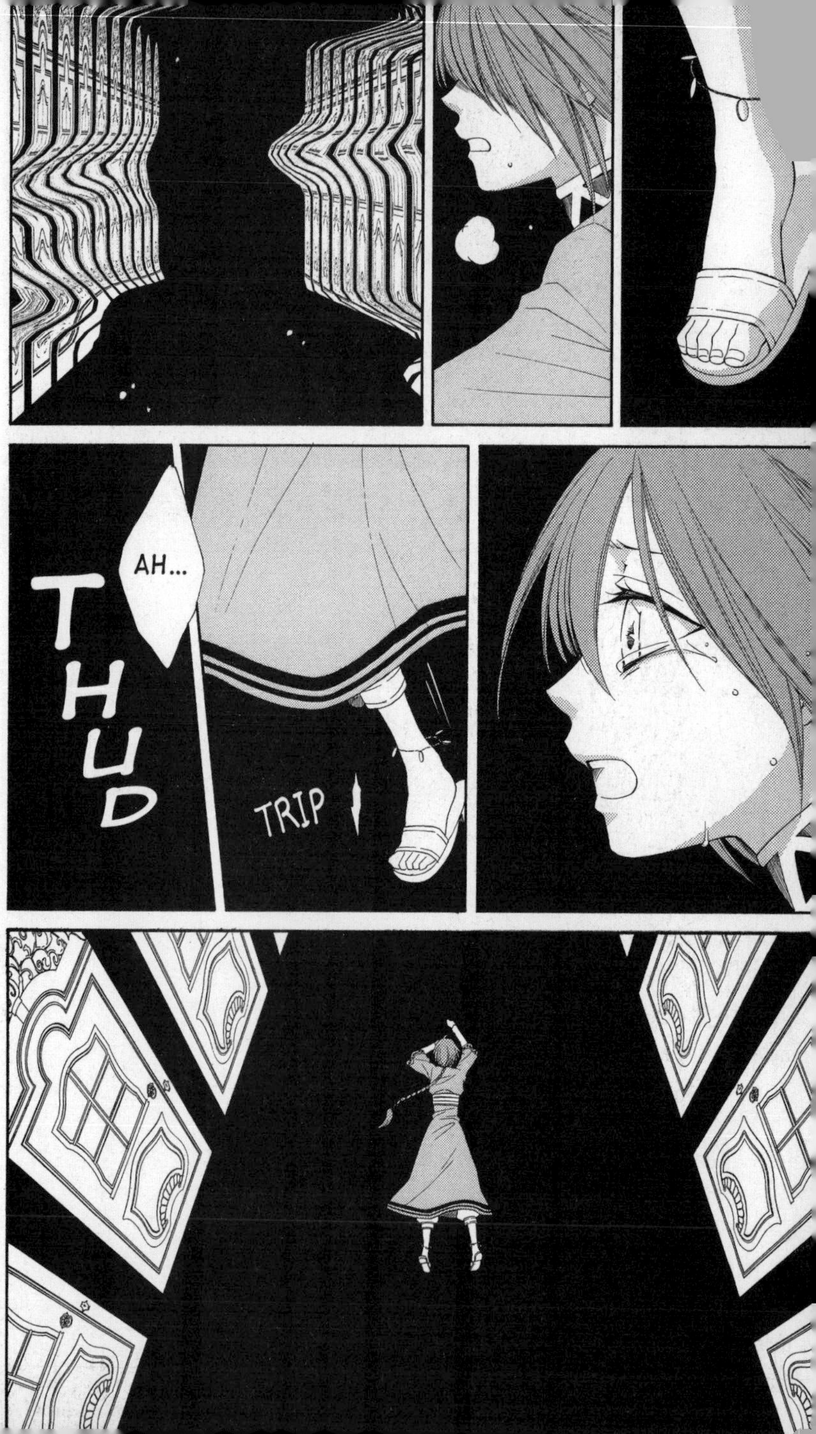
AH...
TRIP
THUD

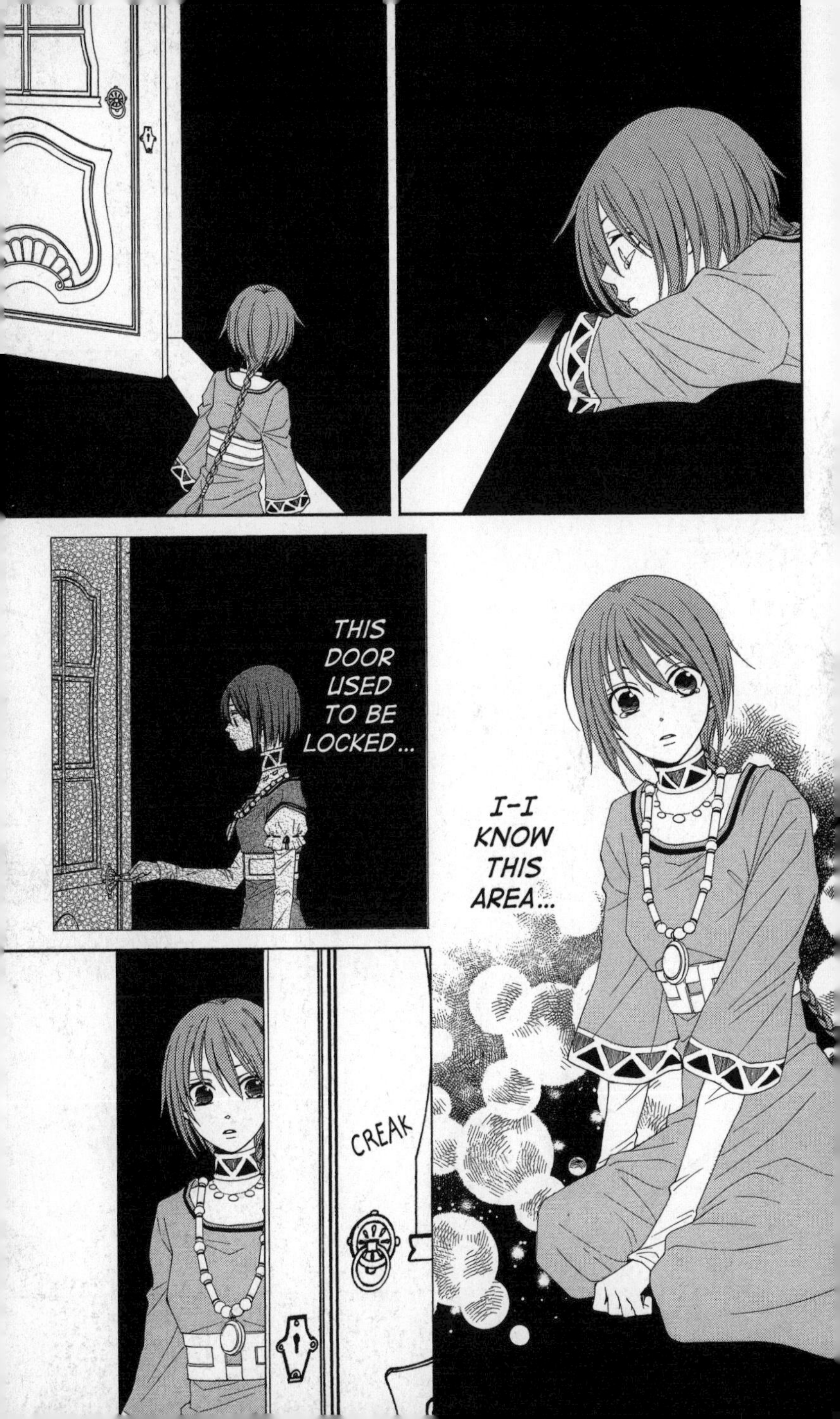
I-I KNOW THIS AREA...
THIS DOOR USED TO BE LOCKED...
CREAK

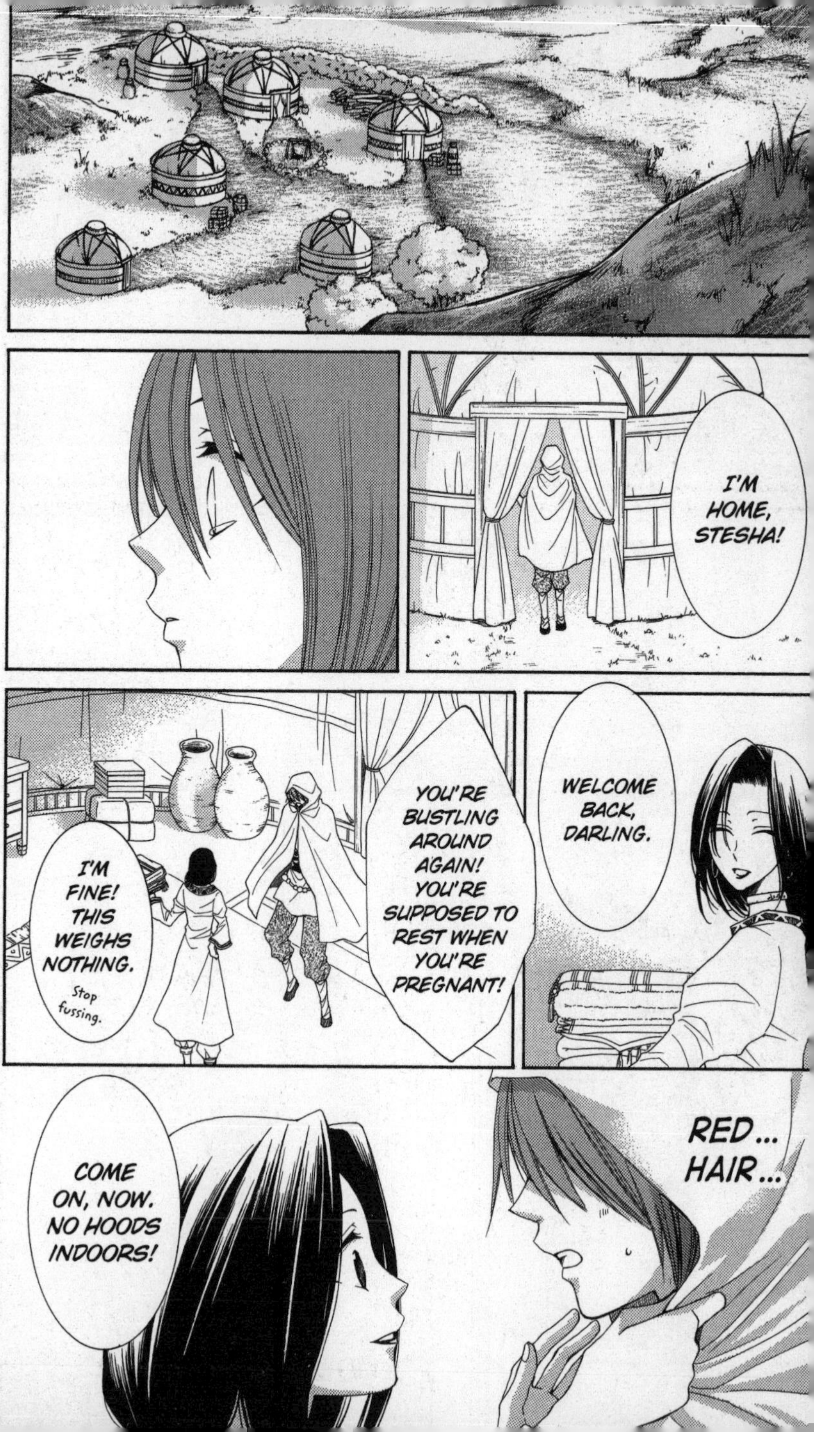
I'M HOME, STESHA!
WELCOME BACK, DARLING.
YOU'RE BUSTLING AROUND AGAIN! YOU'RE SUPPOSED TO REST WHEN YOU'RE PREGNANT!
I'M FINE! THIS WEIGHS NOTHING.
Stop fussing.
RED... HAIR...
COME ON, NOW. NO HOODS INDOORS!

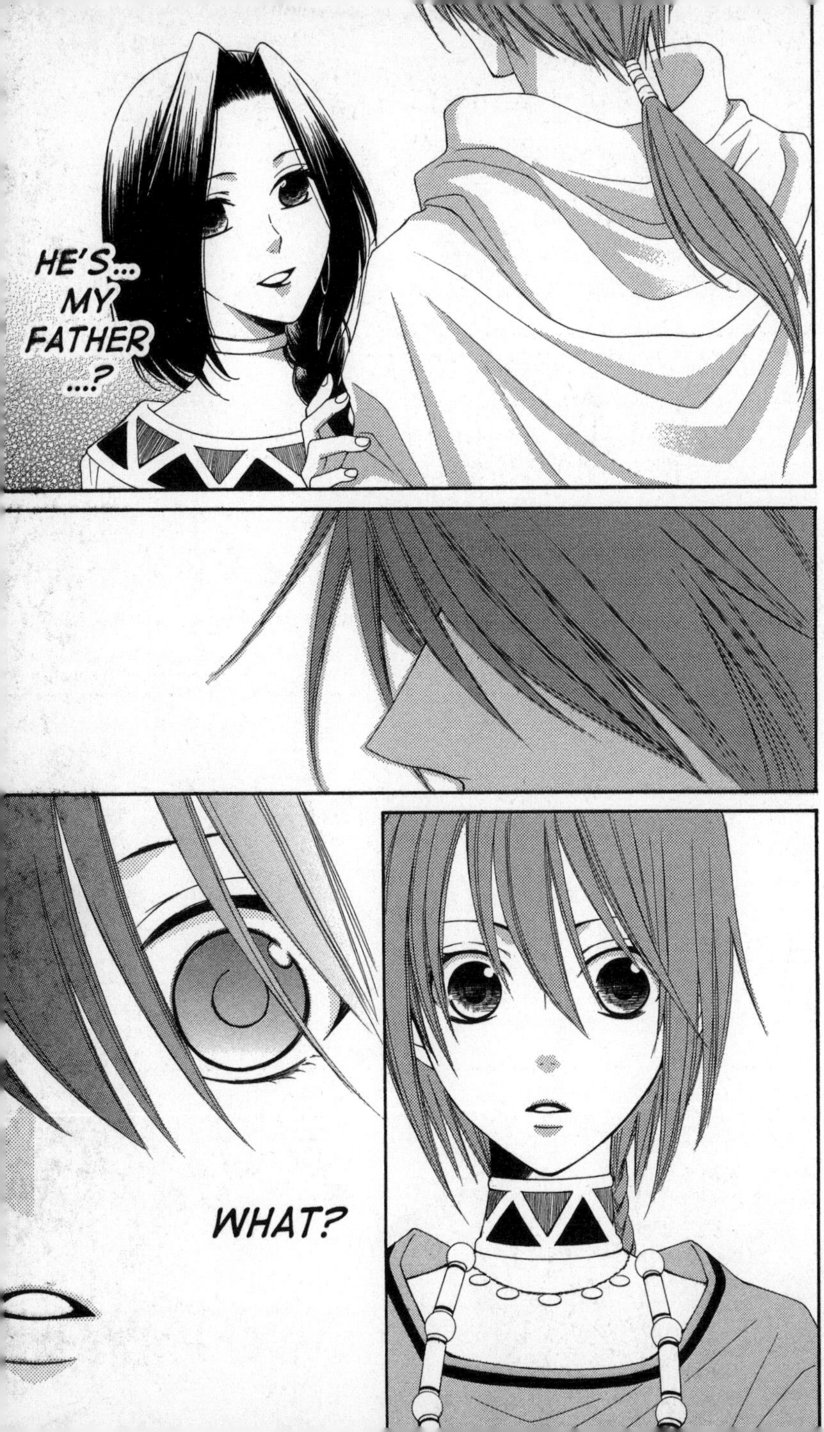
HE'S... MY FATHER ...?
WHAT?

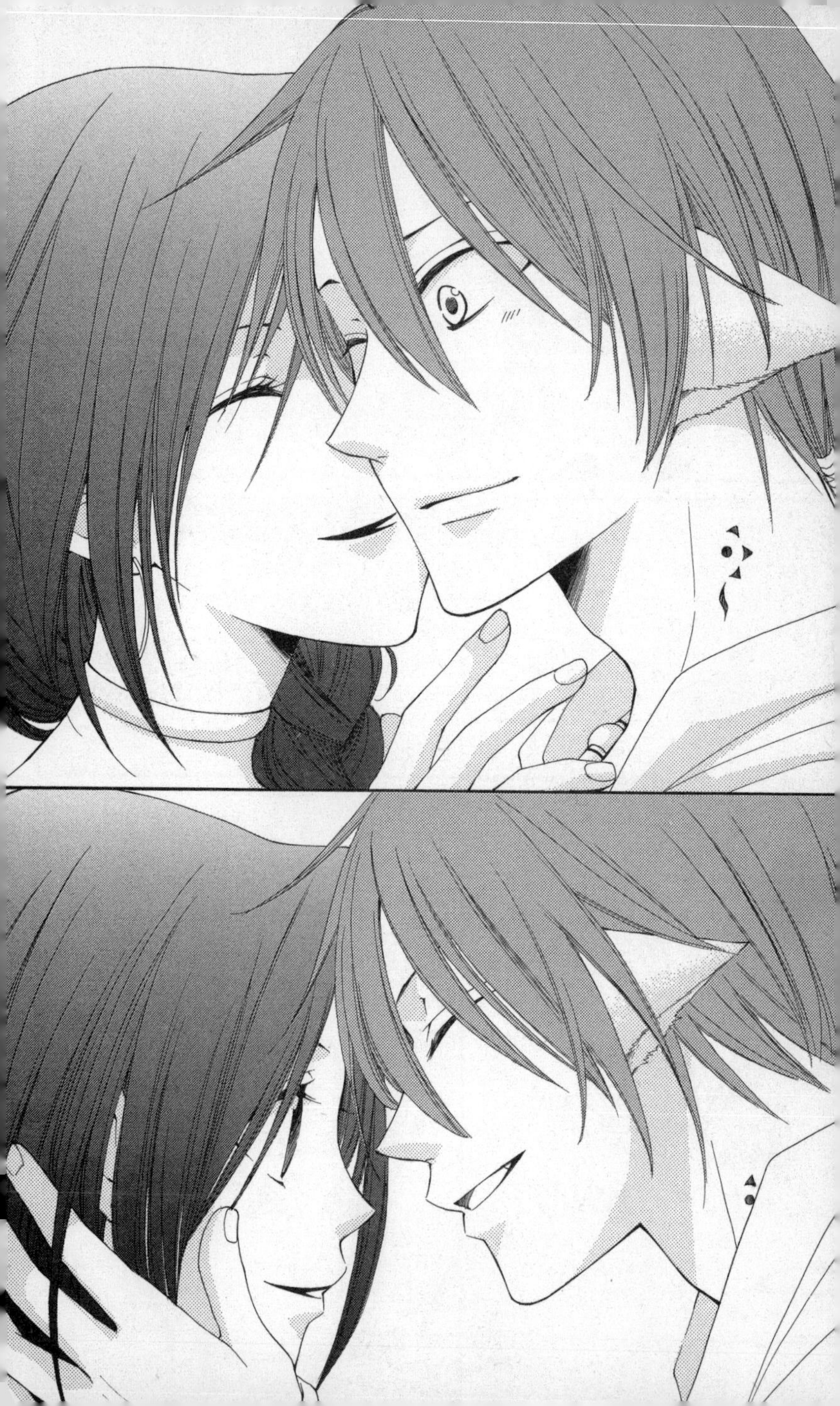

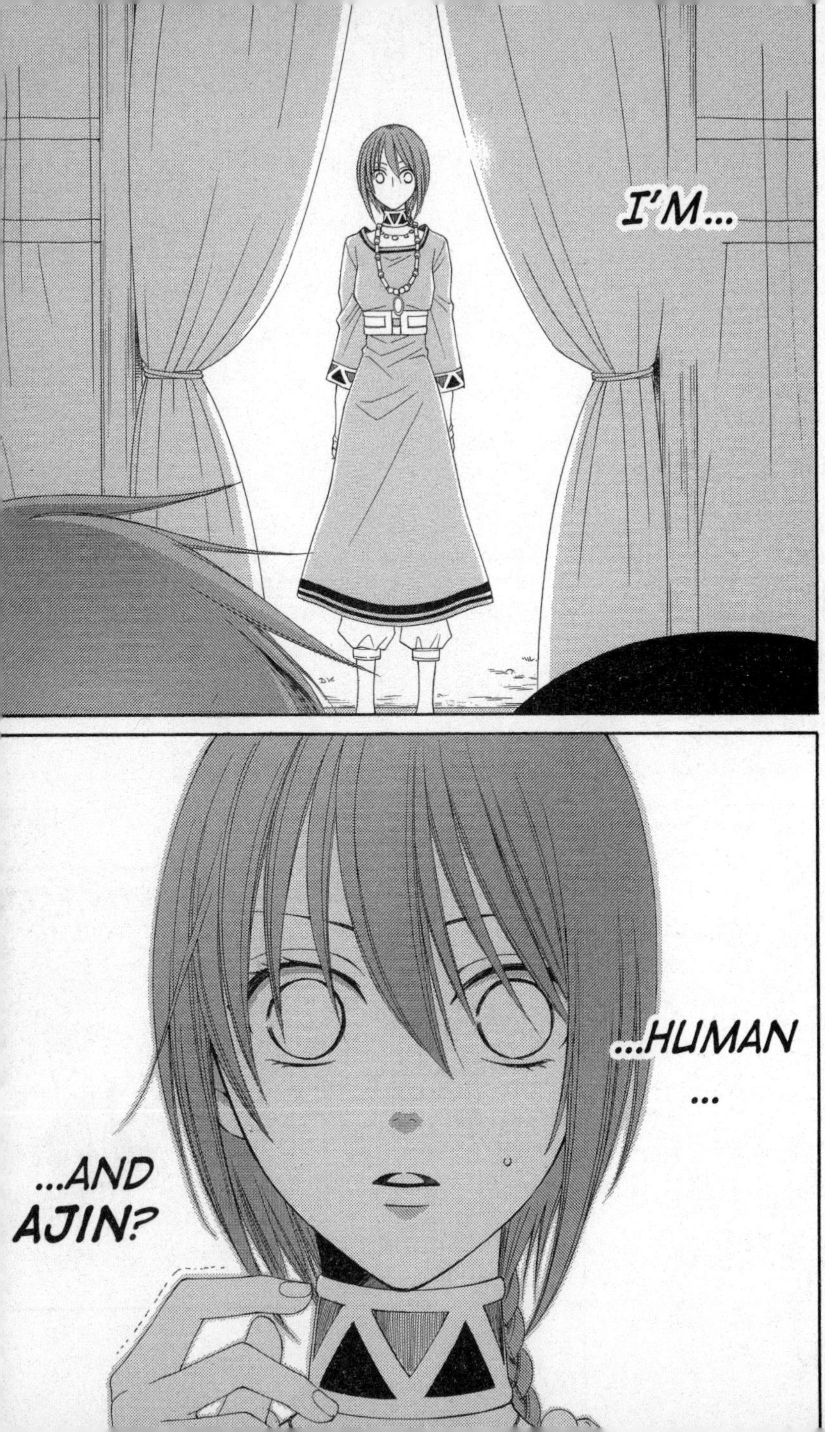
I'M...
...HUMAN
...
...AND
AJIN?

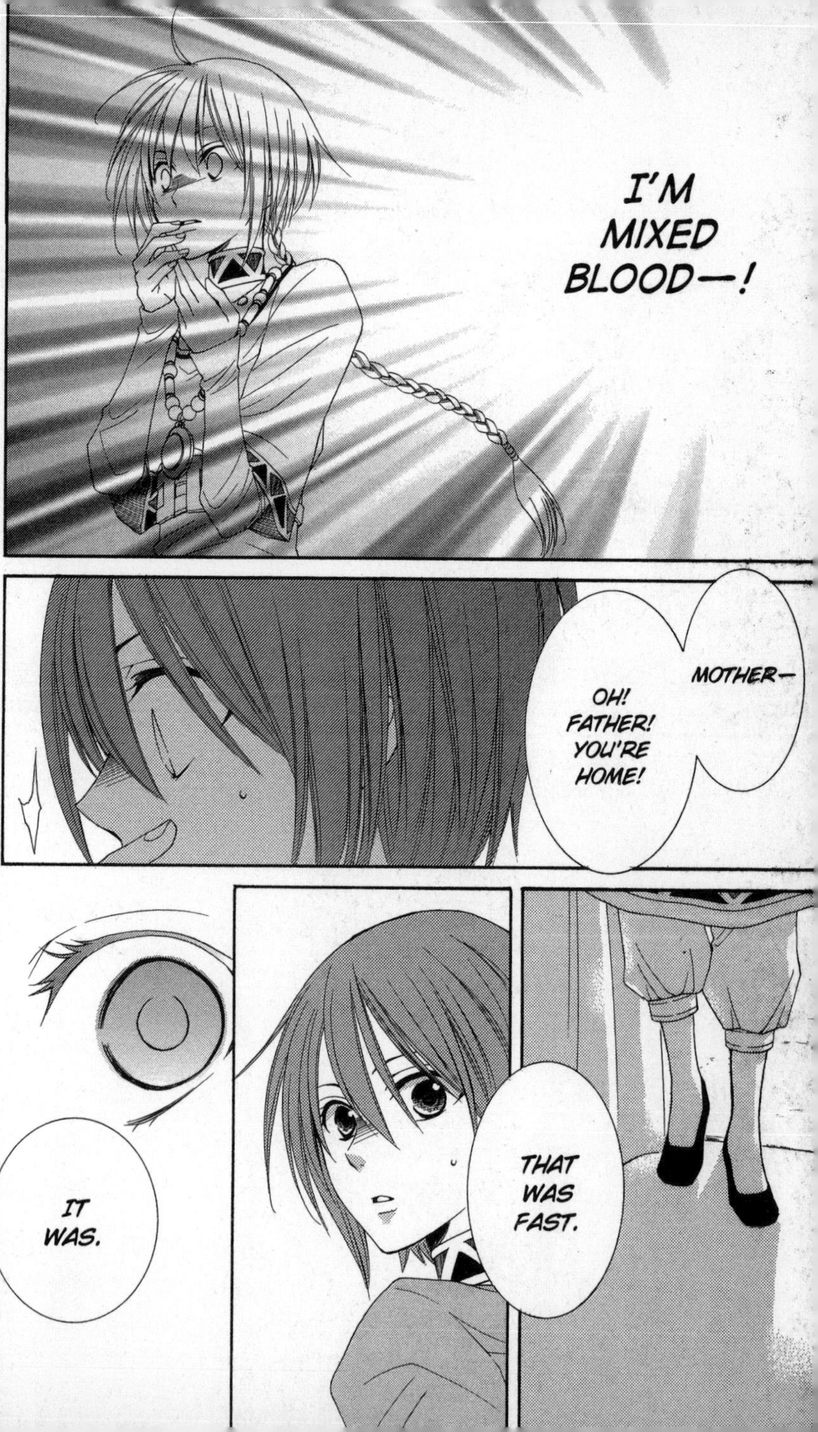
I'M MIXED BLOOD—!
MOTHER—
OH! FATHER! YOU'RE HOME!
THAT WAS FAST.
IT WAS.

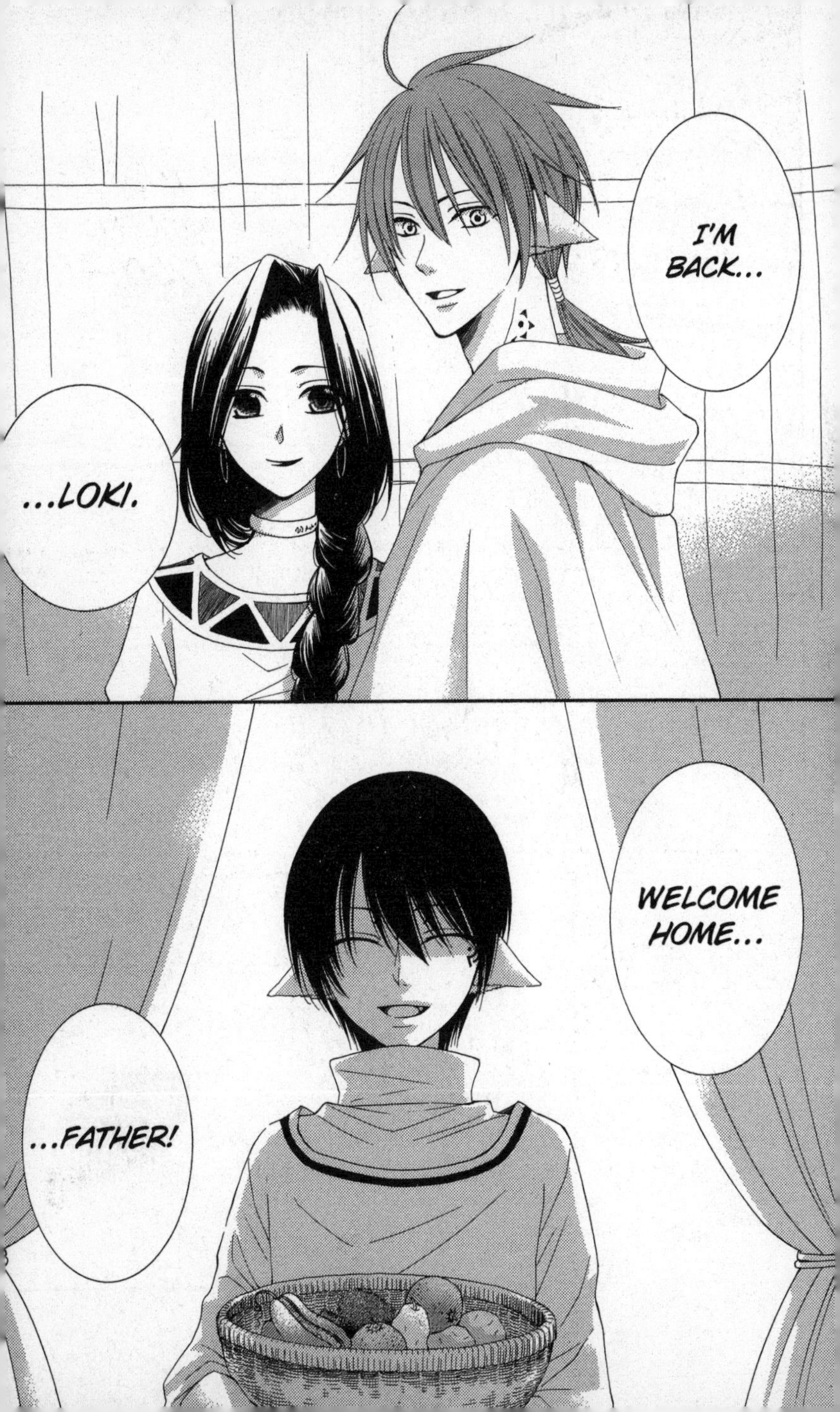
I'M BACK...
...LOKI.
WELCOME HOME...
...FATHER!

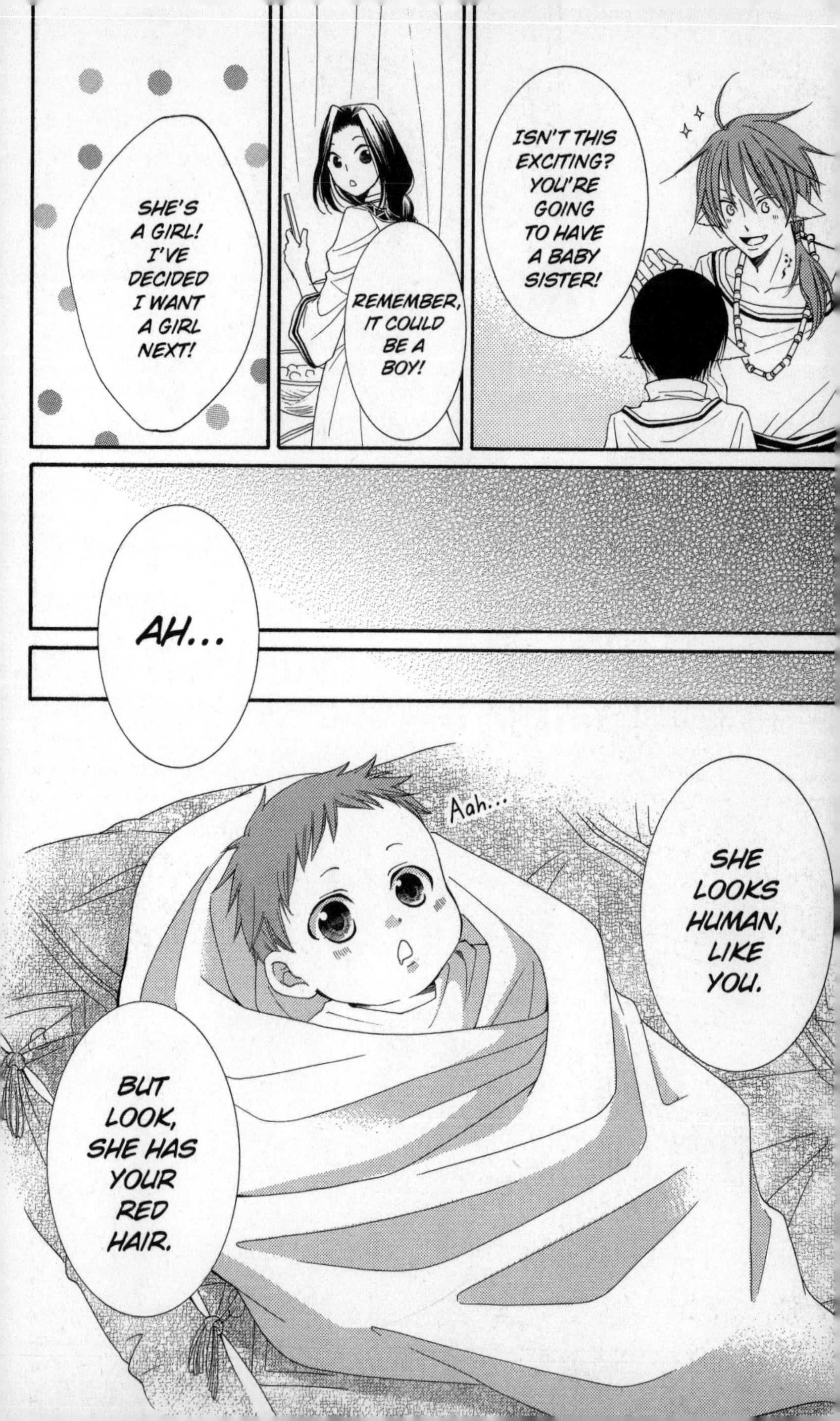
ISN'T THIS EXCITING? YOU'RE GOING TO HAVE A BABY SISTER!
REMEMBER, IT COULD BE A BOY!
SHE'S A GIRL! I'VE DECIDED I WANT A GIRL NEXT!
AH...
SHE LOOKS HUMAN, LIKE YOU.
Aah...
BUT LOOK, SHE HAS YOUR RED HAIR.

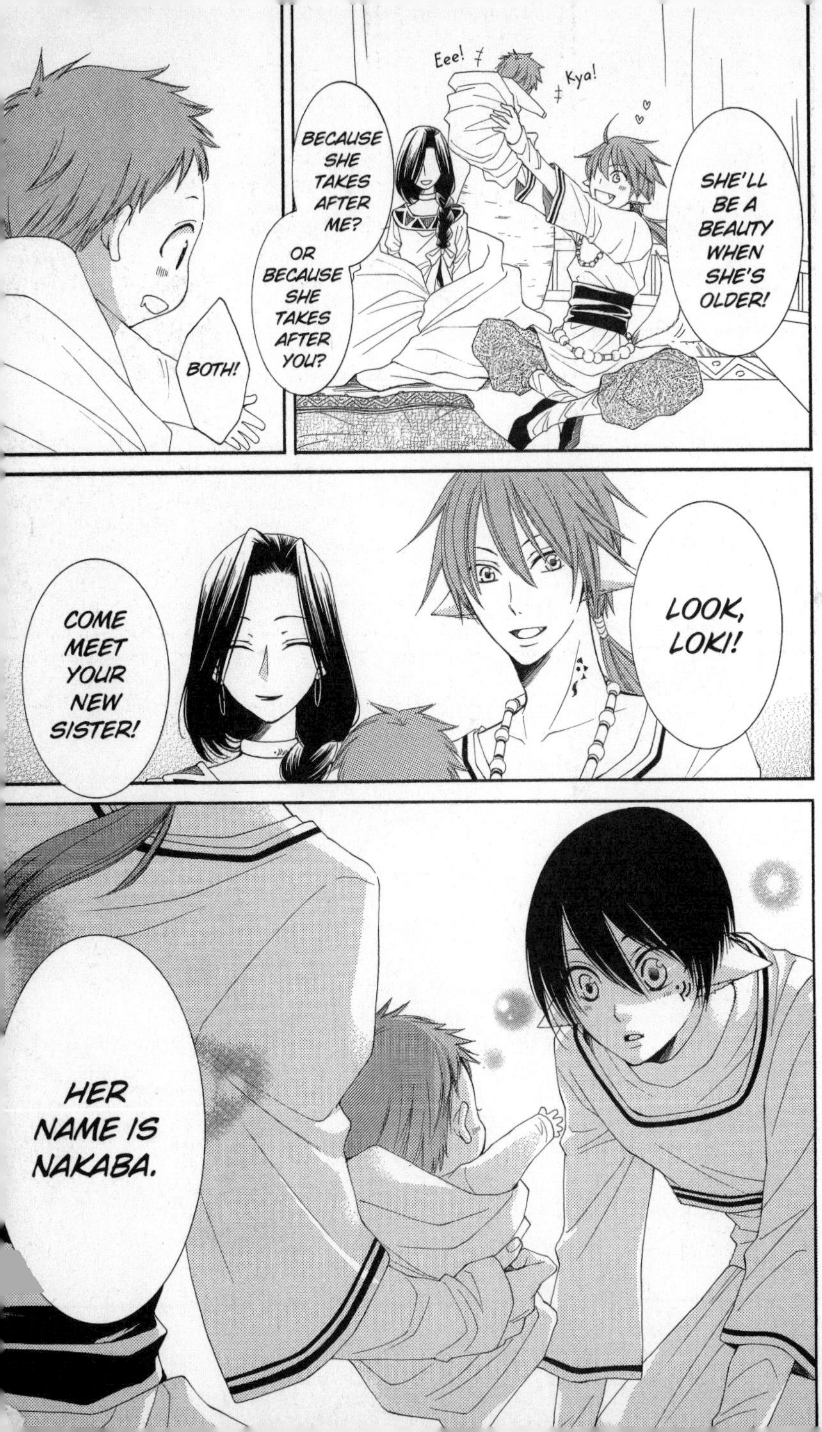
Eee!
Kya!
SHE'LL BE A BEAUTY WHEN SHE'S OLDER!
BECAUSE SHE TAKES AFTER ME?
OR BECAUSE SHE TAKES AFTER YOU?
BOTH!
LOOK, LOKI!
COME MEET YOUR NEW SISTER!
HER NAME IS NAKABA.

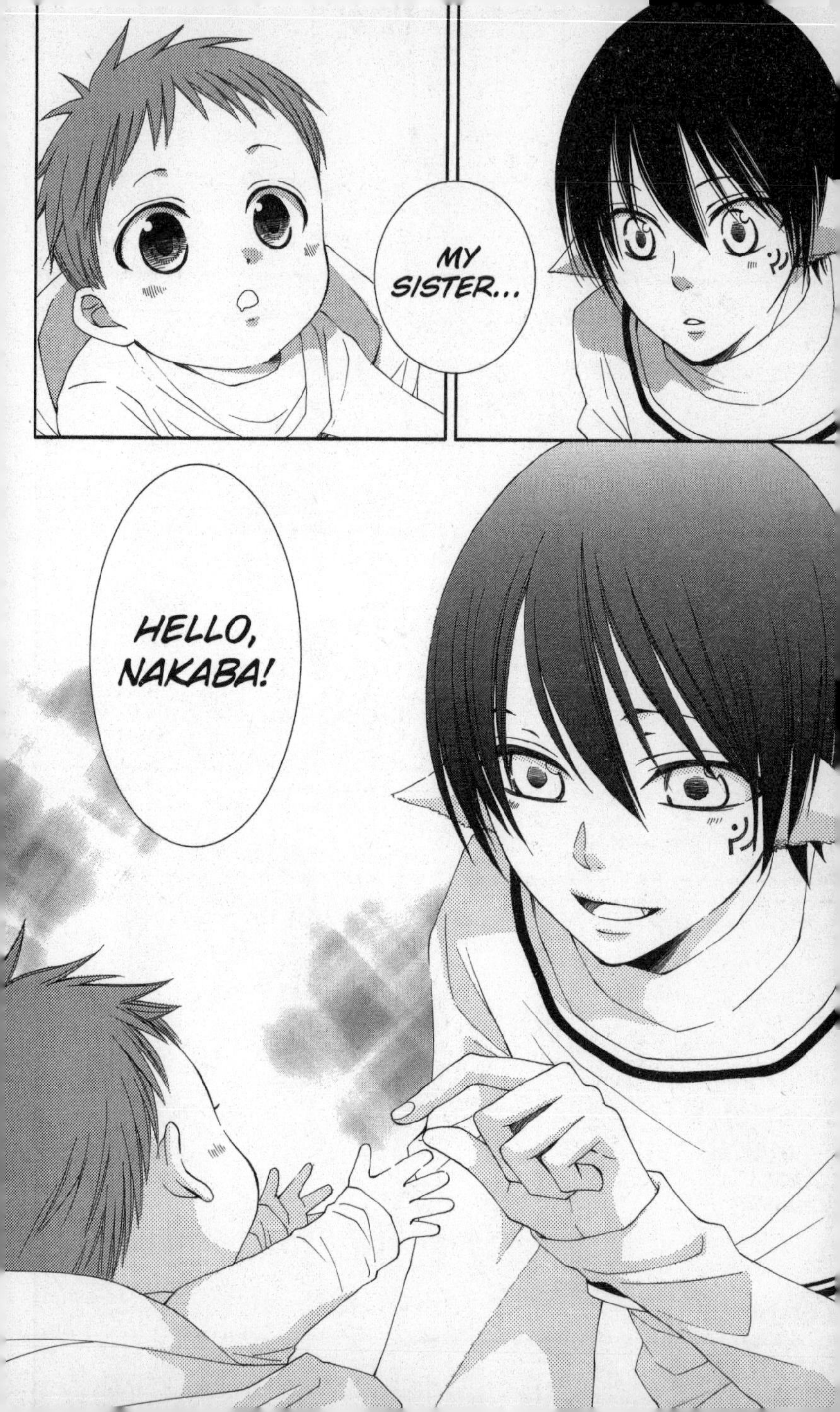
MY SISTER...
HELLO, NAKABA!

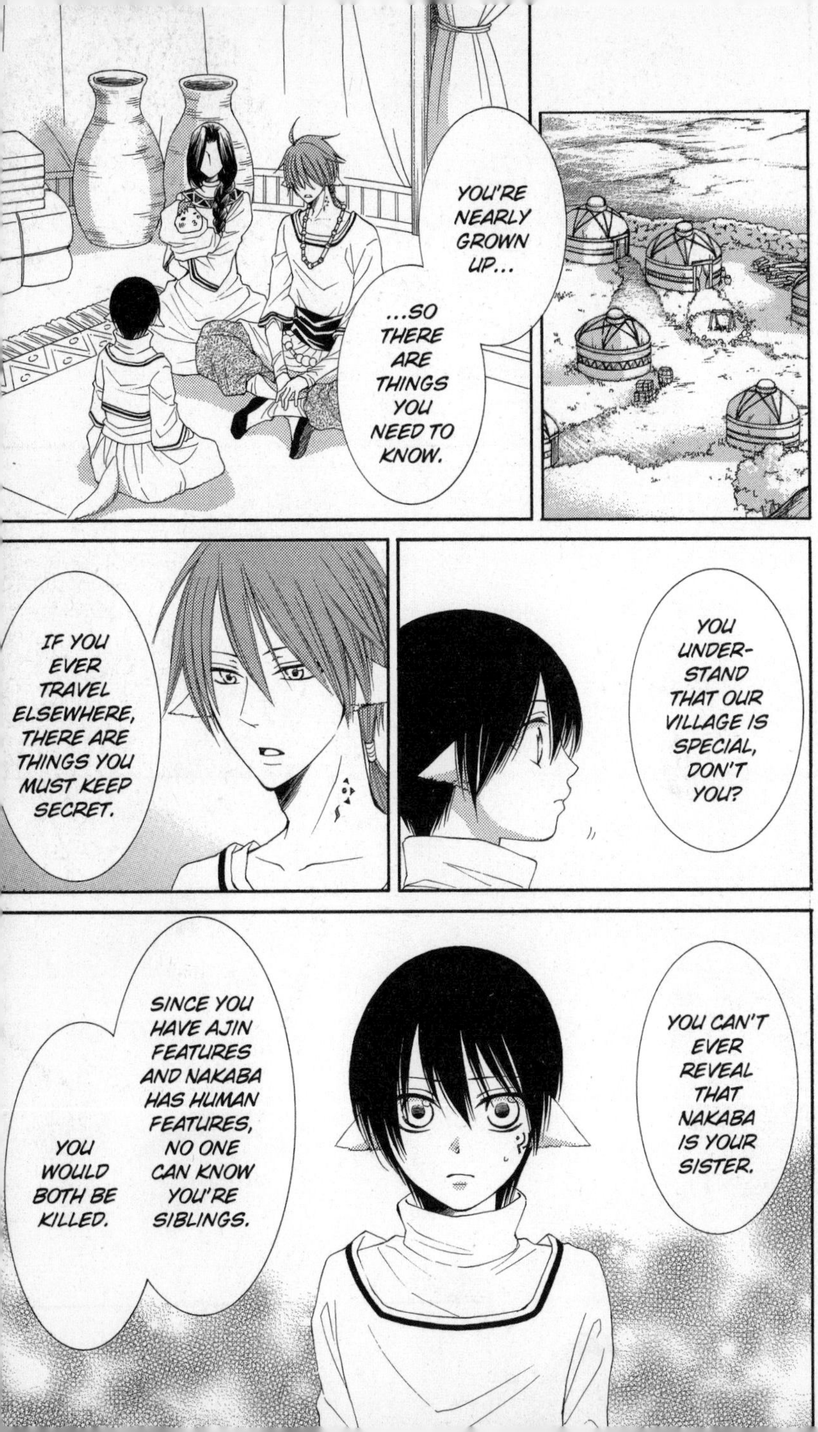
YOU'RE NEARLY GROWN UP...
...SO THERE ARE THINGS YOU NEED TO KNOW.
YOU UNDERSTAND THAT OUR VILLAGE IS SPECIAL, DON'T YOU?
IF YOU EVER TRAVEL ELSEWHERE, THERE ARE THINGS YOU MUST KEEP SECRET.
YOU CAN'T EVER REVEAL THAT NAKABA IS YOUR SISTER.
SINCE YOU HAVE AJIN FEATURES AND NAKABA HAS HUMAN FEATURES, NO ONE CAN KNOW YOU'RE SIBLINGS.
YOU WOULD BOTH BE KILLED.

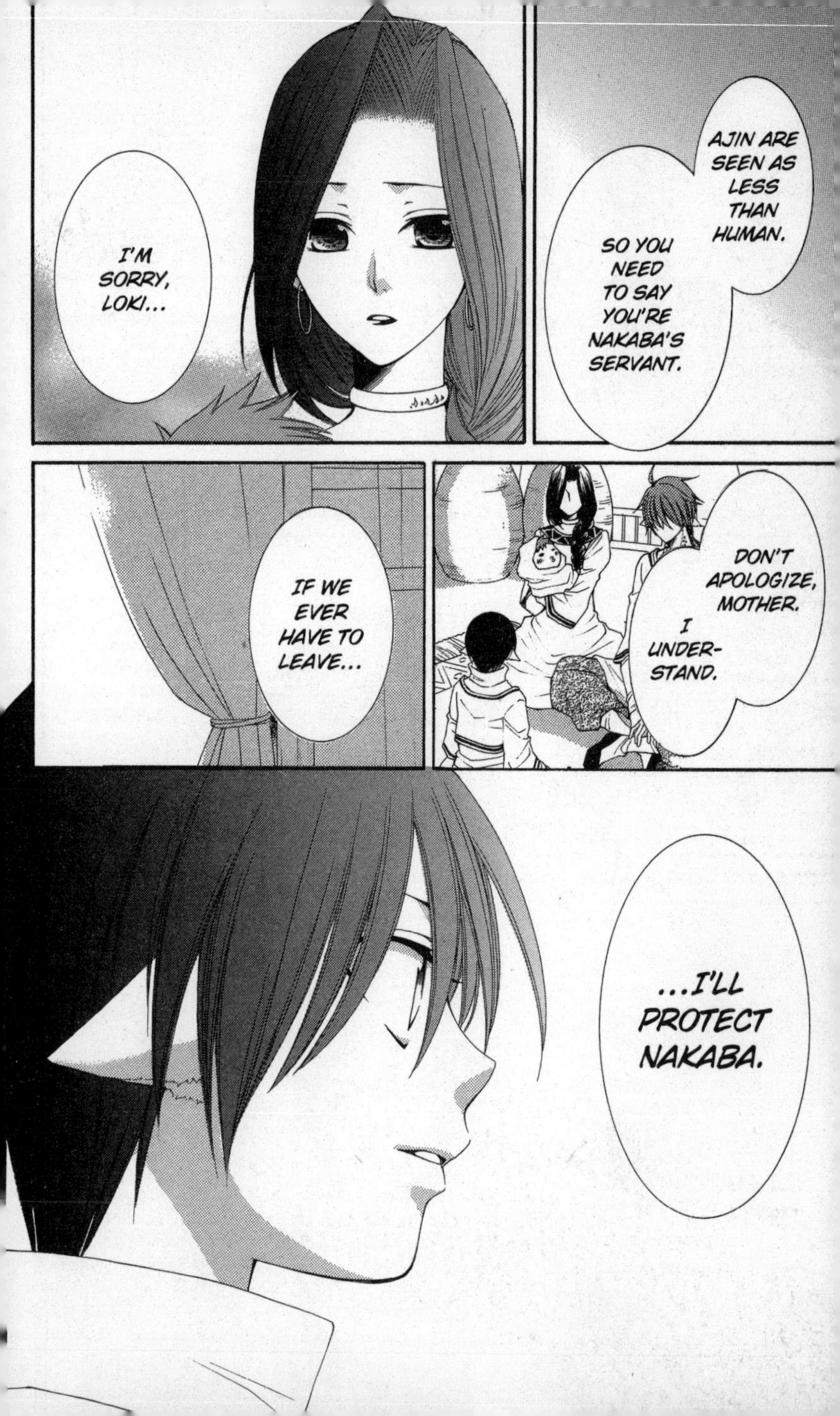
AJIN ARE SEEN AS LESS THAN HUMAN.
SO YOU NEED TO SAY YOU'RE NAKABA'S SERVANT.
I'M SORRY, LOKI...
DON'T APOLOGIZE, MOTHER.
I UNDERSTAND.
IF WE EVER HAVE TO LEAVE...
...I'LL PROTECT NAKABA.

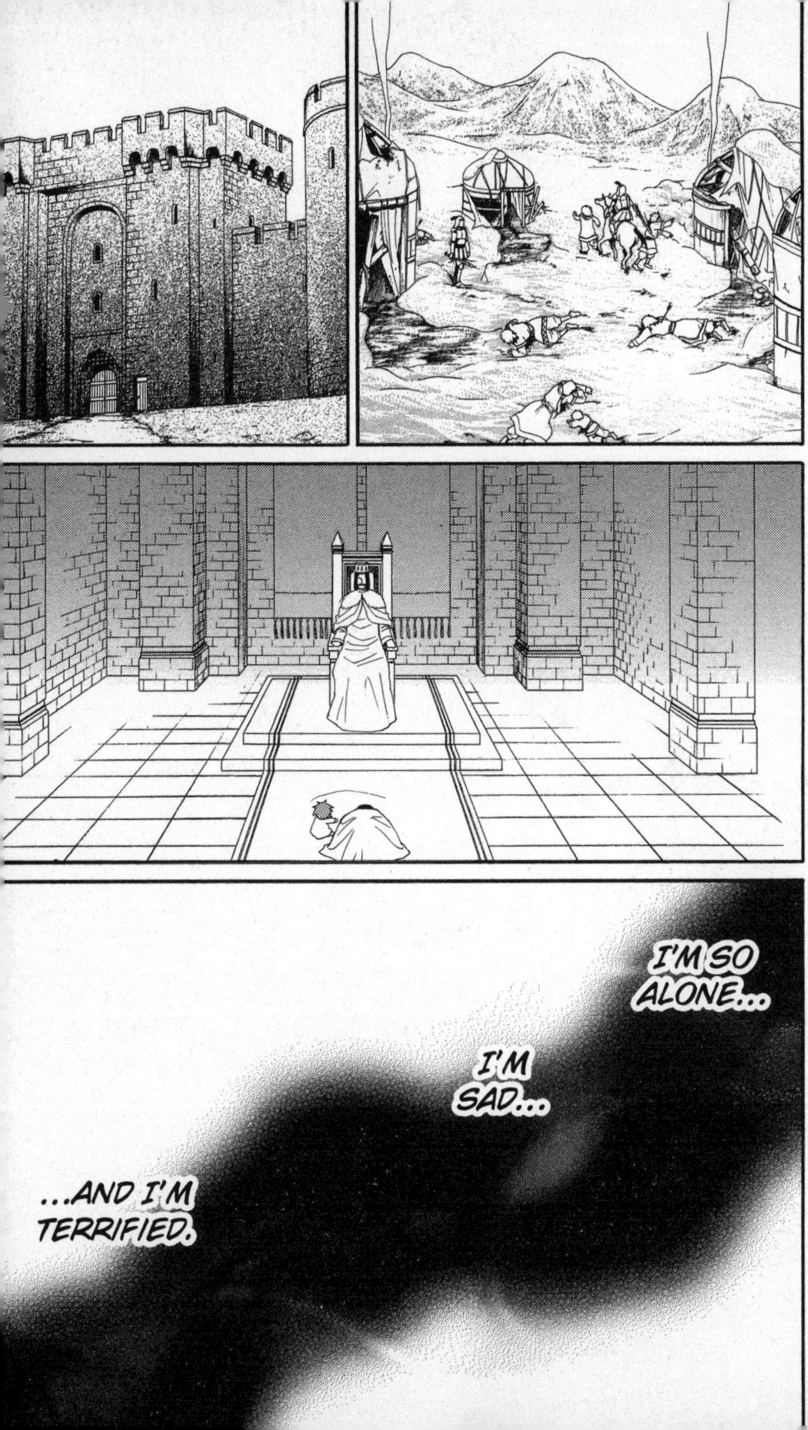
I'M SO ALONE...
I'M SAD...
...AND I'M TERRIFIED.

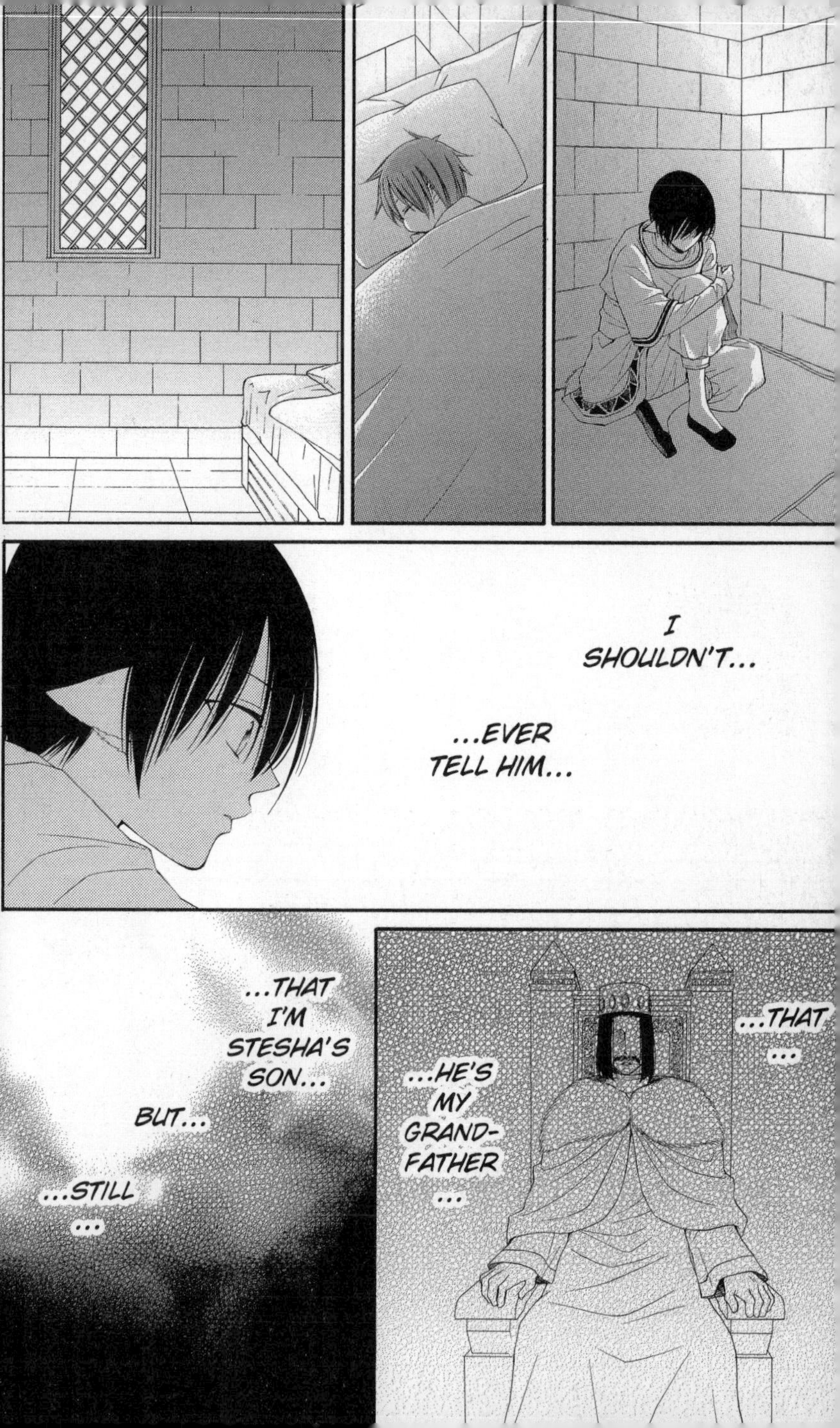
I SHOULDN'T...
...EVER TELL HIM...
...THAT...
...HE'S MY GRAND-FATHER...
...THAT I'M STESHA'S SON...
BUT...
...STILL...

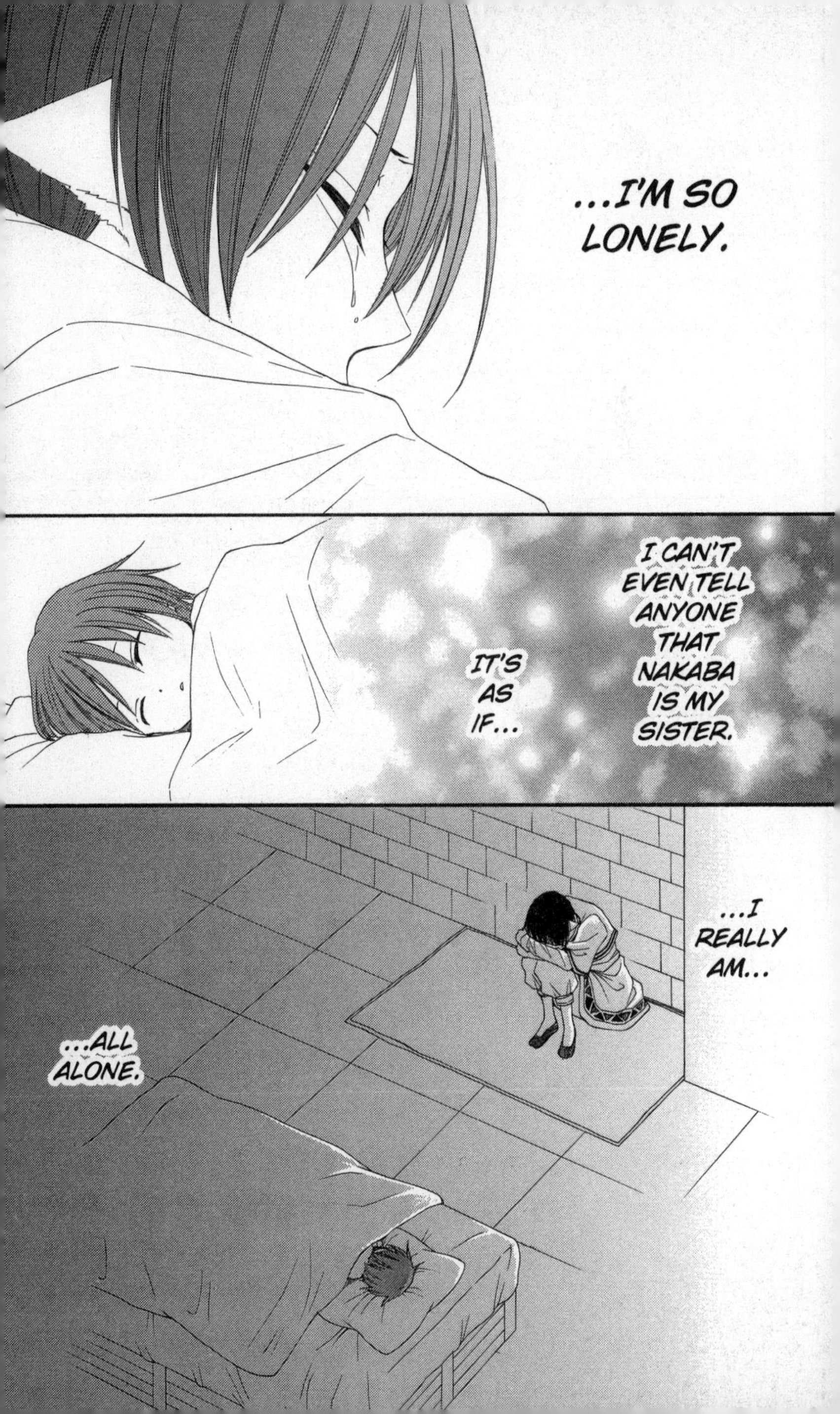
...I'M SO LONELY.
I CAN'T EVEN TELL ANYONE THAT NAKABA IS MY SISTER.
IT'S AS IF...
...I REALLY AM...
...ALL ALONE.

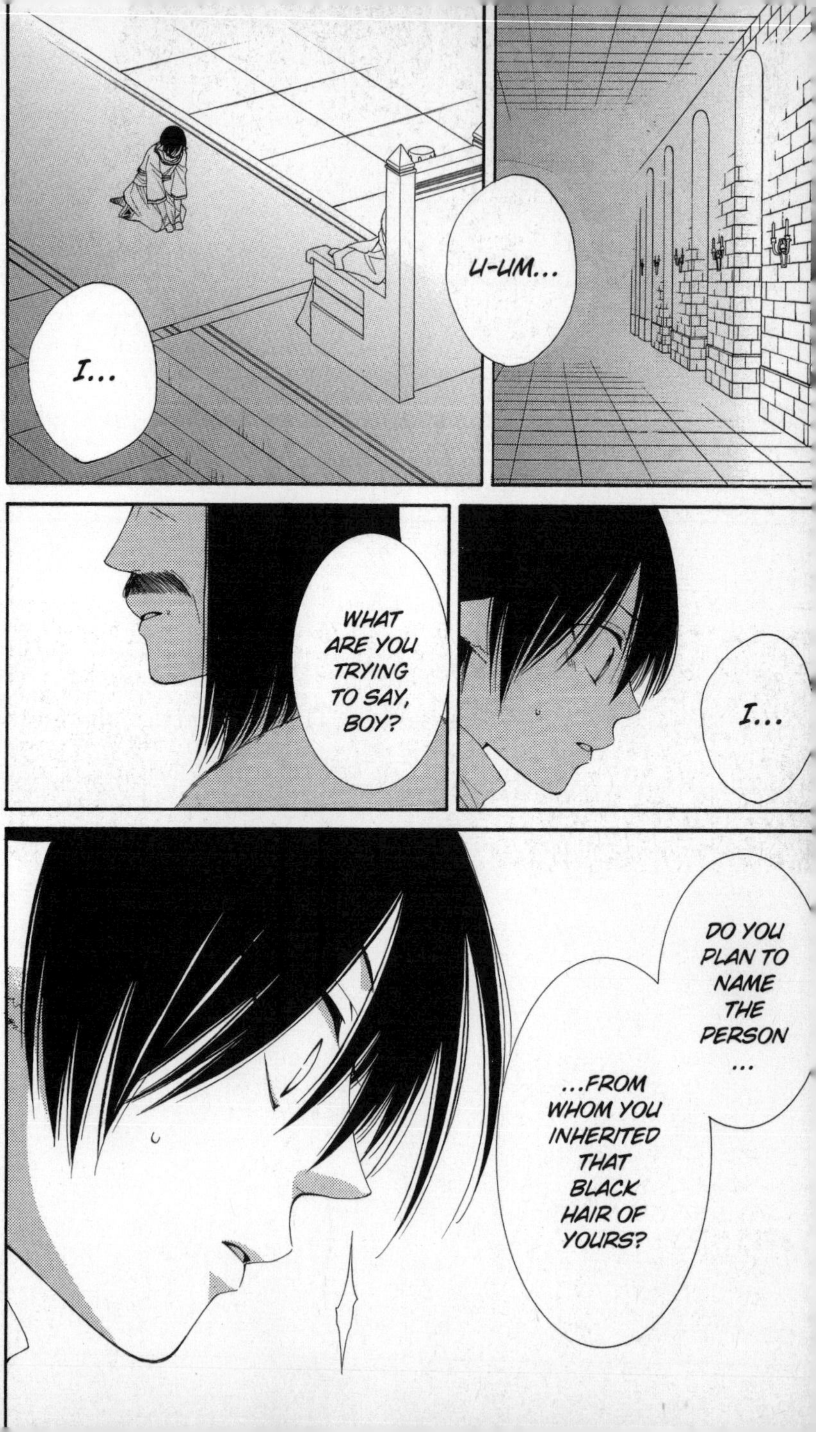
U-UM...
I...
I...
WHAT ARE YOU TRYING TO SAY, BOY?
DO YOU PLAN TO NAME THE PERSON...
...FROM WHOM YOU INHERITED THAT BLACK HAIR OF YOURS?

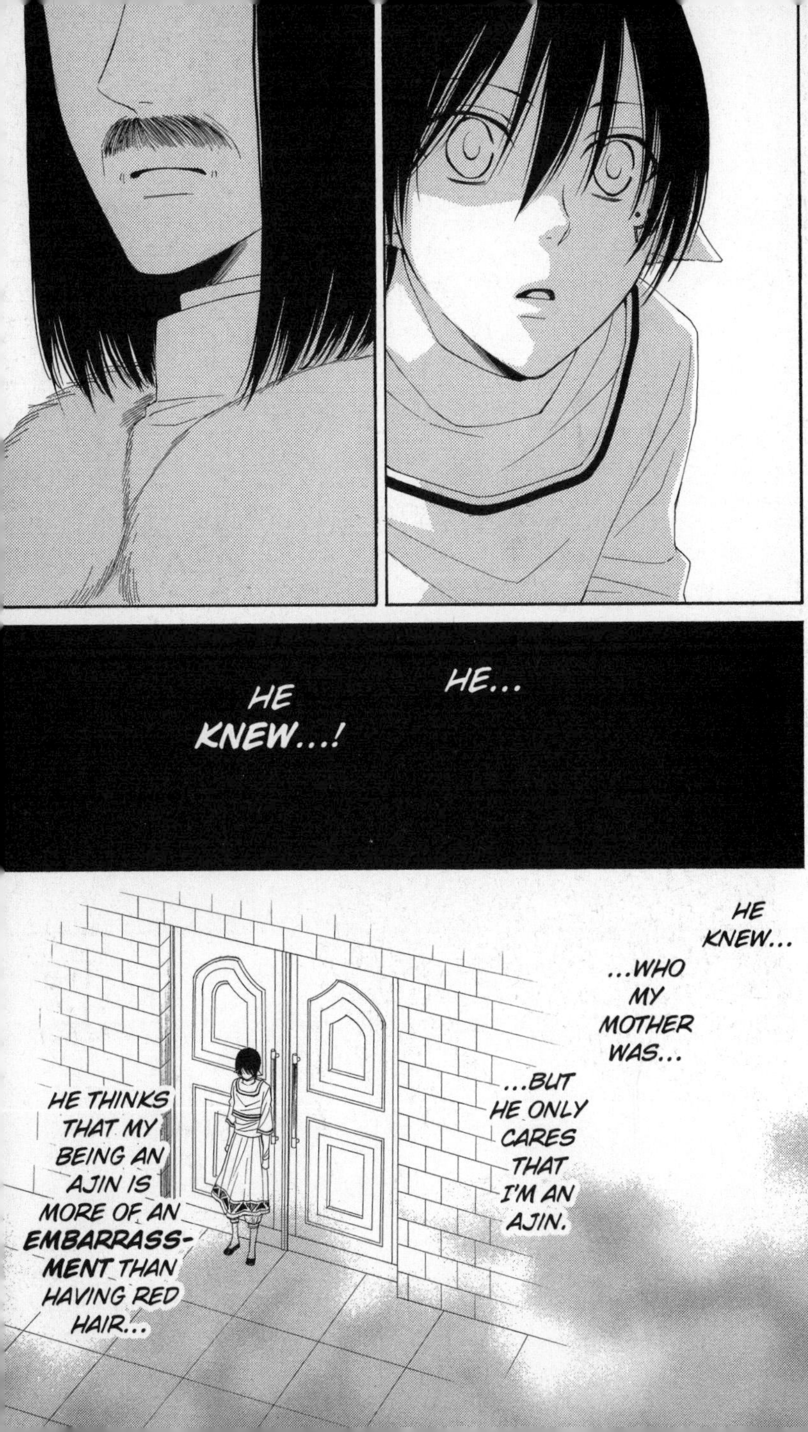
HE...
HE KNEW...!
HE KNEW...
...WHO MY MOTHER WAS...
...BUT HE ONLY CARES THAT I'M AN AJIN.
HE THINKS THAT MY BEING AN AJIN IS MORE OF AN EMBARRASSMENT THAN HAVING RED HAIR...

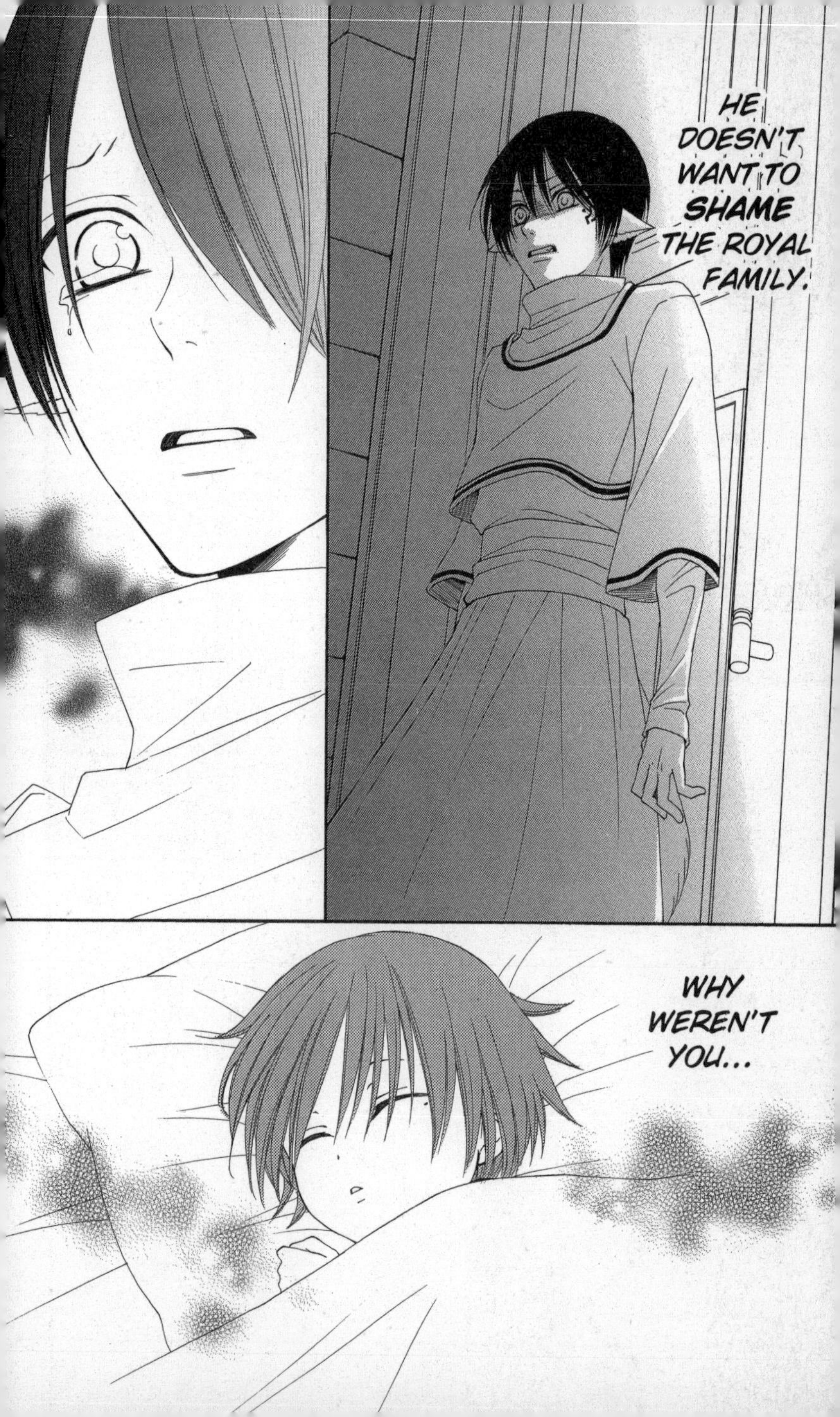
HE DOESN'T WANT TO SHAME THE ROYAL FAMILY.
WHY WEREN'T YOU...

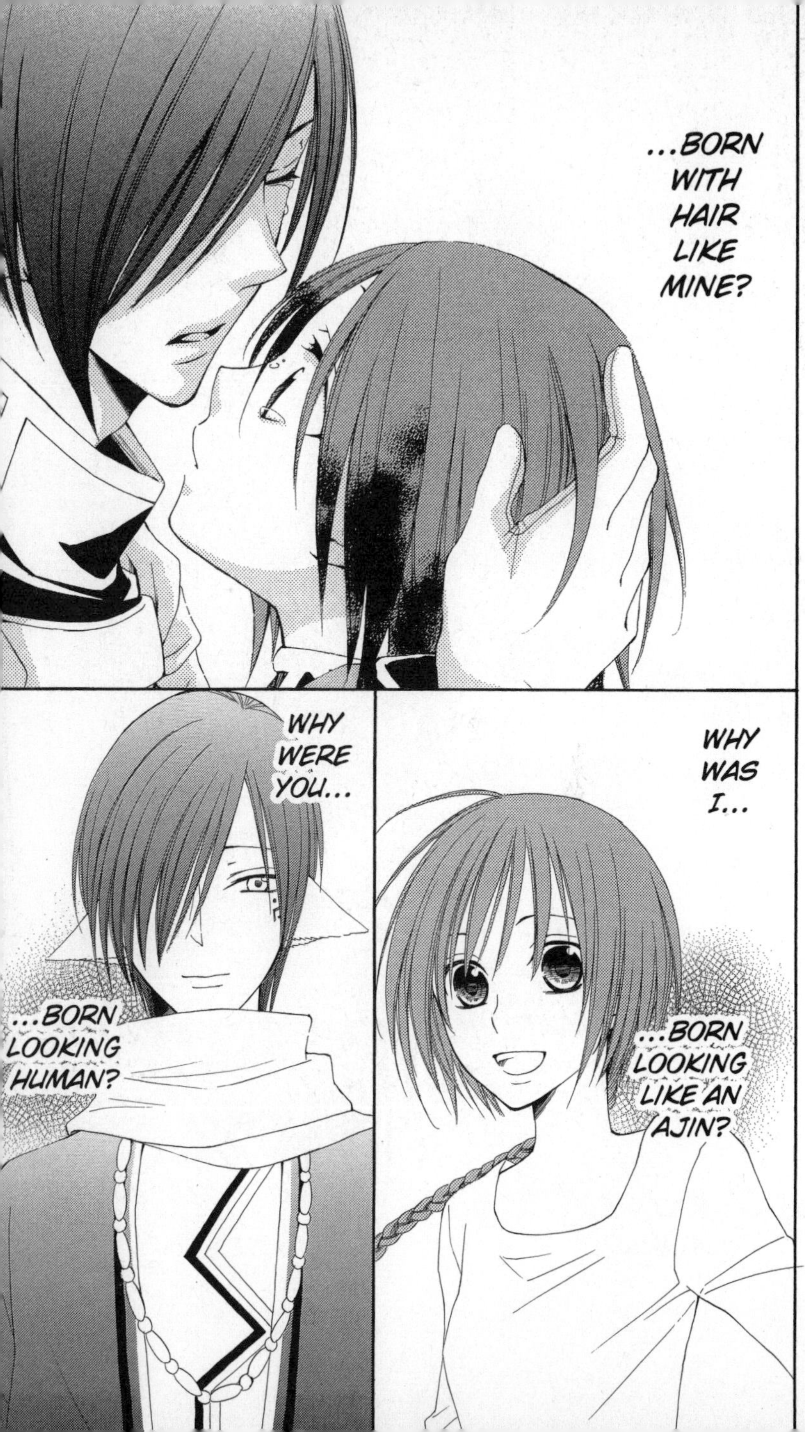
...BORN WITH HAIR LIKE MINE?
WHY WAS I...
...BORN LOOKING LIKE AN AJIN?
WHY WERE YOU...
...BORN LOOKING HUMAN?

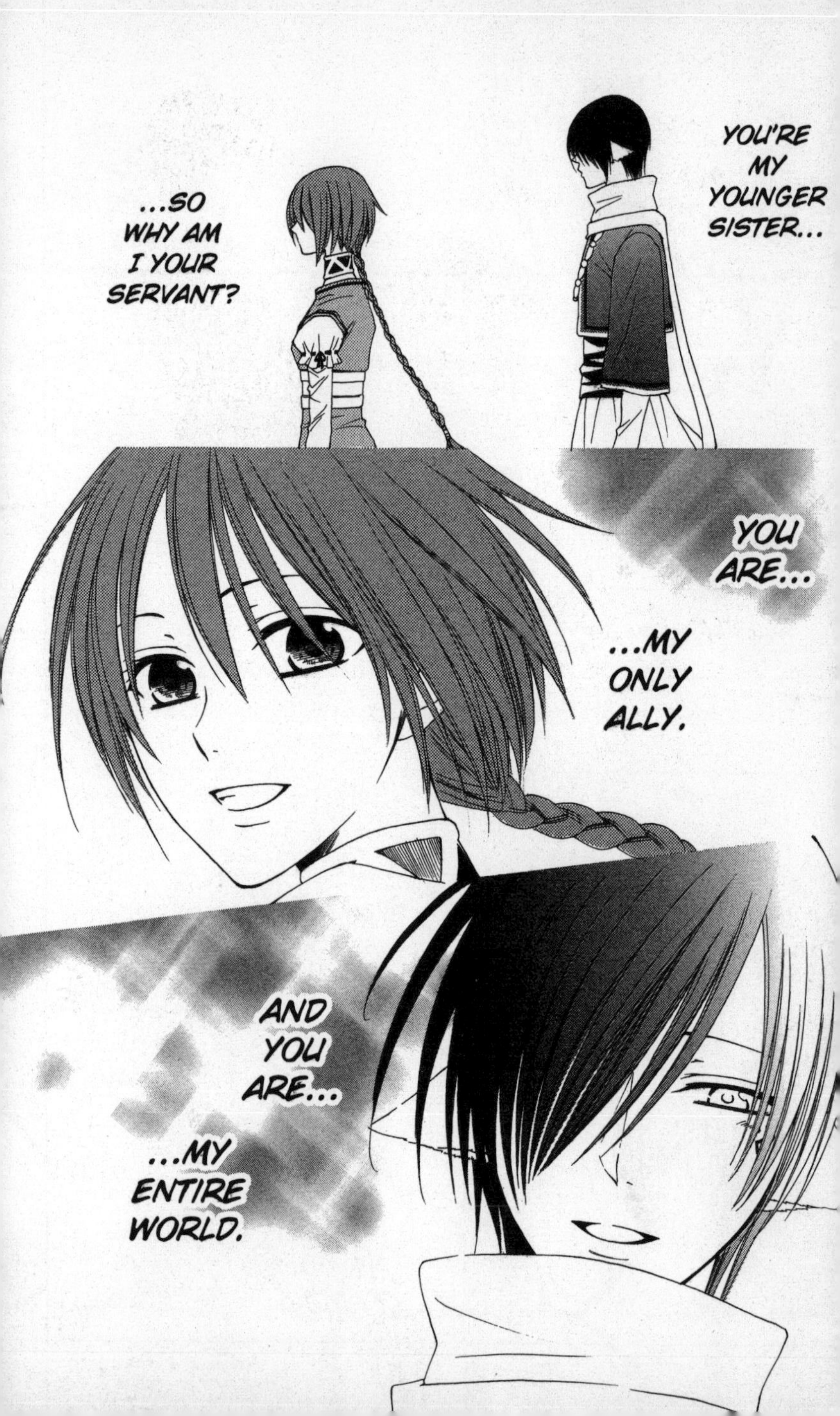
YOU'RE MY YOUNGER SISTER...
...SO WHY AM I YOUR SERVANT?
YOU ARE...
...MY ONLY ALLY.
AND YOU ARE...
...MY ENTIRE WORLD.

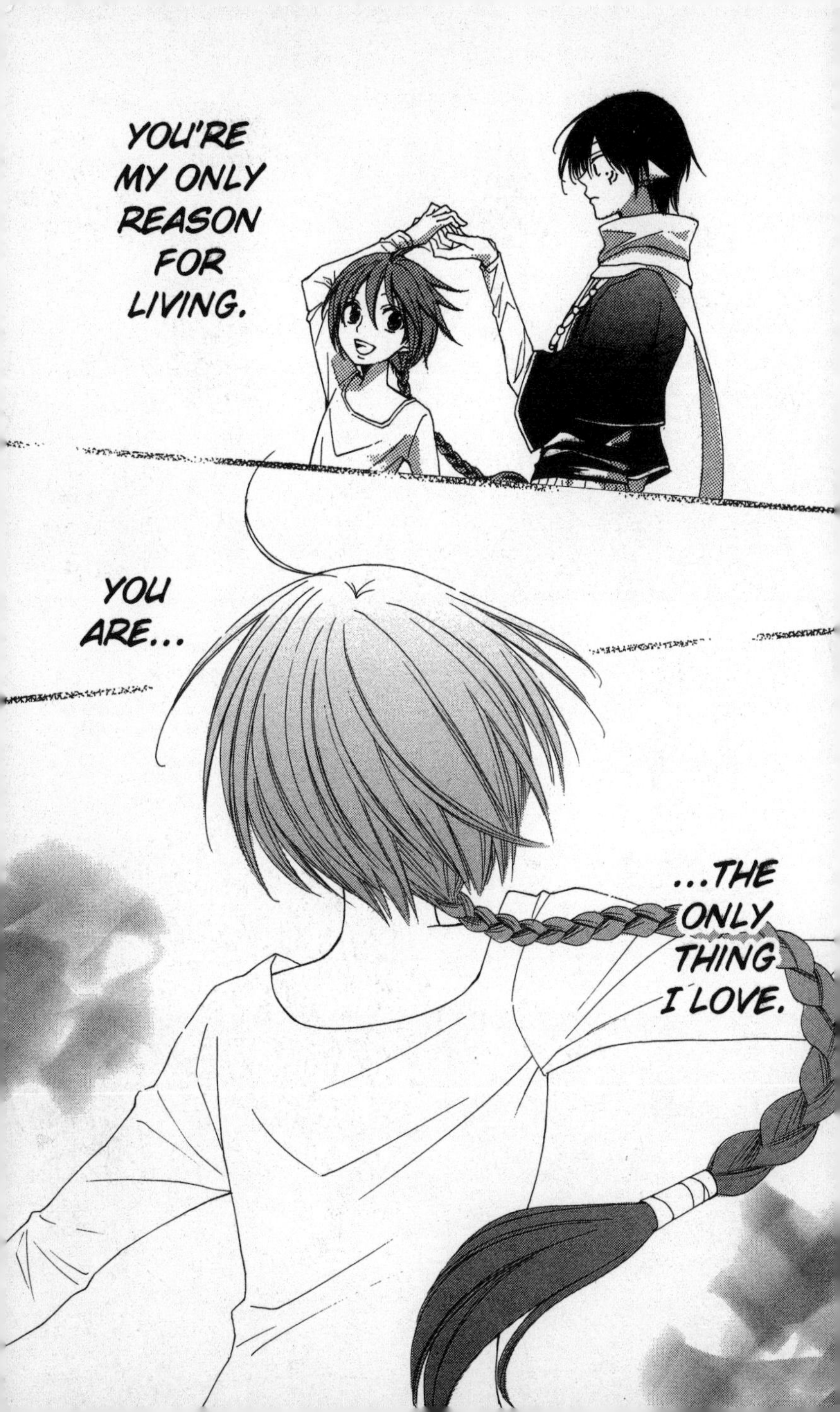
YOU'RE MY ONLY REASON FOR LIVING.
YOU ARE...
...THE ONLY THING I LOVE.

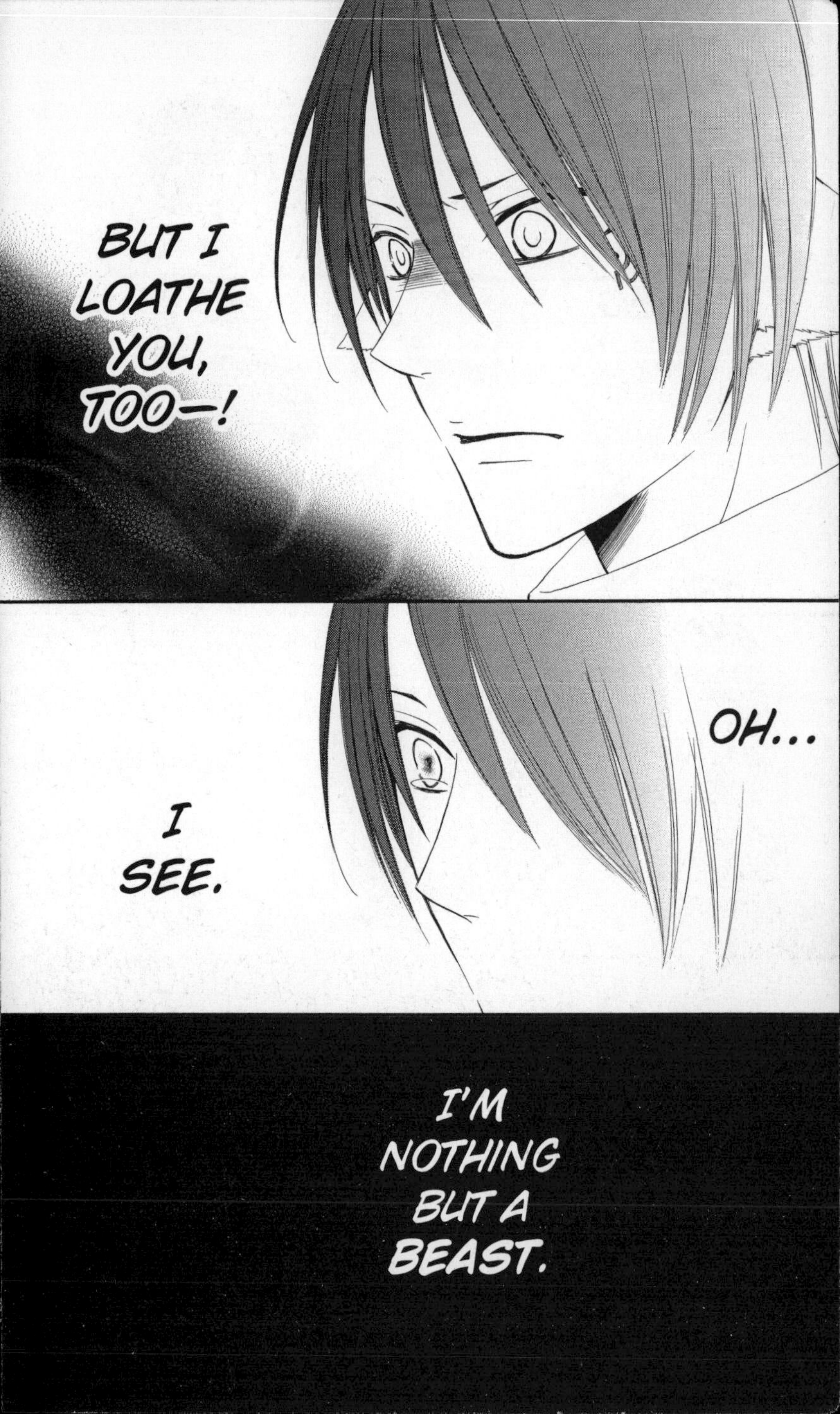
BUT I LOATHE YOU, TOO—!
OH...
I SEE.
I'M NOTHING BUT A BEAST.

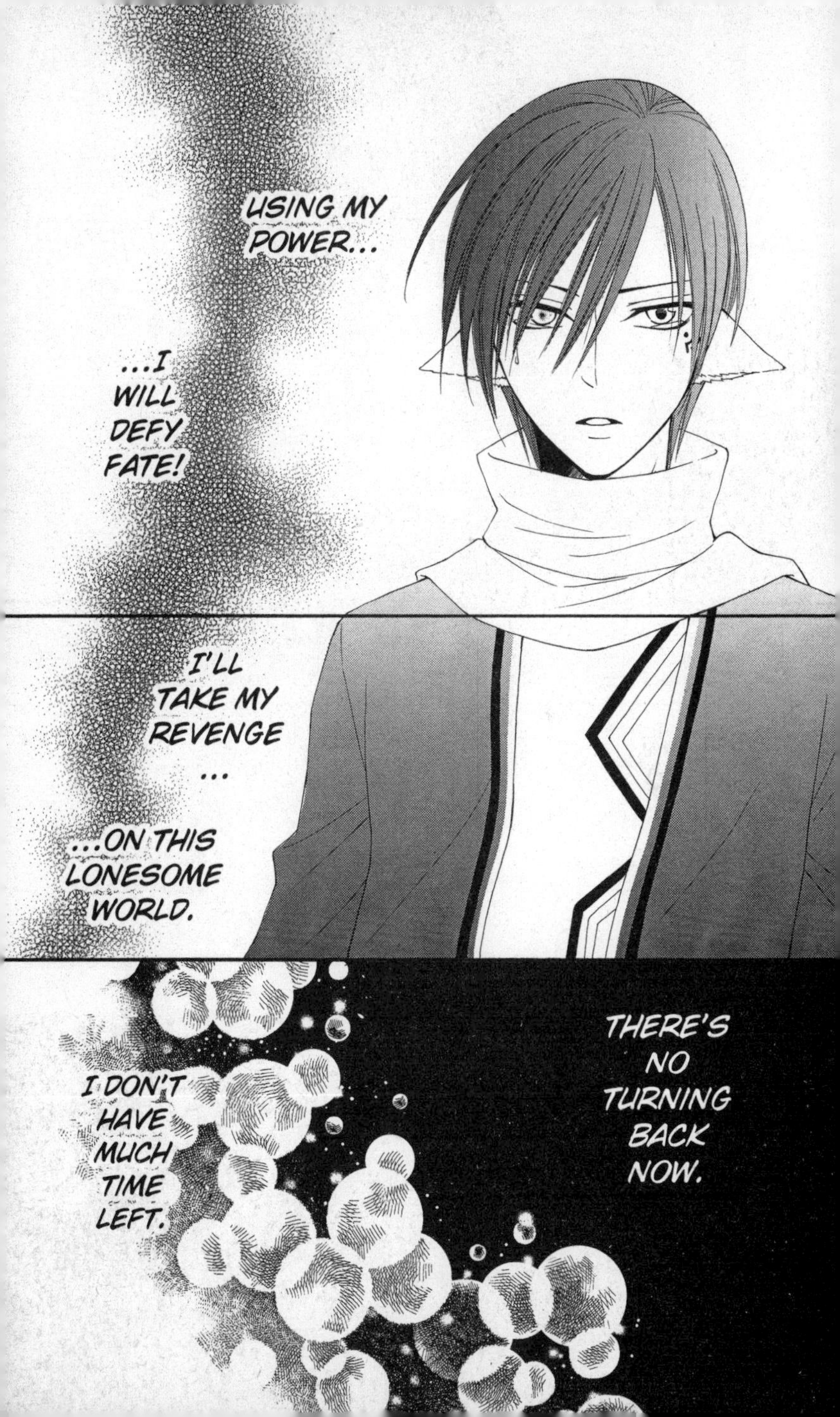
USING MY POWER...
...I WILL DEFY FATE!
I'LL TAKE MY REVENGE ...
...ON THIS LONESOME WORLD.
THERE'S NO TURNING BACK NOW.
I DON'T HAVE MUCH TIME LEFT.

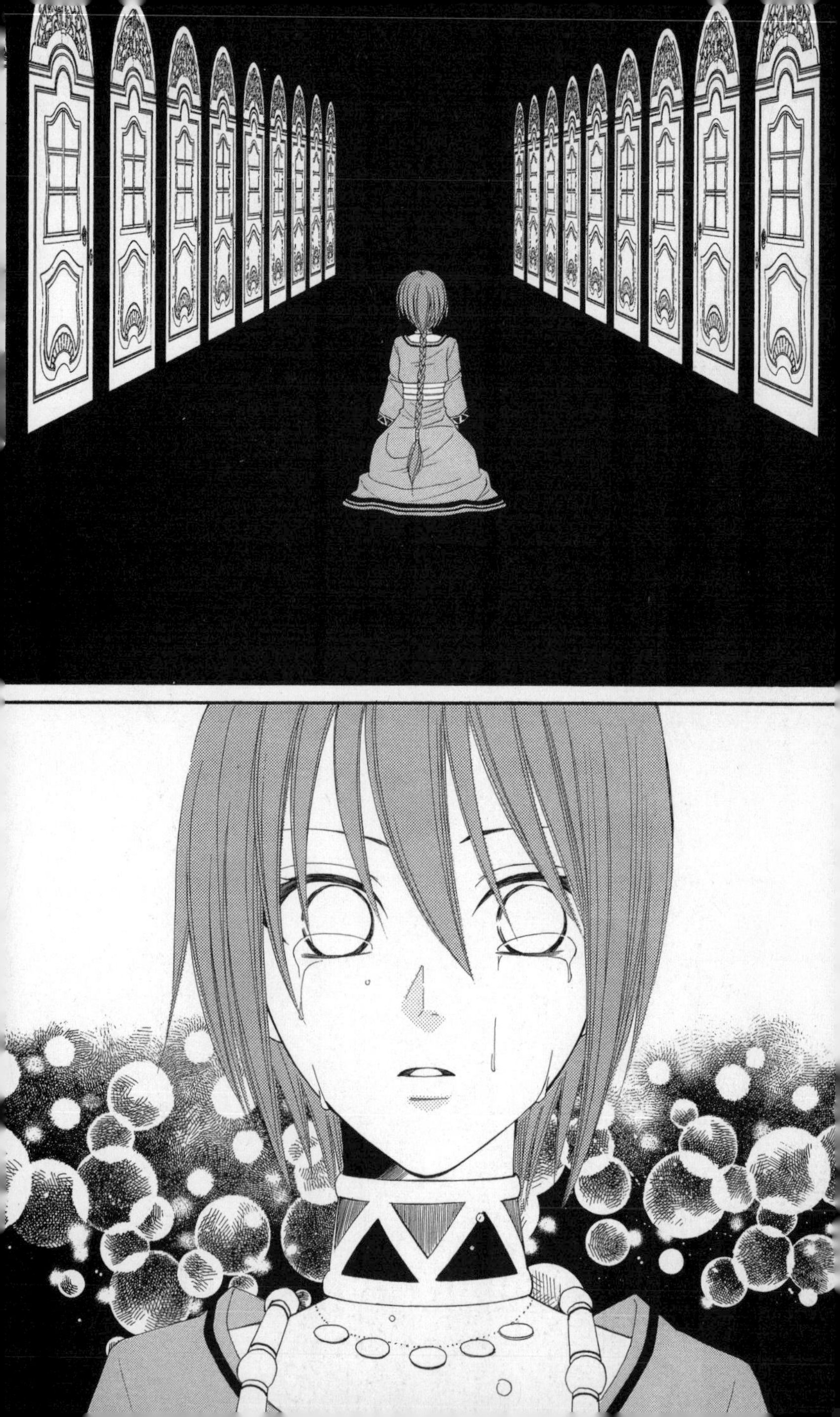

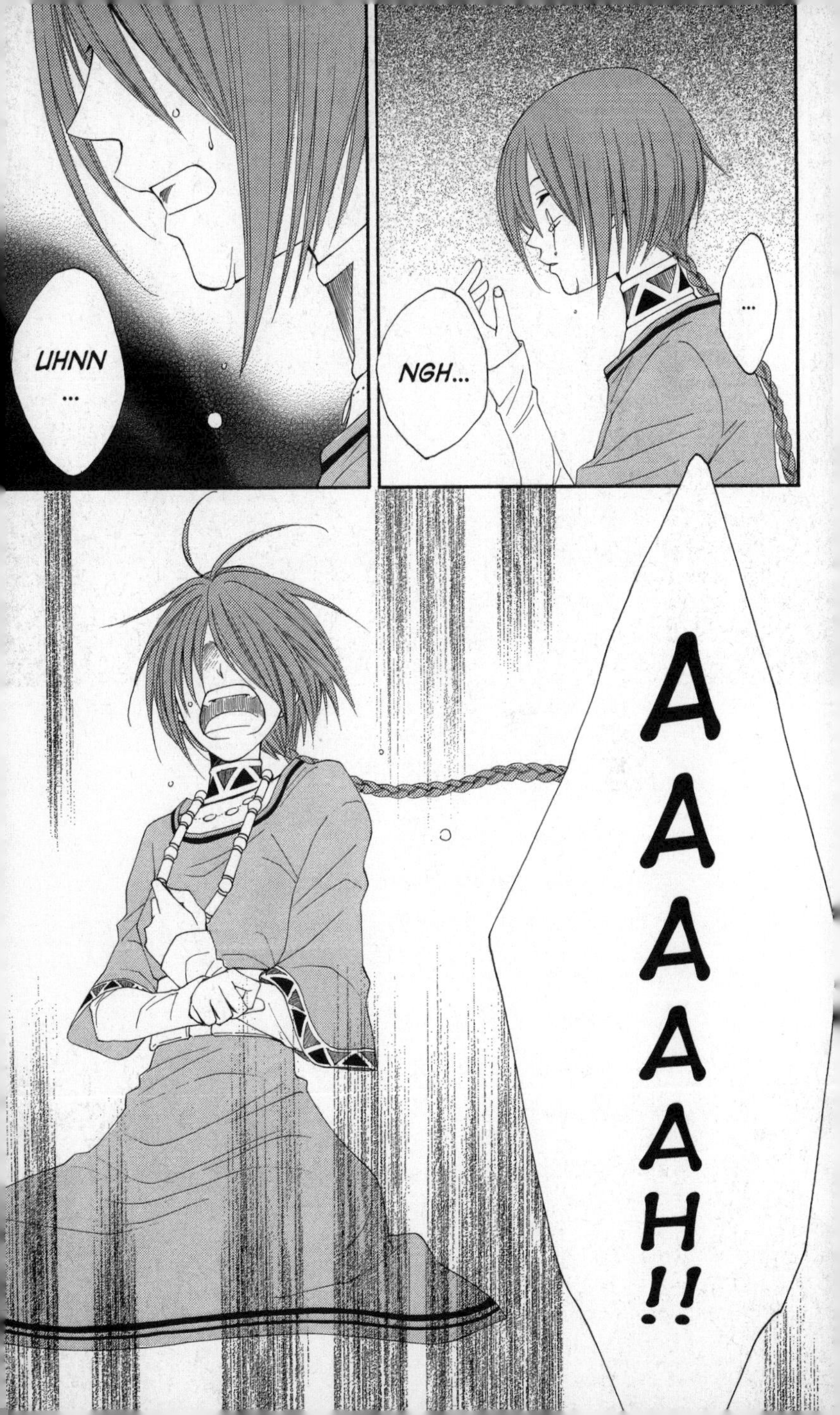
...
NGH...
UHNN ...
AAAAAH!!

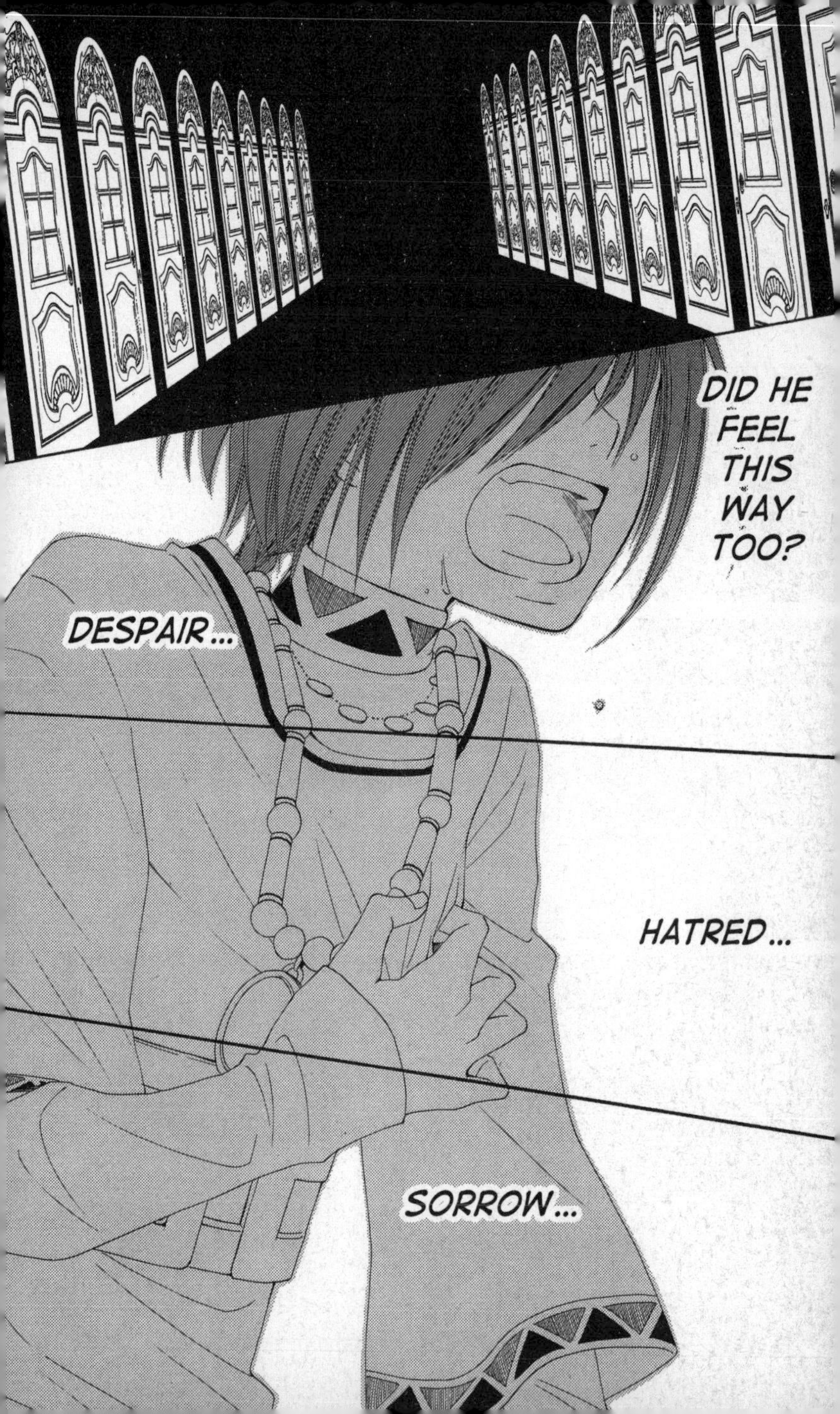
DID HE FEEL THIS WAY TOO?
DESPAIR...
HATRED...
SORROW...

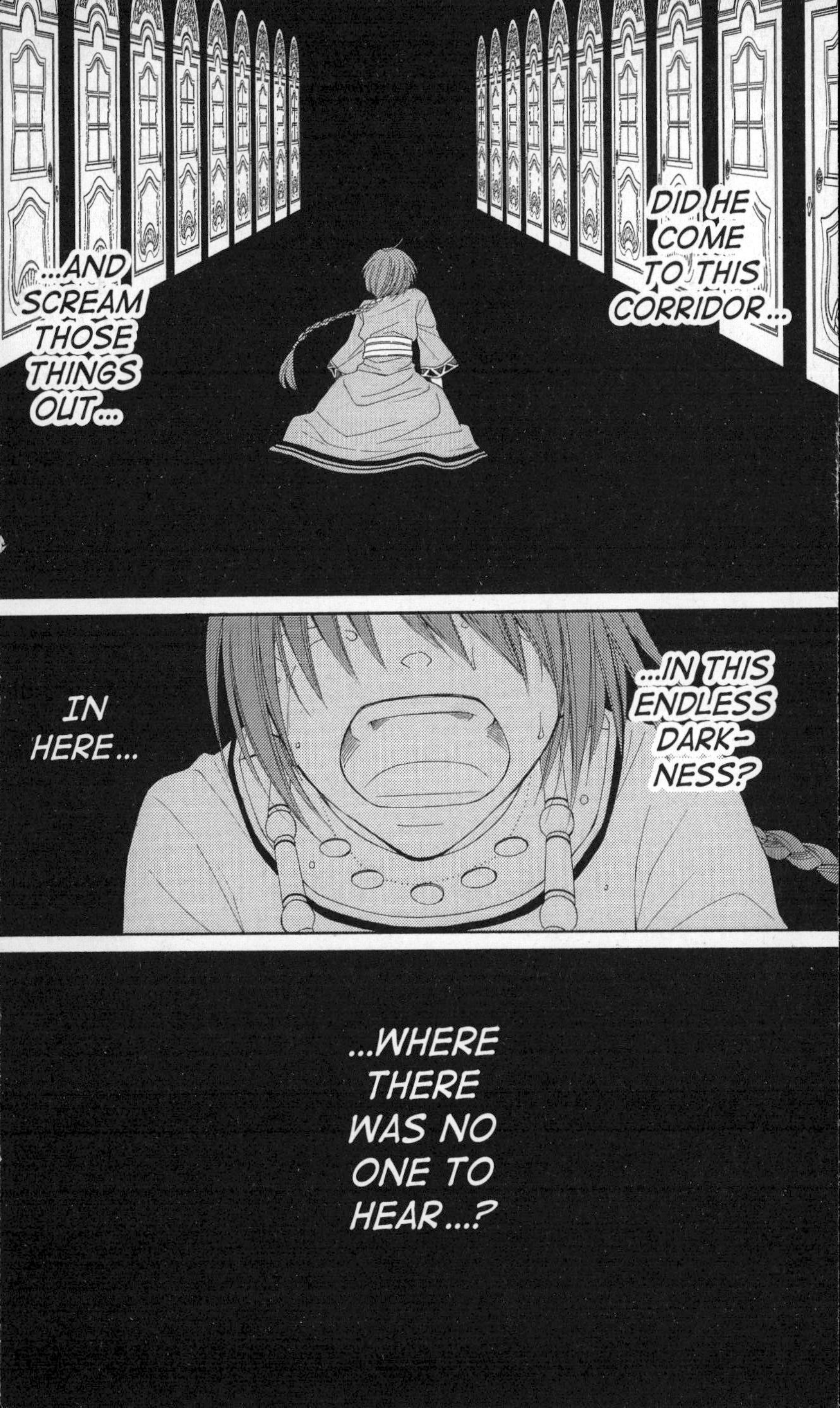
DID HE COME TO THIS CORRIDOR...
...AND SCREAM THOSE THINGS OUT...
...IN THIS ENDLESS DARK-NESS?
IN HERE...
...WHERE THERE WAS NO ONE TO HEAR...?

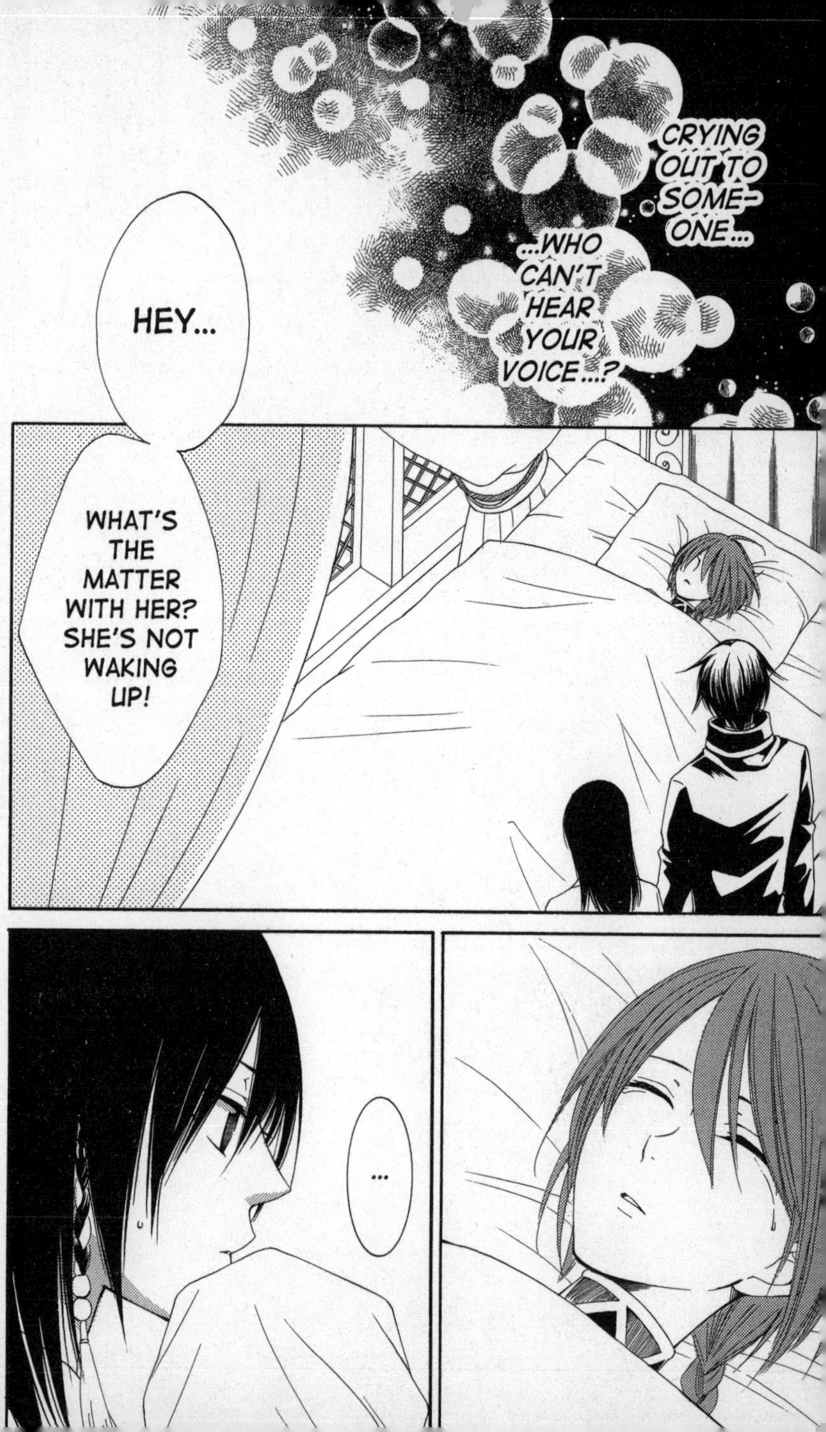
CRYING OUT TO SOME-ONE...
...WHO CAN'T HEAR YOUR VOICE...?
HEY...
WHAT'S THE MATTER WITH HER? SHE'S NOT WAKING UP!
...

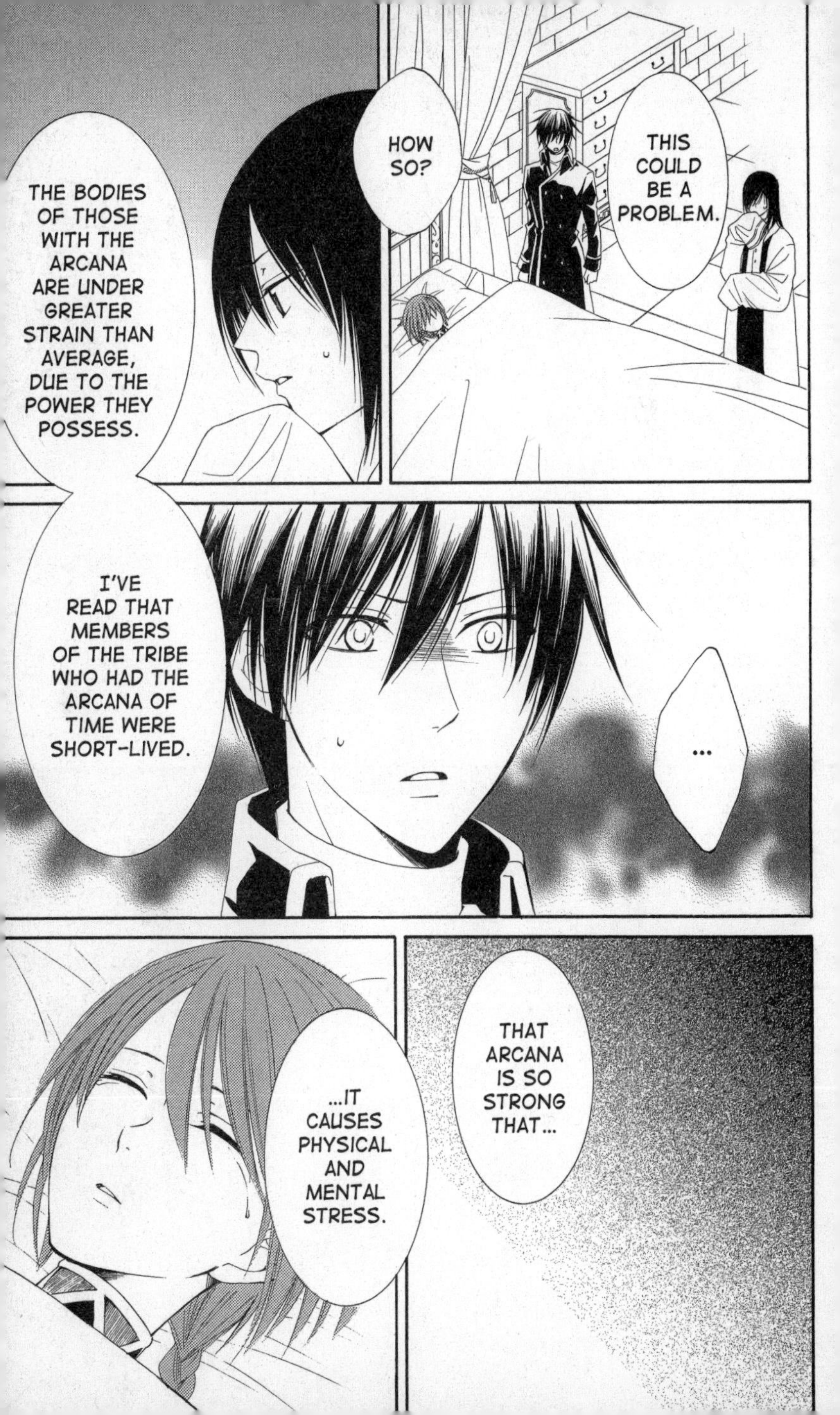
THIS COULD BE A PROBLEM.
HOW SO?
THE BODIES OF THOSE WITH THE ARCANA ARE UNDER GREATER STRAIN THAN AVERAGE, DUE TO THE POWER THEY POSSESS.
I'VE READ THAT MEMBERS OF THE TRIBE WHO HAD THE ARCANA OF TIME WERE SHORT-LIVED.
...
THAT ARCANA IS SO STRONG THAT...
...IT CAUSES PHYSICAL AND MENTAL STRESS.

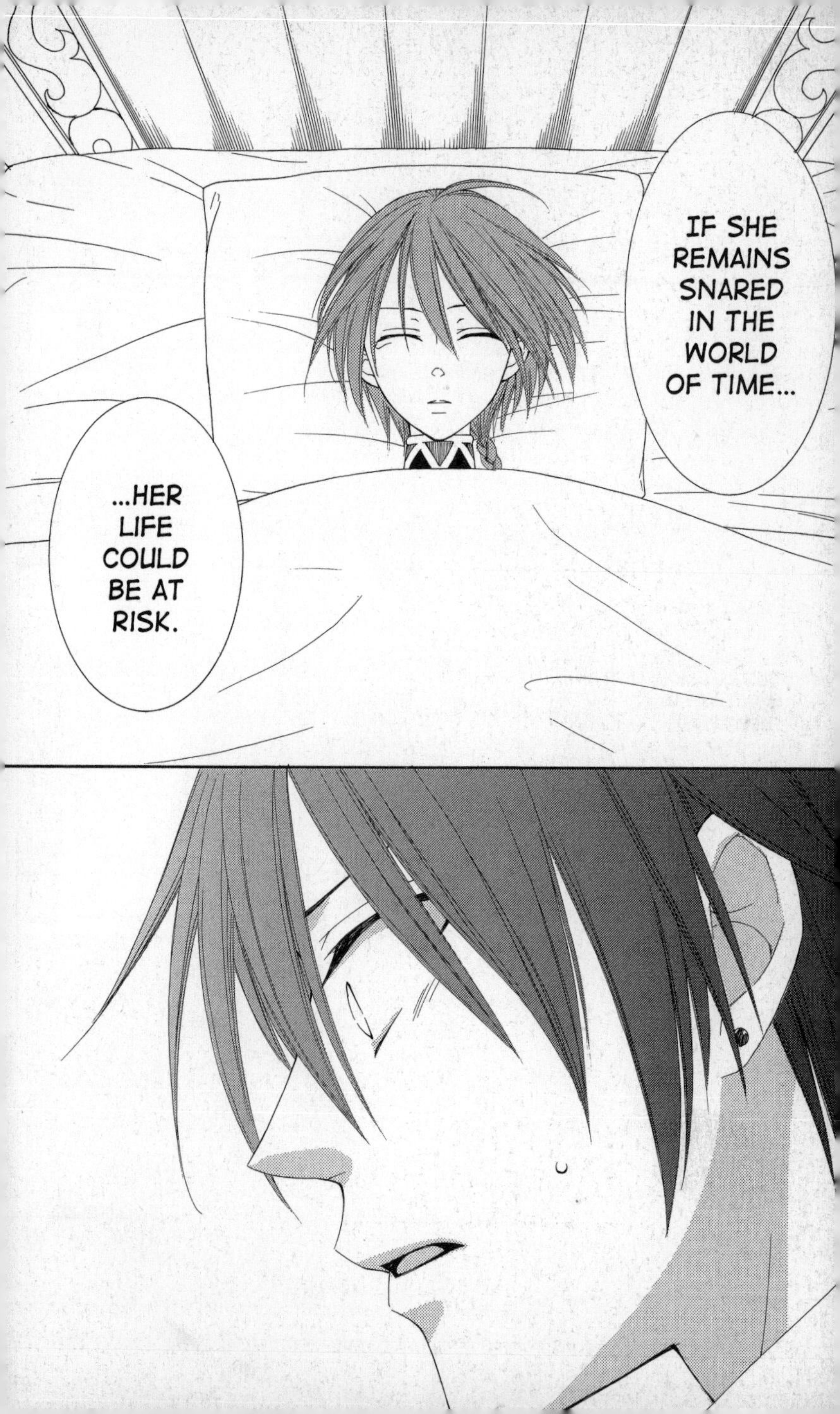
IF SHE REMAINS SNARED IN THE WORLD OF TIME...
...HER LIFE COULD BE AT RISK.

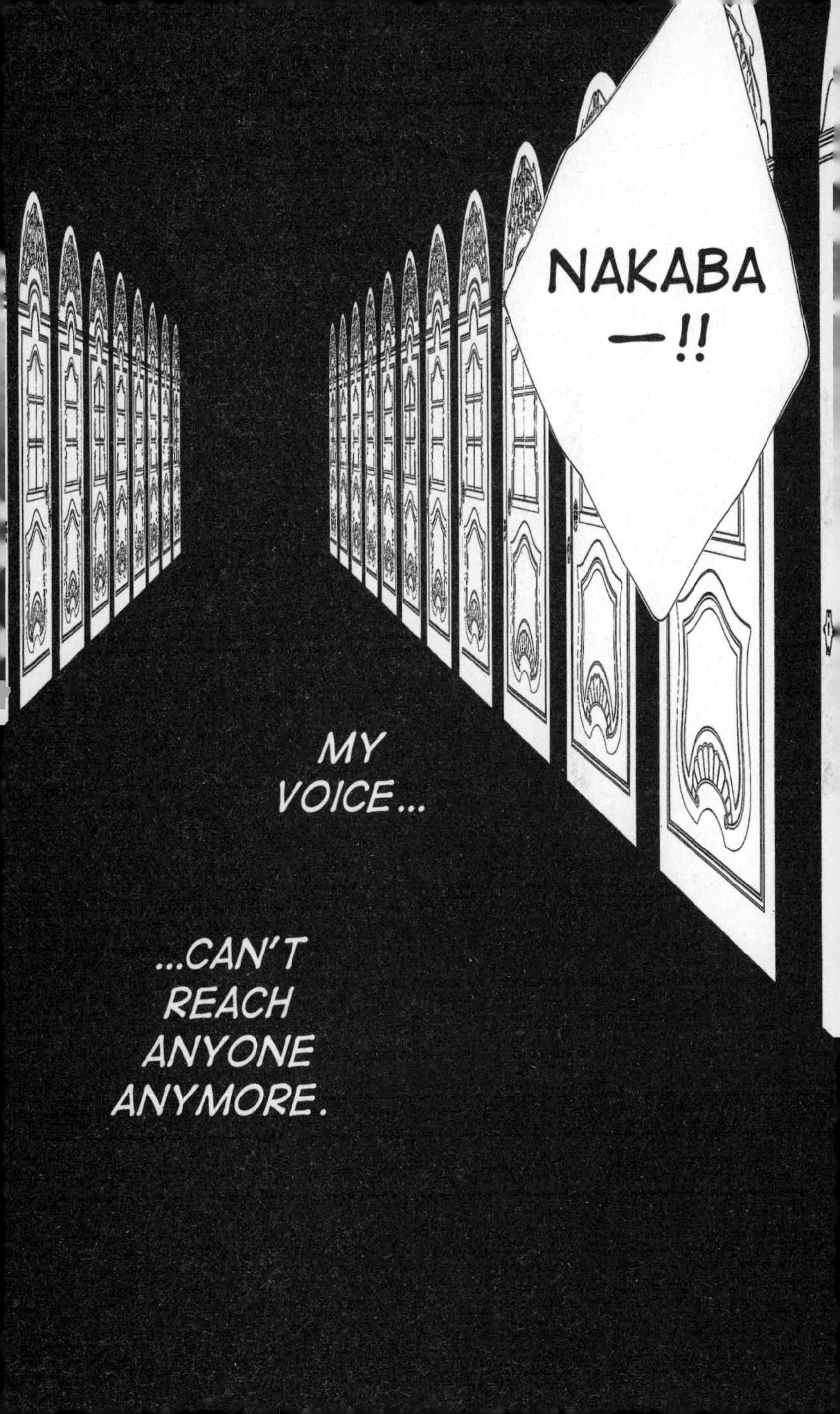
NAKABA—!!
MY VOICE...
...CAN'T REACH ANYONE ANYMORE.

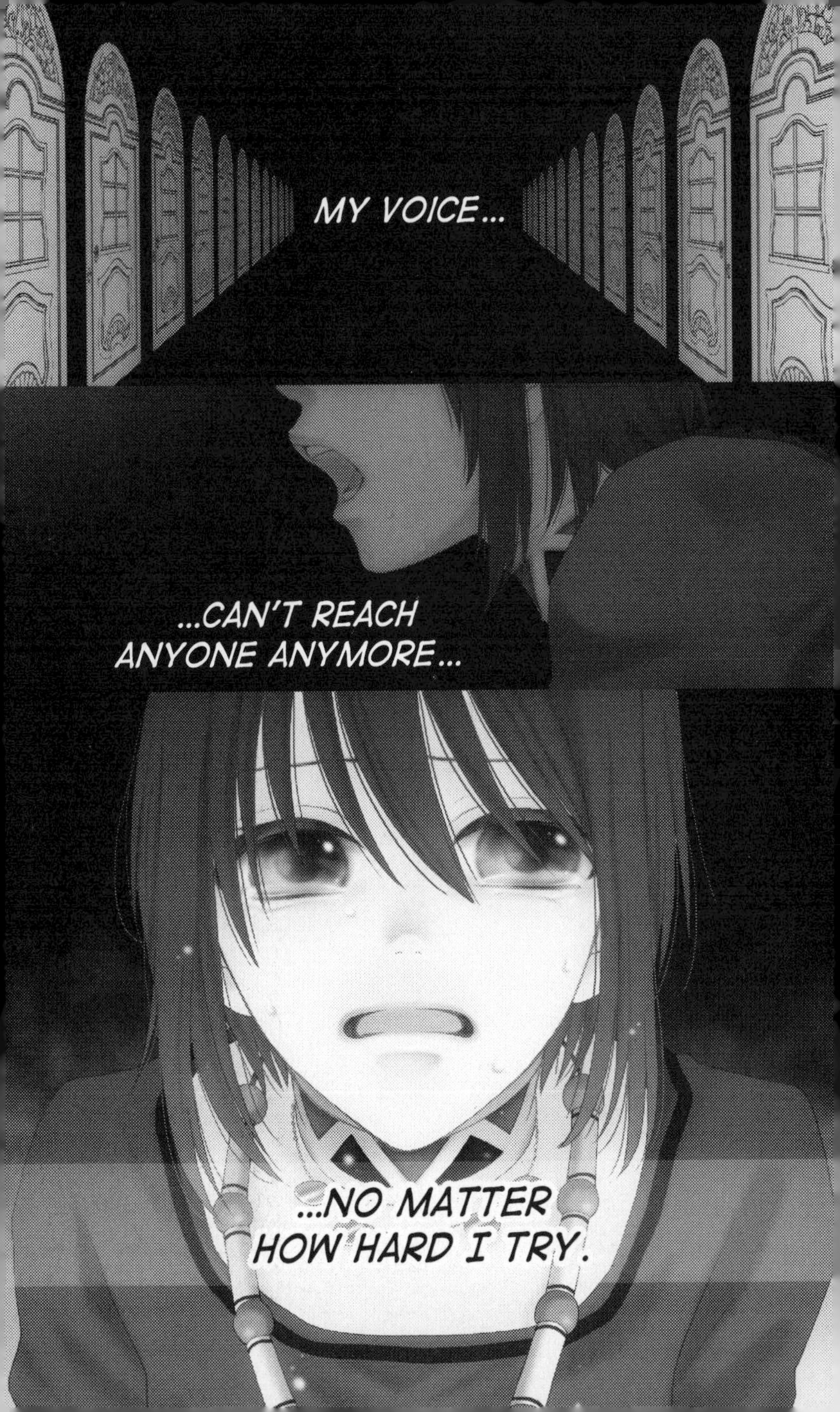
MY VOICE...
...CAN'T REACH ANYONE ANYMORE...
...NO MATTER HOW HARD I TRY.

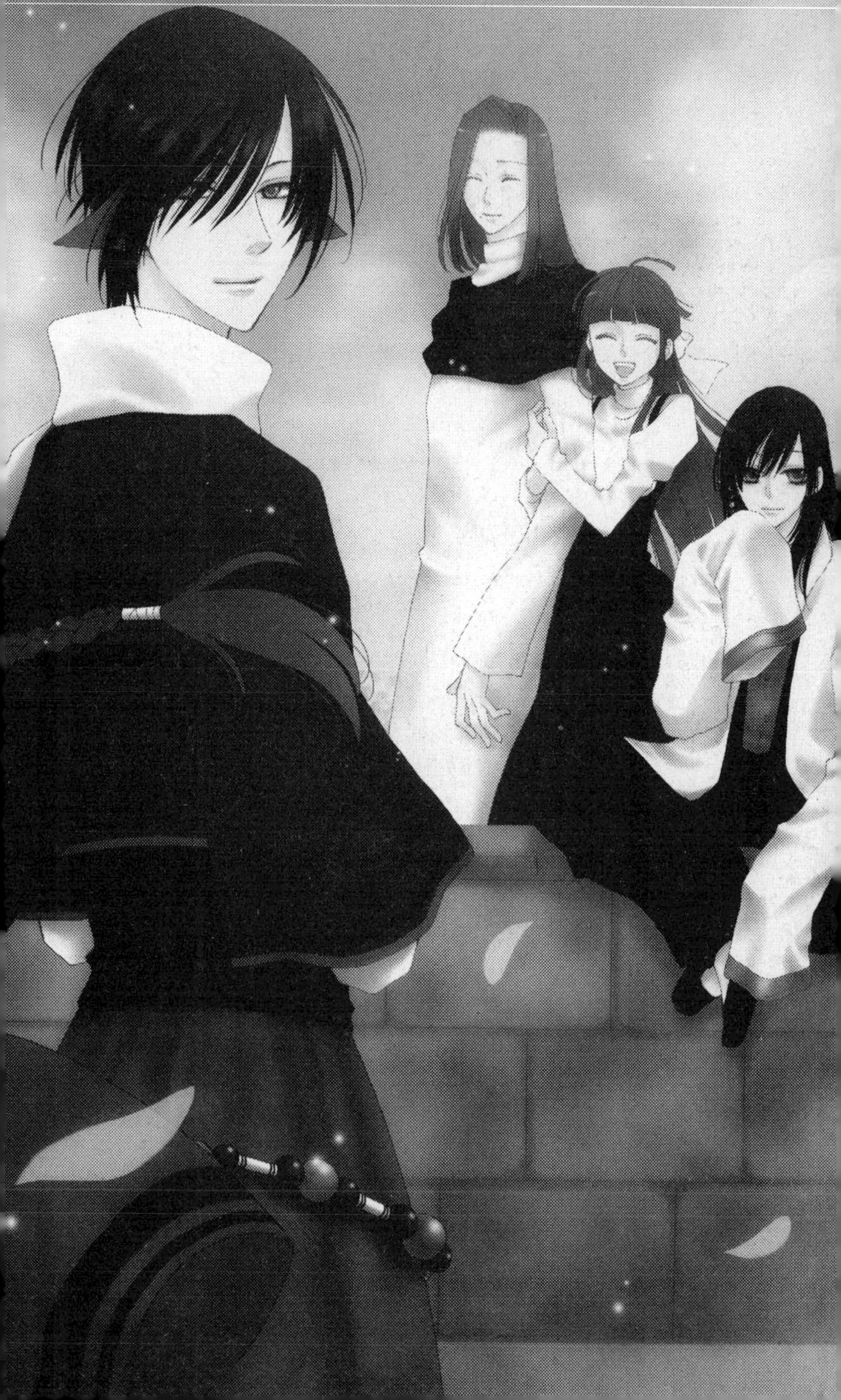

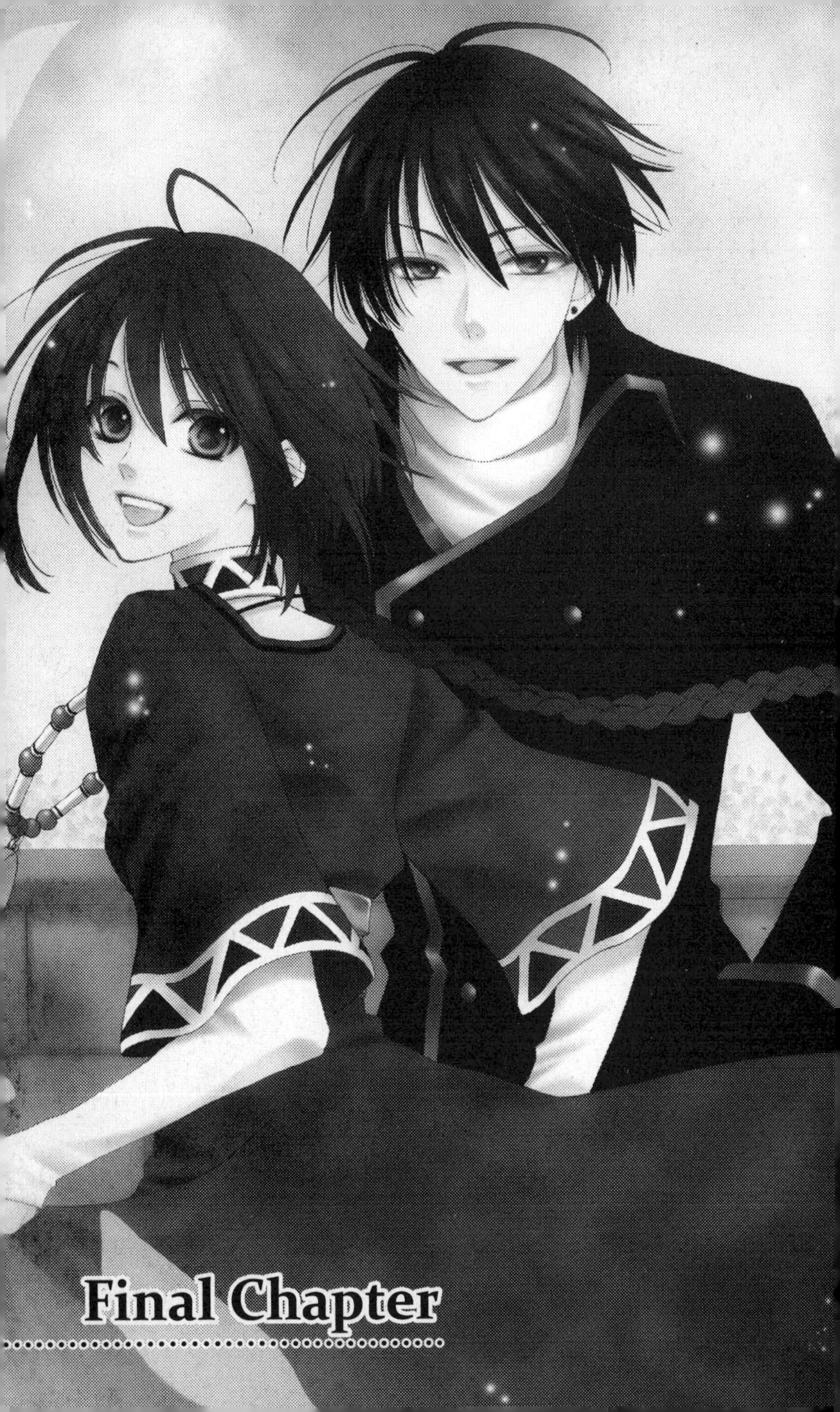

Final Chapter

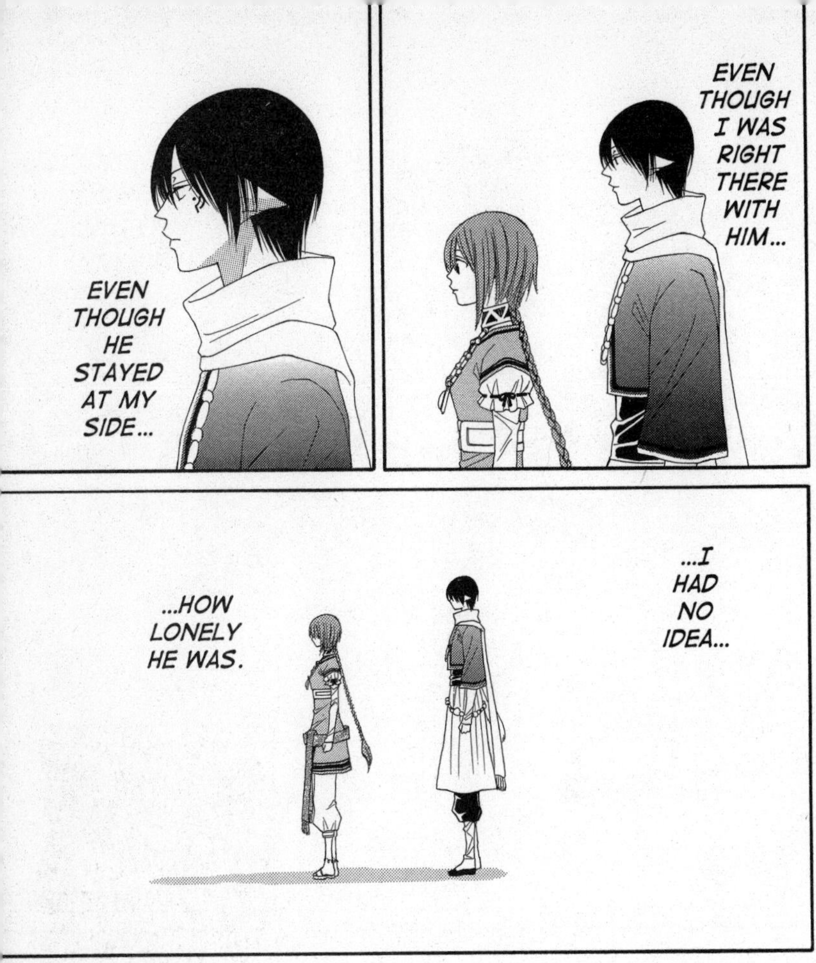
EVEN THOUGH I WAS RIGHT THERE WITH HIM...
EVEN THOUGH HE STAYED AT MY SIDE...
...I HAD NO IDEA...
...HOW LONELY HE WAS.

Dawn of the Arcana

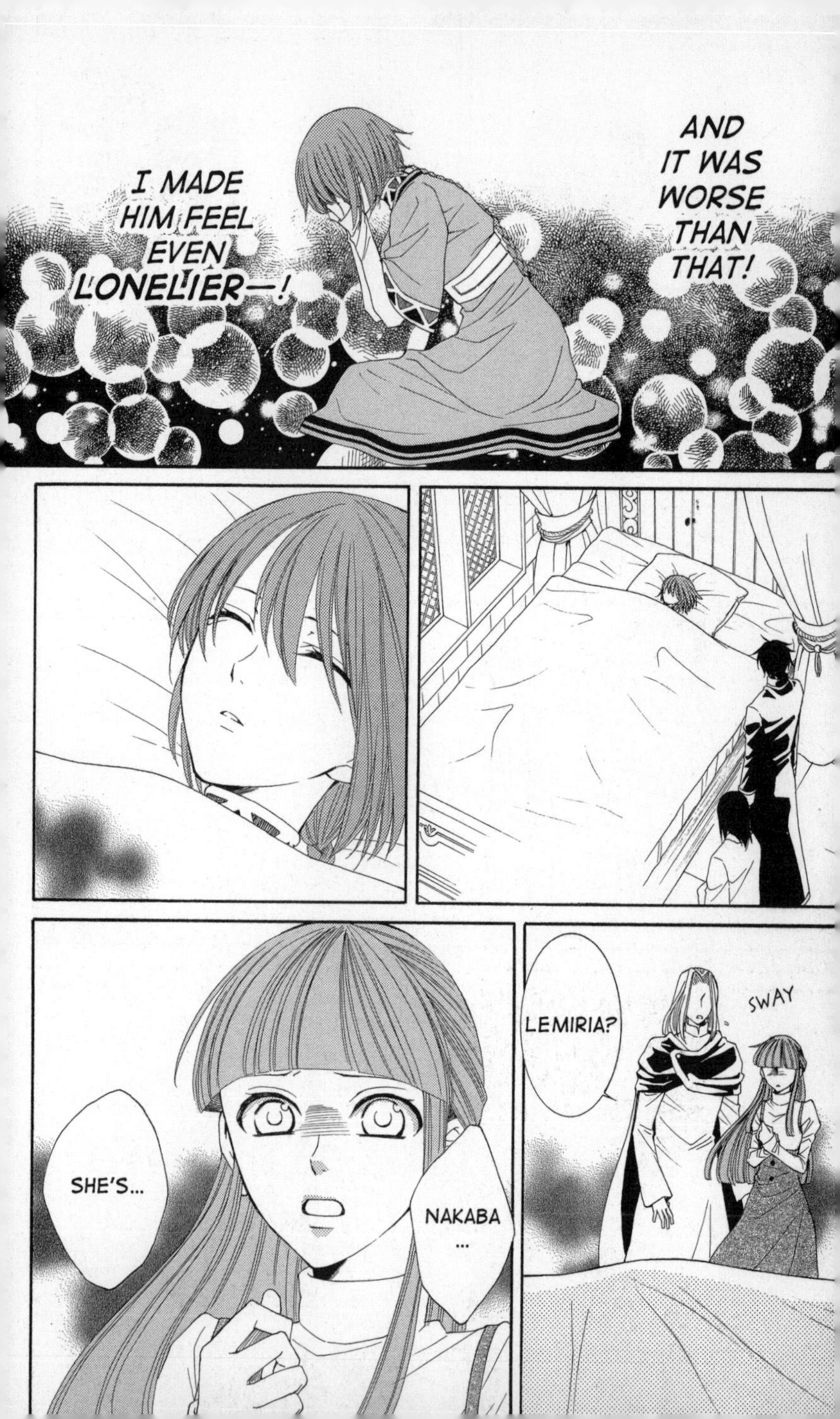
AND IT WAS WORSE THAN THAT!
I MADE HIM FEEL EVEN LONELIER—!
SWAY
LEMIRIA?
NAKABA...
SHE'S...

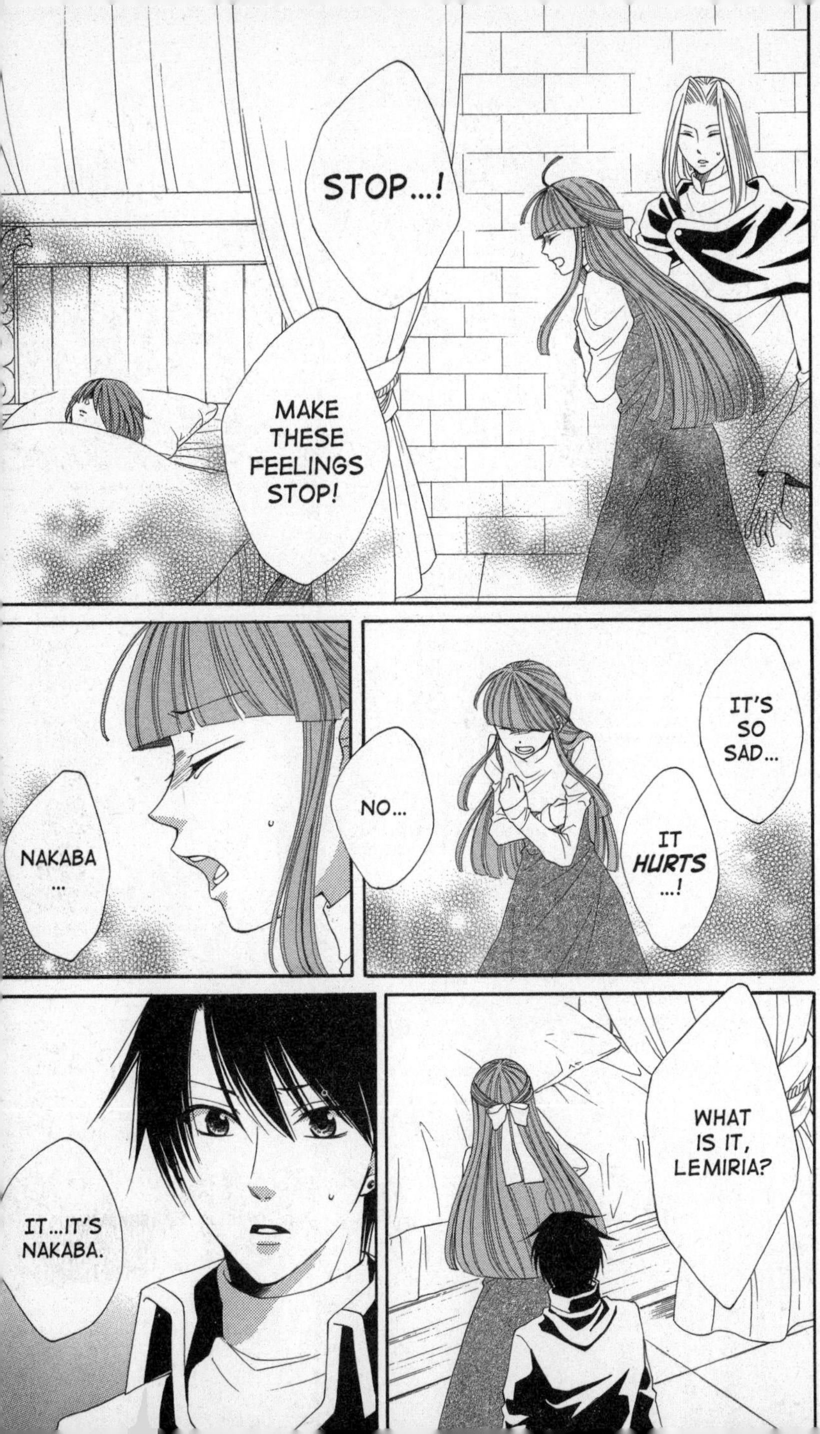
STOP...!
MAKE THESE FEELINGS STOP!
IT'S SO SAD...
IT *HURTS*...!
NO...
NAKABA...
WHAT IS IT, LEMIRIA?
IT...IT'S NAKABA.

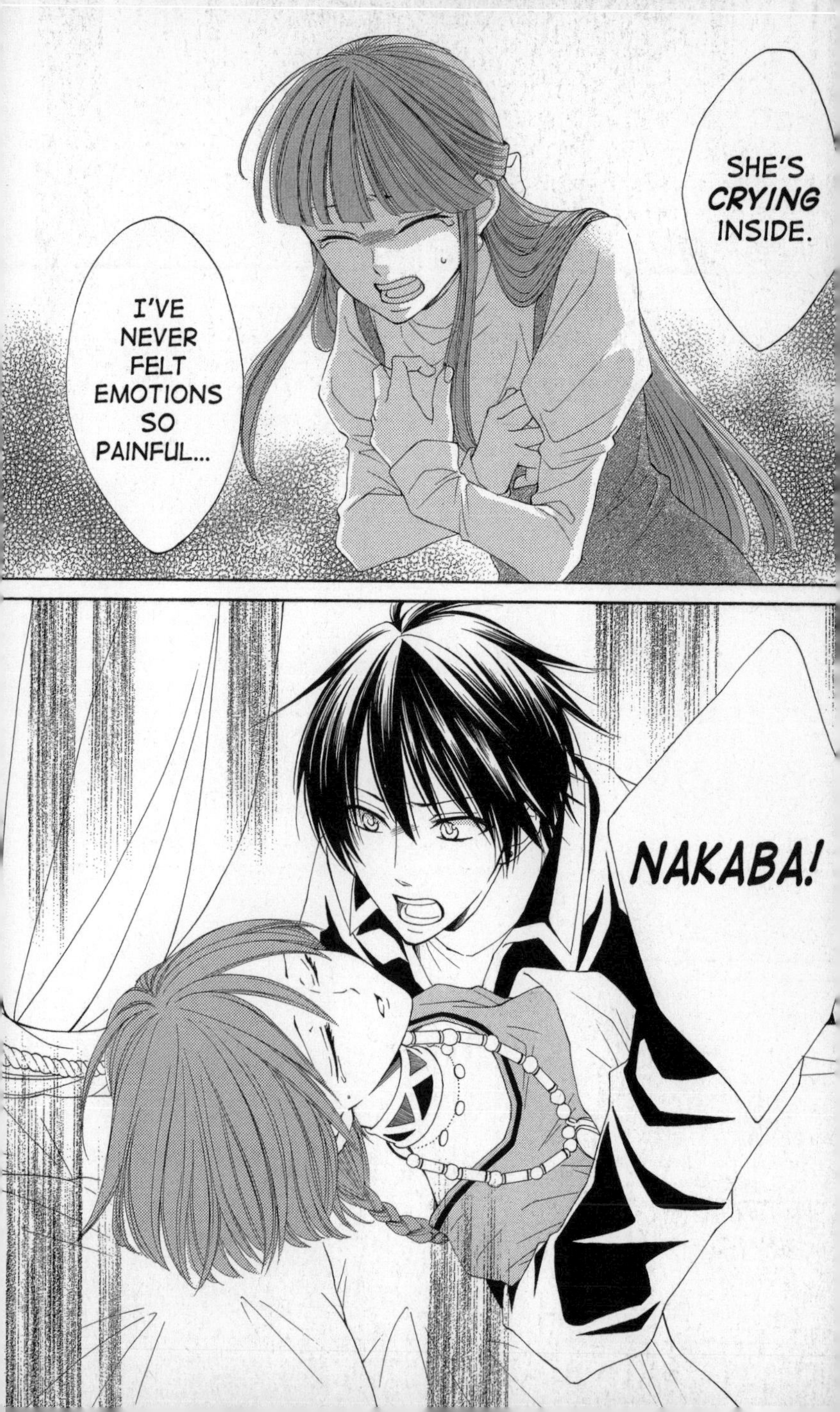
SHE'S *CRYING* INSIDE.
I'VE NEVER FELT EMOTIONS SO PAINFUL...
NAKABA!

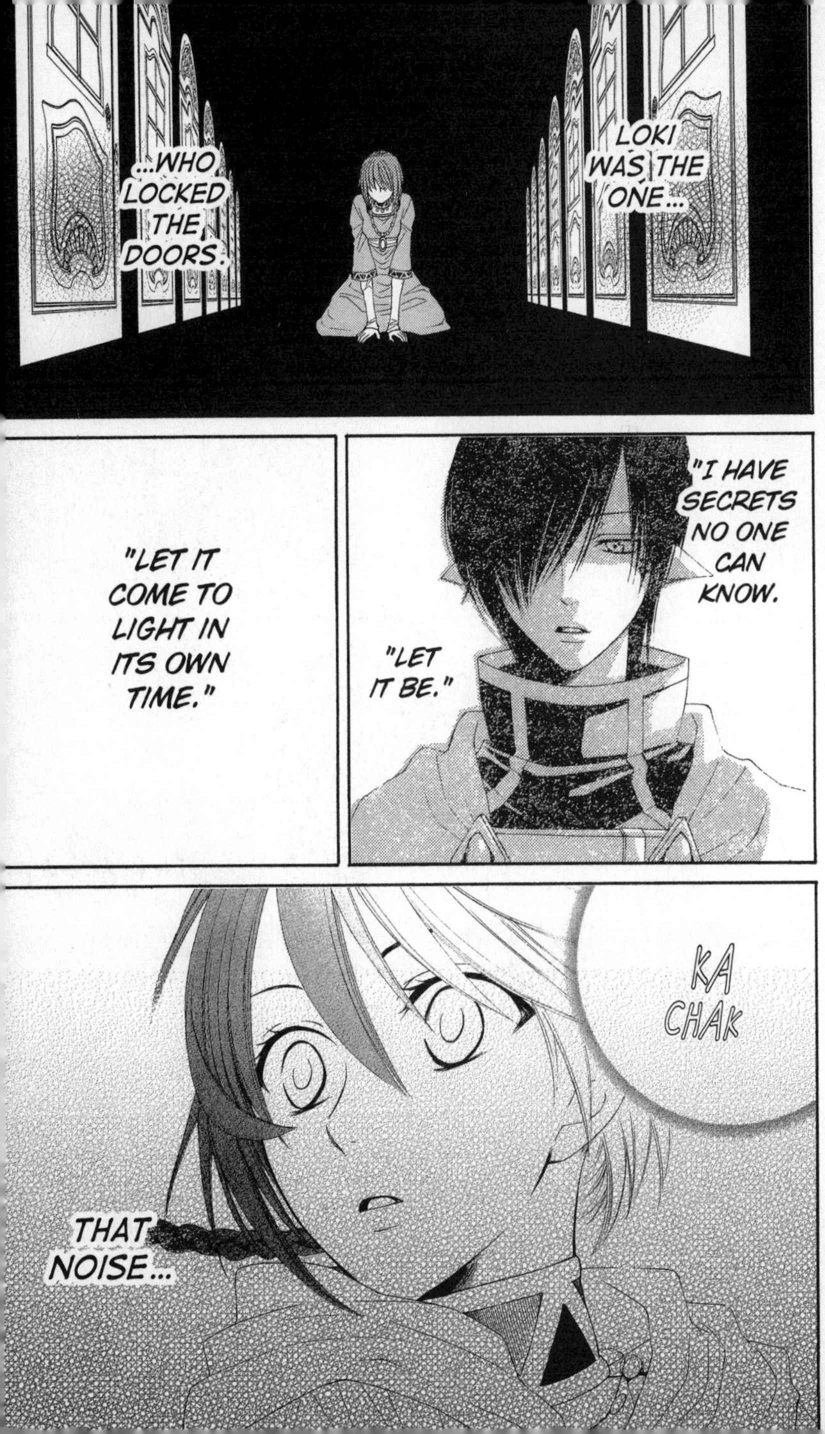
LOKI WAS THE ONE...
...WHO LOCKED THE DOORS.
"I HAVE SECRETS NO ONE CAN KNOW.
"LET IT BE."
"LET IT COME TO LIGHT IN ITS OWN TIME."
KA CHAK
THAT NOISE...

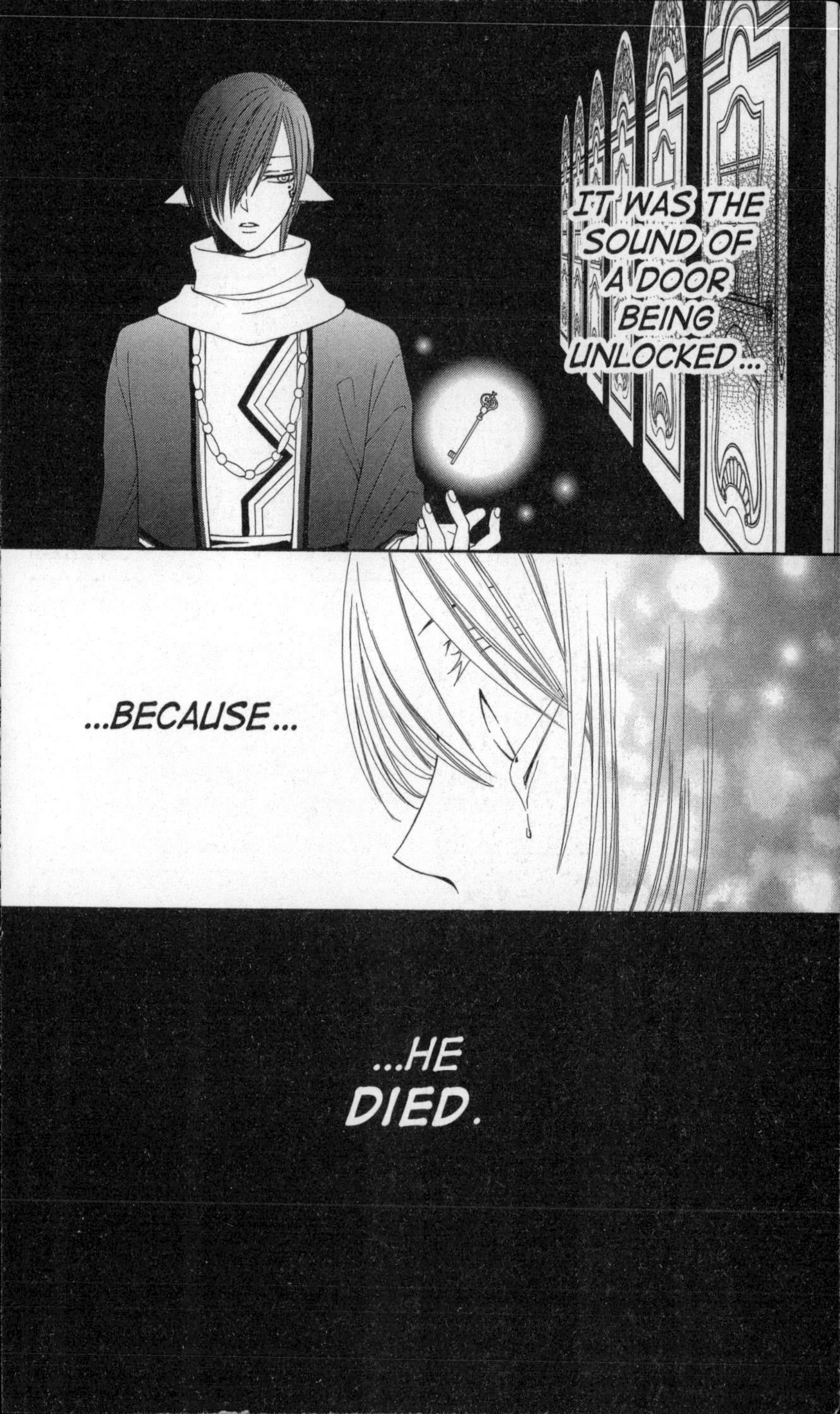
IT WAS THE SOUND OF A DOOR BEING UNLOCKED...
...BECAUSE...
...HE DIED.

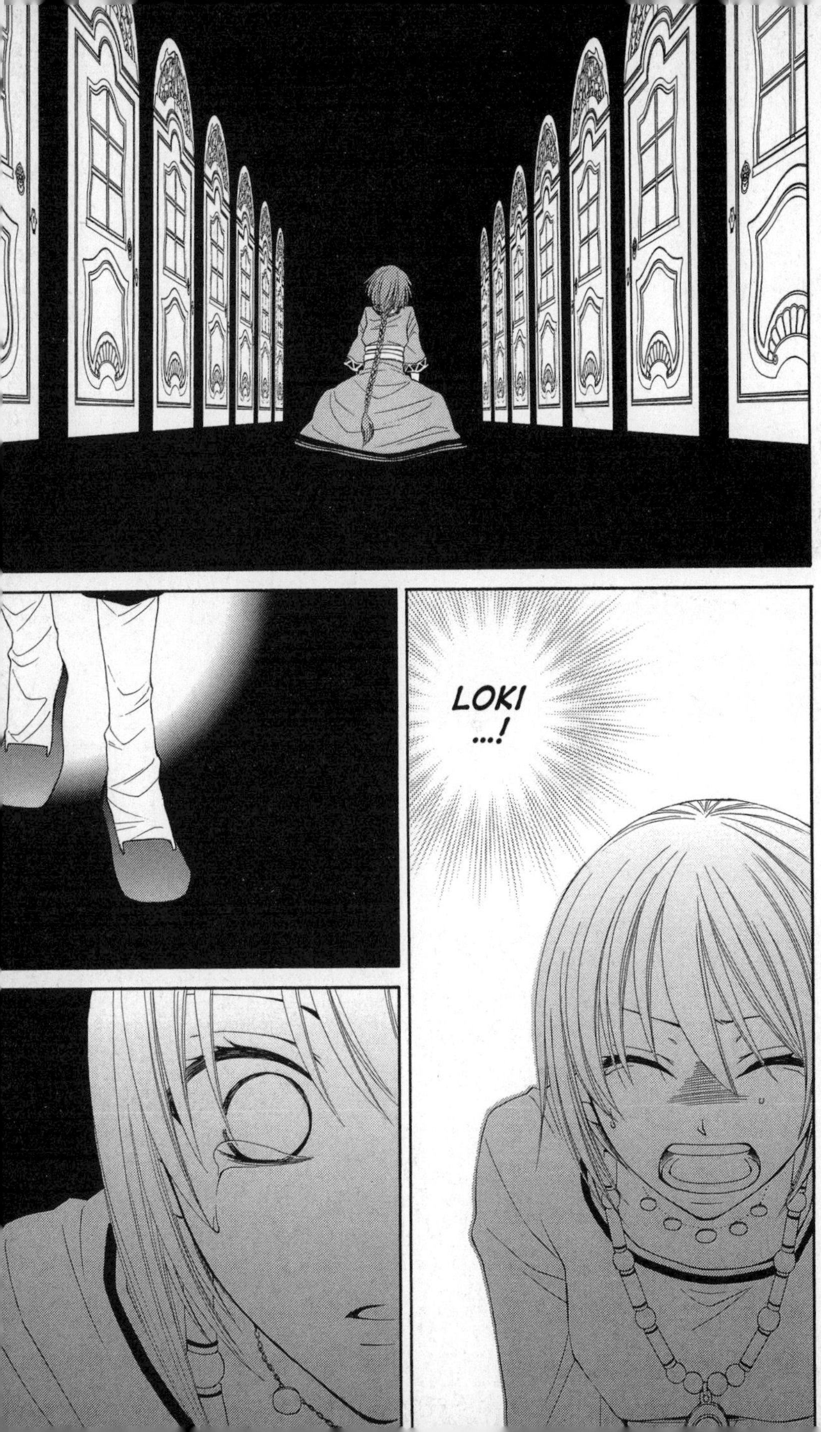
LOKI
...!

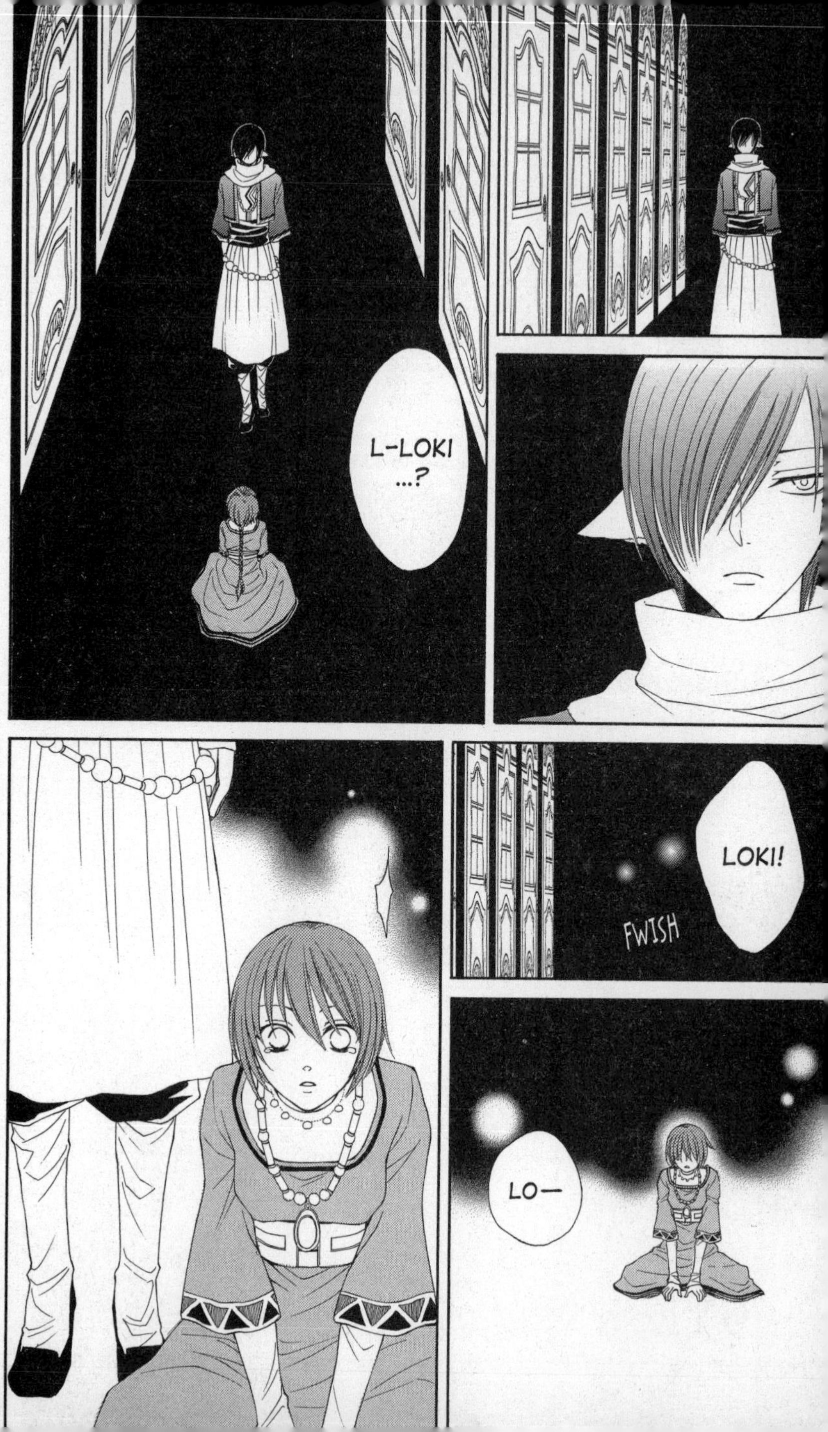
L-LOKI ...?
LOKI!
FWISH
LO—

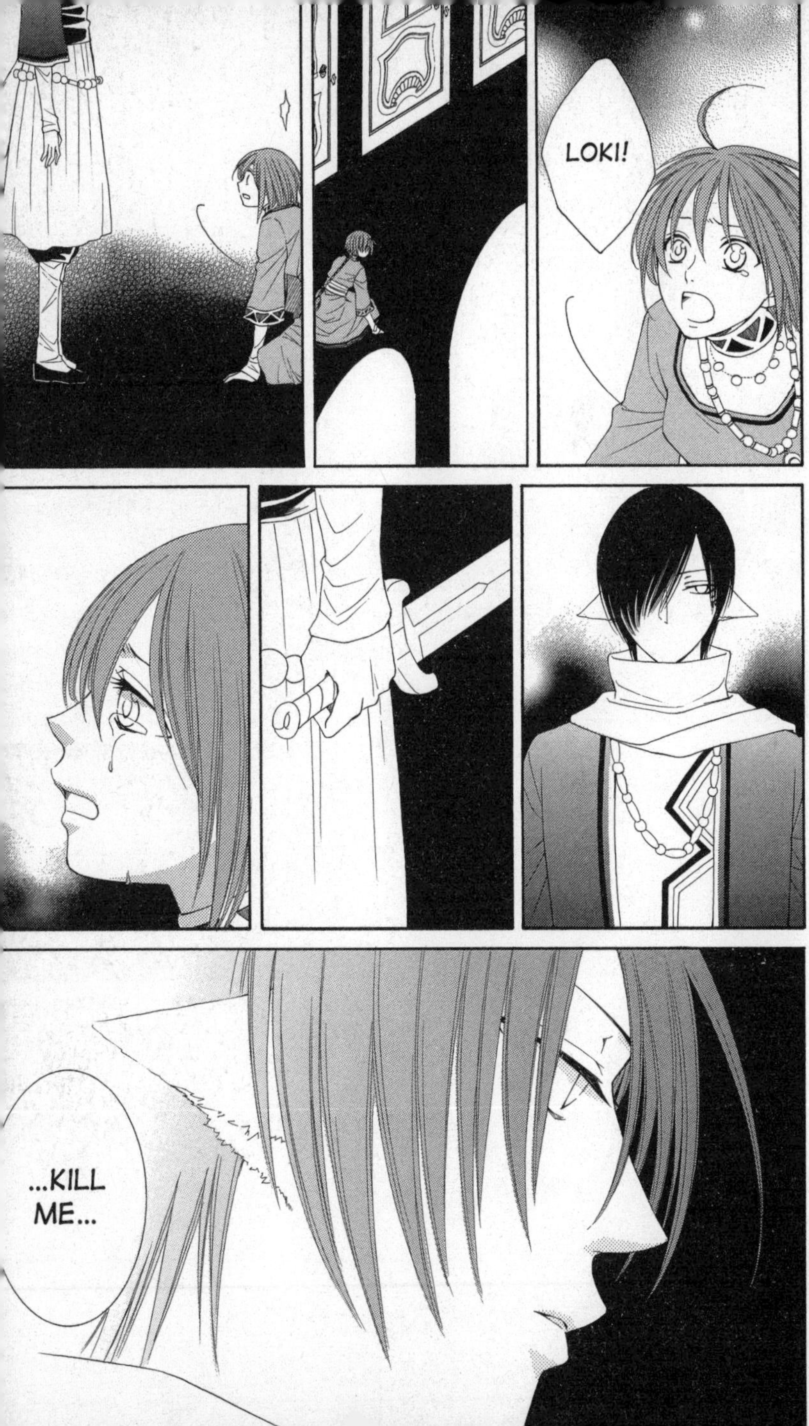
LOKI!
...KILL ME...

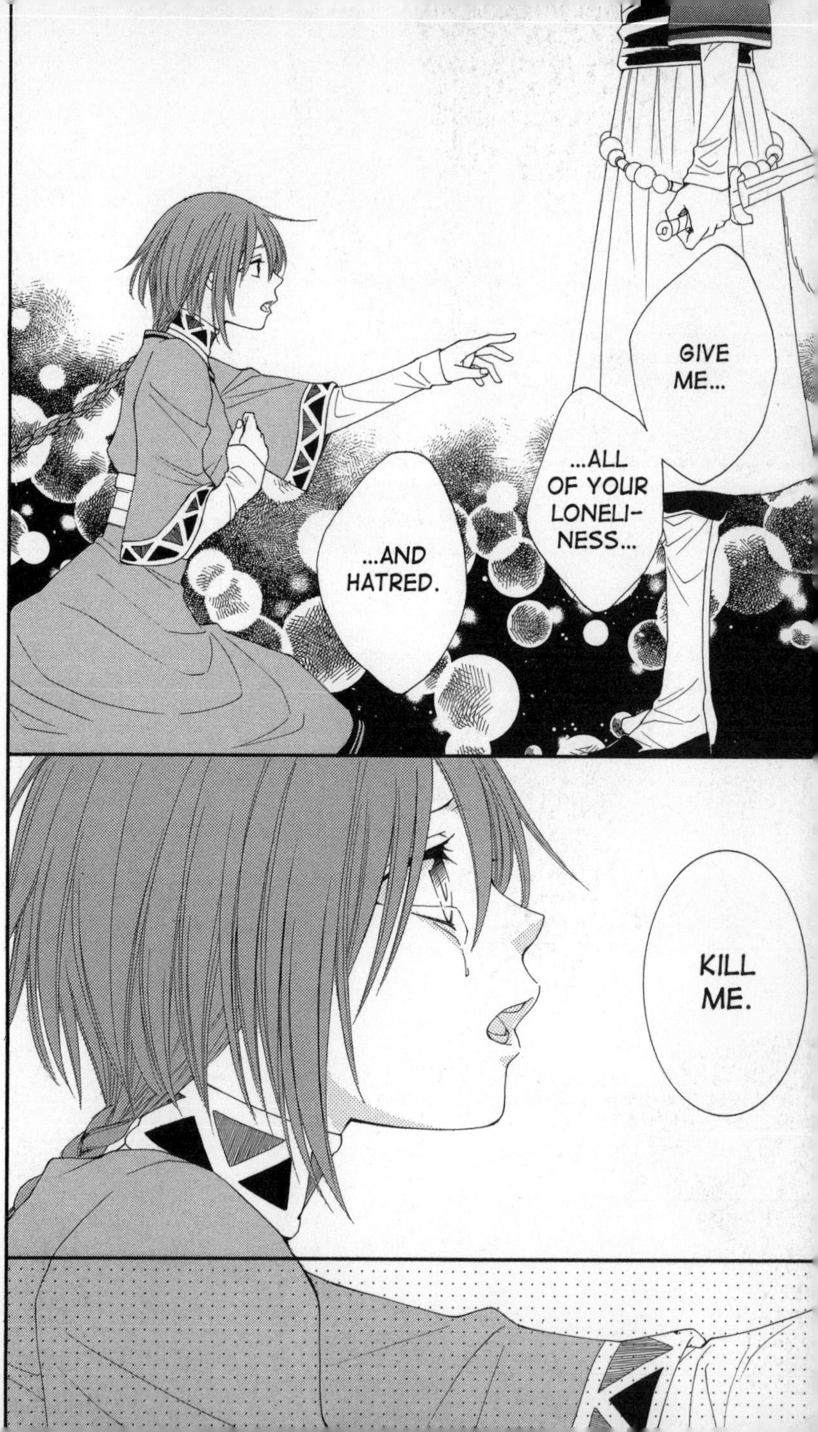
GIVE ME...
...ALL OF YOUR LONELI-NESS...
...AND HATRED.
KILL ME.

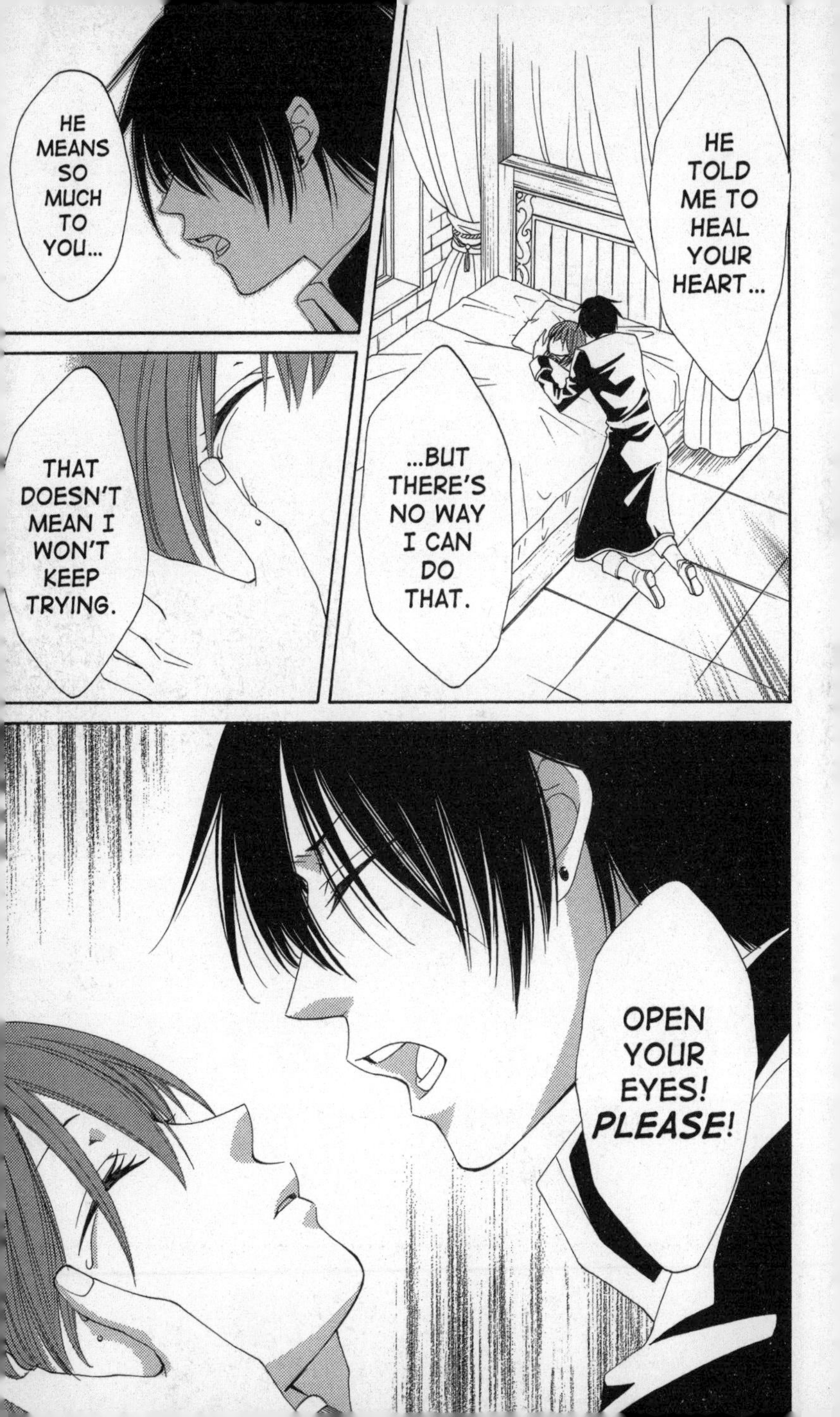
HE TOLD ME TO HEAL YOUR HEART...
...BUT THERE'S NO WAY I CAN DO THAT.
HE MEANS SO MUCH TO YOU...
THAT DOESN'T MEAN I WON'T KEEP TRYING.
OPEN YOUR EYES! *PLEASE*!

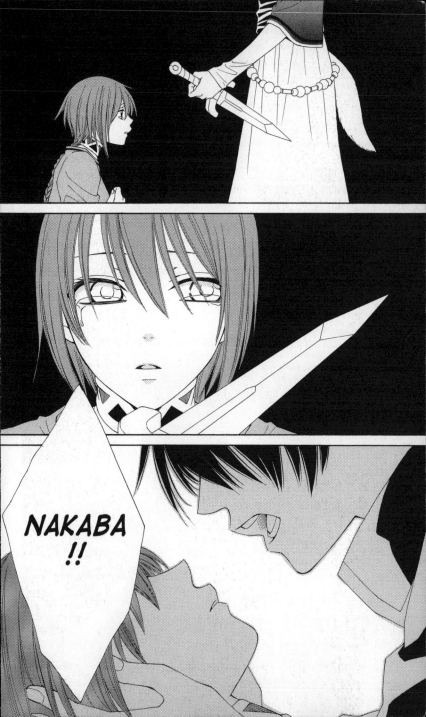

NAKABA
!!

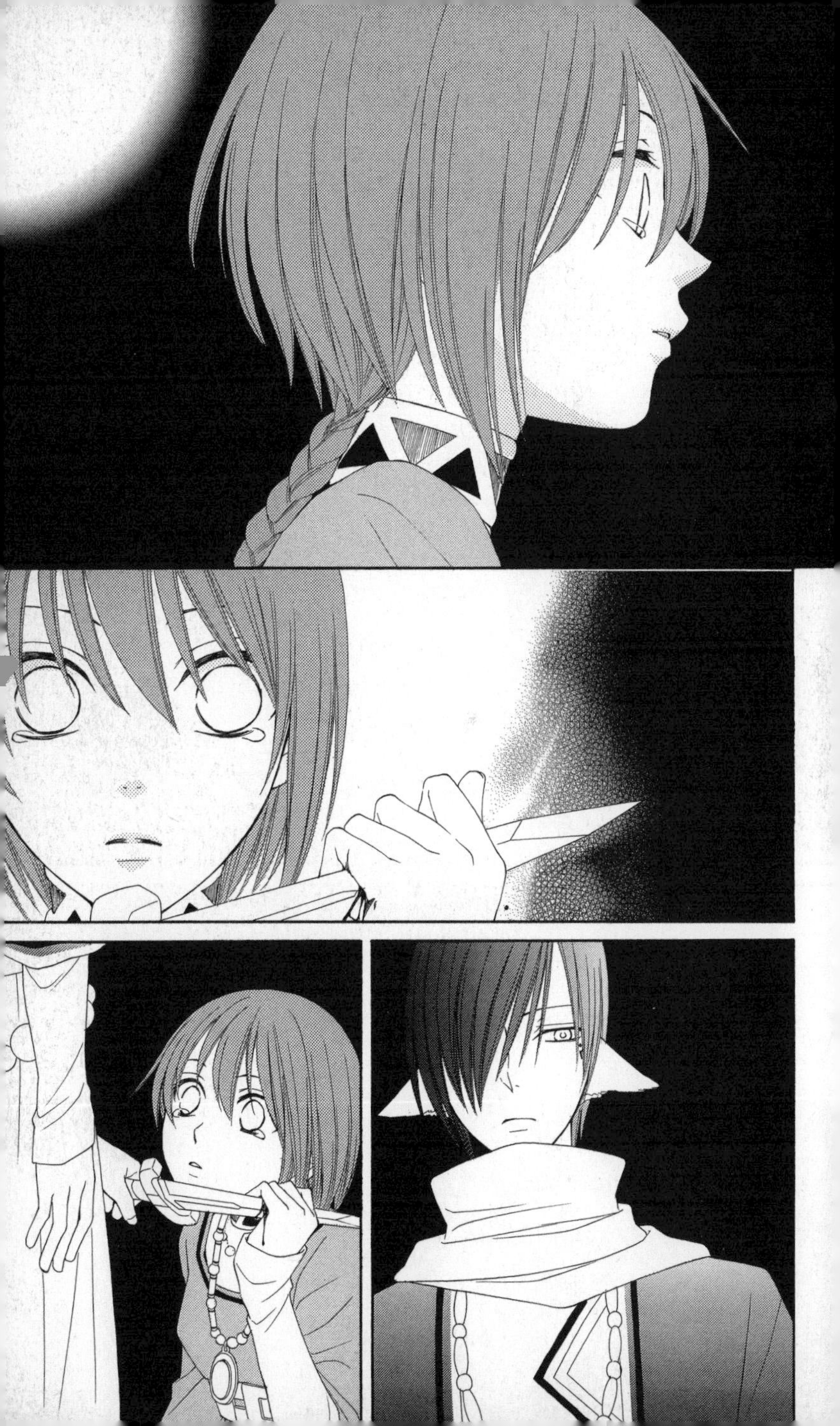

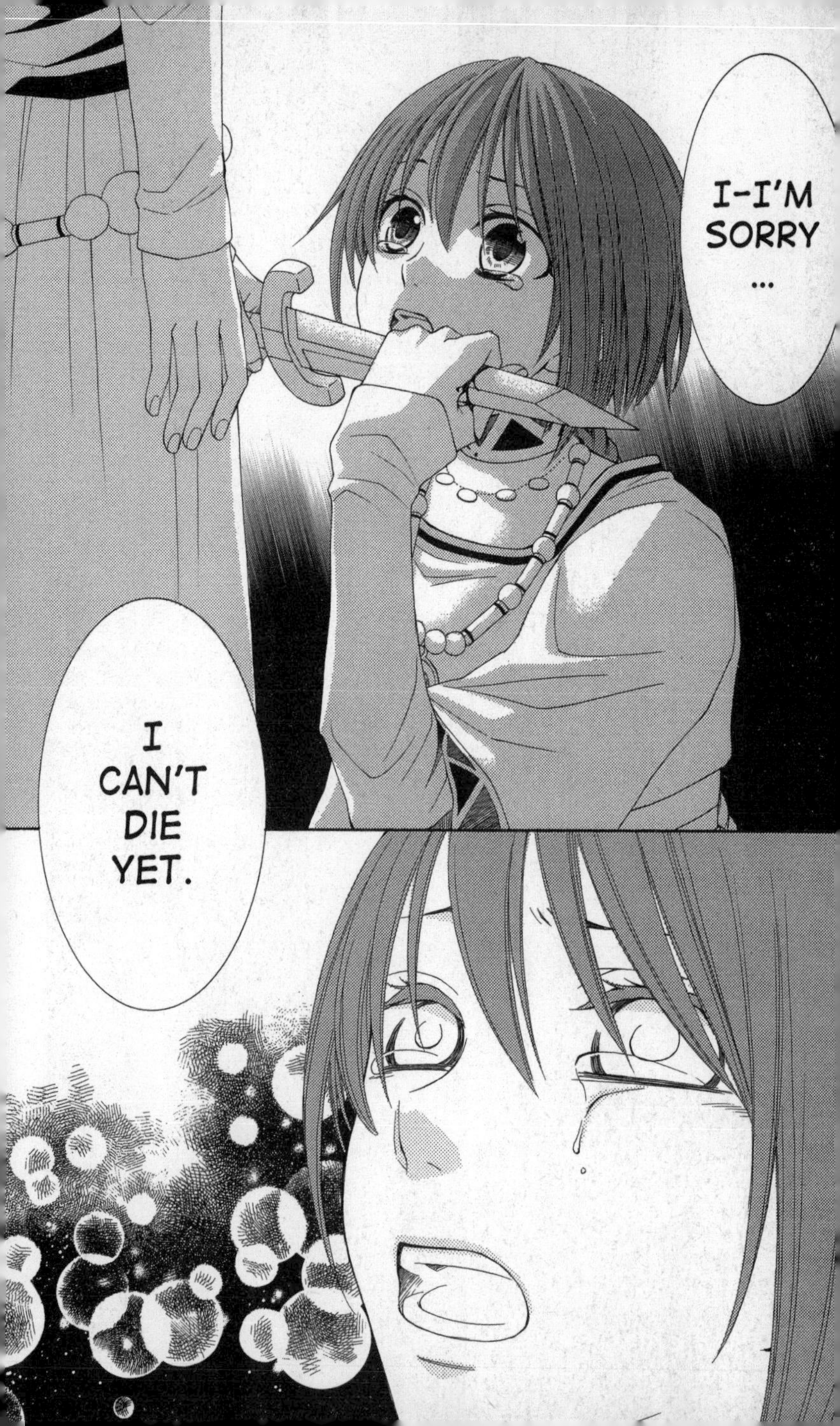
I-I'M SORRY ...
I CAN'T DIE YET.

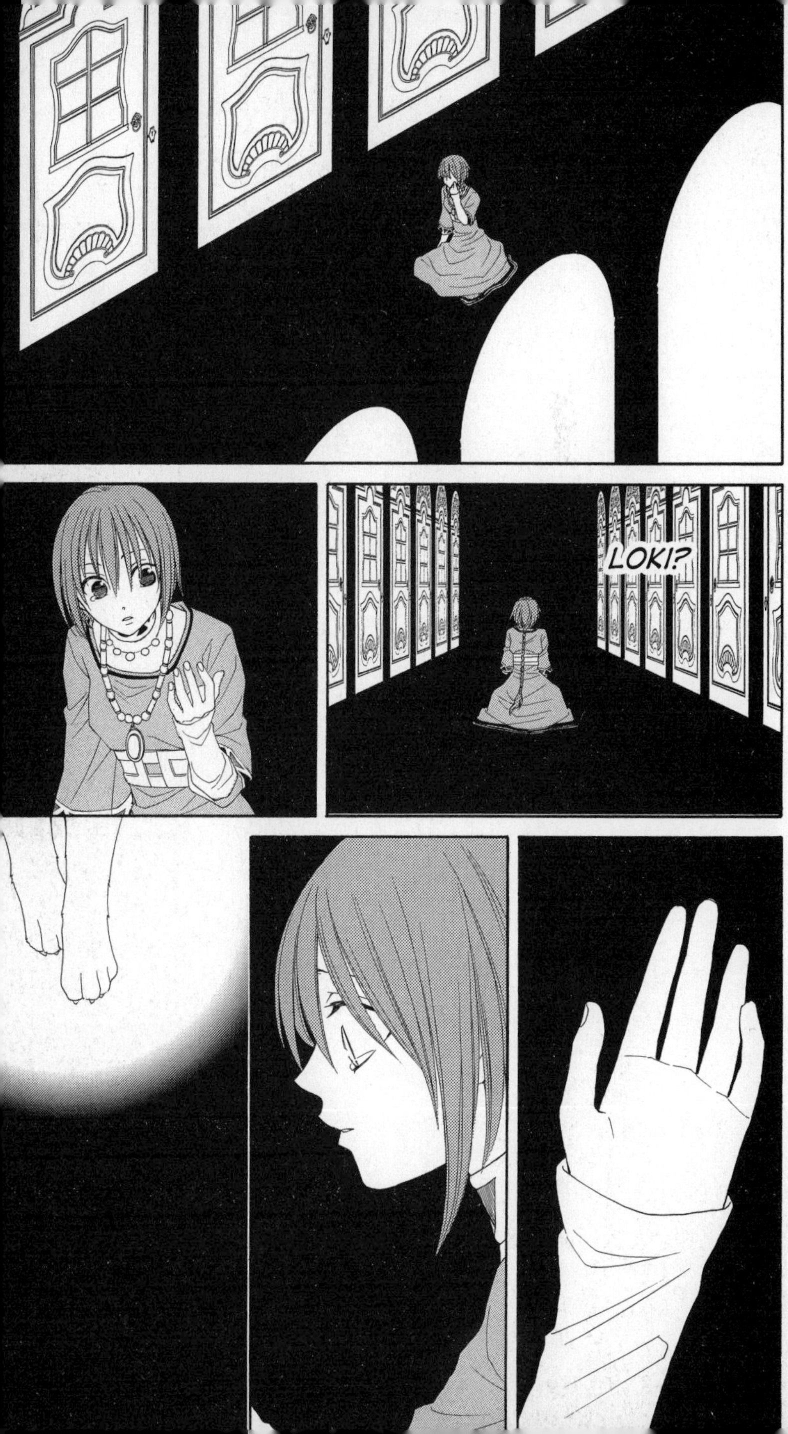
LOKI?

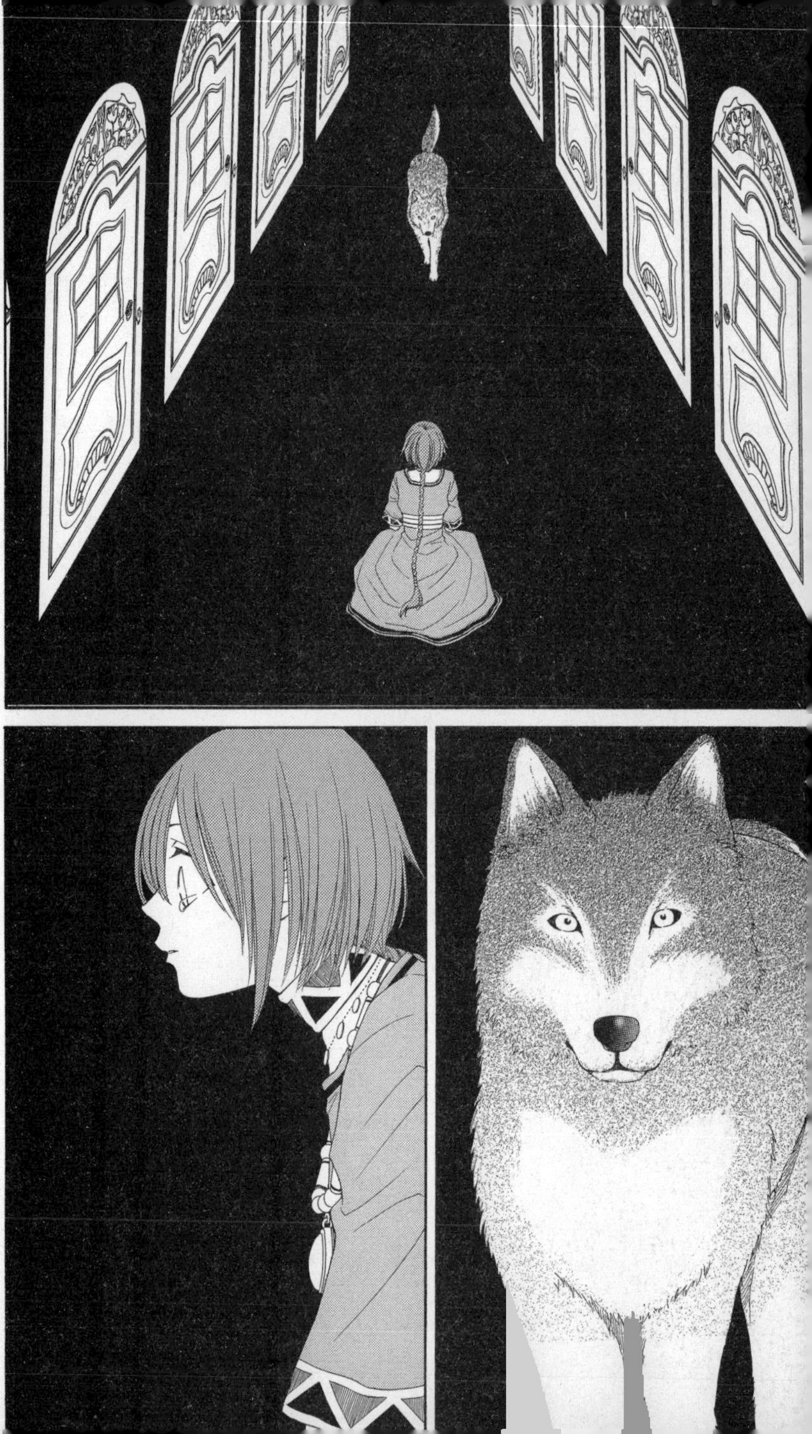

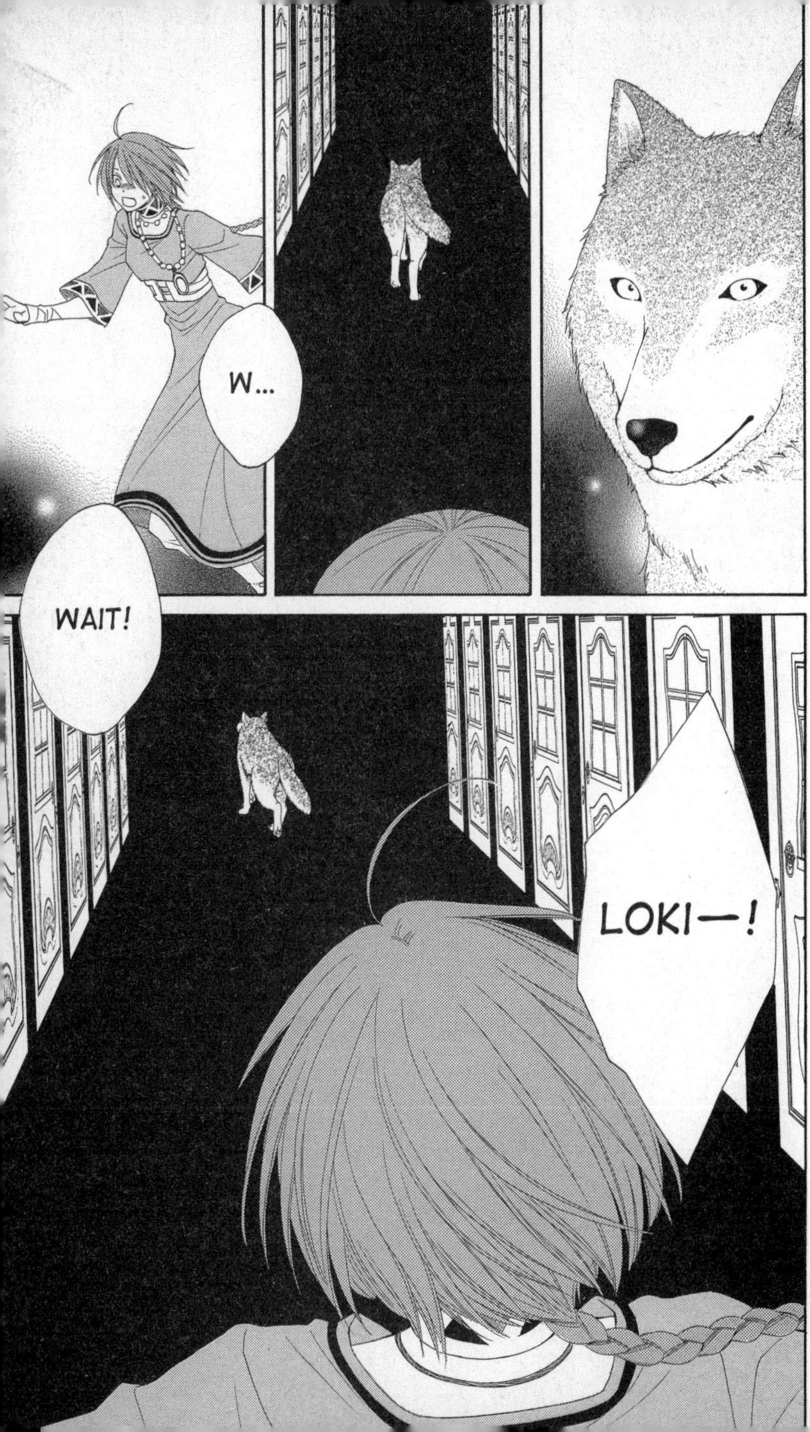
W...
WAIT!
LOKI—!

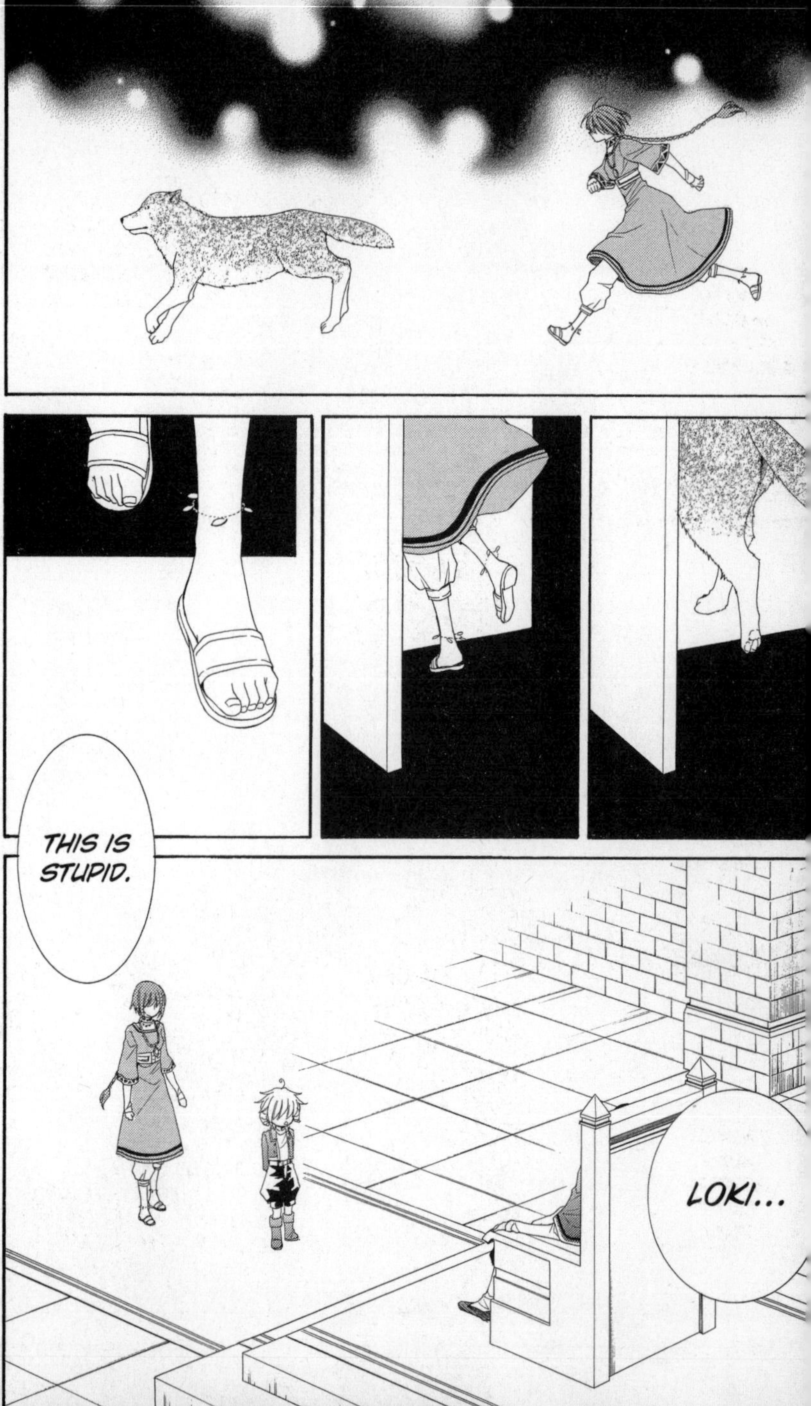
LOKI...
THIS IS STUPID.

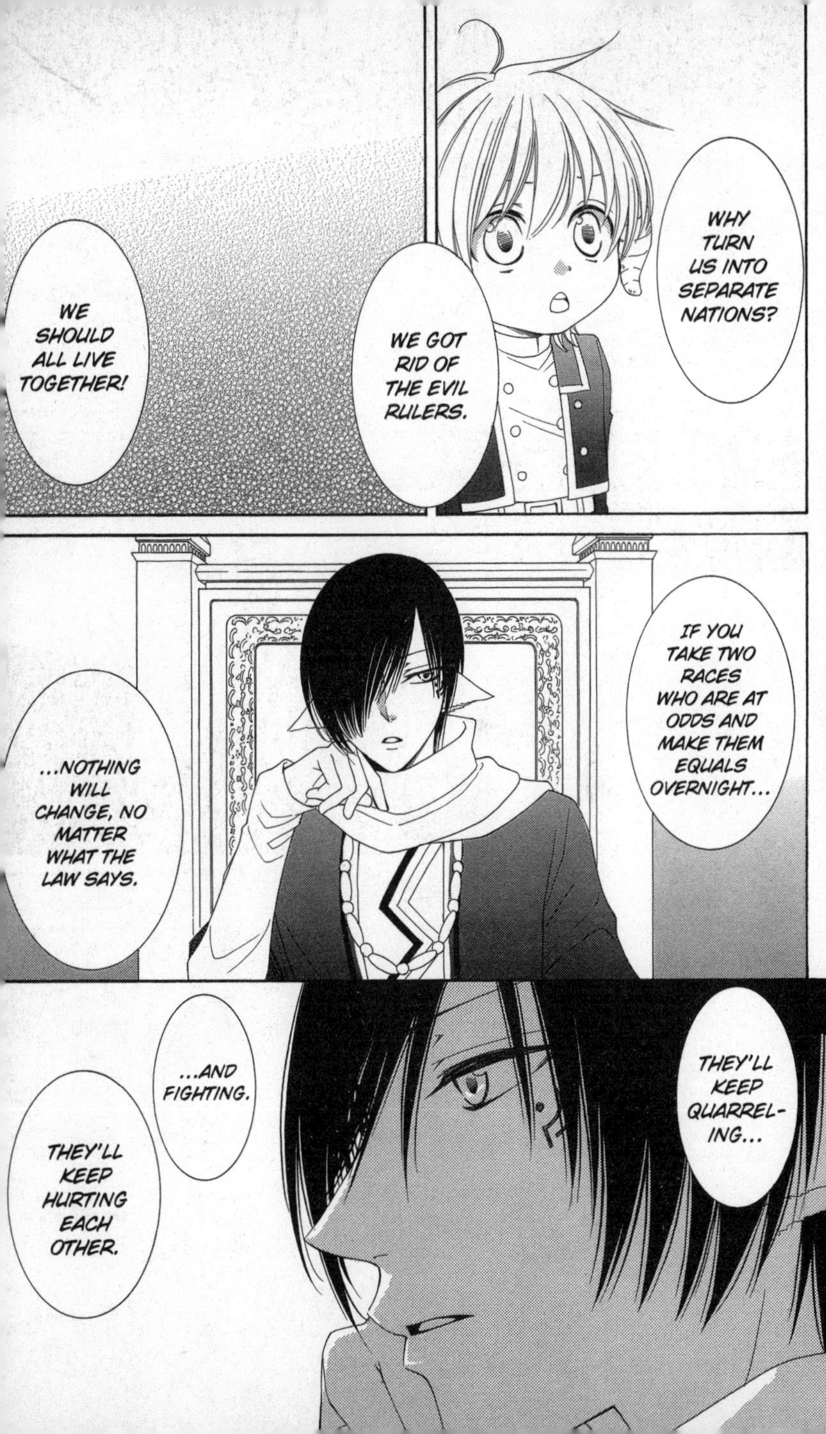
WHY TURN US INTO SEPARATE NATIONS?
WE GOT RID OF THE EVIL RULERS.
WE SHOULD ALL LIVE TOGETHER!
IF YOU TAKE TWO RACES WHO ARE AT ODDS AND MAKE THEM EQUALS OVERNIGHT...
...NOTHING WILL CHANGE, NO MATTER WHAT THE LAW SAYS.
THEY'LL KEEP QUARREL-ING...
...AND FIGHTING.
THEY'LL KEEP HURTING EACH OTHER.

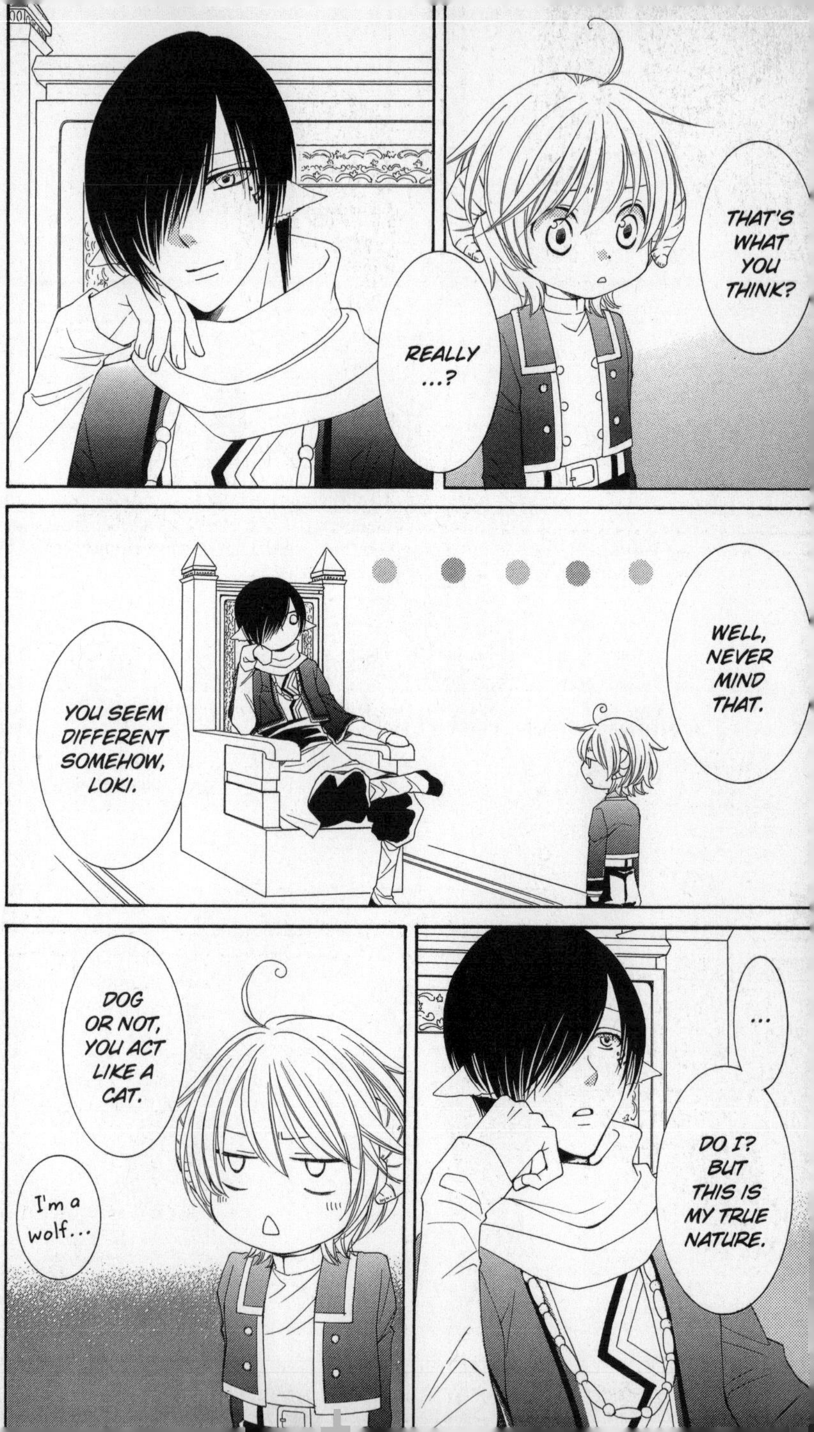
THAT'S WHAT YOU THINK?
REALLY ...?
WELL, NEVER MIND THAT.
YOU SEEM DIFFERENT SOMEHOW, LOKI.
...
DO I? BUT THIS IS MY TRUE NATURE.
DOG OR NOT, YOU ACT LIKE A CAT.
I'm a wolf...

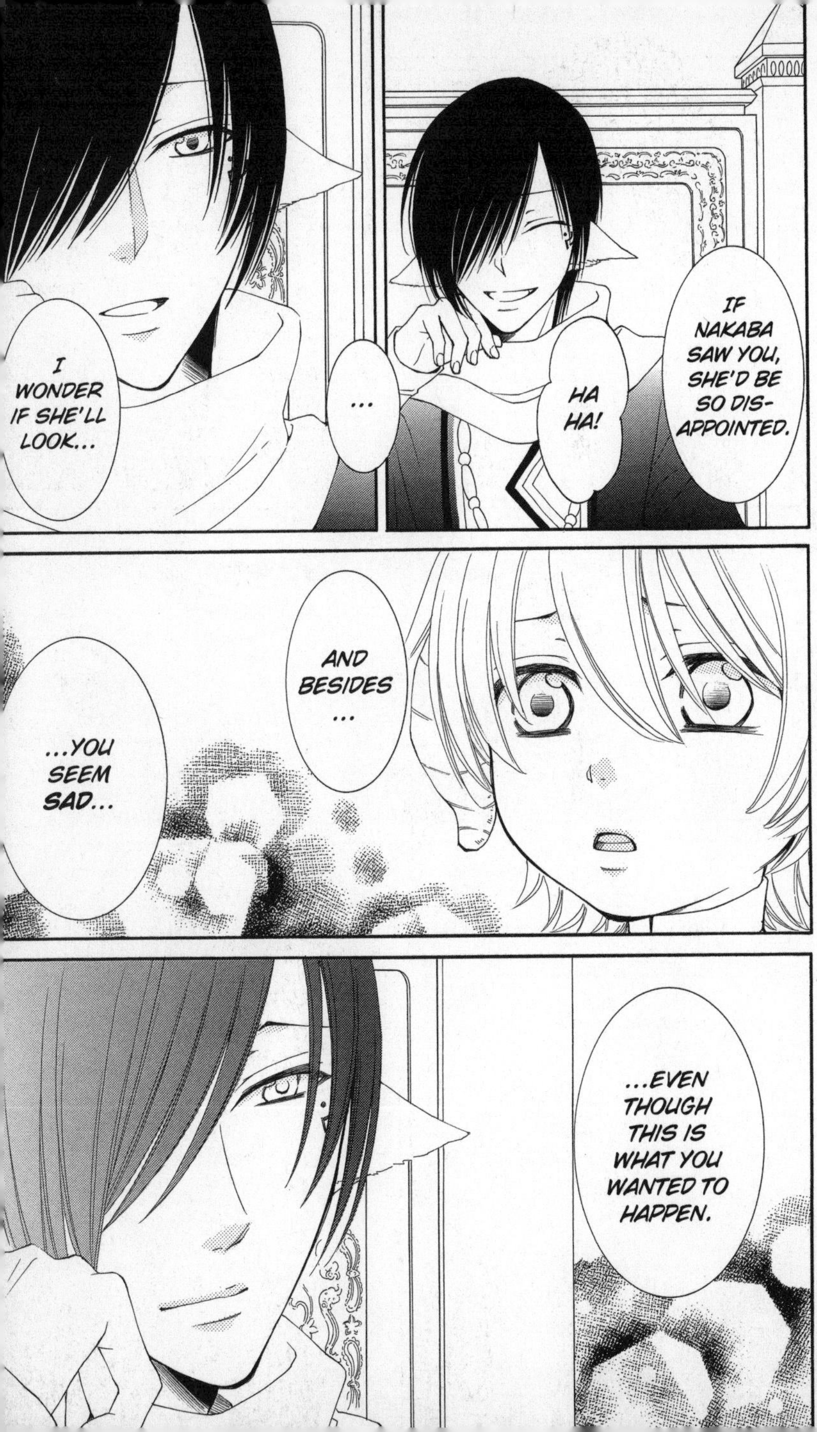
IF NAKABA SAW YOU, SHE'D BE SO DIS-APPOINTED.
HA HA!
...
I WONDER IF SHE'LL LOOK...
AND BESIDES...
...YOU SEEM SAD...
...EVEN THOUGH THIS IS WHAT YOU WANTED TO HAPPEN.

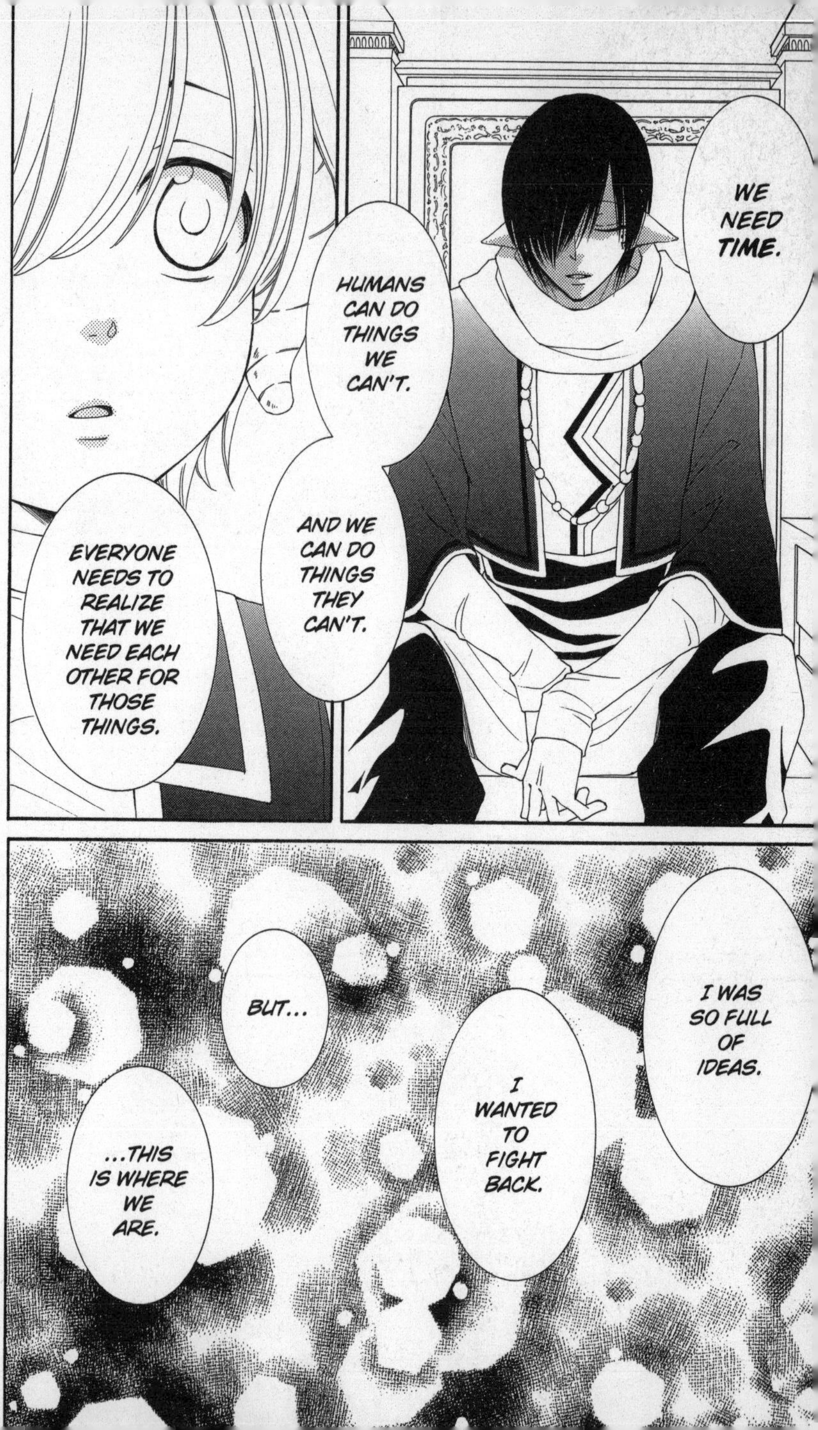
WE NEED TIME.
HUMANS CAN DO THINGS WE CAN'T.
AND WE CAN DO THINGS THEY CAN'T.
EVERYONE NEEDS TO REALIZE THAT WE NEED EACH OTHER FOR THOSE THINGS.
I WAS SO FULL OF IDEAS.
I WANTED TO FIGHT BACK.
BUT...
...THIS IS WHERE WE ARE.

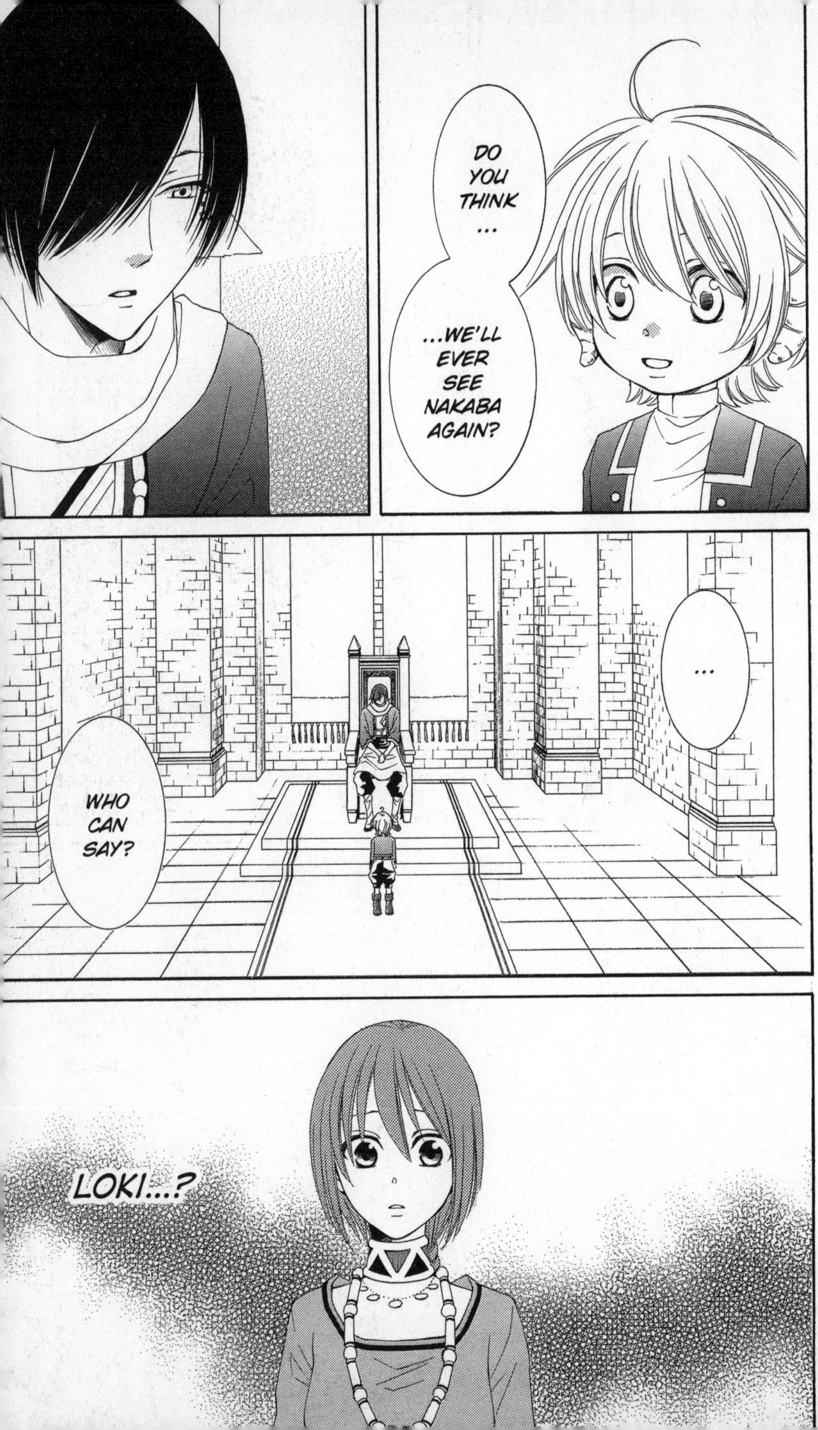
DO YOU THINK ...
...WE'LL EVER SEE NAKABA AGAIN?
...
WHO CAN SAY?
LOKI...?

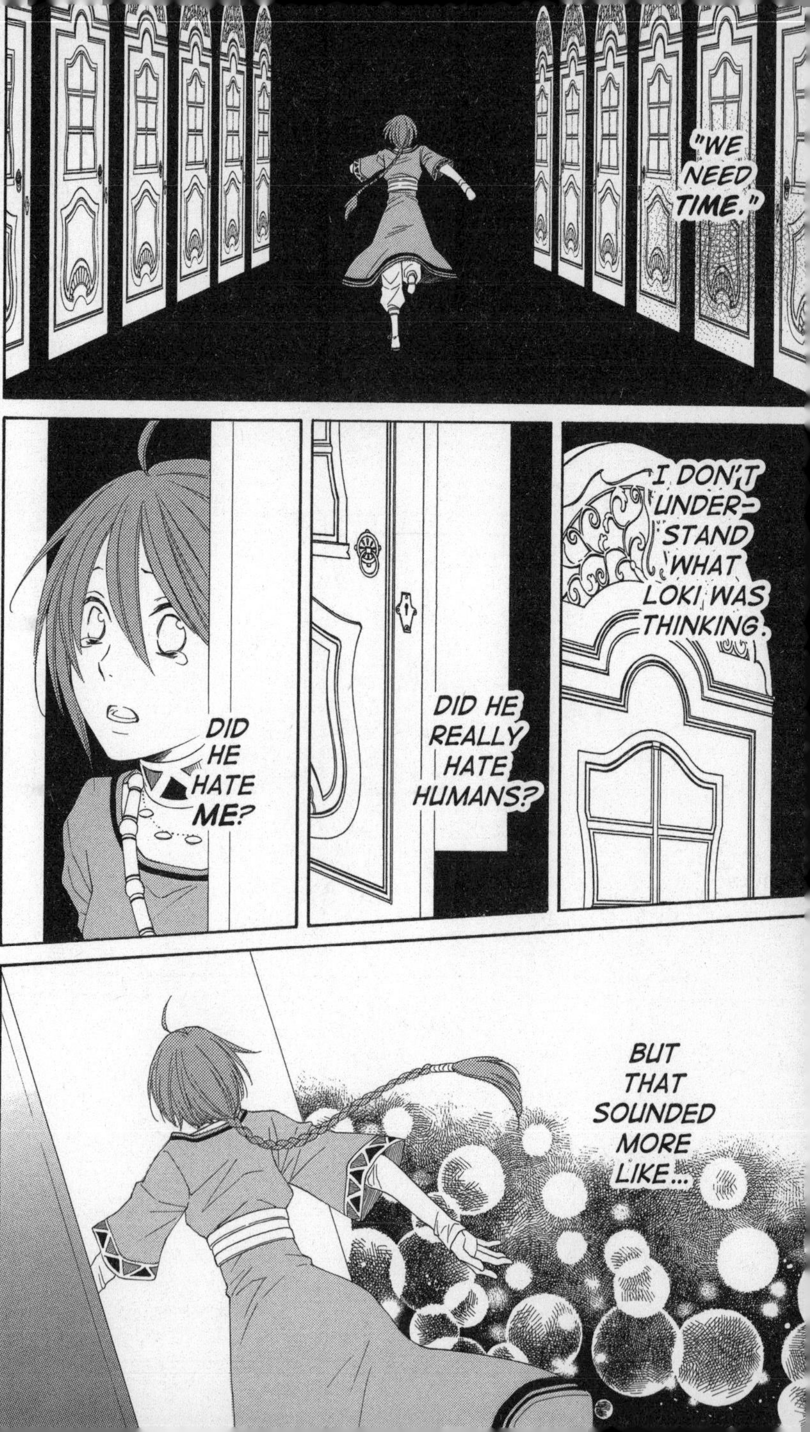
"WE NEED TIME."
I DON'T UNDER-STAND WHAT LOKI WAS THINKING.
DID HE REALLY HATE HUMANS?
DID HE HATE ME?
BUT THAT SOUNDED MORE LIKE...

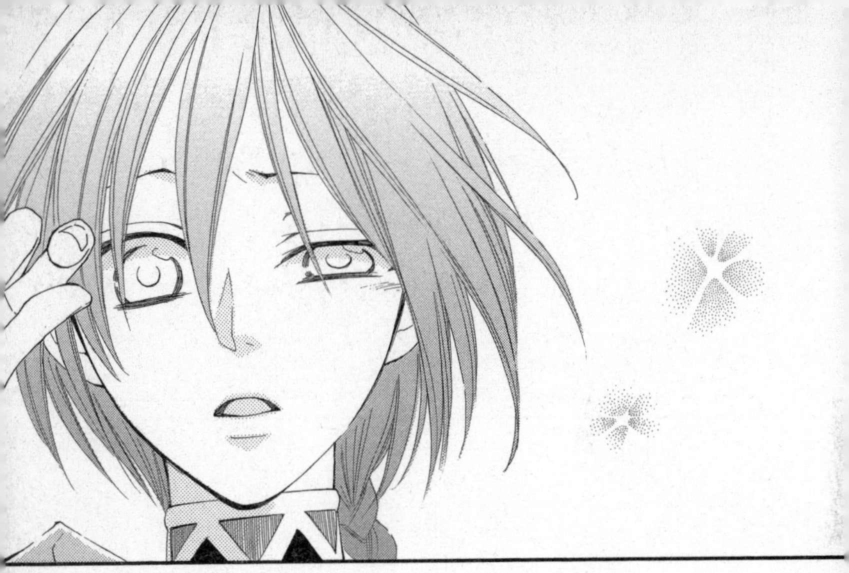
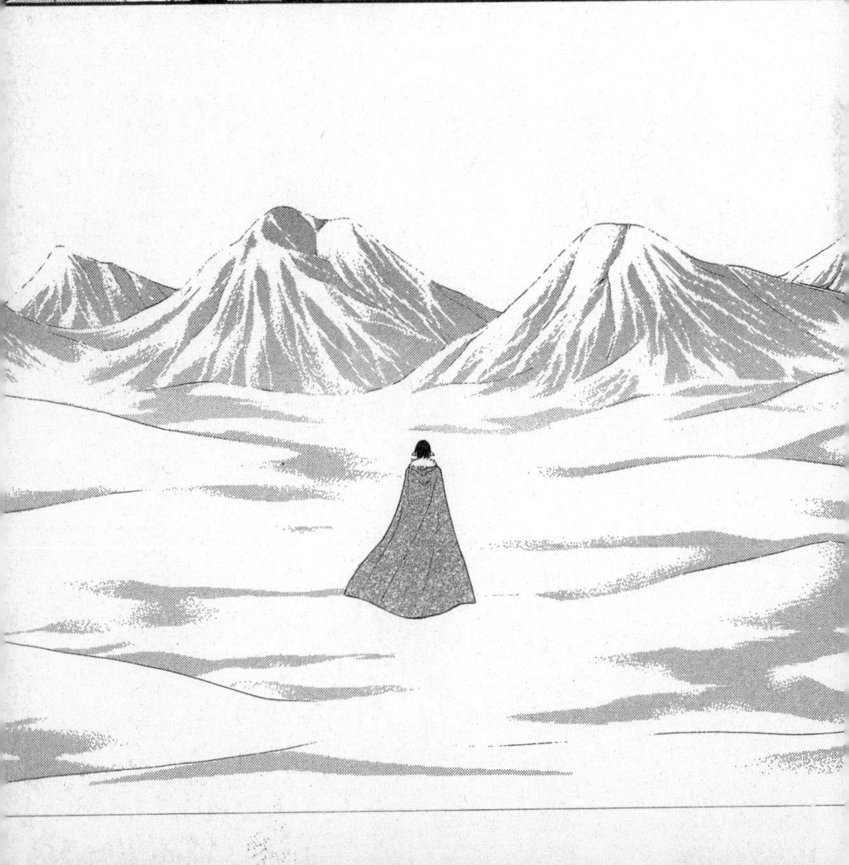

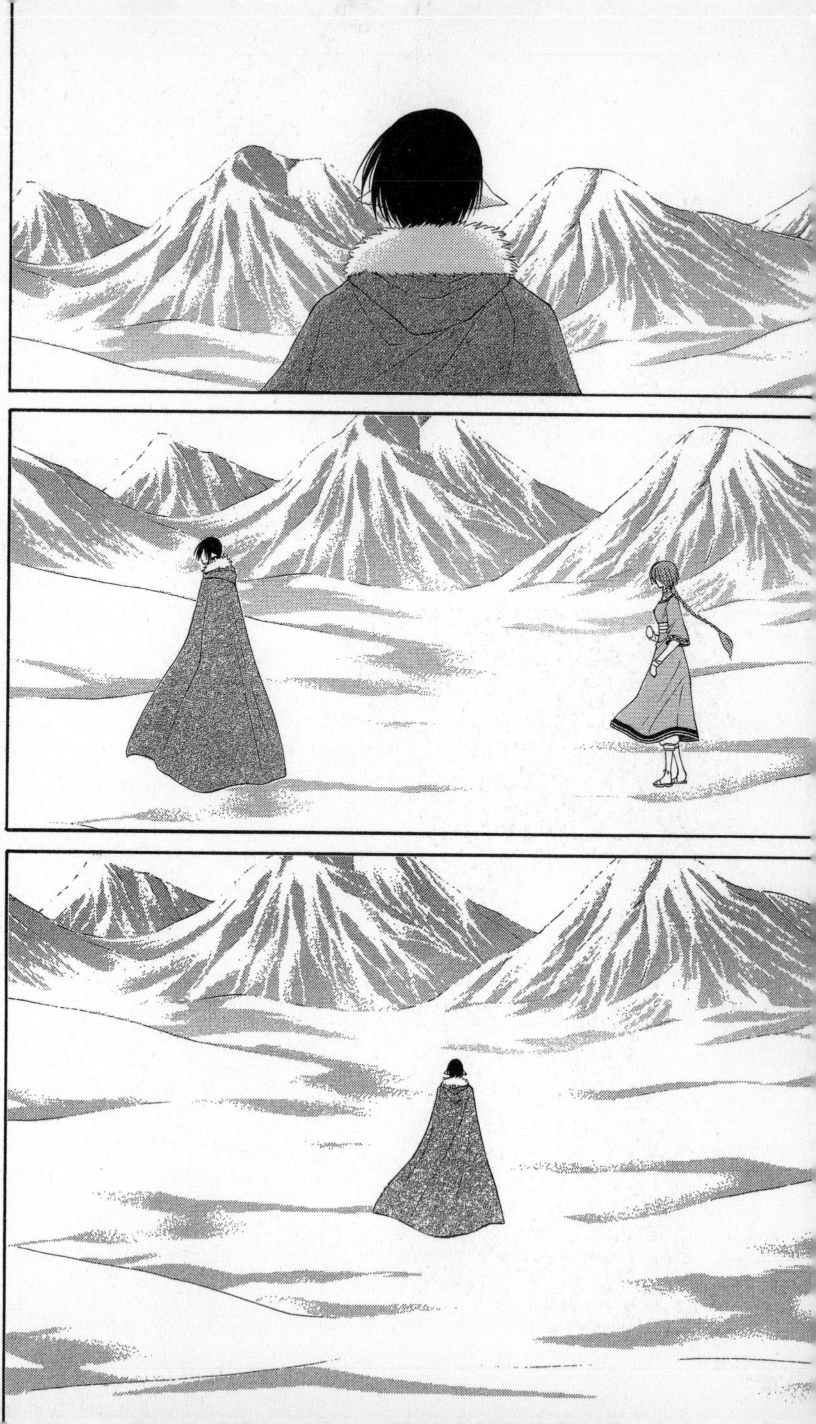

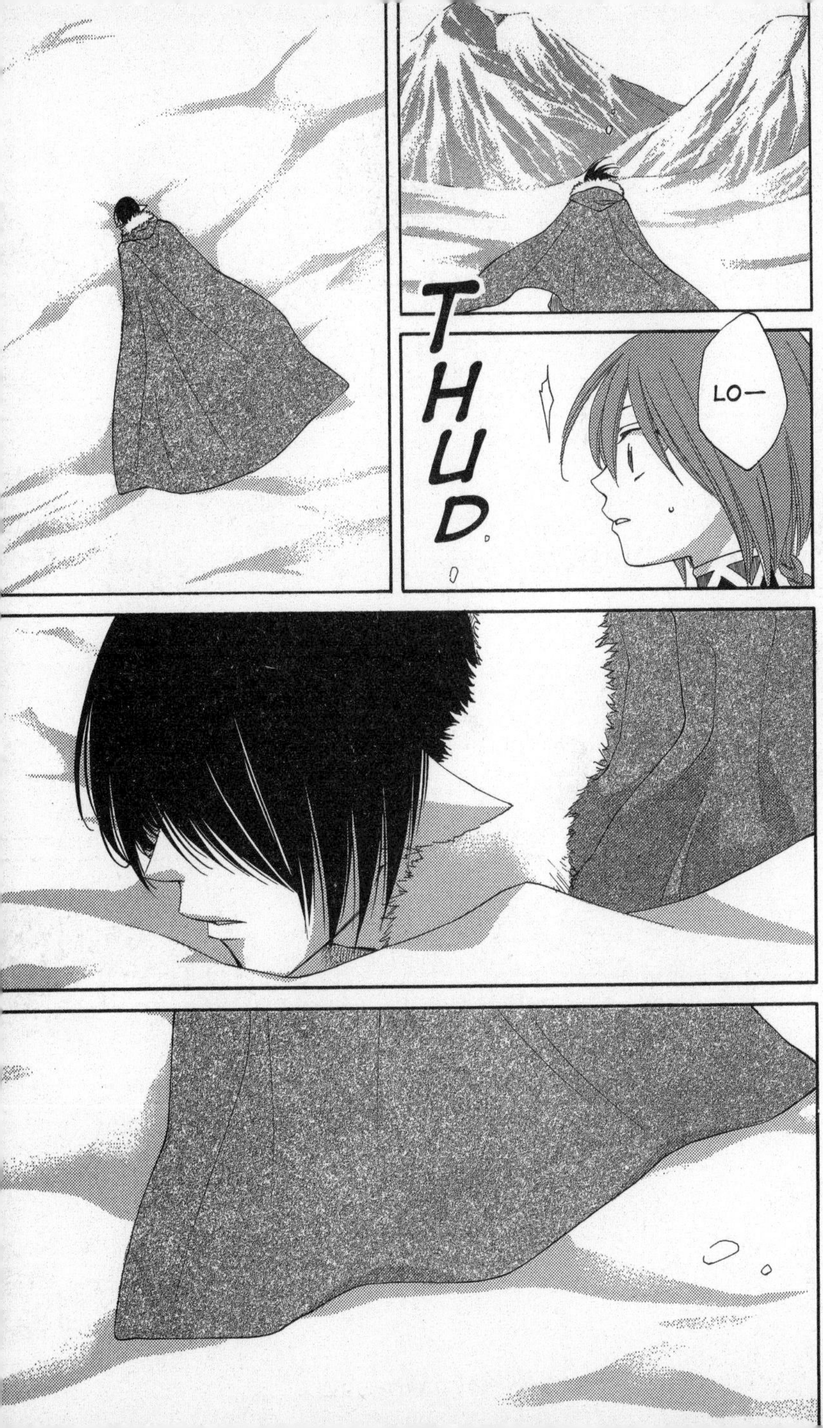
THUD
LO—

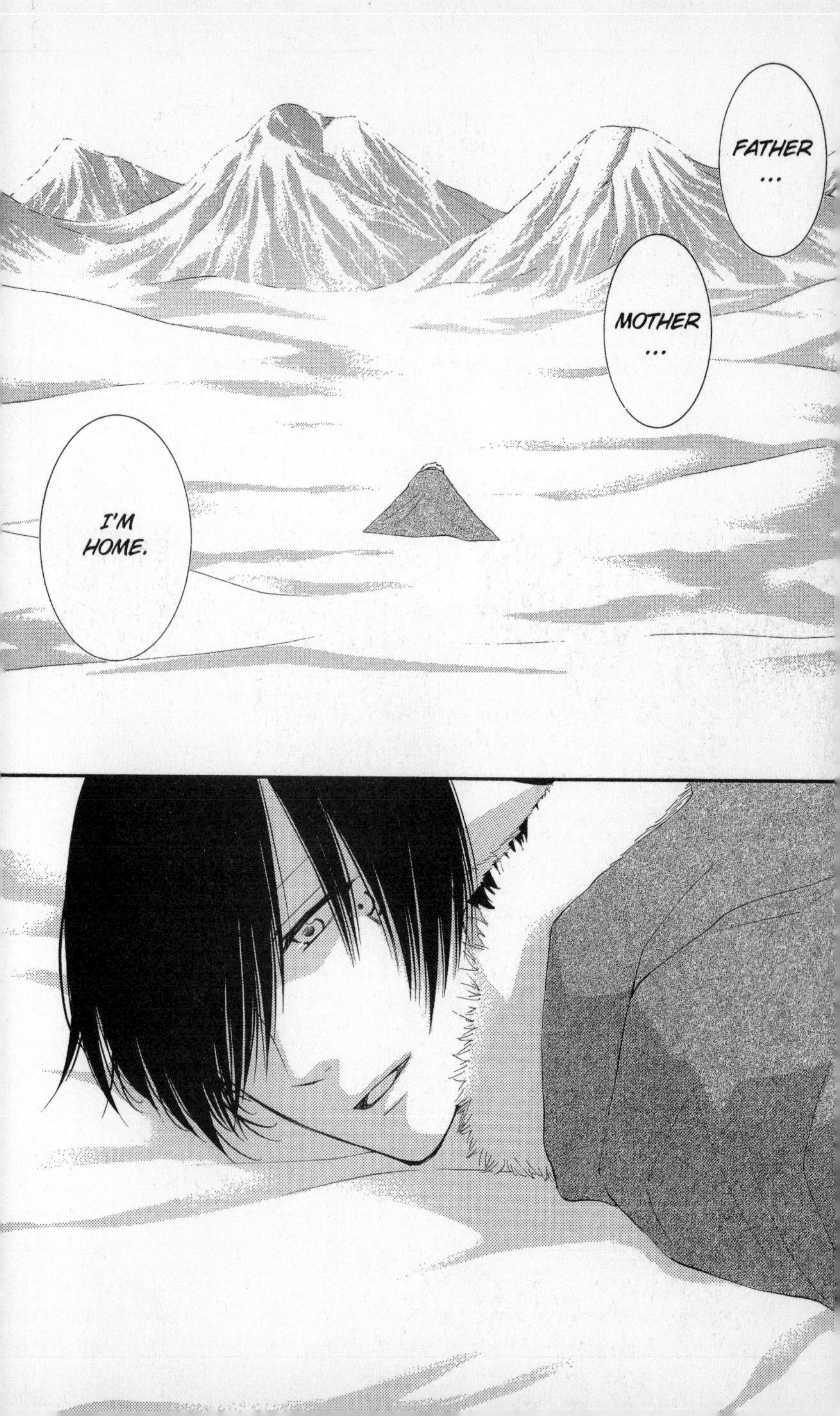
FATHER ...
MOTHER ...
I'M HOME.

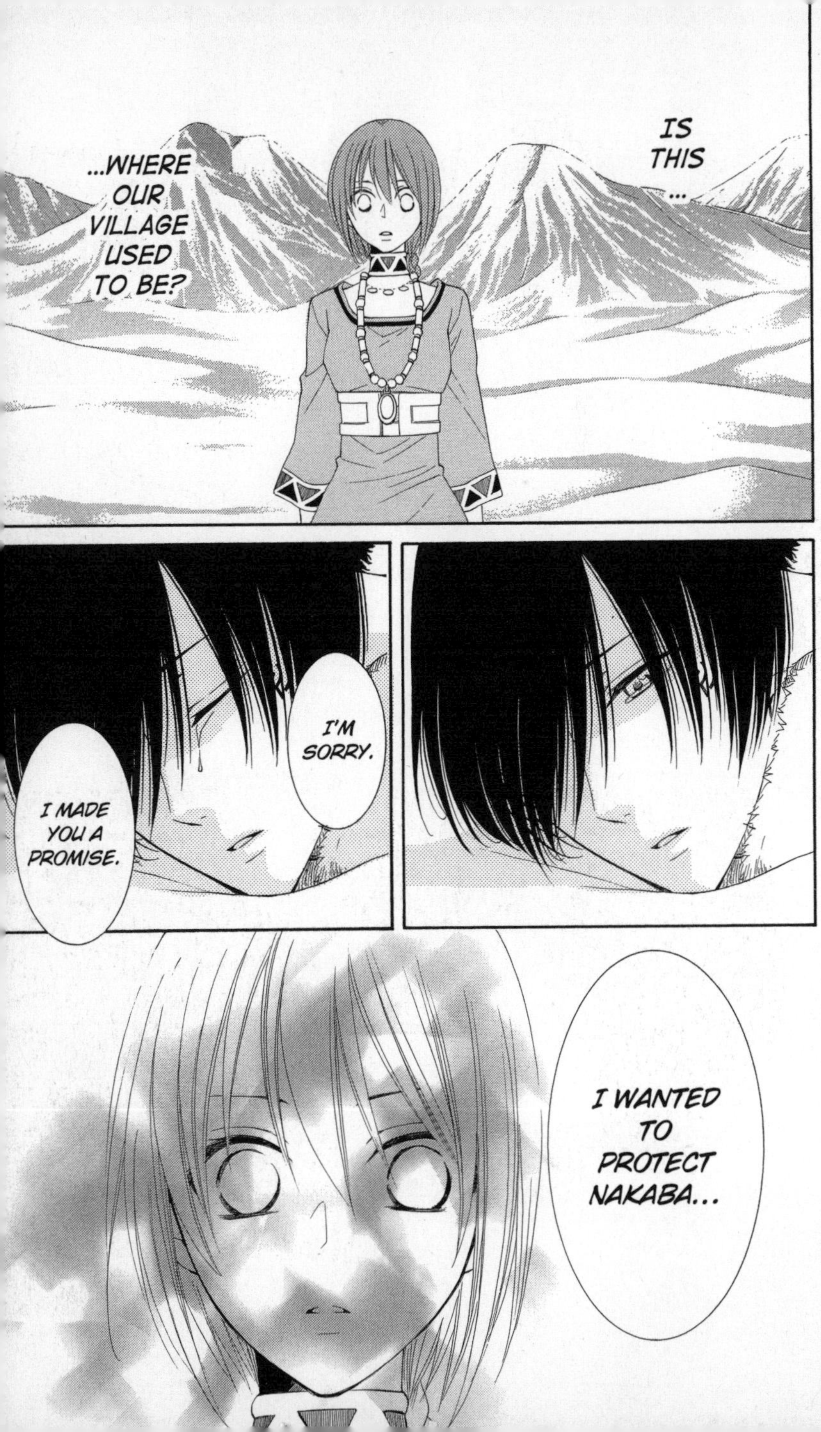
IS THIS ...
...WHERE OUR VILLAGE USED TO BE?
I'M SORRY.
I MADE YOU A PROMISE.
I WANTED TO PROTECT NAKABA...

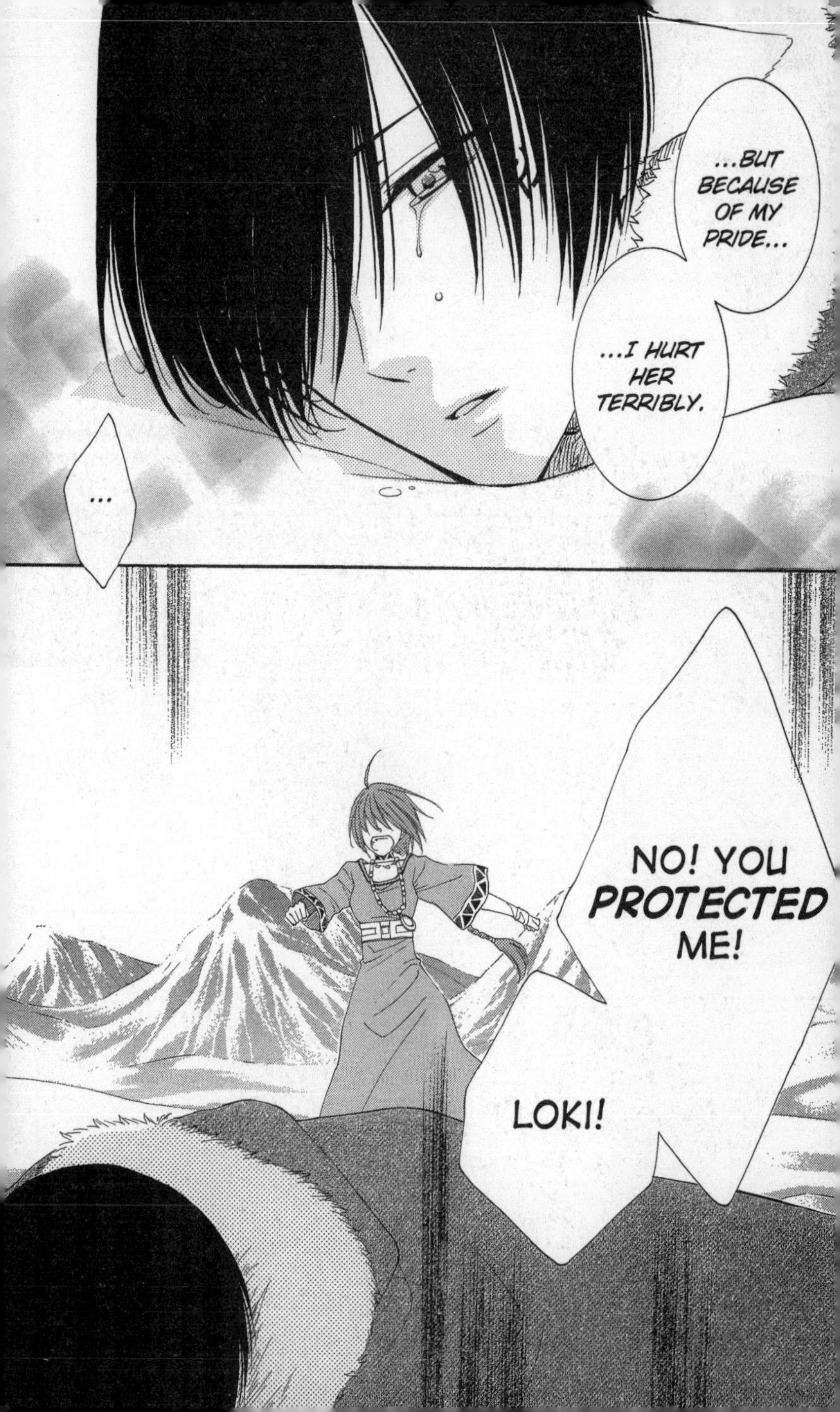
...BUT BECAUSE OF MY PRIDE...
...I HURT HER TERRIBLY.
...
NO! YOU PROTECTED ME!
LOKI!

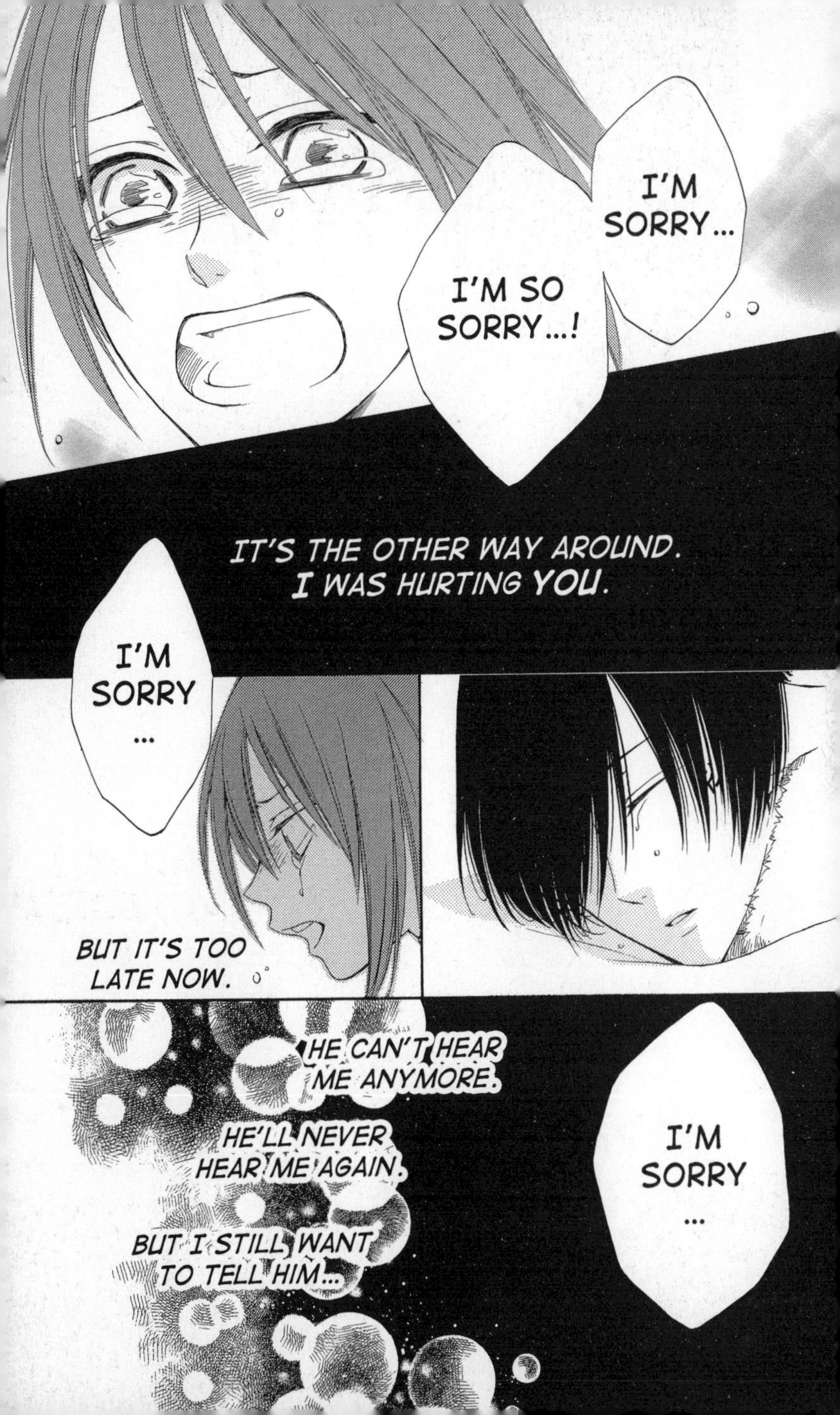
I'M SORRY...
I'M SO SORRY...!
IT'S THE OTHER WAY AROUND. I WAS HURTING YOU.
I'M SORRY ...
BUT IT'S TOO LATE NOW.
HE CAN'T HEAR ME ANYMORE.
HE'LL NEVER HEAR ME AGAIN.
BUT I STILL WANT TO TELL HIM...
I'M SORRY ...

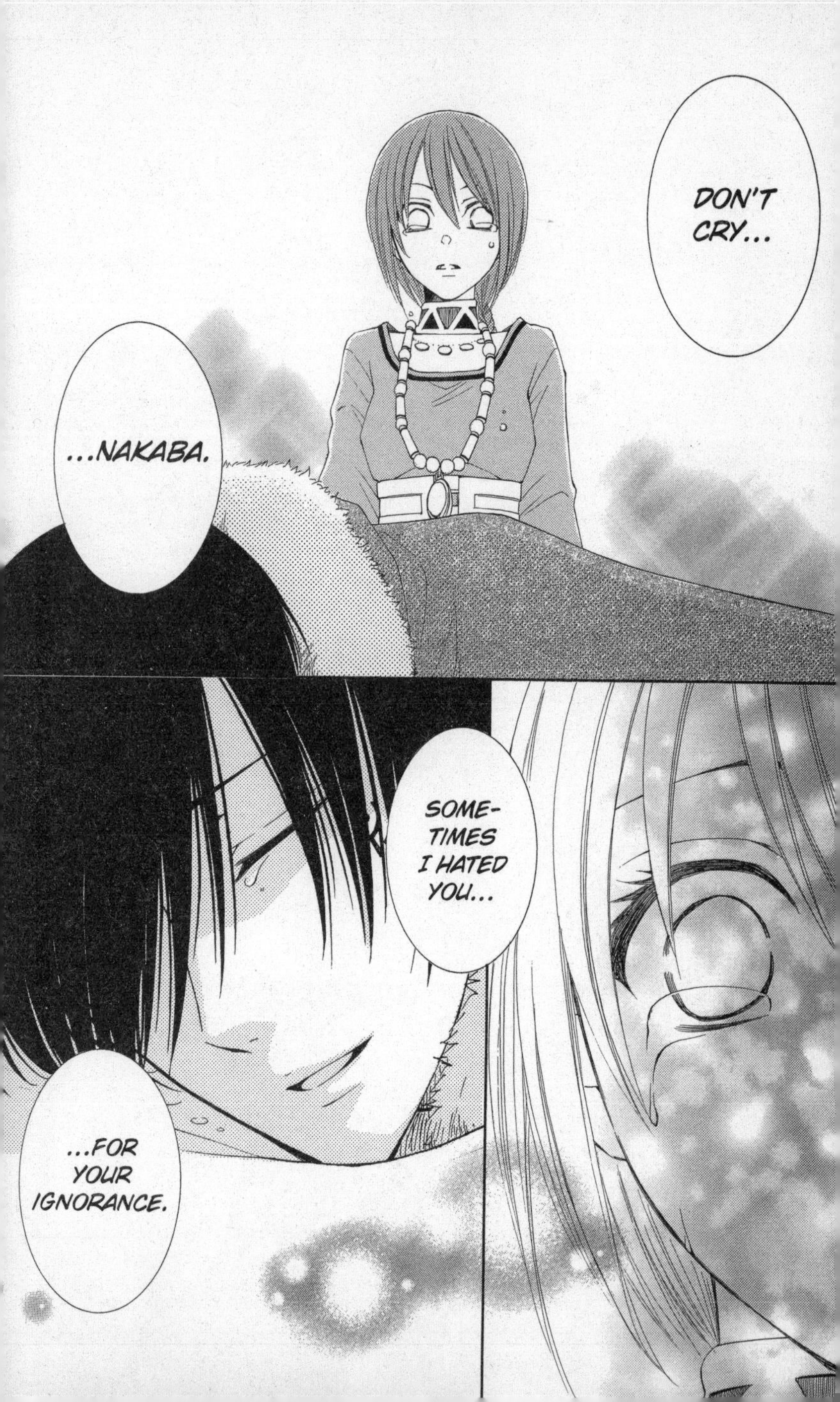
DON'T CRY...
...NAKABA.
SOME-TIMES I HATED YOU...
...FOR YOUR IGNORANCE.

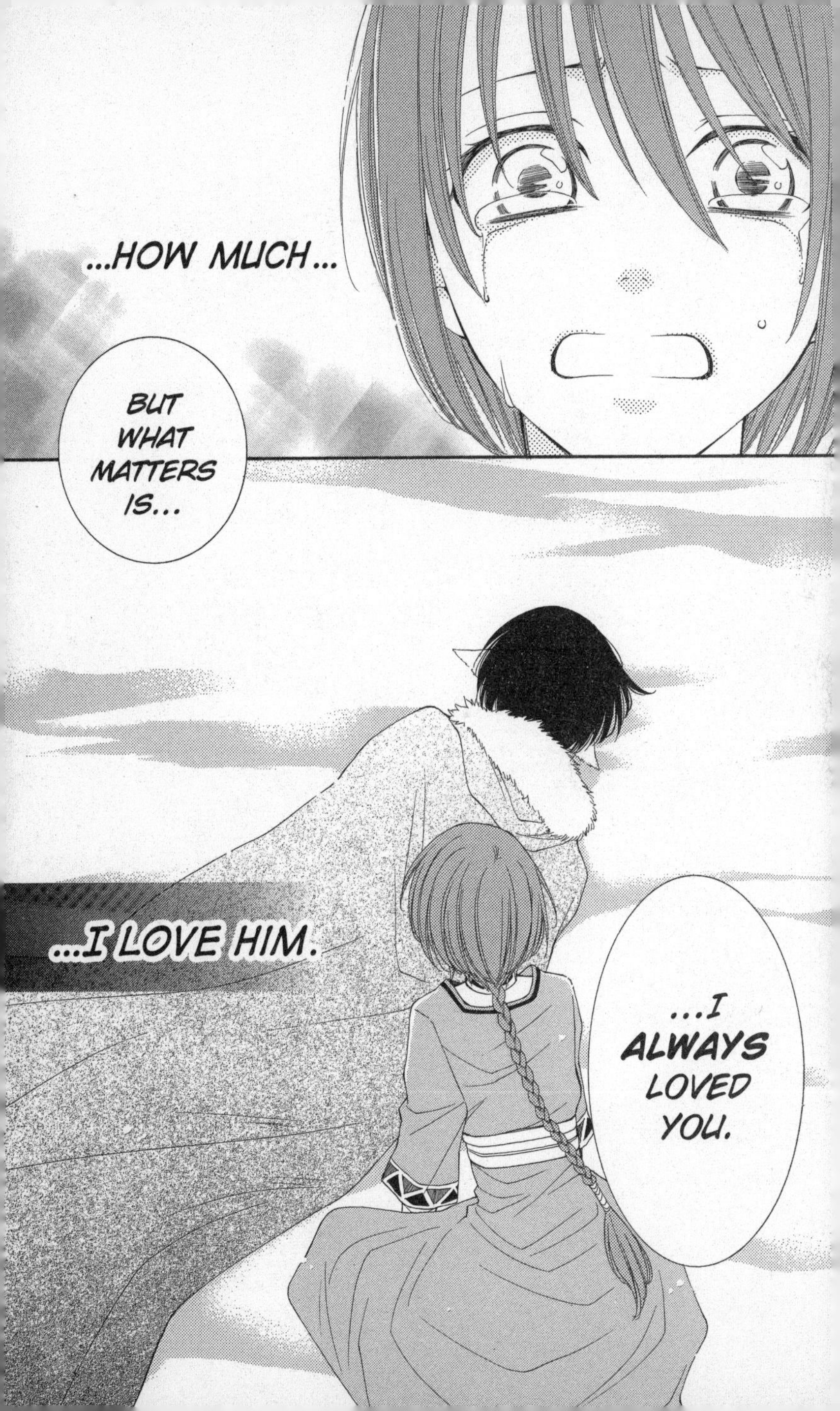
...HOW MUCH...
BUT WHAT MATTERS IS...
...I LOVE HIM.
...I ALWAYS LOVED YOU.

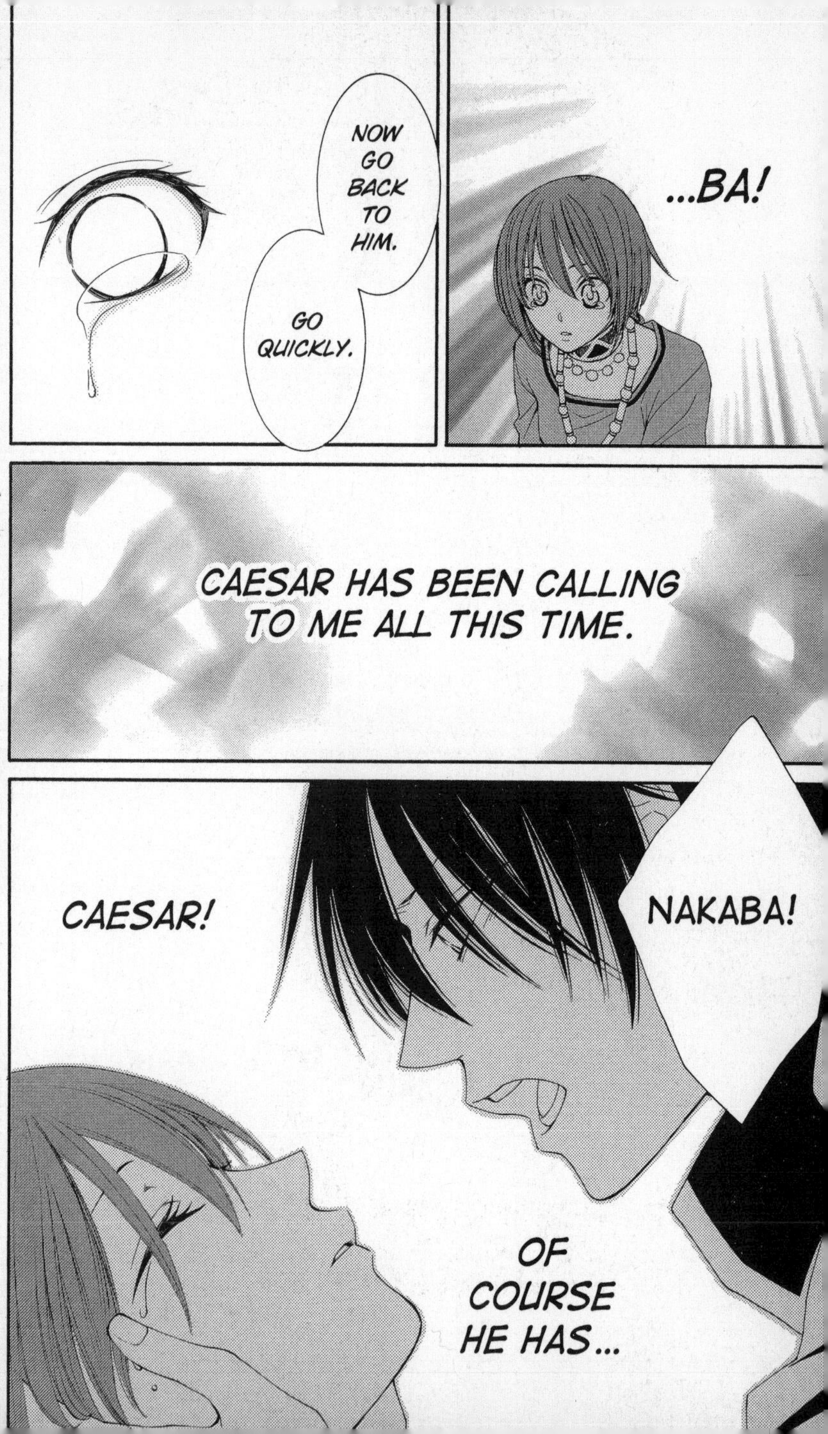

...BA!
NOW GO BACK TO HIM.
GO QUICKLY.
CAESAR HAS BEEN CALLING TO ME ALL THIS TIME.
NAKABA!
CAESAR!
OF COURSE HE HAS...

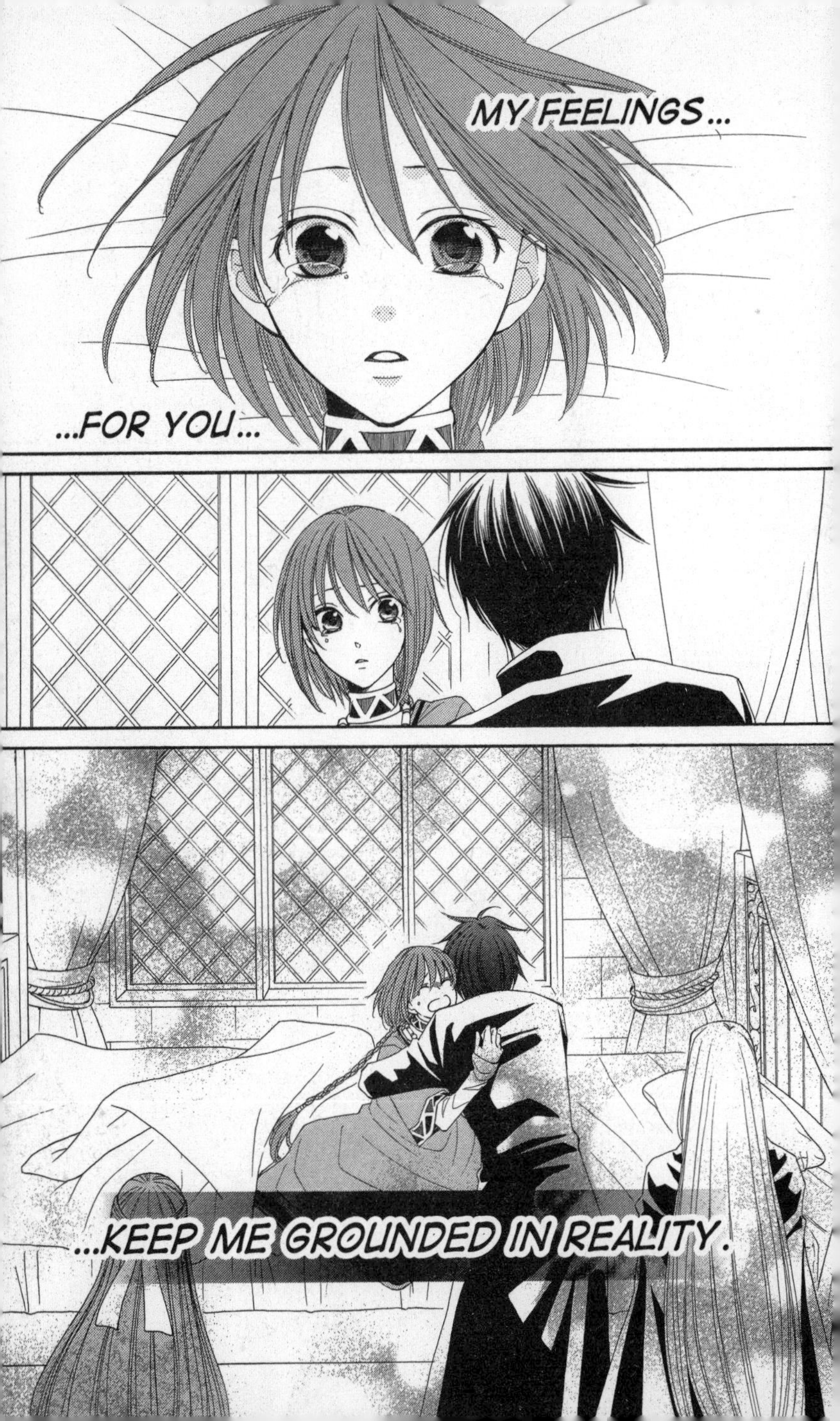
MY FEELINGS...
...FOR YOU...
...KEEP ME GROUNDED IN REALITY.

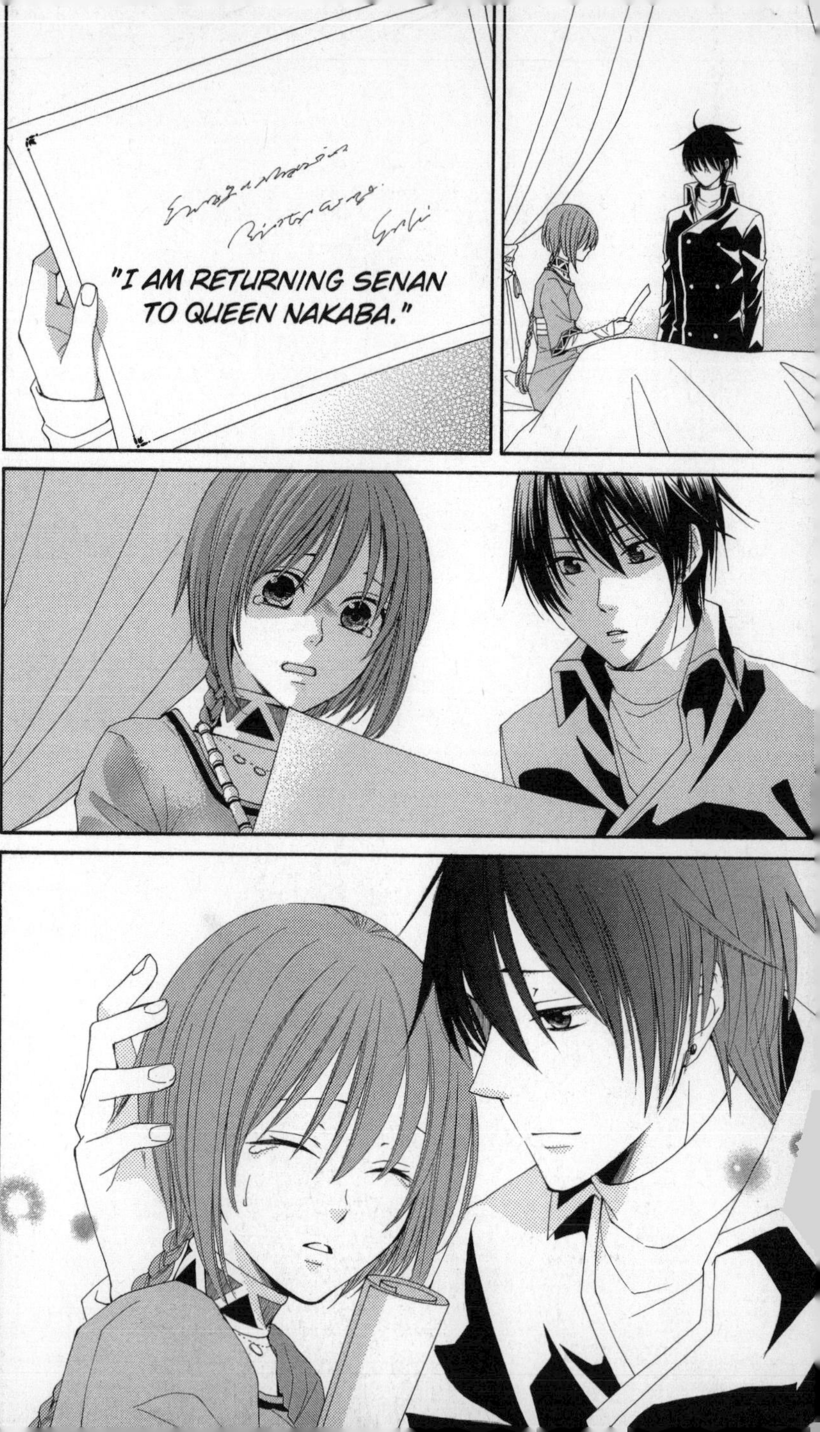
"I AM RETURNING SENAN TO QUEEN NAKABA."

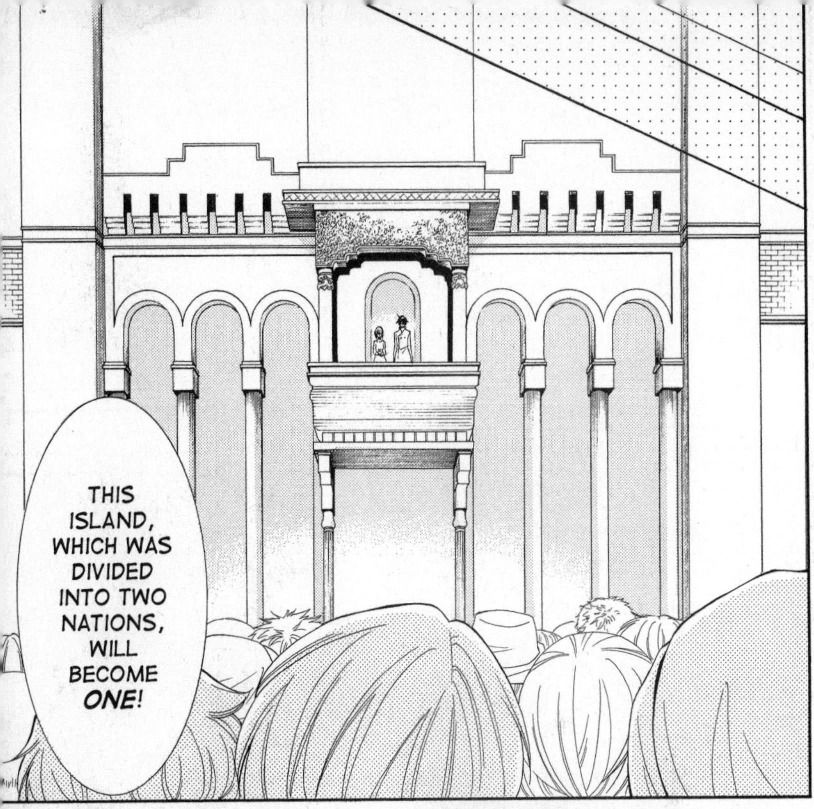
THIS ISLAND, WHICH WAS DIVIDED INTO TWO NATIONS, WILL BECOME ONE!
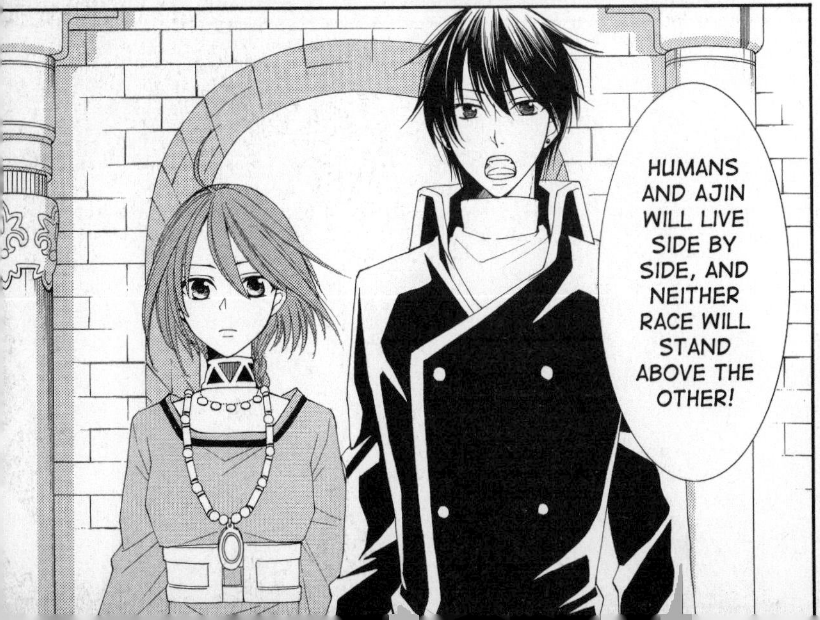
HUMANS AND AJIN WILL LIVE SIDE BY SIDE, AND NEITHER RACE WILL STAND ABOVE THE OTHER!

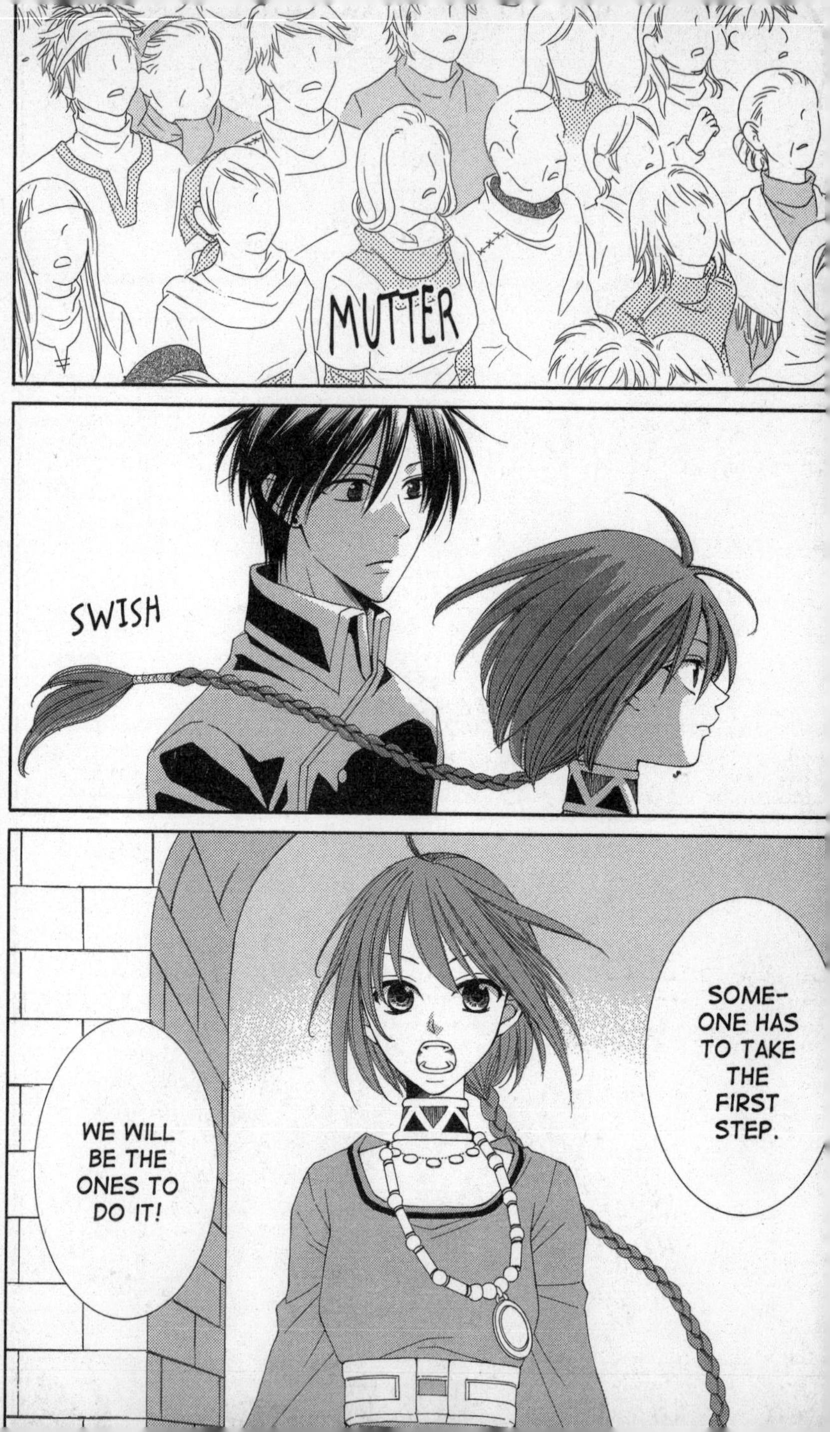
MUTTER
SWISH
SOME-ONE HAS TO TAKE THE FIRST STEP.
WE WILL BE THE ONES TO DO IT!

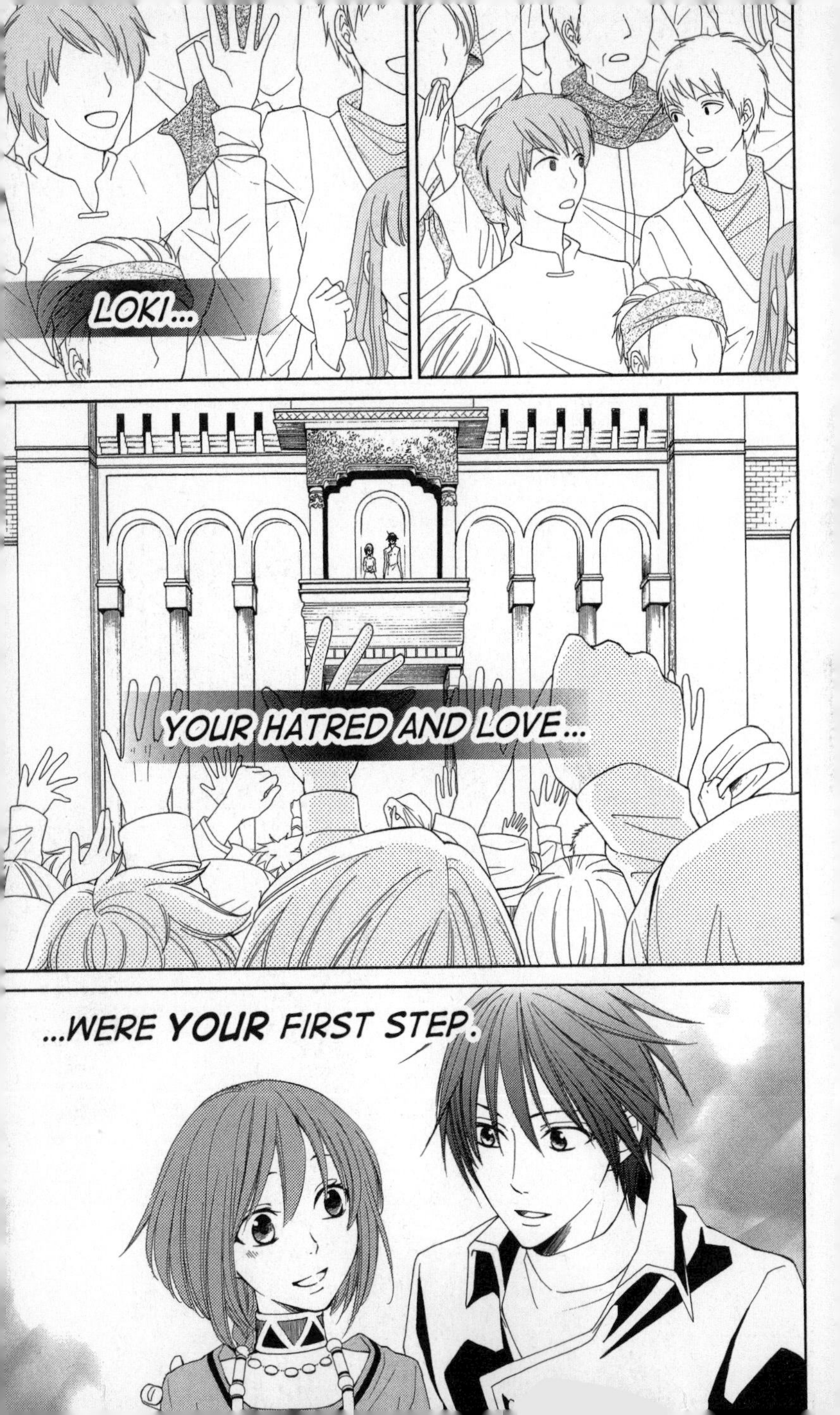
LOKI...
YOUR HATRED AND LOVE...
...WERE YOUR FIRST STEP.

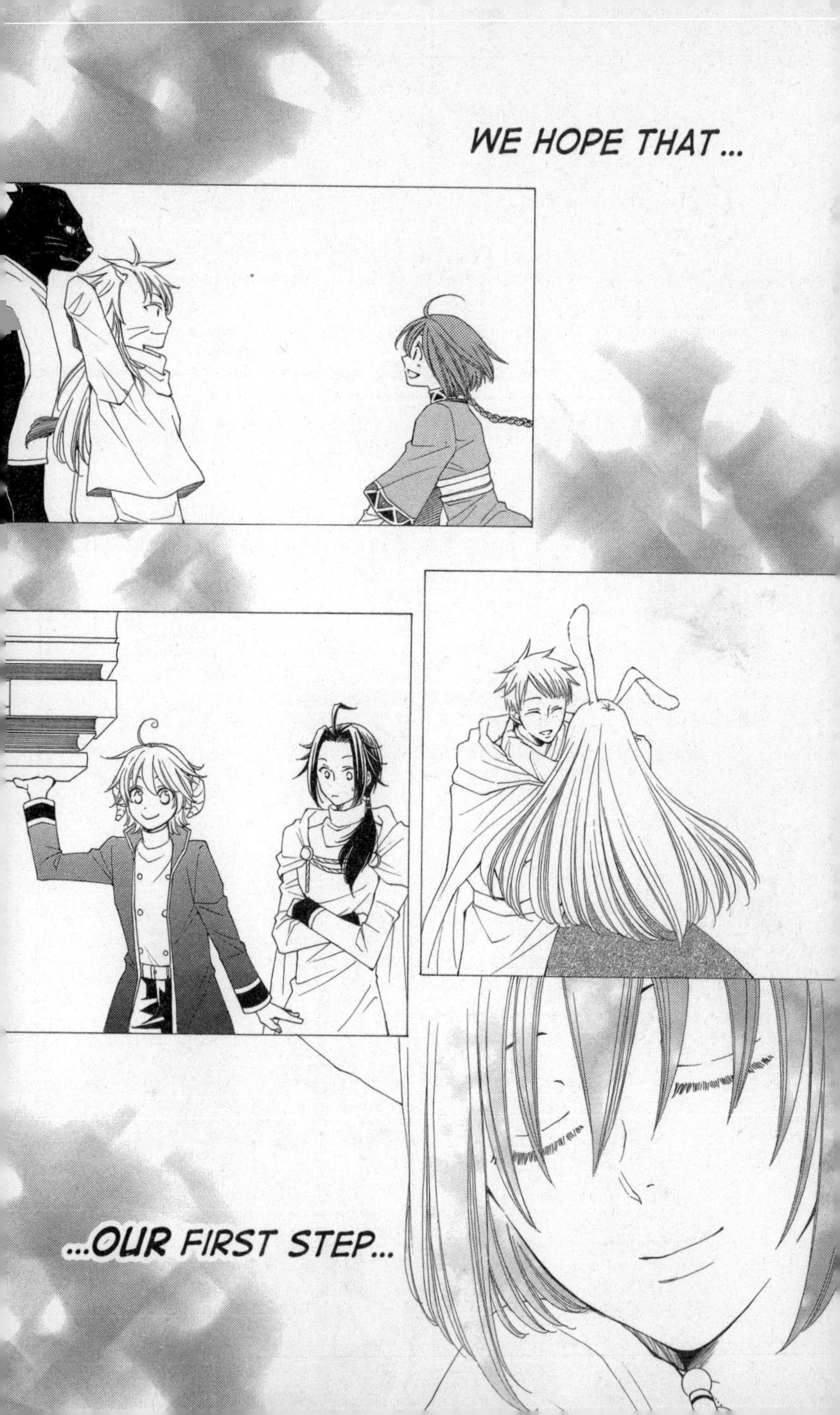
WE HOPE THAT...
...OUR FIRST STEP...

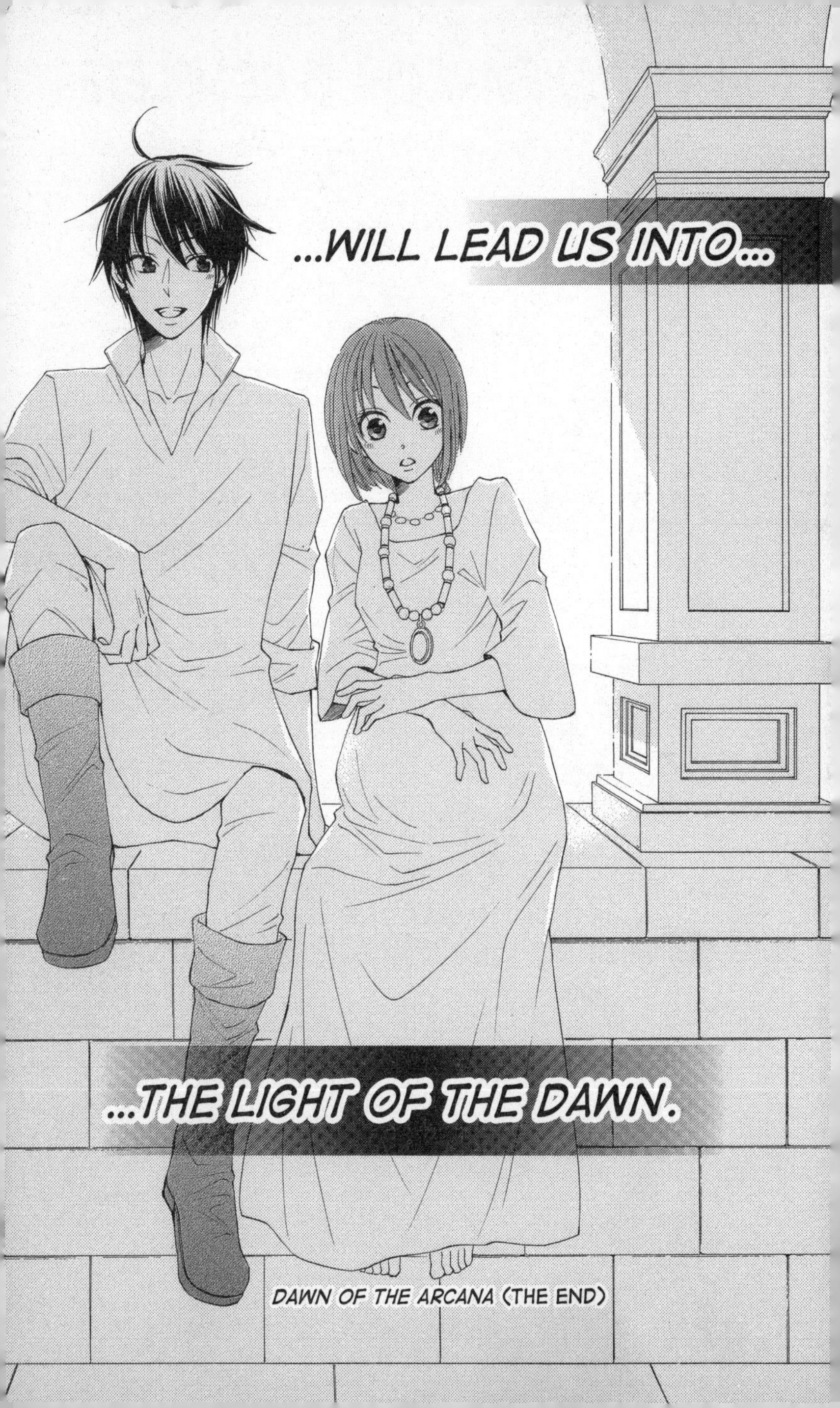
...WILL LEAD US INTO...
...THE LIGHT OF THE DAWN.
DAWN OF THE ARCANA (THE END)

DAWN OF THE ARCANA IS COMPLETE!

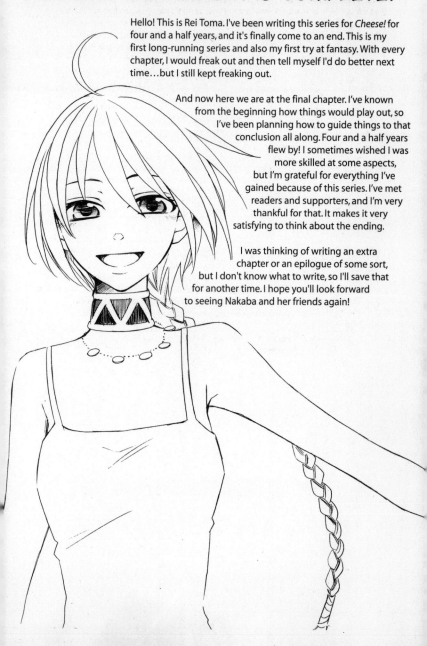

Hello! This is Rei Toma. I've been writing this series for *Cheese!* for four and a half years, and it's finally come to an end. This is my first long-running series and also my first try at fantasy. With every chapter, I would freak out and then tell myself I'd do better next time…but I still kept freaking out.

And now here we are at the final chapter. I've known from the beginning how things would play out, so I've been planning how to guide things to that conclusion all along. Four and a half years flew by! I sometimes wished I was more skilled at some aspects, but I'm grateful for everything I've gained because of this series. I've met readers and supporters, and I'm very thankful for that. It makes it very satisfying to think about the ending.

I was thinking of writing an extra chapter or an epilogue of some sort, but I don't know what to write, so I'll save that for another time. I hope you'll look forward to seeing Nakaba and her friends again!

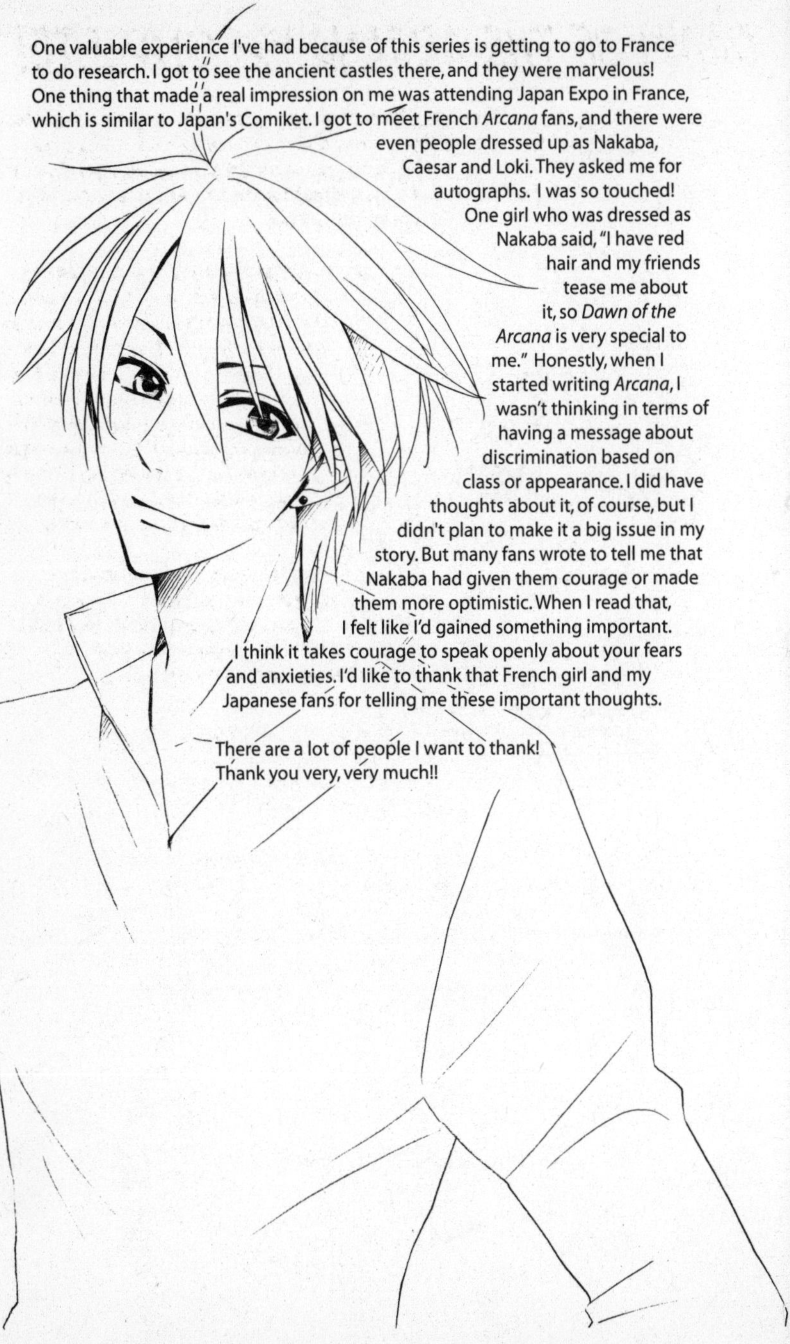

One valuable experience I've had because of this series is getting to go to France to do research. I got to see the ancient castles there, and they were marvelous! One thing that made a real impression on me was attending Japan Expo in France, which is similar to Japan's Comiket. I got to meet French *Arcana* fans, and there were even people dressed up as Nakaba, Caesar and Loki. They asked me for autographs. I was so touched! One girl who was dressed as Nakaba said, "I have red hair and my friends tease me about it, so *Dawn of the Arcana* is very special to me." Honestly, when I started writing *Arcana*, I wasn't thinking in terms of having a message about discrimination based on class or appearance. I did have thoughts about it, of course, but I didn't plan to make it a big issue in my story. But many fans wrote to tell me that Nakaba had given them courage or made them more optimistic. When I read that, I felt like I'd gained something important. I think it takes courage to speak openly about your fears and anxieties. I'd like to thank that French girl and my Japanese fans for telling me these important thoughts.

There are a lot of people I want to thank! Thank you very, very much!!

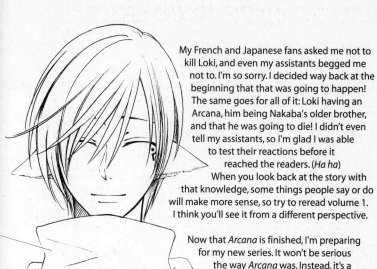

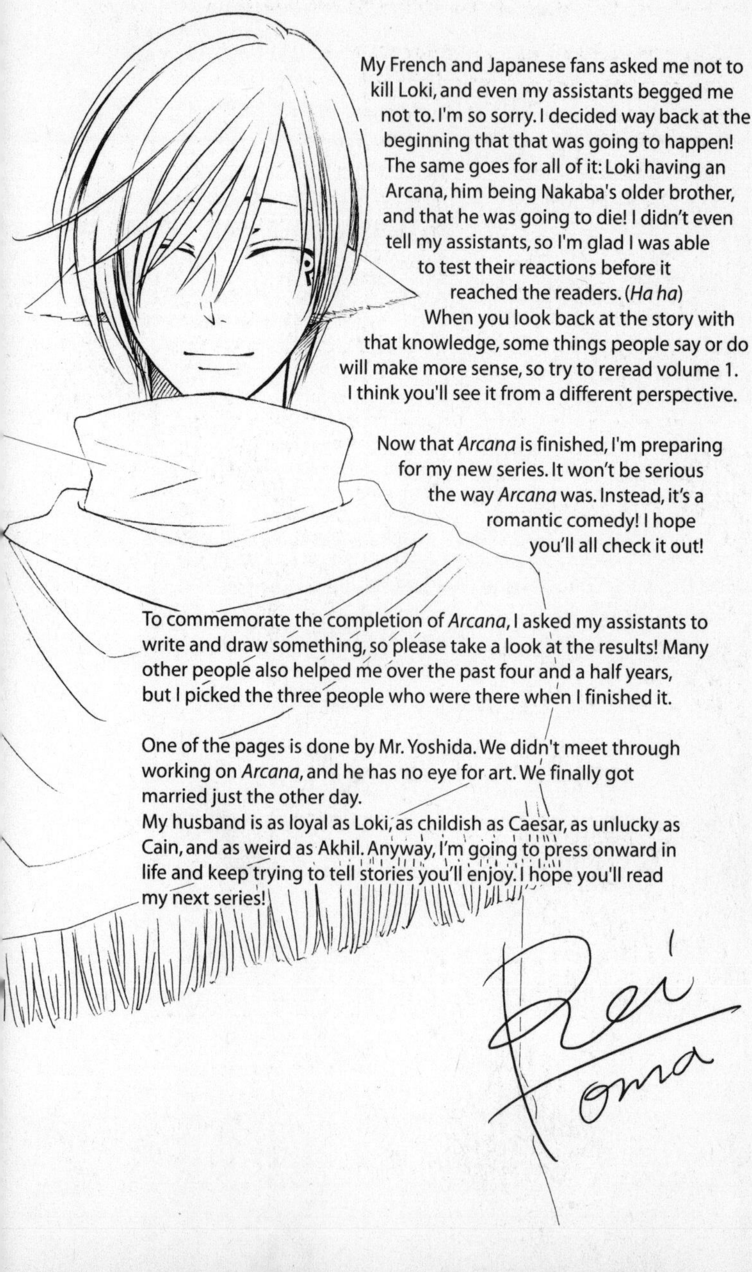

My French and Japanese fans asked me not to kill Loki, and even my assistants begged me not to. I'm so sorry. I decided way back at the beginning that that was going to happen! The same goes for all of it: Loki having an Arcana, him being Nakaba's older brother, and that he was going to die! I didn't even tell my assistants, so I'm glad I was able to test their reactions before it reached the readers. (*Ha ha*) When you look back at the story with that knowledge, some things people say or do will make more sense, so try to reread volume 1. I think you'll see it from a different perspective.

Now that *Arcana* is finished, I'm preparing for my new series. It won't be serious the way *Arcana* was. Instead, it's a romantic comedy! I hope you'll all check it out!

To commemorate the completion of *Arcana*, I asked my assistants to write and draw something, so please take a look at the results! Many other people also helped me over the past four and a half years, but I picked the three people who were there when I finished it.

One of the pages is done by Mr. Yoshida. We didn't meet through working on *Arcana*, and he has no eye for art. We finally got married just the other day.
My husband is as loyal as Loki, as childish as Caesar, as unlucky as Cain, and as weird as Akhil. Anyway, I'm going to press onward in life and keep trying to tell stories you'll enjoy. I hope you'll read my next series!

Rei Toma

GOOD JOB ON THE *ARCANA* SERIES!!

I met Toma when we were students over ten years ago. She doesn't talk about herself very much, but I'd like to show you a side of her you may not know about!!

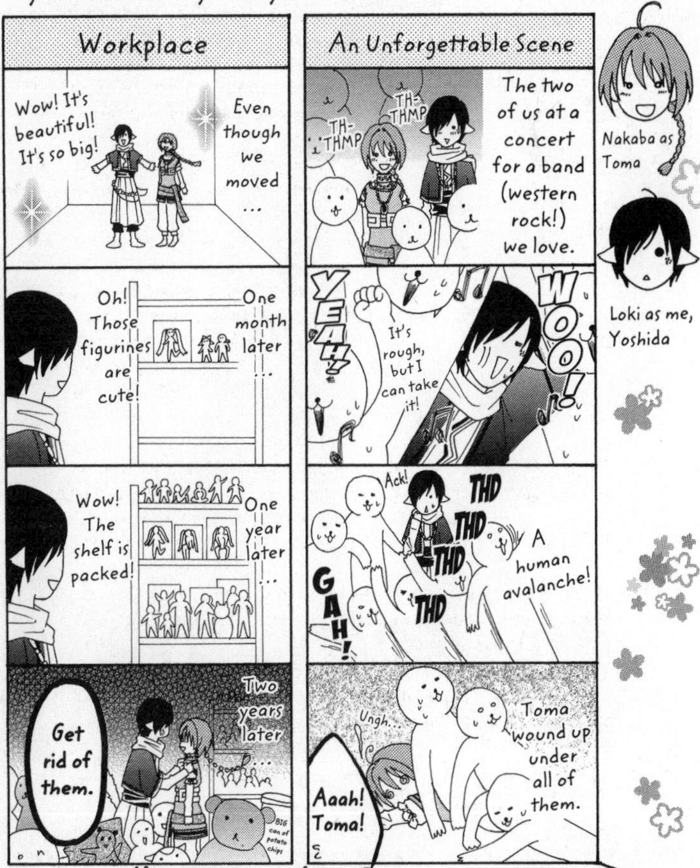
Nakaba as Toma
Loki as me, Yoshida
An Unforgettable Scene
The two of us at a concert for a band (western rock!) we love.
TH-THMP
TH-THMP
WOO!
It's rough, but I can take it!
YEAH!
A human avalanche!
THD
THD
THD
THD
Ack!
GAH!
Toma wound up under all of them.
Ungh...
Aaah! Toma!
Workplace
Even though we moved...
Wow! It's beautiful! It's so big!
One month later...
Oh! Those figurines are cute!
One year later...
Wow! The shelf is packed!
Two years later...
BIG can of potato chips
Get rid of them.

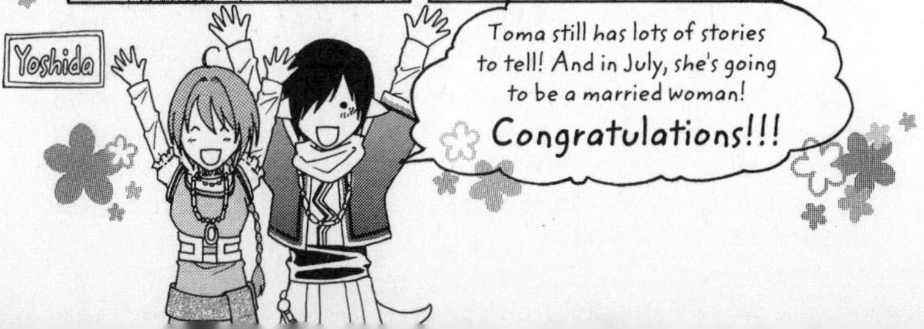
Yoshida
Toma still has lots of stories to tell! And in July, she's going to be a married woman!
Congratulations!!!

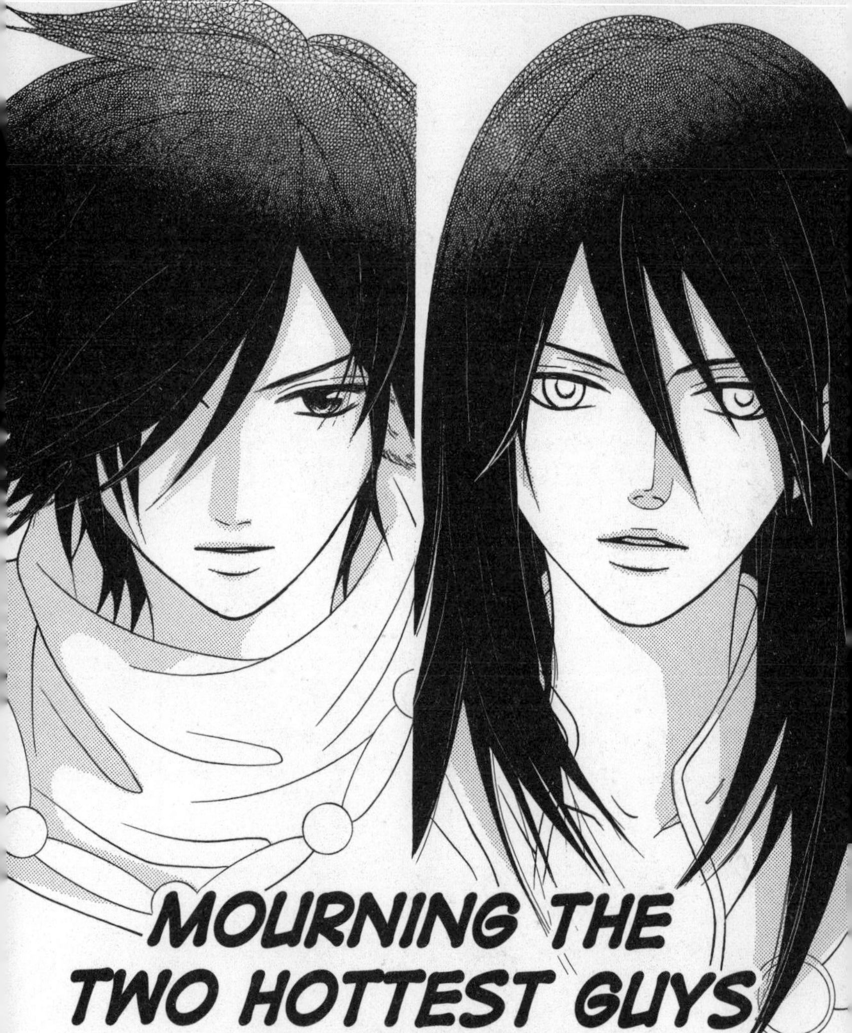

MOURNING THE TWO HOTTEST GUYS IN ARCANA

"GIVE BACK THE PEOPLE I LOVE!!"

Great work on this series! I am truly honored to have been able to work so closely with you. I'll keep supporting you, both as a reader and as an assistant! Thank you for this opportunity. It's still too difficult for me to read the final chapter, even though I helped work on it. I might not be able to read this volume through the tears...

Jun Toura

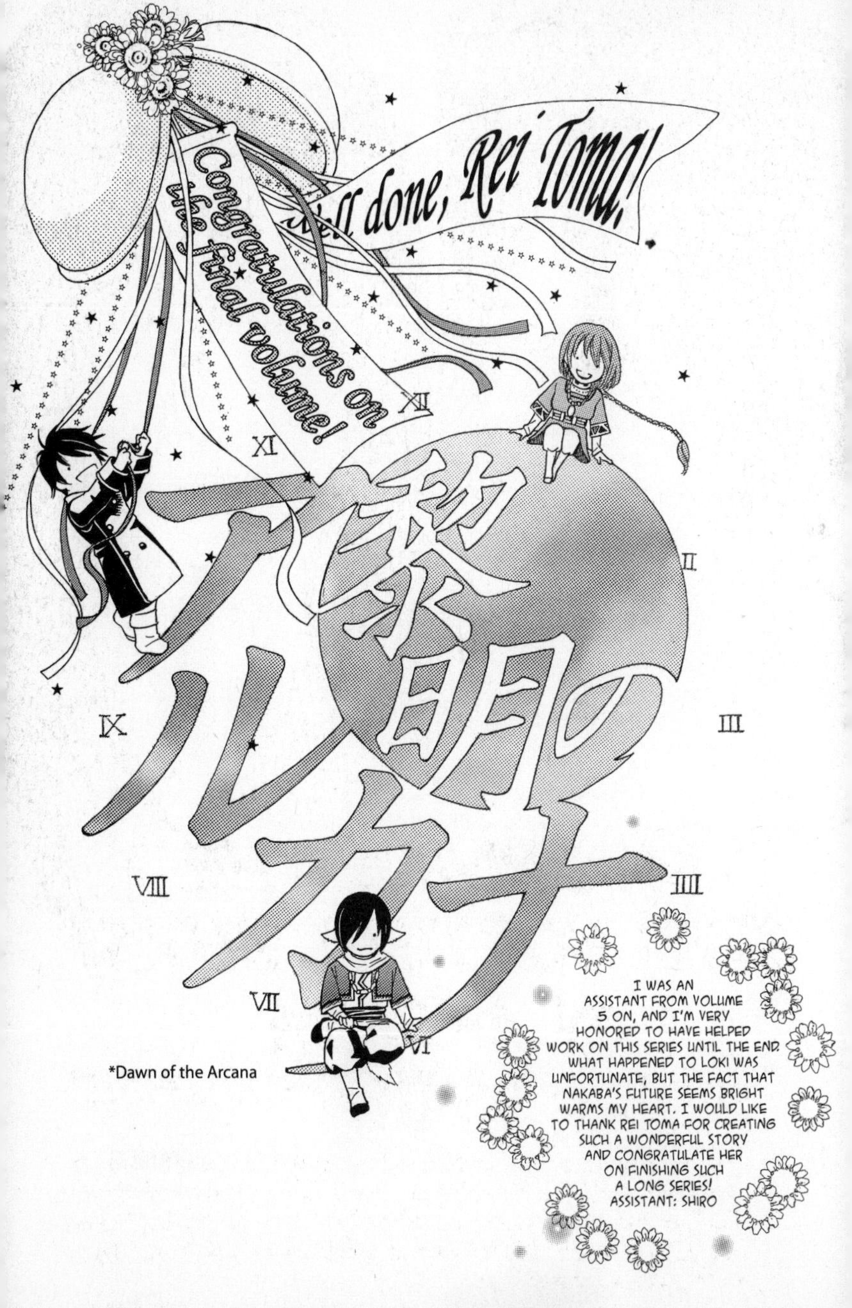
Well done, Rei Toma!
Congratulations on the final volume!
黎明のアルカナ
I WAS AN ASSISTANT FROM VOLUME 5 ON, AND I'M VERY HONORED TO HAVE HELPED WORK ON THIS SERIES UNTIL THE END. WHAT HAPPENED TO LOKI WAS UNFORTUNATE, BUT THE FACT THAT NAKABA'S FUTURE SEEMS BRIGHT WARMS MY HEART. I WOULD LIKE TO THANK REI TOMA FOR CREATING SUCH A WONDERFUL STORY AND CONGRATULATE HER ON FINISHING SUCH A LONG SERIES!
ASSISTANT: SHIRO

*Dawn of the Arcana

To all of my readers, all those
who helped me, and all
those who supported me,
thank you very much!

Send your letters here: ↓

Rei Toma
c/o Dawn of the Arcana Editor
VIZ Media
P.O. Box 77010
San Francisco, CA 94107

We're finally at the final volume! To all of you who gave me your support, thank you very much!

–Rei Toma

Rei Toma has been drawing since childhood, but she only began drawing manga because of her graduation project in design school. When she drew a short-story manga, *Help Me, Dentist,* for the first time, it attracted a publisher's attention and she made her debut right away. Her magnificent art style became popular, and after she debuted as a manga artist, she became known as an illustrator for novels and video game character designs. Her current manga series, *Dawn of the Arcana,* is her first long-running manga series, and it has been a hit in Japan, selling over a million copies.

DAWN OF THE ARCANA
VOLUME 13
Shojo Beat Edition

STORY AND ART BY
REI TOMA

REIMEI NO ARCANA Vol. 13
by Rei TOMA

Original Japanese edition published by SHOGAKUKAN.
English translation rights in the United States of America, Canada, United Kingdom, Ireland, Australia and New Zealand arranged with SHOGAKUKAN.

English Adaptation/Ysabet MacFarlane
Translation/JN Productions
Touch-up Art & Lettering/Freeman Wong
Design/Yukiko Whitley
Editor/Amy Yu

Printed in Canada

Published by VIZ Media, LLC
P.O. Box 77010
San Francisco, CA 94107

10 9 8 7 6 5 4 3 2 1
First printing, September 2014

www.viz.com www.shojobeat.com

RATED T FOR TEEN

PARENTAL ADVISORY
DAWN OF THE ARCANA is rated T for Teen and is recommended for ages 13 and up. This volume contains suggestive themes and fantasy violence.

ratings.viz.com

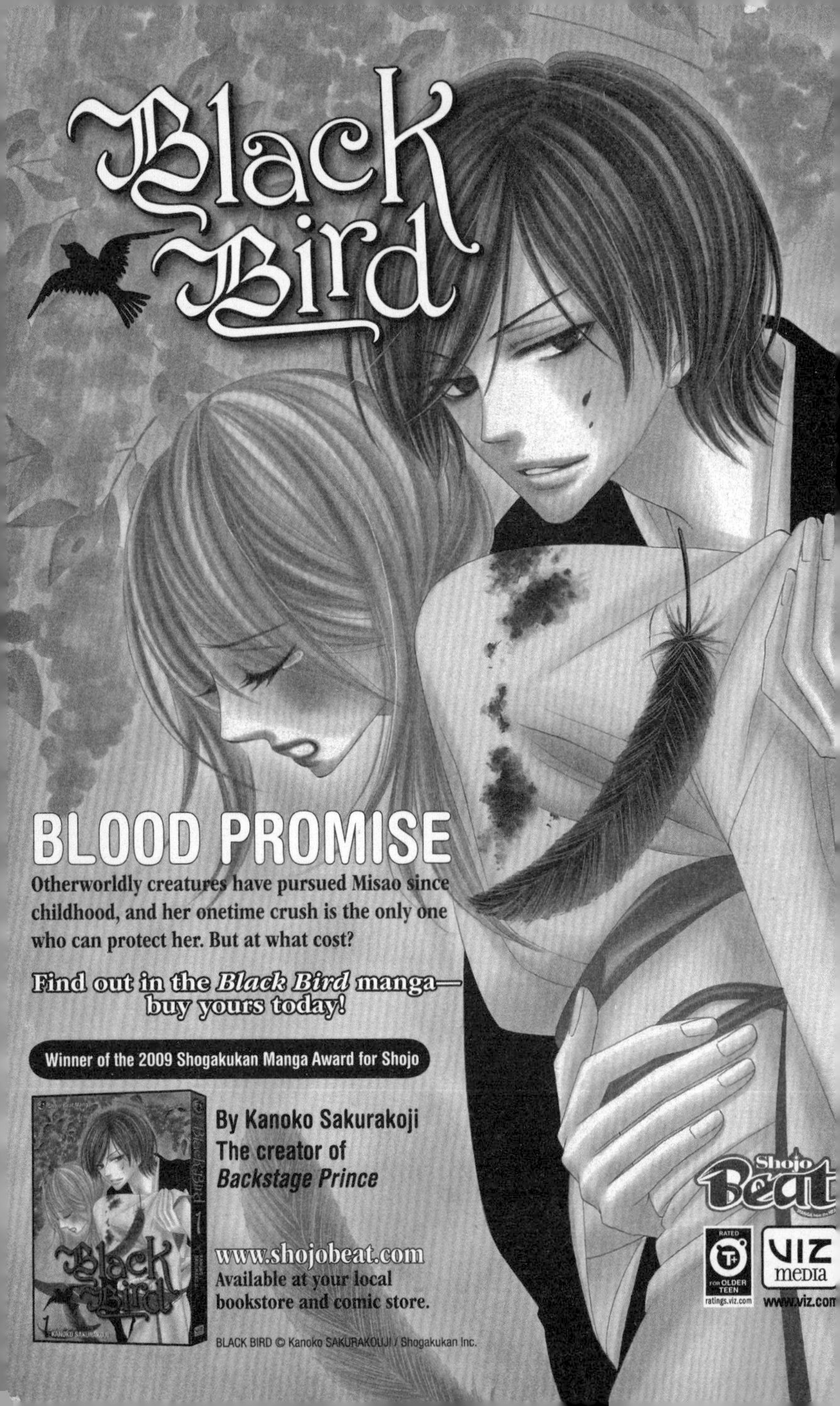
Black Bird
BLOOD PROMISE
Otherworldly creatures have pursued Misao since childhood, and her onetime crush is the only one who can protect her. But at what cost?
Find out in the Black Bird manga—buy yours today!
Winner of the 2009 Shogakukan Manga Award for Shojo
By Kanoko Sakurakoji
The creator of Backstage Prince
www.shojobeat.com
Available at your local bookstore and comic store.
BLACK BIRD © Kanoko SAKURAKOUJI / Shogakukan Inc.
Black Bird
1
KANOKO SAKURAKOJI
Shojo Beat
RATED
T+
FOR OLDER TEEN
ratings.viz.com
VIZ media
www.viz.com

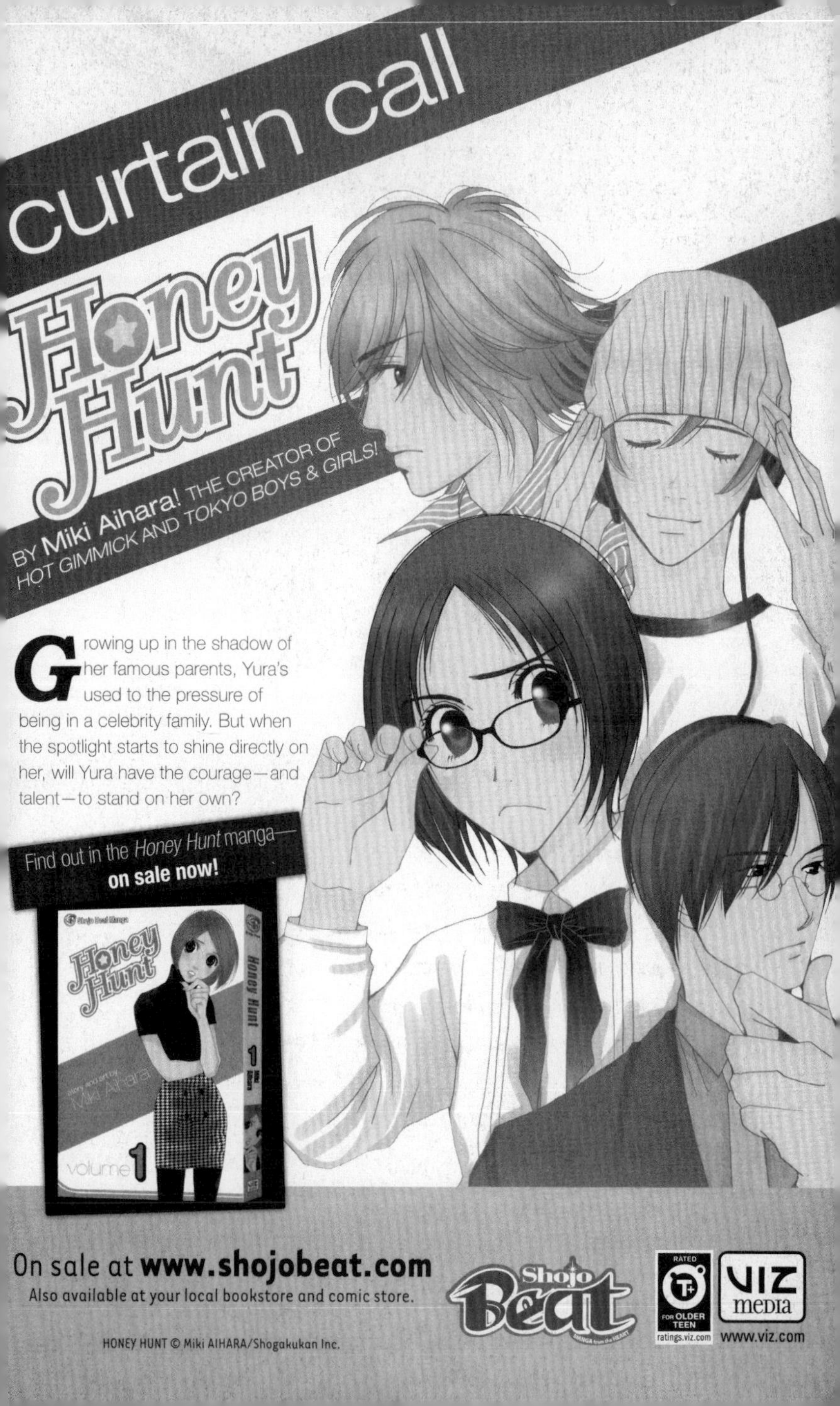
curtain call
Honey Hunt
BY Miki Aihara! THE CREATOR OF HOT GIMMICK AND TOKYO BOYS & GIRLS!
Growing up in the shadow of her famous parents, Yura's used to the pressure of being in a celebrity family. But when the spotlight starts to shine directly on her, will Yura have the courage—and talent—to stand on her own?
Find out in the Honey Hunt manga—
on sale now!
Shojo Beat Manga
Honey Hunt
story and art by Miki Aihara
volume 1
On sale at www.shojobeat.com
Also available at your local bookstore and comic store.
Shojo Beat
RATED T+ FOR OLDER TEEN
ratings.viz.com
VIZ media
www.viz.com
HONEY HUNT © Miki AIHARA/Shogakukan Inc.

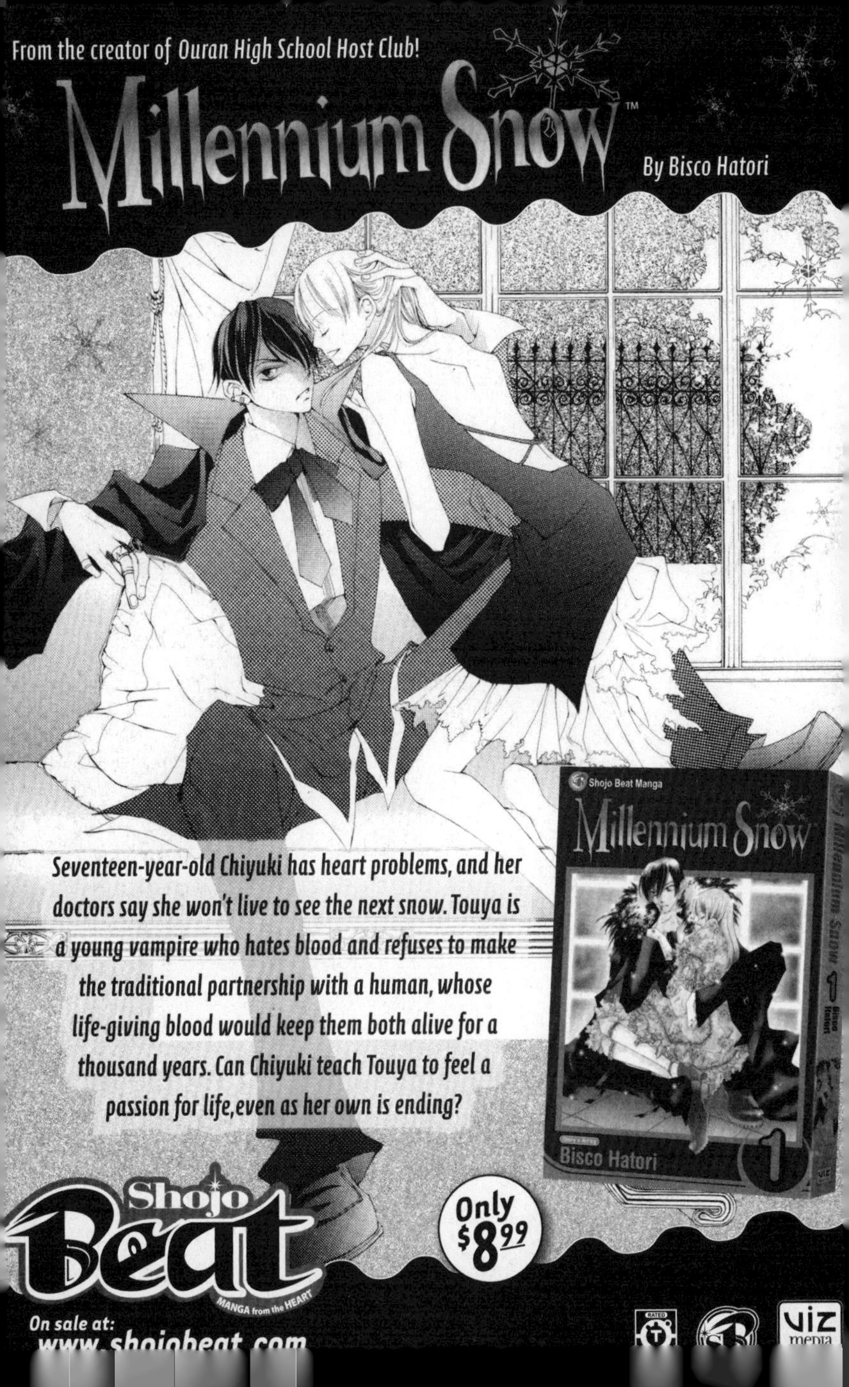
From the creator of Ouran High School Host Club!
Millennium Snow™
By Bisco Hatori
Seventeen-year-old Chiyuki has heart problems, and her doctors say she won't live to see the next snow. Touya is a young vampire who hates blood and refuses to make the traditional partnership with a human, whose life-giving blood would keep them both alive for a thousand years. Can Chiyuki teach Touya to feel a passion for life,even as her own is ending?
Shojo Beat Manga
Millennium Snow
Bisco Hatori
1
Shojo Beat
MANGA from the HEART
Only $8.99
On sale at:
www.shojobeat.com
RATED T
viz media

This is the last page.

In keeping with the original Japanese comic format, this book reads from right to left—so action, sound effects, and word balloons are completely reversed. This preserves the orientation of the original artwork—plus, it's fun! Check out the diagram shown here to get the hang of things, and then turn to the other side of the book to get started!

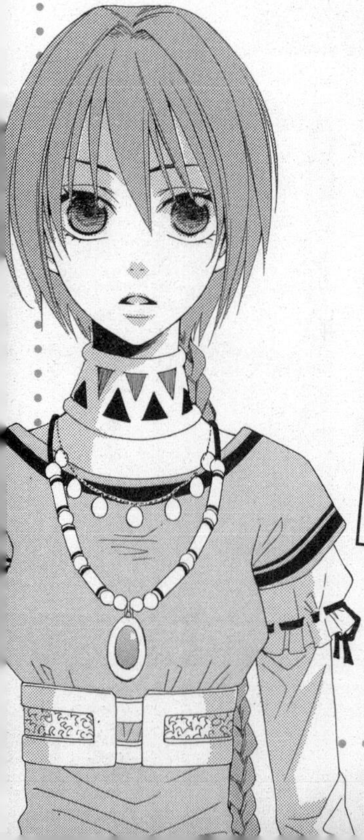

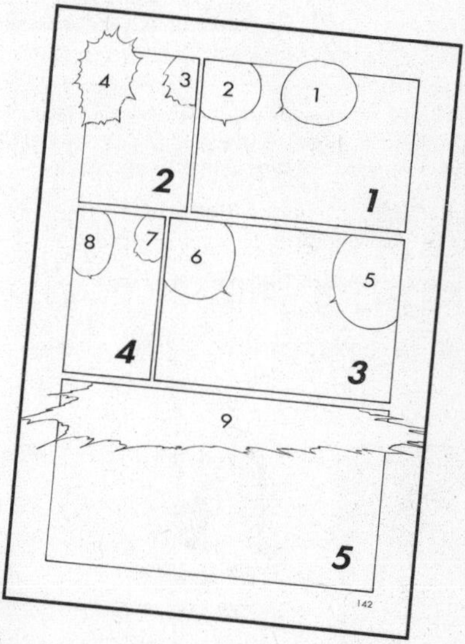

1
2
3
4
1
2
5
6
7
8
3
4
9
5
142